ORGANIZATIONAL BEHAVIOUR

■ ■ ■ ■ ■ ■

Canadian Cases and Exercises

Seventh Edition

Randy Hoffman
York University

Fred Ruemper
Retired

Captus Press

Organizational Behaviour: Canadian Cases and Exercises
Seventh Edition

Captus Press Inc.
Units 14 & 15
1600 Steeles Avenue West
Concord, Ontario
Canada L4K 4M2

Phone: (416) 736–5537
Fax: (416) 736–5793
E-mail: info@captus.com
Internet: http://www.captus.com

Library and Archives Canada Cataloguing in Publication

Organizational behaviour : Canadian cases and exercises / [edited by] Randy Hoffman, Fred Ruemper. — 7th ed.

ISBN 978-1-55322-229-3

1. Organizational behavior—Canada—Case studies. 2. Personnel management—Canada—Case studies. 3. Organizational behavior—Case studies. 4. Personnel management—Case studies. 5. Organization—Case studies. I. Hoffman, Randy, date II. Ruemper, Fred, date

HD31.O74 2010   658   C2010-904496-7

Canada ▮◆▮ We acknowledge the financial support of the Government of Canada through the Book Publishing Industry Development Program (BPIDP) for our publishing activities

0 9 8 7 6 5 4 3 2
Printed in Canada

Table of Contents

EXERCISES

Preface

The managerial profession requires, as do other professions, that practitioners be competent in the application of the skills and knowledge of their field. Your course in organizational behaviour is an essential component of this needed expertise. This book includes case studies and experiential exercises, because rote learning of theoretical content alone will not create that competence. The purpose of these learning tools is to present or simulate organizational opportunities for applying the abstract theories and principles of organizational behaviour. In this way, you will be better prepared for the real-world administrative issues that will arise in a career in management.

Each exercise focuses on a single issue that is identified at the beginning of the activity. By following the directions in the book and those from your instructor, you will see how a theory may be put into action. Sometimes it is as simple as filling out a form and comparing your results with those of other students, while at other times the activity involves a more complex simulation and more elaborate activities.

By showing you how to put the theory in action, we hope that you will avoid the common tendency to fall back solely on the use of "common sense". Applied psychology can help you develop analytical skills that enable more sophisticated solutions to organizational problems. The first exercise, "Earning Your Mark", is an application of equity theory to a familiar situation. For example, if you have ever worked on a group project for a course and received a group mark for your efforts, you will recognize the potential for forming beliefs that people did not get a mark that reflected their contribution. This exercise builds on this experience.

There are also exercises on group behaviour that encourage you to employ principles from the field of social psychology. The focus is on the behaviour of individuals as they interact within small groups. Whenever students study in groups or do group projects, it is inevitable that they will also learn something about the way groups operate.

A portion of the exercises are focused on the organization and based on the application of the theories of sociology and anthropology to business life. These activities will help you to come to recognize the formal and informal structure of organizations, including the rules, policies, and norms that govern organizational life. The study of organizations is the study of the broad patterns that exist in all organizations.

The cases will enhance your learning in a different, but equally valuable way. Since cases are based on real life situations, they seldom illustrate a situation that can fall into a single category or topic like the exercises, although the story of each case will tend to relate more to particular topics in organizational behaviour. The medium-sized and longer cases may be examined several times for different issues and purposes during your course. For that reason, we have grouped the cases together neutrally, in alphabetical order by title. At the end of each case you will find a series of questions designed to bring out certain salient issues. They have been prepared to help you focus on areas of organizational behaviour that are strongly illustrated in the real life situations depicted. The value in these cases is that, over the duration of your course, you will have the opportunity to become acquainted with a more diverse variety of organizational situations than would occur over many years in an administrative career.

Students need some guidance in the method of analyzing cases, so we have provided you with a guide to case analysis. The guide is comprehensive in nature; so when using it, feel free to refer only to those parts relevant to your assignment.

Randy Hoffman
Fred Ruemper

Cases

The Purpose and Analysis of Case Studies

Cases are included in many courses in Administrative Studies to give students a feeling of the hard realities of business and the constraints involved in decision making. By exposing herself or himself to a variety of situations and diverse problems, the student should experience the challenges and dilemmas of the decision maker. Cases are usually based on real situations. For reasons of privacy and confidentiality, the persons, the companies, and the locations involved are concealed.

It is intended that a student will study the information provided in each case, attempt to diagnose the true nature of the problem or problems involved, search for alternative ways in which the problems can be resolved, and then recommend and justify the most plausible course of action.

Sometimes students feel disappointed because the cases sometimes do not appear to be "dramatic". However, because the cases do represent the realities of organizations, they are often likely to be somewhat mundane, at least to the outside observer. Most of the incidents are based on events that were actually faced by managers and their subordinates on a day-to-day basis.

Very often, cases do not contain all the information that the student would like to have. This is often done intentionally, or at least knowingly, by the case writer. In real life, a manager must frequently make decisions on the basis of limited information.

Essentially, a case study allows the student to experience, to some extent, the realities of a problem situation and to react to the pressures and demands made on the decision maker. It is therefore important for the student to identify closely with the decision maker in the case by trying to put himself or herself in that person's shoes. This is the only way in which he or she will experience the constraints, limitations, frustrations, as well as the joys of effective decision making. As a learning aid, the case method tests the student's ability to diagnose problems and identify, evaluate, and choose the appropriate alternative as the best course of action. Ideally, before making a decision, he or she should have considered all the possible alternatives and evaluated the advantages and disadvantages of each. Each alternative must be considered in terms of its chances for achieving the best results.

Sometimes students look desperately for the "correct answer" or the "one best solution" without realizing that, in case studies, the stress is not on the "right" or "wrong" answer. Instead, the emphasis is on the student's ability to take into account all the variables that might have a bearing on the situation and then find an answer that is feasible using a process that is correct in terms of theory. Rarely are there situations for which there is only one solution. Most problems confronted by managers are multifaceted, involving motivational, cultural, structural, technological, communicational, and inter-personal aspects. In dealing with an organizational problem, a student has to be able to comprehend all its aspects, including the complex personal interrelationships involved.

The learning objectives of a case study can include many of the following:

(a) To improve a student's ability to think logically and imaginatively;
(b) To improve her or his ability to communicate;
(c) To provide an opportunity for experiential learning, particularly when it involves group work;
(d) To develop analytical ability and personal involvement in problem solving;
(e) To reinforce theoretical learning and provide the opportunity to understand and use previously learned theories and models;
(f) To bring about an awareness of the constraints in real-world decision making; and
(g) To integrate the knowledge and skills gained studying the diverse areas within a administrative studies or business program.

A METHOD OF CASE ANALYSIS

There are many different methods that can be used to analyze successfully an organizational problem. Each, however, requires a comprehensive understanding of the case information and its interrelatedness; a correct decision as to which principles, models, and theories of organizational behaviour should be applied; and a competent application of that selected area of knowledge to the problems or issues at hand. Outlined below is one method of incorporating those criteria into a step-by-step procedure for case analysis. It is not the only feasible approach, but it is a method that will work, if applied carefully.

1. Read the case study two or three times (more, for a long or complex case) in an undirected manner. "Undirected" means do not think about the questions asked or the method of analysis. The goal here is to become familiar with the management situation that is described without filtering that perception with a premature focus on solutions or answers. If the assigned questions are considered prematurely, the case reader will unavoidably become solutions-oriented from the very first perusal. These solutions are likely to be both superficial and very hard to change as the study of the case proceeds.

2. During the final reading, make notes regarding salient issues. These issues will not necessarily conform to those upon which the assigned questions are based (although there will most likely be a strong relationship that will eventually become clear).

3. Now read and study the assigned question. Record information from the case that appears pertinent to its analysis. Do not, however, attempt to answer the questions. At this stage the focus is on an organization of the previous impressions of the case in terms of the assigned areas of inquiry. It will usually be necessary to return to the case for further information.

4. Decide which principles, theories, or models of organizational behaviour, if any, can be applied to the observed data in order to generate solutions. The goal here is to match the theories, etc. to the case information and assignment. The temptation that must be avoided is to generate solutions based mainly upon intuition and then try to force-fit some handy theoretical rationale to the preconceived answers. Theories of organizational behaviour are to be used in the analysis and solution of organizational problems, not as an afterthought.

5. Apply the selected general principles, theories, or models and determine what solutions are suggested by this application. Select the ones that best deal with assigned problem(s). Often, more than one answer is supportable for a particular question. A search for additional theoretical rationale and an application of informed judgment will eventually resolve this difficulty. Part of the answer to the case study assignment may require that the rationale for the alternatives and solutions presented also be given. The major strength of any case report cannot reside chiefly in the specific solutions offered, as these are always arguable. Rather, it is the reasons given for the solutions that will either support or ultimately undermine the student's efforts. They will be correct or incorrect applications of management science and refined judgment.

WHEN SPECIFIC QUESTIONS ARE NOT ASSIGNED

Occasionally, case studies are assigned for analysis without specific questions. The student must then devise a framework that will enable the analytical and/or synthetic treatment of strategic issues. One general approach is as follows.

1. Follow steps one and two of the procedure given above.

2. Identify the salient problems (no more than three or four can be treated in a typical five- to ten-page case report). The problems may also be divided into symptoms and root causes, thus providing an opportunity later on to suggest measures that might be effective at either or both levels. Notes should now be made, categorizing the information in the case according to its relationship with an identified issue.

3. Employ internal and external constraints and relevant values to establish criteria by which the proposed solutions to the identified problems may be judged. Wherever possible, ensure that these criteria are objective. Qualitative indicators of success tend to be ambiguous and subject to argument. Too short a list of criteria will result in an incomplete judgment of solutions. Too long a list may be unsatisfiable and unwieldy. Typically, about four to eight criteria will usually do the job for each salient problem. They must, however, be very

carefully chosen to reflect the essential areas that will mean success or failure to the firm's general management.

4. Follow steps four and five relating to the use of organizational behaviour concepts from the procedure outlined above. Again, the list of alternative solutions will emerge, and the rationale for the final selection (refer to the criteria) should constitute an important part of the case report.

5. The final selection of a solution from alternatives is based upon how well it meets the criteria you have established. Any solution to a strategic problem will be, at best, an optimal approach that satisfies the criteria reasonably well. Sometimes, all that can be found is the lesser among evils. Rarely, indeed, is any solution a perfect match, meeting or exceeding all criteria. Students are advised to moderate their enthusiasm with a realistic assessment of the merits and drawbacks of their solutions.

6. Present the chosen solution(s) in detail and realistically. Section titles for a case report following this format might then be: "statement of the problem"; "selection of criteria"; "selection and evaluation of solution alternatives"; and "conclusion" (presentation, rationale for its selection, and detailed assessment of the chosen solution).

FOUR COMMON PITFALLS

1. **Salience of Data and Issues**
   Most comprehensive cases (as do real-world situations) contain much information of little real importance to the main problems or issues that must be confronted. Many problems or issues may themselves be spin-offs of deeper, more important root causes; or perhaps they are incidental and of little consequence to more major concerns. One of the tasks of the case study analyst is to "separate the wheat from the chaff", or identify and focus upon the truly essential elements of the problem at hand. To do otherwise is to become sidetracked by issues of little gravity, and therefore to neglect, in direct proportion, the real goal of the exercise. Often, students are asked to take the role of employees, management, upper level executives, or of a consultant to those groups. This viewpoint should form the filter by which the case material is perceived. A careful balance must be struck between the rigorous case report and the scattering and weakening effects of being diverted by too many minor matters.

2. **Superficial Solutions**
   These often arise due to an inadequate analysis of too little data; the failure to establish comprehensive, rather than vague, criteria; overlooking root causes; or some other way in which the case report was not pushed far enough in important directions. For example, suppose the case refers to an ineffective work group and the assignment is to make corrective recommendations. If the case report states, "The managers must improve their leadership skills", that is probably a superficial recommendation. A detailed description of precisely what changes are required and why, and perhaps also how to carry out these

improvements would constitute a proper response. Students should strive to be specific and to include as much detail as possible, relevant to the major issues, their analyses, and solutions. The test of a superficial statement includes: first, does it apply equally well to many firms or specifically relate to the one at hand; and second, would it constitute only vague hints to management, or would it give specific directions or criticisms.

3. **The "I Need More Information" Syndrome**

It is often a temptation in a case report to "reluctantly" conclude that the data is woefully incomplete, and thus a firm conclusion is impossible. It would be necessary (as the next line usually reads) to get more information before reaching any definite conclusion. In the real world, this sometimes is precisely what happens. In a case study, it is almost always tantamount to ducking the issue. The goal of a case study is usually to depict a behavioural or management situation for the purpose of analysis and recommendations, and that cannot be accomplished if the information is said to be incomplete and the student does not proceed further. The student will of course never receive that additional information, and the exercise's aim is thus frustrated. It is therefore important to complete the case report with the information at hand. If there is legitimate cause to seriously question the quantity or quality of information, then this can be noted as qualifying the competence of the solution. A complete answer should still be attempted.

4. **Finally, Answer the Question**

Just as the organizational decision-maker must ultimately reach some conclusion, so the preparer of a case report must avoid "waffling" or sitting on the fence when a specific recommendation is requested. Many times it may seem difficult to decide between two or more alternatives. The wisest course is to make the best choice possible and then note that other alternatives may be almost equally attractive. After completing the writeup of the case, the student should always look at the question again and ask himself or herself, "Did I answer that question?"

Action Realty Inc. (A)

What was once a small real estate office has evolved into Action Realty Inc., a medium-sized, prestigious brokerage firm specializing in the buying, selling, and management of residential and commercial real estate. It is a young and aggressive company based in Vancouver that started out four years ago as a partnership between two licensed real estate brokers, Harvey and Paul. Beginning in an 800 sq. ft. office, the partners first generated most of the company's sales themselves, and Harvey's wife, Marie, was the entire administrative staff. However, in 2003 they incorporated and moved into a new office with 3,500 sq. ft. of prime office space. This year, the company perceived a need for even more space to accommodate their growing organization and added another 2,000 sq. ft. from next door to accommodate a new commercial real estate division. The company now employs some 200 registered agents, of which 50 are full-time and the rest part-time. An administrative staff of 11 people performs the bookkeeping and clerical functions.

Harvey and Paul are the only shareholders of Action Realty Inc. Even though the company has expanded so rapidly, the two men and Marie still personally oversee the operations of all the staff. Harvey's principal managerial role is to make sure the company reaches or exceeds sales goals. Paul does most of the hiring of new agents, and Marie manages the accounting and clerical personnel. All managerial activities to plan, direct, control, and otherwise administer the firm are performed by the three of them in one capacity or another.

GOALS OF THE COMPANY

The two men's original goal was to establish a large, profitable, and prestigious organization as soon as possible. In other words, their goal was to make "Big Bucks", with sales volume being the key determinant. But since the real estate environment is of a changeable nature, the company must always try to adapt. Each year, new goals are set according to the economic situation at the time. The two brokers often find it difficult to achieve these goals because, in many years, survival alone is hard to ensure. A current goal is to open a branch office and eventually to establish a multibranch brokerage business. According to the agents and the office staff, "We'll have to see it to believe it."

POLICIES

Action Realty has issued a booklet describing company policies and setting out the rules and regulations the agents should follow when pursuing business. These policies, rules, and regulations, which the company enforces, are concerned mainly with business ethics — that is, standards of business practice. Employees must abide by these policies to maintain the company's reputation. Agents join the company in order to benefit from the firm's name and to promote personal sales through the use of the firm's image. It is not the goals of the company that concern agents, but the reaching of personal objectives. Often, few agents are really sure what the company's current goals are. Sometimes, whoever attends the company meetings tries to pass the word around.

It would be difficult for Paul and Harvey to enforce other rules and regulations concerning work practices with their prevalent management style — which can be described as relaxed. Probably, this style was adopted because all agents work strictly on a commission basis and develop their own clientele. Action Realty's goal-setting philosophy for individual agents is to "do your best", and agents are responsible for their own productivity. It is essential that they enjoy working for the company, however, for they could leave at any time. The company cannot afford an agent staff that consists only of transients. All agents registered with the company incur overhead expenses, regardless of whether they produce any sales. That expense can sometimes be kept minimal if they do not occupy a permanent desk within the office. If an agent generates commission revenue of over $25,000/ yr., he/she is considered a full-time agent and has the privilege of occupying a desk. Those who do not maintain that quota are considered part-time. The latter group does not have any minimum sales level; they are only required to maintain their licence by paying an annual fee to the provincial government and the local real estate board.

STRUCTURE

The organizational structure of the firm appears to be simple and somewhat flat. The agents all report to the two Brokers, Paul and Harvey; the administrative staff reports to Marie. Figure 1 shows the structure.

The personnel are divided into four separate groups. The first is the administrative department, composed of five secretaries and two accountants, all salaried. They take care of general office duties to ensure that the administration of the company is running effectively and efficiently. The secretaries are constantly barraged with work from the agents, which often causes their own office work to be neglected. The second department is the property management division, which consists of only one agent and his own personal secretary. The property manager also acts (at times) as the company's lawyer. He is paid by salary and is responsible solely to the Brokers. His job responsibility is to look after the company's real estate investments and to manage properties for clients of the company. He was hired because he was a close friend of the Brokers.

The third department is the residential department, which consists of 50 full-time agents. This department contains 50 desks, all separated by partitions to ensure

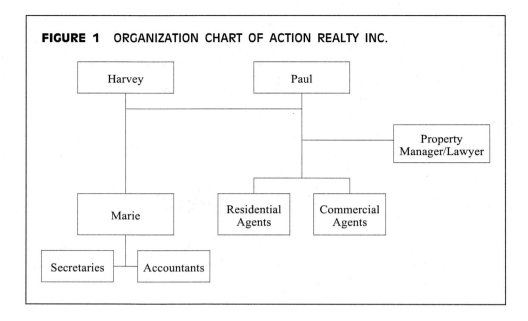

FIGURE 1   ORGANIZATION CHART OF ACTION REALTY INC.

privacy. Out of these 50 agents, approximately 25% work at their full capacity, while the other 75% work at moderate levels to "just getting by". Sometimes, during the evening and, occasionally, during the afternoons, full-time agents get together to play cards in the office, have a meal outside, or sit around a local pub.

The fourth department is the commercial real estate division, which is the most important department because it generates the highest sales per agent. This department comprises small individual rooms restricted to those who deal only in commercial real estate. This poses a problem because all agents would like private rooms. However, even the top salesmen who deal in residential and some commercial real estate do not have their own rooms. Dealing solely in commercial real estate is quite difficult without the right connections and the "know how". It is considered the "gravy" of the business, while selling residential is the "bread and butter". At times, the "commercial only" agents do tend to list and sell residential property, and this upsets the other agents immensely. This places management in a very awkward position. There are so many agents with different needs and desires that it is difficult for the two Brokers to please everyone.

MANAGEMENT

Marie manages the administrative department in a highly centralized way. She tries to control staff and impose certain restrictions upon them. For example, she does not want her staff to socialize too much or to have lunch with the agents. Everything must be done according to the way she wants it done. She feels that her way is the one best way to do the job. There is no room for staff input. Anything done out of the normal procedure must be cleared with her first, yet she is not even present half the time. As a result, there are many complaints within this department. The staff occasionally find their jobs very disorganized and frustrating, and the office does not run as efficiently as it should.

Supplies are locked up after Marie leaves for the evening to prevent "vandalism". Since she is the only one who holds the key, the administrative staff feel as though they are being treated like children or, possibly, criminals. The morale in this department appears to be quite poor. Marie does not have the formal education or job experience to qualify her for this position. The staff find it very difficult to complain or voice their opinions in order to effect any changes because Marie is Harvey's wife. On a personal level, in non-business related matters, the administrative staff gets along very well with Marie and the Brokers. When staff meetings are held (which is very seldom), it is always at staff's request. Management is doing them a favour by holding the meeting, and staff complaints are not taken seriously. Bonuses and promotions are very seldom awarded in this department, and salaries are increased only with the cost of living.

With respect to the agents, Paul and Harvey practically run the entire organization themselves. They do all the hiring and supervision, and make all the business decisions concerning the company. They do not like delegating authority to members of the sales staff regarding non-routine matters. The main operating policy is to hire as many agents as possible because of the belief that more sales agents registered with the company will result in more sales. The hiring of agents is performed almost indiscriminately rather than on merit. All agents work on a commission basis. The Brokers feel that the best way to manage them is to give them free rein to come and go as they please. Harvey and Paul are extremely active themselves, but they try to accommodate the agents in whatever way they can. New agents are encouraged to come to them whenever help is needed. Yet the Brokers are often very busy with company operations, promotion, and their own sales. General meetings and sales training classes for new agents are held by the brokers every Saturday morning. Since they are obviously so busy at other times, agents do not wish to bother Paul or Harvey. Instead, agents tend to form partnerships of three or four persons working together to help one another on deals. As a result, several persons working together end up doing the normal workload of one person. Productivity actually decreases, and overall performance of the company is lower. Management officially discourages these informal work groups. They prefer agents to work on their own and to only come to management for help.

The agents at Action Realty are hired personally by the Brokers. Everyone seems to have some connection with the Brokers either through social contact or family ties. Hiring decisions are solely based on the personal references of the prospective employees. Management tries to operate the system on an impersonal basis so that decisions regarding employees can be made fairly. Yet the agents feel a close affiliation with the Brokers because of the company's cultural homogeneity and family relationships. Therefore, it is hard for management to maintain a very impersonal approach, however much they try. The Brokers are known for being open, honest, and straightforward with employees. It seems everyone gets along with management. Yet there is still a high rate of agent turnover.

WORKING CONDITIONS

The Brokers motivate their sales staff by, in part, working hard and generating sales themselves. Action Realty's profits at this time are mainly generated by the number and the dollar amount of deals the company makes. The agents must be relied upon to produce a large volume of sales in order for the company to cover their overhead and to realize any profits. The "open board", where all the agents' property listings and sales are compiled, covers an entire wall for all to view. Management feels that when agents see how well their associates are doing, it motivates them to work harder.

Overall company morale is very good, and the agents seem to enjoy working there. The office is spacious, comfortable, and pleasantly designed to facilitate good working conditions, which management feels is important for motivating staff to work harder. At times agents arrive ready to work, but end up just socializing all day. Management does not seem to mind. They feel that the agents will mainly socialize only temporarily. In the long run, they are expected to motivate themselves to generate increased sales. The company has an "open door policy", and encourages employees to take advantage of it. Agents are free to talk to the Brokers at any time. It is hoped that this will help resolve any work problems. According to the company, "For people to work together effectively, there must be a friendly, congenial atmosphere based on mutual trust and respect." Informal groups are well established, and rarely does any worker feel alienated. Social gatherings outside of work are encouraged. An Action Realty house newspaper called "Action Times" has been set up to keep employees and outsiders informed as to what is happening within the organization.

To ensure that agents are kept up to date, announcements are placed on bulletins, and letters to each agent are put into their message slots. Policy meetings are held every month on the first Monday morning. Company objectives and new policies are discussed there, giving agents the opportunity to voice freely their opinions and to relate problems. Management is very proud of these meetings as they are evidence of the open communication that exists within the firm. Sometimes guest speakers are invited to these meetings to enlighten the agents on various business-related fields. Since attendance is not mandatory, full-time agents attend whenever they feel like it, or not at all. As for the part-time agents, many are not even aware of the time and date of the meetings.

The company also offers and arranges a variety of planned social activities such as a bowling league every Tuesday evening and a soccer league every Saturday afternoon. Either Harvey or Paul attempts to be present at all these activities. Two major social events are held every year. The management hopes that all of these activities will give staff a sense of belonging.

Management believes that they are doing the best they can to motivate employees by providing great working conditions and by establishing excellent interpersonal relations between them and their staff. However, it seems that employees are still not motivated to work to their full potential. At least, this is the case with the 75% of the agents who do not even generate one sale per year. Some agents are seen constantly to go in and out of the office daily, yet accomplish next to nothing. Every year profits do increase, but expenses increase as well.

QUESTIONS

1. Describe and compare the motivational states of the agents and the office staff.

2. Are these states the result of the leadership styles employed and the organizational structure? Why or why not?

3. Analyze the reward system at Action Realty with respect to:
   (a) part-time agents
   (b) full-time agents
   (c) commercial agents
   (d) office workers

4. What changes would you suggest to ensure continuing growth in the future?

Action Realty Inc. (B)

By late 2004, the Vancouver real estate market in both residential and commercial business became more competitive. Sales became sluggish and commissions to both brokers and sales agents fell substantially. Poor sales expectations among the public meant that properties were withheld from the market. There was increasingly fierce competition among agents for both listings and clients. The only positive sign was that, at long last, mortgage rates were beginning to show signs of a long-awaited decline.

Action Realty seemed to be feeling the effect of the depressed state of the market more severely than many other firms. In response, it had not only shelved its plans to establish branch offices, but management began to worry about whether the present level of business could support even the existing size of the firm.

To make matters worse, one of the two owners, Paul, had developed severe bronchitis during the wet fall weather. He was advised by his doctor to drastically reduce his work hours until his condition improved. Possibly, he would be incapacitated for a few months. Since the poor market conditions were already causing a number of the less productive employees to seek other work, the hiring activities that Paul was now not able to carry out were, at first, much missed. Harvey realized that now there might not be enough business even to keep a part-time agent interested. From a total of over 200 agents at its peak, the firm now had a complement of about 120.

As a barometer for this deteriorating state of affairs, the office atmosphere became decidedly dour. Even the part-time agents, many of whom had previously seemed content to socialize or travel around in groups, were dispirited and frequently complained about business in the office. This was puzzling to the brokers since most of that group had never been dependent on their commissions to maintain their life styles. The productive section of the full-time agents in both the residential and commercial fields, who previously had rarely been seen idle, now often sat in their offices seemingly waiting for the telephone to ring. Arguments in the office were becoming frequent — especially between full-time and part-time agents. Relations between secretarial support staff and agents, never without friction, were now coming close to the point of breakdown. This was also puzzling since the low volume of business should have made for an easier administrative work flow. Even the informal but very popular company bowling league now consisted mainly of only a few bowling fanatics, whose primary reason for coming out had not been social.

With the burden of management responsibilities almost totally on his shoulders for the present, Harvey became increasingly concerned about the declining income and poor morale of the employees of Action Realty. Other firms, he noted, had all lost some people, but most were managing to survive with a more modest level of sales and a committed core of professionally oriented agents. Harvey was traditionally responsible for setting and attaining performance goals and for occasionally supervising administration, but not hiring. Therefore, he had not questioned or interfered with Paul's practice of bringing in any acquaintance with agent certification as a new employee. Harvey had simply done his best with the staff as it existed. Although it had never mattered in the past, he was now beginning to wonder whether this nearly random method of hiring was creating difficulties in the current situation.

With sales and commissions declining even faster than the number of agents, Harvey knew that effective measures had better be taken quickly. Options he was considering included: immediately terminate all employees whose previous year's commissions were less than $12,000 and move the firm into smaller premises; set realistic sales goals for the next two months and terminate those who did not attain them; or simply try to carry on and hope business improves. He gave himself until the next Saturday morning meeting to reach a decision. He had let the word out that important announcements would be made, and he expected a big turnout of staff. That was all to the good, he felt, since his own business activities had always been an important source of income for the firm, and his present preoccupation with this problem was causing him to neglect them.

QUESTIONS

1. Do you believe that hiring practices were responsible for the performance of Action Realty being worse than many other firms during the market downturn? Explain your answer.

2. What other aspects of the firm's management and policies might have contributed to the problem?

3. Evaluate Harvey's measures to alleviate poor performance. Which is likely to be most effective? Do you recommend that either option to downsize the firm be adopted?

4. Suggest a solution that you feel would be optimal in alleviating the motivational problems and improving performance. Provide an implementation plan, including the outline of what Harvey should say at the meeting.

Affirmative Action at the University of Selkirk

The University of Selkirk is a medium-sized institution situated in a prairie province. During the first half of 2001, it conducted an audit of its faculty members with the intention of determining the degree to which males were overrepresented among faculty members. The conclusion of the audit was that, in most faculties, there was indeed a severe imbalance in favour of men.

The direct result was the establishment of a university-wide Affirmative Action Committee. The role of this body was to make recommendations to the vice-president, Academic (who was in charge of academic hirings) concerning how the university could make more strenuous efforts towards hiring women faculty members. By late 2001, the committee had formulated a three-phase proposal which, after some negotiation, was reluctantly approved by the vice-president, Academic and was ratified by the university senate and the president. The proposal contained the following provisions.

1. Each department formulates an affirmative action hiring plan that would outline:
   - how women candidates could be located and be encouraged to apply for forthcoming positions;
   - in the assessment of candidates, how the department will take into account that many women may not have had the same opportunities as men to complete doctorates or to publish as prolifically in academic journals, but should still be considered on a par with men who have;
   - how, at the time when job offers are being made, women candidates with acceptable qualifications would be offered the position prior to any men.

2. Each department's plan would then be submitted to the Affirmative Action Committee for approval. No hirings would take place until an acceptable plan had been worked out between the department and the committee.

3. No men candidates for faculty positions would be submitted to the vice-president, Academic for hiring unless the Affirmative Action Committee and the department agreed that no acceptable woman candidate could be found.

The vice-president (male) had felt that the plan was too rigid, and that it might result in "the best candidates" not being considered. Even in cases where the lack of qualified women finally resulted in approval to hire a man, the vice-president suggested that the best candidates would have taken positions elsewhere by the time the process worked through to the stage where an offer could be made to a man. The Affirmative Action Committee, composed in the majority of women faculty members and librarians, countered that the systems of graduate studies, academic faculties, and scholarly publishing in Canada were so dominated by men that there was an implicit set of values that effectively excluded women. Only by increasing the number of women in academic positions in a direct and forceful manner, the committee stated, would this male-dominated environment be altered.

By mid-2002, almost all university departments had successfully negotiated a plan with the Affirmative Action Committee. An exception was the department of Business Studies. Its plan had been rejected once in January 2002 as woefully inadequate, and the department had not so far attempted to re-open negotiations with the committee. In university circles, it was widely known that many Business Studies' faculty members, 85% of whom were men, had nothing but disdain for the committee and its work, and openly stated it.

Then, in November 2002, an alumnus bequest gave Business Studies sufficient funding to hire a new faculty member in the finance area. Rather than actively pursue approval of their affirmative action plan, however, the department's efforts were put towards attracting and interviewing candidates. As it happened, the best candidate to emerge was a woman. This person's credentials were so strong that unless action was taken quickly, she would certainly take a position elsewhere. The department, believing that it would face no impediments, forwarded its recommendation to the vice-president, Academic. However, once the Affirmative Action Committee found out, they immediately moved to block the appointment, as no affirmative action hiring plan had been approved.

The department, with the concurrence of the vice-president, appealed directly to the president. They put the case forward that the objection of the committee was a politically motivated disruptive tactic. The Affirmative Action Committee replied that it was not this appointment that was important, but rather it was having an appropriate procedure in place that would guarantee better access for faculty jobs for women. Every department in the university had to follow the same rules. They also stated that the woman candidate was an exceptional case, and would find a position regardless. Without strict policies, however, many other deserving women candidates would be out of luck. Catering to the wishes of the Business department now would make it appear that the committee was "selling out".

With seemingly no possibility of a resolution between the parties, the vice-president, Academic and the Affirmative Action Committee appealed to the president of the university for a final decision.

QUESTIONS

1. Discuss the affirmative action policy of the University of Selkirk. Is it practical? Is it fair?

2. In the case of the preferred candidate for the department of Business Studies, does the end justify the means?

3. How would you advise the president to resolve the problem in respect of this hiring and any wider issues?

A-Plus Drywall Limited

THE ORGANIZATION

A-Plus Drywall Limited specializes in finishing the interior space of new public, corporate, and residential projects for developers and construction firms. The company was founded at the beginning of Calgary's current construction boom. From modest beginnings, the two original partners progressed from installing drywall in houses to a company that rates among the top 10 companies in the Calgary area. With approximately $30 million a year in contract work at present, their projects have included some of the largest buildings in the area.

A-Plus is recognized throughout the industry as a low-cost leader. Most often, a supplier of drywall partitioning is chosen on the basis of cost. Among the major firms able to take on large projects, A-Plus is frequently able to out-bid its rivals on the basis of a more attractive price.

The company is currently is managed by three partners, Joseph, Alfie (Joseph's brother-in-law), and Jerry (Joseph's son). Although the three have equal status and authority in the partnership agreement, Joseph and Alfie exercise more authority than Jerry since they started the firm. The remainder of the staff comprises an office secretary, an estimator, seven foremen (two of whom are women, despite the title), and approximately 200 workers. Workers are unionized throughout the industry and vary greatly in knowledge, skills, and ability. The division of labour is as follows: labourers who handle material and clean up; insulators who install insulation; studmen who install steel structures; drywallers who install drywall; and tapers who finish the drywall for painting. A foreman's typical responsibility is to read the blueprints; coordinate the work of the workers with that of the overall project; lay out partitions; arrange for materials; and plan the size and schedule the attendance of the workforce based on the contractor's schedule. As the job progresses, the foremen supervise the ongoing work, coordinate with the other trades, and meet with inspectors.

Jerry became familiar with A-Plus by driving around with his father, Joseph, on Saturdays. He learned the business through his father, and by taking courses in

This case is based on original work by Mandy Lee.

blueprint reading. Joseph, Alfie, and Jerry look after their own projects and workers. In the partnership, all profits are divided equally, but there is pressure on the three partners to be the most profitable, which has led to an informal competition.

Howie is a foreman with A-Plus and now works solely on Jerry's projects. He has worked with the company for the past 12 years (beginning as a drywaller), except for a period of six months when Howie accepted an offer to work for a smaller competitor as a project manager. A-Plus, realizing that they had lost one of the best foremen in the industry, won him back with the promise of a better salary and more managerial control over the projects assigned to him. Howie has the highest qualifications and the most extensive education of the seven foremen. He is often assigned to projects estimated at $2 million or more with the responsibility for supervising 30 to 50 workers. His short-term goals are to exercise more authority over his projects and show excellent performance; his long-term goal is to ultimately gain a partnership. The latter would elevate his status and income.

THE PROBLEM

Currently, Howie is frustrated with inconsistencies and difficulties in his role as a foreman. He is not seeing the progression of responsibilities he expected on his return to the firm, and he has become aware of some questionable management practices. On two previous projects for Joseph, Howie was responsible for scheduling the workers and ordering material. On his projects for Jerry, where he is now permanently assigned, he assumed that it would be the same, but he was wrong. Jerry was personally scheduling the workers and ordering the material. However, when Howie noticed that they had run out of a particular material and brought it to Jerry's attention, Jerry showed disappointment and blamed Howie for the problem. Howie almost said, "Since when did it become my responsibility?" but he held his tongue and placed the order for replacement supplies. Similar problems have often arisen for Howie due to Jerry's leadership practices.

After one particularly annoying incident, Howie decided that he would no longer discipline or dismiss any workers. It happened after Howie noticed one worker arriving an hour late for work three mornings in the same week. When Jerry was collecting the worker's hours, Howie advised him to dock the man three hours of his pay, and Jerry did so. Later, the worker confronted Howie, waving his reduced paycheque in the air in front of Howie's face. Howie explained that as he had showed up late three times during the past week he had reported fewer hours to Jerry. The worker said, "Well, I asked Jerry why and all he said was to ask you!" Frequently, Howie needs support from Jerry but gets mixed messages. Howie now just tells Jerry when workers are being unproductive and sometimes, although rarely, Jerry does something about it.

Jerry's goals are all about the bottom line — enhancing profits above all else. Often, he wins the informal competition to achieve the best profit margin among the three partners. While the other two partners are more straightforward and even-handed with their subordinates, if Jerry sees the opportunity, he cheats the workers on their hours, benefits, and overtime payments. When confronted about not compensating the workers fully, Jerry would say, "It's tough competing with your uncle and your old man. Sometimes, we need to cut a few corners so I can get a little respect when the final numbers come out on the project." When the workers' pay rates were increased due to the union's efforts, Jerry waited several paycheques before paying his men the revised union rate. In return, the workers sometimes "borrow" materials, take longer breaks (occasionally going off on personal business), lie about the hours they have worked, etc. This put Howie in a predicament: should he blow the whistle on his boss and/or on his workers, or does he just look out for number one — himself? Blowing the whistle on his boss, when he and the other partners are all members of the same family, might not be a wise thing to do.

Howie reviews his pay carefully to ensure Jerry hasn't scrimped on paying his hours or benefits. When a project is especially profitable and the foremen have worked long days and many weekends, some of them ask for a bonus. Jerry has never rewarded his first line supervisors on his own initiative, not even providing a Christmas bonus. He waits until he is pressured. Howie has adjusted to this practice by requesting extra compensation when he feels it is justified. However, he is uncomfortable with this informal solicitation of extra pay. He would rather see a formal overtime arrangement and profit sharing in place for foremen and workers. However, he realizes Jerry could not be relied on to follow such a plan.

Howie had originally believed that as time went on he would become more involved in project administration. Now, in meetings with the general contractor and other trades, Howie feels that he has such limited ability to supervise the workers that he can't promise to meet deadlines. He lets Jerry make whatever commitments are required.

Jerry has recently told Howie that he will be leaving A-Plus to start his own company. He is encouraging Howie to join him, promising Howie that he would be given full authority to manage projects within the new company and be offered a partnership within three years if the business goes well. Despite his questionable management practices, Jerry is very effective in dealing with clients, and Howie believes that the new firm will likely obtain large and profitable projects. Howie realizes that staying with A-Plus and transferring to work under Joseph or Alfie would probably delay his career progress. Howie is wondering whether he should just welcome Jerry's departure and hope to excel in a better working environment with Alfie or Joseph, or whether he should approach Jerry with his misgivings about joining him in order to seek a firmer assurance that things would be better in the new company.

QUESTIONS

1. Compare and contrast Jerry's and Howie's values.

2. After Howie requested Jerry to change his unethical practices and discipline the workers and Jerry failed to do so, should Howie have informed the other two partners of what went on in Jerry's projects? Why or why not?

3. What other actions could Howie have taken in response to the poor working environment he had under Jerry?

4. If Howie takes the job with Jerry in the new firm, what do you think would be the likely outcome?

5. What should Howie do now (as of the end of the case)?

Alice's Expense Account

THE CASE

Alice Bigelow worked for the Beaver Basket Company. She was the newest member of their sales department and the first woman. The Beaver Basket Company was an old and established Canadian company that got its start manufacturing wooden baskets. These were used by the fruit and vegetable industry, but they also manufactured a line used in the home as laundry baskets.

They kept abreast of the times, and, when technology changed, they switched to more modern packaging methods and expanded their product line to serve the growing manufacturing industry of southern Ontario. They moved their offices and plant from Minesing, Ontario, which had an abundant forest, to Ajax, which was close to major highways.

Members of the sales team visited manufacturers and helped them package their product in a visually pleasing manner. The Beaver Basket Company would then make the packages and ship them to the manufacturer. Many of their customers were importers who required domestic packages for their products.

Most of their current packages were made of paper and plastic. Despite this modernization, the Beaver Basket Company was still privately owned by the original family. The corporate culture was filled with the traditional rural values of the founders, even though they no longer manufactured any wooden laundry baskets.

Alice had a problem with her expense form for her first sales trip to western Ontario. She had been away for a week, and her actual expenses came to $730. She was about to hand it in when one of the older salesmen asked to see it. He said that it was far too low, and that she ought to pad it the same way all the men did. He showed her how to do this by faking restaurant receipts, adding mileage, parking charges, and customer entertainment. He suggested that the past average for her trip was around $800–$850 and, if she didn't put in that much, then the accountants would start to wonder about the previous expense forms. He made it clear that, if she wanted to be one of the boys, she had better play ball on their team.

The problem that Alice had was that her great grandparents were from Minesing, Ontario, and had founded the Beaver Basket Company. She was the first member of her family in a generation to take any interest in actually working for the business, and she had not told anybody that she was a part of the family that owned it.

She did not know whether to blow the whistle on the salesmen, choke on it, or to save it for a rainy day.

QUESTION

1. List the options Alice had, and identify the pros and cons of each option. Consider all aspects of her situation, including her immediate circumstances as well as her long-term plans to work at the Beaver Basket Company.

2. Discuss the morality of the salesmen, in particular, the older salesman who undertook to teach Alice the tricks of the trade. Expense account padding is a fairly institutionalized practice. How is it justified by the participants? What rationalizations would they give for their unethical behaviour? How deviant is it?

The Auto Finance Centre

The Auto Finance Centre is a department of a much larger financial institution that was created to provide financing for car dealerships across the country. In June of 2004, the Centre expanded its financing program to other areas such as recreational vehicles, home improvements, RSP investments, boats, pianos, computers and other motorized vehicles such as motorcycles and snowmobiles. The Centre consisted of Data Entry, Customer Service, Administration, Credit Analysis and overall Management, for a total complement of 35 different positions. Each of the four former functions was supervised by a manager and two assistant managers. To provide coverage for the time zones from Atlantic to Pacific, there were 44 full- and part-time employees in the Centre. This staffing was designed to provide same-day service on 400–500 credit applications. The bulk of the applications pertained to car financing.

The business in the Centre was carried out as follows: A dealership would fax a handwritten credit application for a client who was purchasing a car and wanted to finance it. This application would be entered into the computer system, which automatically pulled a credit reference, and then was forwarded to the credit analysts for a decision. The dealership would ultimately be informed of either an approval or a disapproval of the application. (There may also have been a series of communications by fax and/or telephone, requesting additional information about the applicant or for additional support of the application by means of cosigners.) If the application was approved, funding took place when the dealer submitted properly completed sales documents. These documents also required verification by Centre staff. Finally, a new loan account was set up on the computer system that was then transferred to one of the financial institution's branches in order that the purchaser of the car would have a local contact for his/her loan.

The Centre had grown very rapidly, starting with two employees in 2003. Serious management problems began in April 2006 when the newly appointed Vice-President, Mr. Jones (who served as the general manager of the Centre), decided to replace both the Credit Manager and the Administrative Manager with outside appointments, and the two incumbent managers were transferred to different areas of

---

This case is based on original work by Eldeh Michael.

the financial institution. By hiring Ms. Green as the Credit Manager and Ms. Johnson as the Administration Manager, the Vice President had violated, in the opinion of all the staff, an unwritten rule that existing personnel should be considered first for such promotions. Everyone in the Centre felt that the promotions should have gone to one of the existing Assistant Managers, as they had put a lot of time and effort into building the Centre almost from its inception. Their backgrounds and years of experience in the financial institution were not taken into consideration. In fact, the staff felt that neither Ms. Green nor Ms. Johnson had the expertise and ability to handle a Centre with a high volume of applications and a large portfolio on in-house loan balances [mostly RSP loans]. Ms. Green's previous position was as Credit Authorization Officer for the Visa Centre of a trust company that was purchased by the financial institution. Her credit experience was limited to deciding whether to accept charges by merchants on customer credit cards. It seemed that Mr. Jones appointed Ms. Green due to the fact that she had worked for him in the past and they had become, over the years, very good friends.

As for Ms. Johnson, her previous experience was as a lower level supervisor for an insurance company, and she had no experience or understanding of how things are done in a lending institution. The staff of the Auto Finance Centre wondered for months about the reasons for hiring Ms. Johnson. The truth emerged that Ms. Green and Ms. Johnson were good friends, having in the past shared an apartment as roommates. This lack of recognition and failure to promote the skilled personnel in the Centre caused low morale among the remaining managers and staff. Many questioned why they should bother to do a good job if it was not going to enhance their careers. The remaining two managers kept a low profile, as the department now seemed to be run by Jones, Green and Johnson.

Green and Johnson apparently knew that the majority of staff would not be supportive of them in their new positions, and adopted the practice of making decisions without consultation. For example, Ms. Green felt that she had to promise a faster turnaround time for credit applications to improve customer service to the dealerships. She neglected to discuss the logistical side of this decision with the staff who had intimate knowledge of the time needed to input and analyze the application, nor did she consider the time it took to perform the administrative and accounting functions of processing the application. Everyone, including the assistant managers, was shocked when Ms. Green made an announcement that the maximum time to spend on an application should be ten minutes, and that she had also signed up 200 new dealers across the country to start sending in new business to the Auto Finance Centre. The new dealerships alone meant doubling the amount of work for the existing staff, not even considering the reduction in the processing time target.

Ms. Green also failed to include the opinions and the points of view of her assistant managers and staff who would be responsible for performing the tasks associated with the increased workload and reduced turnaround time. As for Ms. Johnson, she felt that by extending the business hours daily and on weekends, the Centre could attract more business from the network of coast to coast dealers. Again, this was decided without any discussion with the staff. On the 28th of June, 2006, Ms. Johnson surprised everyone with a new schedule that required the staff to work more late night shifts and two out of every four weekends. Ms. Johnson felt, as the Manager of Administration, that she was exercising her right of authority to organize the Centre, regardless of how her staff would react to the change or whether they had any family commitments or other concerns affecting their ability to work different hours. Her response to their concerns was, "People are lucky to have a job."

In order to try to accommodate the increased workload, the management of the Auto Finance Centre applied different rules every day based on the volume of work that had been received that day. On a busy day policy was adjusted to meet the demands of the volume of work and the commitment to the ten-minute turnaround time. The management was very concerned that they not receive any complaints from the dealerships about turnaround time. For example, in the case of a credit application where the customer had a history of slow payment, or was perhaps looking for amounts that were higher than the credit analyst's lending authority, the formal rules stated that such an application should be reviewed by the Assistant Credit Manager or the Credit Manager. But the policy was suspended when there were a lot of deals with decisions pending. The Credit Manager felt that credit analysts should make the decisions on those deals, and obtain their supervisor's signature later, to keep to the turnaround target. Much misunderstanding with regard to the Centre's policies, and when they should be followed, was the result. The credit analysts were blamed for not doing their jobs according to the rules when the Auto Finance Centre was audited by the Internal Inspectors of the Financial Institution. Moreover, some credit analysts took advantage of the absence of rules and regulations and approved some marginal credit applications for specific dealerships where friendly relations had developed through dealing with them frequently.

Other problems involved Ms. Green's and Ms. Johnson's treatment of their staff. When they extended the business hours, they did not include themselves in the scheduling for more weekend coverage. They also made promises of training and advancement to data entry staff. They were to learn the work of the credit analysts, and would therefore be eligible for promotion when such a position became available. While a small amount of cross-training occurred during slow periods, the promises of full training and eventual promotion were never realized. In one particular case, a qualified staff member's promotion to become an analyst was blocked, apparently because it would cause an inconvenient vacancy that would have to be filled.

Staff lacked motivation when they had few goals to achieve and few opportunities to direct their personal ambitions. Individuals who performed well were not rewarded. Neither Ms. Green nor Ms. Johnson talked to individual staff members to learn their needs and expectations. The few employees who still put a lot of time and effort into meeting the Centre's targets were taken for granted. When the Credit Manager decided to hire a third assistant manager, she hired someone from outside who had limited credit experience. This position was not even posted internally, so none of the qualified staff had a chance.

The managers also treated people in the same positions differently. Credit Analysts were all paid on different scales, and some of them were given more authority and higher credit limits than others. These decisions were not based on years of experience in credit, nor on their performance in the Centre, but strictly on favouritism.

With all these problems, however, the Centre still seemed to function adequately in the six months following the appointment of Johnson and Green. At this time, employees were being laid off throughout much of the financial sector, including in other areas of the institution to which the Auto Finance Centre belonged. It was probably the only reason many of the Centre staff stayed.

QUESTIONS

1. Classify the organizational type. In what ways is the Centre operating as a bureaucracy, and in what ways is it not?

2. Identify the motivational problems in the organization.

3. Relate these motivational problems to the practices of its leaders. In what ways are the leaders' styles dysfunctional?

4. Assuming continuing financial sector job losses, can you foresee any development, in terms of performance problems at the Centre, that will be likely to cause the financial institution to examine the Centre's Management with a view to discovering possible deficiencies?

Automation in the Book Store

My name is Lisa and I am a fourth year student in honours Biology at the University of Southern Ontario. Last summer I took a part-time job three evenings a week in a book store. My regular summer job provided me with good work experience, but it didn't pay too well. This story is about my experience in the book store.

I worked for a medium-sized book store, part of a chain that had two outlets in different malls in our city. The manager was glad to hire me because I had retail experience with Eaton's and Zeller's, and I was glad to work for them because I like to read and didn't want a part-time job that included weekend hours. I like to go camping with my friends.

The store was not very large. There were only three full-time employees: the manager, her assistant, and another woman. There were five part-time employees. One woman worked days, and the rest of us worked evenings and weekends. Only one other employee was a student; he worked the opposite shift to me. The rest were older women.

I liked the sales work. Employees were expected to serve a customer from our first contact with them through to the end of the sale, so it meant that I would approach a customer and offer assistance and stay with them until I had rung up any purchase the customer made. This made the work varied and interesting. It was a lot more personal than just standing at a cash register ringing up sales.

Shortly after I arrived, the manager announced that the store was going to join the company computer system. We had been managing with a simple system using a till and written record of sales. The computer system would record cash sales, credit card sales, and inventory, as well as maintain other records that were not explained to us. It was supposed to make our work go faster because it included a scanning device to read the product code on the books and other items in the store. We also assumed that the switch-over had something to do with the imposition of the new Goods and Services Tax that was expected in the new year. Books had not previously been taxed, and this would greatly ease the registering of this new sales tax.

The older staff were quite apprehensive about this new system. None of them had any previous experience with computers. I had worked with this kind of system at Eaton's, so I was curious to see how this one would work. The other student was experienced with computers, but had never worked with this kind of machine.

There was a great deal of discussion about what the computers could actually do. We were all assigned an ID number to use when recording our sales, and the people realized that it meant their work could be watched by the computer. Nobody liked that, although we really didn't know what could or could not be monitored.

The training was pretty skimpy. Head office sent the manager to the other store in the city to learn on their system. When she got back, our system was installed and our training began. There were two parts to the training. First we watched training tapes. There were two of them, each half an hour long. I found them to be boring and insulting. A man in the tape taught a dumb woman how to run the system. It was very patronizing.

The second part was better. We were given a training manual containing a series of exercises to do. The technician who installed the machine told us the system was in the training mode for the next week, and we could go ahead and do the exercises in the book. Later the machine would go "on line".

For two days we made progress. Even the most hesitant employees relaxed a bit as they rang up thousands of dollars in fictitious sales. We read how the main computer would keep track of these sales and maintain a record of our store inventory and decide when we needed more supplies, and so on. The scanner used to read the bar code worked pretty well. People were worried about having to read those long numbers and punch them into the register. The credit card system was terrific. It automatically made up the slip and phoned to get authorization for the card sale.

On the third day things fell apart. It turned out that our register was not in the training mode at all. It was on line and loaded with fictitious sales. This unfortunate incident confirmed the worst fears of those who had doubts about the change in the first place. There was lots of talk. The best comment was, "If you really want to make a mess, use a computer." The manager was dismayed, and head office wanted to assign blame. The technician said it was our fault since the system says when it is in the training mode, and we should have noticed that it was not. I told him he had it backwards. We had never seen the training mode, and what we saw looked exactly like it showed in the manual.

By the next week this mess was cleaned up, and we got down to regular use of the new system. There were three lingering problems. The first was an omission in the training. It did not include instructions on how to close up at the end of the day. Somehow nobody noticed this until the first day. The manager had to come in and prepare a hand-written set of instructions about this routine.

The other two problems were related. The employees continued to be concerned about work monitoring. I had experienced this at Eaton's, where my supervisor had told me that if my sales were much higher than the others in my area, they would take it to mean that I was not helping out on the floor, but rather was just standing there ringing up the cash register. Our manager at the book store would not confirm or deny any of these concerns.

The other problem had to do with signing in and out. We were supposed to sign in with our ID number when making a sale, and sign out after. We found this was time consuming. The actual registering of a sale was fast, and this additional step was unwelcome. The procedure seemed to be at odds with the previous standard of providing individual service to customers, and might have encouraged a system of having one person on cash while the others dealt with customer enquiries. We opted to ignore the individual sign in/out step. This also had the effect of scuttling any worker monitoring that the system might have done.

It took about a month for everything to settle down. I don't think the change to the new system was handled very well.

QUESTIONS

1. Conduct an analysis of this change.
   (a) Identify the forces supporting the change, the forces opposing the change, and the currently neutral forces that might be tipped one way or another once the change process has begun.
   (b) Develop a better change strategy that is based on strengthening the forces in favour of change and weakening the forces opposing change, and that covers the contingencies arising from the tipping of currently neutral forces.
   (c) Develop a strategy for "unfreezing" the status quo to begin the change process.

2. Why did the change, as it was carried out, create motivational dysfunctions for Lisa and the other participants?

Barry Wilson

Barry Wilson is Executive Director of the Communications Division of the Ontario Ministry of Transportation and Communications. The communications division has a staff of about 120 people divided into four offices: Policy Development, Cable/ Broadcast Research Office, Engineering, and Regulatory Affairs. The division also has an Administrative Services unit that supports the work of these four offices. Each office, including the unit, is headed by a manager. Wilson is the senior ranking officer in the division, and is responsible for the efficient and effective operation of the division, including the cooperative efforts and team work of all managers.

On one occasion, Wilson was called into the deputy minister's office and was directed to start preparing a briefing manual for the minister for an important upcoming federal-provincial conference on communications. Since the federal government would be represented by the minister of communications, the minister wanted to use this opportunity to press the federal government for further control over cable television within Ontario's boundaries. The minister's briefing manual for this conference had to be completed in one week. It had to include background on the issue, where the other provinces stand, possible tactics and strategies to gain support for the objective, possible consequences for Ontario if the federal government accepts Ontario's demands, and the consequences if it does not. In short, the briefing manual was quite detailed and comprehensive. A special meeting had been scheduled for the following week to review the briefing manual with the minister.

As Wilson leaves the deputy minister's office, he is wondering how to allocate this obviously sensitive and important project among his managers in order to produce a quality briefing manual within the limited timeframe he has to work with. He knows that the staff members have not always successfully collaborated on major projects in the past. He is also aware of the uneven quality and talents of his management team. The best manager is Ms. Edwards, who is in charge of the Policy Development Office. He often thought that Edwards could be his successor when he moves on. But Wilson is aware of how jealous and resentful the other

This case was written by James Simeon.

managers can be if Edwards, yet again, gets the choice project. Wilson must decide on how best to delegate responsibility for this project. He is also aware that by successfully completing this project he could be in a better position for possible promotion to assistant deputy minister or deputy minister status.

QUESTIONS

1. What leadership issues arise in this case?

2. Is it always best to choose the most competent person to work on an important project, regardless of the consequences?

3. What should Barry Wilson do about allocating responsibility for this project?

Best Food Grocer

COMPANY PROFILE

Best Food Grocer was a small, high-quality store located in the northwest area of Toronto that employed 50–60 full-time and part-time employees. It was opened 20 years ago by an experienced butcher, Aaron McDonald, who loved high quality and rich-tasting foods. The store sold everything from specialty cakes and pastries to exquisite cuts of meat and premium fruits and vegetables. The store also stocked standard grocery items and freshly prepared hot and cold dishes to provide a "home-cooked" meal experience. The store consisted of seven departments — bakery, grocery, produce, kitchen, cash, deli, and meat. Exhibit 1 shows that each department had its own supervisor, who reported directly to Aaron. Aaron made all the staffing schedules. All other day-to-day issues, not including time off and compensation, were to be taken up with the department supervisor. Aaron was rarely seen in the store for more than an hour or so at a time. He came in occasionally, but was often at the food terminals at night gathering fruits and vegetables or spending time dealing with suppliers. He was also busy with his kids during the day. They needed to be dropped off and picked up at school. When the weather permitted it, he would also fit in a weekly round of golf with his friends. Payroll was done on the weekends when the store was very busy with customers. Aaron would be in his office and unavailable to directly supervise the staff. The department supervisors would run the store. Any issues that needed Aaron's attention could be brought up to him at a later time or introduced at staff meetings, which were held irregularly and only when needed. If there was a serious problem, Aaron's home telephone number was on the bulletin board located in the lunchroom. It was to be used only if the situation was extremely urgent and there was no other means of contacting him.

THE PROBLEM

Christina was a meat clerk at the store. She was a 19-year-old culinary arts student who attended Humber College. She had no family obligations and spent most of her

---

This case is based on original work by Julia Cuzzolino.

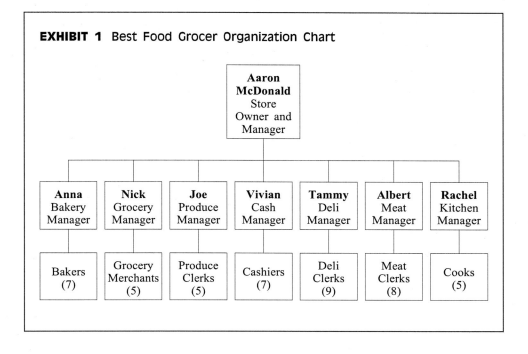

EXHIBIT 1 Best Food Grocer Organization Chart

- Aaron McDonald — Store Owner and Manager
  - Anna — Bakery Manager
    - Bakers (7)
  - Nick — Grocery Manager
    - Grocery Merchants (5)
  - Joe — Produce Manager
    - Produce Clerks (5)
  - Vivian — Cash Manager
    - Cashiers (7)
  - Tammy — Deli Manager
    - Deli Clerks (9)
  - Albert — Meat Manager
    - Meat Clerks (8)
  - Rachel — Kitchen Manager
    - Cooks (5)

free time working. The salary she received was necessary to pay all her expenses, including books, tuition, parking and new car payments for the vehicle she had recently purchased. She had been working at the grocer for five years now, starting off in bakery, moving on to cash, and then to the kitchen, based on her training and experience in cooking. The meat department was her latest assignment, as that area was short-handed. The owner had decided to move her there to supplement the existing staff. That enabled Christina to continue working part-time, as they now needed a full-time person in the kitchen, her previous assignment. Although she worked mainly in the meat department, if another department was ever in need of help, Christina was willing to assist and put in extra hours. After a while, her extended and flexible availability was expected by the owner, Aaron.

All working schedules were made by Aaron, and any changes to the normal availability of any employee were to be taken up with him in writing. All such requests were required to be placed in his mail box at least two weeks prior to the day that the employee needed off. Aaron said that he did all the scheduling because he would best meet everyone's preferences for hours of work, treat everyone evenly, and ensure that all departments were properly staffed. In this way, the supervisors wouldn't have to do any extra work after the staff left the store.

In 2007, Aaron created an incentive program to motivate his part-time employees. For every 1000 hours they worked, he would give them a $0.25 hourly rate increase to recognize the quality of their work and their dedication to the store. On average, an employee who worked 20 hours a week would get the raise after 50 weeks or approximately once per year. Aaron felt this was an affordable and adequate way to keep his employees happy. He didn't formalize this incentive in writing, because he didn't have an employee handbook. Instead, he told his employees about this reward on an individual basis. Since he felt that the full-timers worked equally as hard, Aaron thought that instead of the $0.25 raise for every 1000 hours, he would give them one paid day off a month to compensate them and keep them happy. They could take off any day they wished, except Saturday, as it was the busiest day of the week. The only event that would stop them from having the day of their choice would be if another full-time employee in their department already had that day booked off. The day off had to be used within the month and could not be banked or carried forward to be combined with a second day. If they failed to request a day off in a given month, they were not allowed to ask for it at a later time. They also received a higher rate of pay than the part-timers, and a two-week annual vacation, which needed to be booked well in advance.

During the spring of 2007, Christina was out of school and decided that she should put in more hours for the next several months before she had to pay for all her expenses, which would be due in the early fall. Christina worked full-time hours consisting of 44+ hours per week from April 2007 until September 2007. She didn't book any time off all summer. Customers and other employees liked Christina's constant presence and willingness to help out whenever needed. Over time, she gained experience in various tasks throughout the store. Before the end of the summer, she was doing much of the ordering for the meat shipments, staying after hours with the meat supervisor to prepare for the next day, making gift baskets for customers, and even making special deliveries with her own car to customers' homes when they were unable, through age or illness, to come to the store. This was a lot more than any other part-time employee was doing, and more than most of the full-time staff. Considering her youth, she felt important in the store. She had a lot of responsibility, and her work was recognized and appreciated by her department head, Albert.

In September, Christina returned to her part-time regular hours, but it seemed that she was still expected to do all those other tasks she had performed during the summer, including helping out in other departments. In the beginning, Christina didn't mind. She thought she was doing something good for her fellow employees as well as for the customers. However, over time Christina began to feel as if the extra work was no longer being appreciated as exceptional service, but had become an expectation of her manager and of the employees she assisted. Even a simple "thank you" was rarely received. Lists of extra things for her to do were still being compiled by Albert and her co-workers. Christina started to feel overworked and underpaid. Even the full-timers, who were not doing as much as she, were being paid more and receiving all the perks, such as one paid day off a month, which Christina didn't feel was fair. Prior to Christmas and the holiday season, Christina decided to approach Albert. She told him she felt she was being compensated unfairly, that her work was no longer appreciated, and that she deserved a raise. Albert replied that he did not have the authority to give her the raise, but if she wished, she could present her case to Aaron. Feeling shy and apprehensive about such a meeting, she decided to write him a letter. She asked for either a higher pay rate — the same as a full-timer, pro rata with the hours of work she did, or at least the $0.25 raise for all the hours she put in. She was very open and honest in the letter and left both her home and cell phone numbers so that he could contact her. She put the letter in his mail box and never heard from him.

Over the holiday season, Christina put in many extra hours and even decorated the meat department for the festive season without any recognition or appreciation from Aaron. He was in and out of the store frequently, but never stopped to acknowledge her. By January, Christina had become very unhappy. She had approached her department supervisor, written a letter to the owner, but still nothing had been done — not an even an acknowledgement of her request. Finally, one Friday, Christina came to work early to see if Aaron was in, so that they could talk before her shift. He wasn't there at the time, and when she tried to speak to him during the weekend, he said that he needed her to get back to her department, as the store was busy. He said they would talk at a later time. After store hours, he had already left, and again Christina was unable to talk with him. Feeling extremely frustrated, she obtained his home number from the bulletin board and called him one night at home with the hope of discussing her letter, which she had submitted almost two months earlier. He suggested that she come in one day during the following week prior to her shift to discuss her letter.

When they finally were able to have their discussion, Aaron stated that he did not appreciate being called at home and that if she needed to speak to him, it could have been done at the store. She tried to explain that between school and work she never had the chance. When he was in the store, it was busy and he couldn't speak to her. She reiterated that she still felt unappreciated and unfairly compensated as she still hadn't seen an adjustment to her pay. He responded that she had gotten a raise two years ago and that she was already being paid higher then most part-timers. Therefore, he didn't feel she needed yet another raise. Based on the hours she had put in from the time he began the $0.25 raise per 1000 hours policy, she was not eligible. That was another reason why he wouldn't grant it to her. She tried to explain to him that the raise she had received was prior to the $0.25 policy and that two years was a long time without any increase. She presented him with the argument that since her last raise she had worked a sufficient number of hours and was entitled to the pay increase. She mentioned that although she was a part-time employee, she did more work then anyone else in her department, aside from the meat manager. Aaron claimed he couldn't give her special treatment and apply the same policies as for full-time employees. If the other part-time employees found out, they would be upset and so would the full-timers.

It was then time for Christina's shift to start, and Aaron said he had paperwork to do. He ended their conversation with the statement that he needed to think it over, but he didn't feel that there was much he could do for her. She left his office saying that if she didn't get the pay increase she deserved, she would be forced to look for other means of employment to obtain the money she needed to pay for her expenses. As she walked away, he responded through the open door that if she felt she needed to do that, then to go ahead. That comment made her feel very depressed.

Since early fall, Christina had been working 12 hours per week at a restaurant for her co-op placement at school. The restaurant was close to home, and she could use the skills learned at Humber College in a pleasant working environment. The day after her altercation with Aaron, the head chef at the restaurant, John, could tell that she was upset when she arrived for work. She told him about the problem she encountered and that she didn't like to work at the grocery. Knowing that she was a productive employee and dedicated to her work, he offered her as many hours as she wished in a part-time position at the restaurant. Since the pay at the restaurant would not be high enough, however, Christina decided to take the job at the restaurant during the week and keep the grocery job on Sundays when minimal work was needed to be done. Also, neither Aaron nor the department manager, Albert, was in the store on Sunday. Christina felt that she could still work at both places if she did not have to deal with Aaron, in particular.

Aaron soon realized that Christina wasn't working as many hours and that the various tasks she used to do were either not being done well or were not done at all. He was not pleased that she was available only on Sundays. He told Albert that she needed to give him more hours and days or there was no reason for her to be there. Later that week, Albert called Christina at home and told her that she had been taken off the schedule until she provided Aaron with at least 2 days or 12 hours of availability. Christina, now very upset, immediately wrote a resignation letter addressed to Aaron.

QUESTIONS

1. Assess the likely motivational benefits of the two incentive programs for part-time and full-time employees.

2. Identify all the root causes of Christina's worsening attitude and decreasing level of job satisfaction.

3. Identify and critically assess Aaron's leadership style.

4. To what extent are the organizational structure, policies, and practices responsible for the problem?

5. How should Christina's letter to Aaron and subsequent confrontation with him have been better handled and why?

6. Should part-time employees be treated differently than full-time employees, even if their contribution to the organization is similar?

Blossom Inc.

Blossom Inc. has been assembling and selling personal computers and networks for many years. Typical of small companies in the computer business, it began in the back of a retail computer shop operated by Alfred Wong. He was a computer wizard and a smart businessperson. His retail business flourished, and soon he was able to add the assembly of computers and systems. He then phased out the retail store and focused on business clients, expanding his product line to include office networks, sales and inventory control systems, human resource information systems, payroll and accounting systems and other, similar products. Blossom worked with a client all the way from the initial inquiry, through the custom design of the system, its assembly and installation, employee training and follow-up service.

A key to Blossom's success was its focus on highest quality of its product and services. Blossom stood behind everything it sold, and would replace hardware and software that didn't live up to the advertised standards of performance or customer expectations. In the early days, the typical Blossom customer wanted to install their first PC network in their business. Customers like that were nervous about what they were doing, often had to deal with a lot of internal resistance to the change, and needed a lot of hand holding. This was Blossom's niche. The customer wanted the best in product quality and service and was prepared to pay for it. Blossom satisfied this need and its price reflected that. Blossom monitored the prices of its competition, but generally was not concerned about meeting the lowest prices, feeling that its market wasn't very price sensitive.

Wong managed the growth of Blossom by developing a highly organized company divided into functional divisions. He created a corporate structure with control centred in his office, where all the important decisions were made. There were many levels of management, each with elaborate rules, regulations, and policies. The formal communication channels followed the hierarchical distribution of authority, status and rewards. The job descriptions of subordinates were based on what Wong felt would achieve efficiency and effectiveness.

This case is based on original work by Yiping Luo.

The business transactions consisted of a relatively small number of large sales. This made it possible for each sale to be managed at the highest level in the company. Wong didn't personally manage every sale, but he was never far away. The employees who dealt directly with the clients were not given much authority over details of the transaction; their role was to carry out the orders from above. For their part, the clients were comforted by the knowledge that their business was being handled by senior management, and they felt that involvement of the principals was important.

Employees were provided with above average pay and commissions and good working conditions, and generally maintained outstanding client relations. Many of the employees in sales, installation and trouble shooting were able to deal directly with the clients. Even the employees in the assembly plant would have occasional contact. Customers liked Blossom because they made the transition to a PC network a comfortable process. The employees felt a strong connection with the clients, which was often stronger than was felt towards their own senior management.

However, there were problems within the firm. The most serious was the limited nature of the internal communication. For example, employees in the assembly division failed to report that the poor quality of some equipment purchased externally for the systems they assembled resulted in abnormal shutdowns and excess setup times. Substantial costs were incurred due to these failures. There were also problems in that managers were sometimes too brief in their instructions, and employees couldn't understand the reasons for a particular set of directions or procedures. When this occurred, it meant they didn't know whether they were producing the desired results from their work, as the goals were not communicated to them.

However, on the whole, Blossom generally was a successful business during the early years. To build on this success, in the seventh year of operation Wong took on some silent partners to obtain the capital he needed for expansion. Through a few rounds of investment, these partners ultimately acquired a majority holding. Their contribution enabled the construction of a new plant in Toronto and branch sales offices in six different locations in Canada. By the tenth year, it had a total of 200 employees.

After 11 years of successful operations, the business started to slip, and Blossom had two consecutive quarterly losses. At first, Wong tried to reverse this downturn by imposing even more centralized control. He insisted on personally approving all sales contracts. After a disastrous third quarter in which Blossom lost $6 million, the silent partners became vocal and forced Wong into retirement. He made a graceful exit by selling them his remaining shares in Blossom.

The partners Hired Jimmy Bao as the new CEO and gave him a wide mandate to salvage the firm. Bao came from a smaller competitor and had earned a reputation as being very knowledgeable about the computer business. After meeting with his senior management team, Bao set out to meet with the various employee groups within the company. He quickly learned that the structure of the company was making its operations costly and ineffective. The sales team told him that despite its reputation for high quality, Blossom had a low rate of repeat business. Bao knew that the PC network business had become price sensitive. Businesses might pay for high quality initially, but once clients developed their own expertise they would then select vendors with attractive prices.

Bao met with the partners and proposed a revitalization plan. First they would change to a product-based structure with three divisions — networks, PC's and peripherals such as printers and monitors. This led to the second change — decentralization. Each product line would become a profit centre, and the managers for that area would be given the authority and independence to run their own show. If a particular product couldn't be made profitable, then it would be replaced by one that could. In the previous structure, there was only one profit centre, Blossom, and the profitability of individual product lines was almost impossible to determine. This would greatly reduce the need for senior level management and would enable major cost savings. The third proposed change was a decision to become very price competitive. This meant that Blossom's product departments would not be forced to buy from their own plant, but could outsource at will. This would probably mean the closure of the plant unless it was able to compete with outside suppliers.

The partners were very impressed by this new plan, and were inclined to give it their immediate approval. One of the partners asked Bao how he planned to implement it, and he said he intended to call the employees together and announce it on Monday morning as a plan that would be put into effect immediately. This evoked a very strong reaction from several of the partners. One said he had been involved in this kind of change before, and that it was not as easy as it seemed. He said that if Bao just went ahead with that announcement on Monday morning, the company would be in turmoil for months. Productivity would collapse, and once the layoffs started, the company could be tied up with lawsuits for a long time to come.

Bao countered that he was the CEO and he had been given a mandate by the partners to make Blossom profitable as he saw fit. He said that he would spend day and night on the job to get it done. Blossom needed a lightning strike to turn it around, and he would provide that stimulus. The end result was a lengthy and heated discussion among the partners and Bao about how to implement the change. Some partners supported Bao, while others saw the quick approach as a design for disaster. The turning point of the discussion came when the partners engaged in a lengthy discussion about the assets of the company. They had a strong customer base with a reputation for quality, even if they had been losing out in the price wars. They had an assembly facility that could do excellent work and could probably become price competitive if given an opportunity and the right internal environment. Their sales force was widely based, very knowledgeable, and well received by businesses. Their reputation for customer satisfaction was first rate. They had a large range of products, and were always on top of the latest changes in hardware and software. They had excellent alliances with suppliers and a strong reputation with them for stability and reliability. This meant a lot in the ever changing business computer market. Finally, they had a skilled and loyal group of employees.

In the end the partners prevailed, and Bao reluctantly conceded that the lightning strike would not be in his best interests. He would spend too much of his time fighting resistance and problems, and he would not have enough time to build up the new organizational design he wanted. The alternative strategy was a more gradual change that would tap the knowledge that resided in the firm to help itself to change. It was decided that an outside consultant would be engaged to work with Bao to help turn the company around. The partners also decided that during the change period they would meet regularly to monitor and support the change process.

QUESTIONS

1. Evaluate the pros and cons of Bao's plan (disregarding implementation method) to change Blossom Inc. Is it based on an effective decision-making process?

2. Would you have supported Bao's original timing or the directors' approach of a slower rate of change, and why?

3. Identify what are likely to be the forces in support of Bao's new design and the forces opposed. Identify any opposing forces that might be converted to support the new design.

4. Assume you are the change consultant. What is your plan of action for the first week? What is your goal for the first month? How long do you think it will take to fully implement the change and regain profitable operations?

5. What behavioural challenges are likely to be faced by Bao and the consultant, as they launch the implementation?

Brewmaster Limited

Brewmaster Limited is a broadly based food and beverage company with major participation in the brewing, consumer foods, and agricultural products industries. Its head office is in Alberta. It employs 12,500 people and had gross sales in the last five years averaging $800 million.

Employee alcohol abuse is not unique to Brewmaster itself, but is experienced in most, if not all, industries. The case will deal with a situation concerning approximately 300 employees at the Brewmaster brewing plant in Calgary.

ALCOHOL ABUSE IN INDUSTRY, CANADA WIDE

The "alcohol abuser" or "problem drinker" presents problems to his employer, fellow workers, friends, and family. The cost of maintaining the "alcohol abuser" on the payroll is estimated to cost Canadian industry $1 million a day in sick benefits, job-related absenteeism, property damage, and low production. The average rate of absenteeism for those not regularly indulging is six to ten days, but for the "problem drinker", it is 24 to 36 days a year, a four-fold increase. Not only is the cost to industry enormous, but there is also the question of safety for the worker and fellow employees. With the industry being highly mechanized, the accident rate has risen sharply due to intoxicated personnel operating machines.

It has been estimated that approximately 3–10% of the working population is classified as being either alcohol abusers or problem drinkers. The many problems associated with these employees have prompted many industries to initiate their own programs. Management wants to identify these people and reduce costs to the company. Statistics repeatedly point out the savings in dollars after successful programs have been inaugurated.

"Alcoholism Programs Needed", *Labour Gazette*, Vol. 8, August 1975, p. 485.

HISTORY OF PROBLEMS AT
BREWMASTER BREWERY, CALGARY

At Brewmaster's, the worker was in constant contact with the very product whose consumption management was trying to restrict. This situation alone created problems that most other companies do not have to deal with.

The company had been plagued with an alcohol abuse problem since its early days of operation in 1990. Because the workers were producing beer, management initially decided it would institute a policy whereby no alcohol consumption was allowed at any time on the premises. By outlawing it completely, management hoped that employee drinking would drop for fear of breaking company rules and of having their positions terminated. Unfortunately, this approach of restriction had the same effect on the workers as happens when many desired things become restricted; the demand for it became more intense. Management found that production per worker was dropping, absenteeism related to alcohol abuse was increasing, and the

---

EXHIBIT 1 BREWMASTER POLICY

Management believes that alcohol or drug abuse is an illness requiring treatment. It is the policy of the company to provide such treatment through its medical and personnel departments.

GUIDELINES

1. It is essential for the general well-being of the Company and its employees that high standards of job performance be established and achieved. An employee with an alcohol or drug problem will be unable, over time, to live up to his responsibilities at work.

2. Where unsatisfactory performance is suspected to be due to alcoholism or drug abuse, the supervisor should encourage the employee to consult the Company doctor to obtain treatment.

3. When unacceptable performance is clearly due to drinking or to drug abuse and medical or professional treatment is required, such treatment is mandatory.

4. An employee who is absent from work while undergoing medical treatment for an alcohol or drug problem will receive normal benefits through the Company's Weekly Indemnity, Sick Leave, and Salary Continuation programs with the concurrence of the Medical department.

5. The Company will make every reasonable effort to help the employee back to normal health and job performance. Only when it has been established that medical treatment and other measures have failed should dismissal be considered.

6. The Company will encourage the involvement of the union in its Alcohol and Drug Abuse Program.

7. Through contacts with governmental and other agencies, the Company through its Medical and Personnel departments will make available to supervisors and other interested employees training and information on the control of alcoholism and drug abuse.

EXHIBIT 2 Signs of Job Performance Decline That
May Be Noted by Supervisors & Managers

1. Excessive lateness
2. Excessive absenteeism
3. Excessive sick leave
4. Morale problem (difficulty with other employees or supervisors)
5. Accident prone
6. Work output or quality decline
7. Abuse of lunch and break periods
8. Leaving the job without permission
9. Excessive overstaying on company property
10. Inability to cope with unexpected change in routine
11. Unexplained memory lapses
12. Inconsistent or drastic change in job performance

EXHIBIT 3 Some Helpful Hints for Supervisors and Managers

DO

- remember alcoholism is a progressive illness
- remind that help is available through the Medical department
- make it clear that the company is concerned only with job performance
- emphasize that all aspects of the program are confidential
- remember the importance of documentation

DON'T

- cover up for a friend or fellow employee
- be misled by manipulation and sympathy-evoking tactics — the alcoholic is an expert
- accept substandard job performance from anyone
- moralize — restrict discussion to job performance
- discuss drinking unless it occurs on the job
- try to diagnose the problem
- try to counsel an employee

EXHIBIT 4 Some Responsibilities of Union Representatives

1. To be familiar with the policy and procedures of the alcohol and drug abuse program.

2. To provide information on the program and encourage employees who may have an alcohol or drug problem to seek assistance voluntarily before job performance is affected.

3. To ensure that the rights of bargaining unit employees are explained to them.

4. To advise employees of their options should they refuse the help offered through the program.

5. To participate in ensuring support and follow-up on the job to facilitate the employee's rehabilitation.

morale of the workers was hitting a new low. The temptation to obtain a beer over-came many employees. During working hours when production was low, it was noticed that breaks became longer, as did lunch time. The frequency of a worker leaving a machine to go to the men's room was also increasing.

It was soon clear to management that the prohibition currently in force was not working as well as had been hoped. It became necessary to develop a new approach. This new policy would allow the employees to indulge for 35 minutes after their shift had been completed. An area off the cafeteria was provided as a "bar" or "pub". The beer was kept (Brewmaster brands only) in a huge cooler, and consumption was not restricted, as it was a self-serve bar. Each man was also given a 12-pack each month, or a case of 24 beers for production rates that approached plant capacity. These measures were implemented with the hope that the employees would restrict their consumption until after work and that time lost during the day and accidents would decrease.

If it was determined by the supervisor that an employee's absenteeism and effi-ciency were deteriorating, he would be referred to the medical department for tests and a checkup to determine the reasons. Should it be discovered that the problem was alcohol abuse, the worker would then be offered assistance. In cases where the employee refused the assistance, the union was informed of the refusal, and the employee was warned and given one more chance. If the employee was caught in a less than sober state or in the act of consuming alcohol on the job again and refused treatment, it led to job termination. In cases where the workers accepted help, they were usually referred to the Western Institute for alcohol abuse for approximately three to four weeks. The employee paid half the fee ($600–$700) and management paid the remaining 50%. During this time all employment benefits were paid, including 70% of the employee's salary. If, after treatment, male workers still had a recurring alcohol abuse problem, they were again referred to the Institute or to Alpha House (rehabilitation centre for hard-core male alcoholics), and the treat-ment steps were repeated. A third recurrence led to management terminating employment. (See Exhibit 5.) It should also be mentioned that all privileges with respect to indulging after work were lost by the offending worker for anywhere up to one year. As management proceeded with each step, the union was notified of each recurrence. Once management attempted to terminate employment, the union required that the case go to arbitration for the final decision.

BACKGROUND

The reasons for an alcohol abuse problem are many, and are of varying degrees of importance. Management and the union have tried to determine some of these fac-tors. Both tended to shift the blame to the other side. Some of the reasons both groups have given are: the age of the employee; the relationship between union and management; the nature of the work itself (whether it is shift work or not, and what type of work it is, e.g., specialized, physical, non-skilled, and interesting); the avail-ability of alcohol; the policy currently in effect; and the social situations over which the company has little or no control.

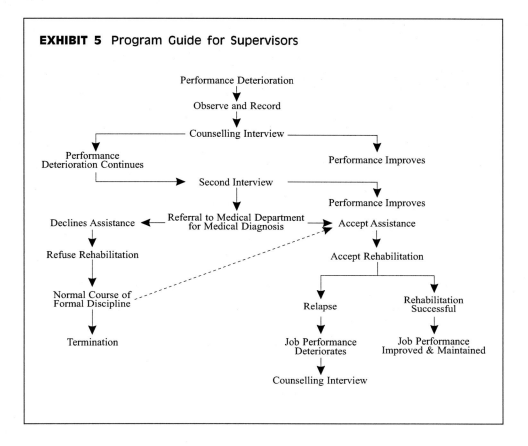

EXHIBIT 5 Program Guide for Supervisors

Performance Deterioration → Observe and Record → Counselling Interview

Performance Deterioration Continues / Performance Improves

Second Interview → Performance Improves

Referral to Medical Department for Medical Diagnosis → Declines Assistance / Accept Assistance

Refuse Rehabilitation → Accept Rehabilitation

Normal Course of Formal Discipline → Termination

Relapse → Job Performance Deteriorates → Counselling Interview

Rehabilitation Successful → Job Performance Improved & Maintained

It appeared to management that, as they hired younger employees (20–29 yrs.), there had been an increase in the alcohol abuse reports related to this age group. This seemed to be the result of the general lack of education regarding the "problem drinker" as well as the temptation of the novelty of free beer. At first the younger employee attempted to "keep up" with his older, more experienced counterparts. This led to drinking while working (usually done when the supervisor was known to be in another part of the plant), as well as indulging after work. Unfortunately, as the novelty wears off, the dependence on alcohol does not.

Union and management were in a rather difficult position. Management's main concern was the increased productivity of the worker and reduction of lost time. Both these results would have increased profits for the company. The union would have liked to get its hands on the extra profits in the form of increased wages, or extra benefits. However, they had to protect the employee, even if it meant that the company took the extra profit and put it into an alcohol abuse program. This reduced the amount of money available to increase wages or extra benefits, but the alcoholic worker was entitled to representation by the union. Supervisory personnel were also in a very unfortunate position. Management was relying on the supervisor to identify the alcohol abuser or problem drinker. Otherwise, the policy would break down at the very start. The union, on the other hand, questioned the qualifications of the supervisor when he had to determine who he felt was a problem drinker or alcohol abuser. To keep the supervisor from reaching a too hasty decision, some union members would bring a grievance against the supervisor or would instigate a slight slowdown in production. Both these methods caused management to re-evaluate the supervisor, bringing more pressure to bear on him. This type of situation usually resulted in the supervisor being concerned only with the most blatant violations.

The nature and type of work has been shown to be a factor in the alcohol abuse problem. The brewery is a very highly mechanized plant employing the latest computerized and high-speed equipment. Except for three or four stations on the "assembly line", all other work took the form of visual inspection and ensuring that conveyors moved along smoothly. Any problems that resulted in "down time" were delegated out to mechanics or electricians. The men on the line were not allowed to deal with the problem or to attempt to correct the situation. The work was neither physically demanding nor interesting. There was no reward for working at an increased rate or contributing more to the production of a line's output. Each worker was paid the same wage as well as benefits, and each had to do shift work. This routine work and lack of incentives seemed to encourage the employee to leave a station for a drink (usually hiding behind a full pallet of beer). Or, if they remained at the machine, they would hide beside it and quickly consume as much as they could. They were not missed unless a problem developed at that checkpoint. To try to reduce the monotony, management started a rotation system whereby the worker rotated from one position to another down the line each hour. It seemed to work well for a period of time, but eventually the rotation system itself began to become tedious and boring to the employee. He knew each hour exactly which task he would be performing and how monotonous it would become. When asked how a worker can tolerate the monotony, John Smith replied, "After a few beers, things seem to pick up, and you don't really think about what you're doing."

The availability of the alcohol presented a unique problem to management. It was impossible to keep the line running and not have the workers come in contact with the beer. The ease of obtaining a beer created situations that most other industries or organizations do not face. How could a supervisor determine that the person had been drinking, just because he happened to be holding a beer bottle in his hand? The handling of the product was a necessary part of producing it. Arriving at a hasty decision would have repercussions for the supervisor. The person must have literally been showing signs of intoxication before action could be taken. By this time though, the problem had already developed into a serious concern.

A NEW POLICY

The policy that was in effect has now been slightly altered to better come to grips with the abuse problem. Management had tried in vain to deal with the problem by allowing the workers access to all the beer they could consume after hours. As could be expected, the company could not revert back to the original policy of prohibition; first, because that particular policy did not work; and second, now that workers were given the privilege of indulging after work, they were not about to let management take it away from them. Management's next move was to remove the self-serve cooler and build an enclosed "bar", serviced by a bartender (a union worker) who was allowed to serve beer 15 minutes **after** the shift was over for 35 minutes. It was hoped that by not allowing the employees easy access to the beer until shifts had changed, they would be restricted from indulging before work and having too much afterward. The bartender was also to refuse beer to anyone he felt might be overindulging. This measure has not proved to be effective. The workers now began hiding cases of beer in the various refrigerated storage rooms, which ensured them of relatively easy access to a cold beer. Those men who could not leave their station would signal a fork lift driver by wiping their brows or stroking their throats. This indicated a thirst, and the appropriate relief would be brought from the storage rooms.

THE JOHN GROOVER CASE

John Groover had been working at Brewmaster Breweries for the past eight years. He was 35 years old, married with three children. John was working on the docks loading and unloading trucks as well as stacking full pallets of beer as they came off the line.

John was proud of his status on the loading docks. He was known by his fellow workers as a "rough neck", who didn't really care about the work at hand. He would not rush his job to accommodate extra production. John felt that if they wanted him to move faster, they could either pay him more or hire more help to get his job done. Along with his independent state of mind, John had a flagrant attitude towards company rules when he reported for work. One day John had one of his frequent disagreements with his wife regarding the time spent at work. His wife felt he was spending too much time at work and not enough at home. John would leave about an hour and a half before his shift (although it was only a 15 minute drive from his home to the plant) and arrive home two hours after his shift ended, usually with the smell of beer on his breath.

As usual, the argument ended with John storming out the door and rushing off to work. He arrived an hour before his shift and headed straight for the cafeteria and the bar for a quick beer to calm himself. He had little trouble gaining access to the bar, even though it was to be locked until the shift previous to John's was over. A quick-witted remark and a plea for a thirst-quenching brew were enough to convince the bartender to open up. Besides, George (the bartender) was a good friend of John's, so that made it all the easier. John sat down and began indulging. At the same time he started to discuss his domestic argument with a couple of truck drivers who had just finished their delivery run.

As John drank more, the problems being discussed included not only his wife, but work, supervisors hassling him, and general discontent with his lifestyle. By the time John's shift was due to start, he had consumed enough beer to make walking difficult. As he was leaving the bar, he stumbled into a chair, which he grabbed and tossed aside. It crossed four tables and crashed noisily against the wall. John then barged through the door narrowly missing his supervisor, Dave, who was on his way up to the cafeteria for a cup of coffee. Upon seeing John in an apparently ine-briated state, Dave called him over to the side, and asked if he felt well enough to carry on with his job. To this, John answered with an obscene remark in the affir-mative. Dave, relying on his better judgment, asked John to go down to the staging office and wait for him, saying that he would be about 10 minutes. While John went down to the office, Dave headed for the supervisors' lounge to get the help of Todd, a senior supervisor. This was common practice whenever a supervisor was anticipating a problem with an employee. It was used for documented protection so that the employee report could be written up. While Dave was speaking with Todd, John found the waiting a bit aggravating, so he went to the cold storage for another beer. Dave, Todd, and John walked into the staging office at about the same time. Todd immediately saw that John had had too many beers, so he recommended that John lie down and rest until he felt he was able to continue his job. To this, John retorted with his customary phrase, pushed both Todd and Dave aside, and headed for his fork lift. Todd and Dave realized the danger if John were allowed to con-tinue on with his job. They again approached John, and this time recommended that he go home and take the rest of the shift off. This seemed to aggravate John even more, and he took a wild swing at Dave. He missed Dave, lost his balance, and ended up falling against a pallet of beer. John picked himself up and screamed that he wasn't drunk, and that they had no right to classify him as being so. The com-motion brought other workers running. Eventually, a heated exchange of words erupted, with the workers vowing to walk out, and the two supervisors vowing to recommend termination for John.

CONFLICTS

The company's chief medical officer and the personnel manager feel that the current alcohol abuse policy is an effective, comprehensive attempt at dealing with the prob-lem. There seem to be conflicting opinions from both supervisory staff and the med-ical department at the Calgary plant. Supervisors feel that the policy is too general and leaves too much room for misinterpretation by supervisory staff, as well as the union. The medical department feels the policy is adequate, but that it is not being implemented properly or consistently enough by the supervisors. They view this hes-itancy as a lack of personal conviction. They feel that the supervisors and upper managers are too concerned with moving up the corporate ladder. They believe that the less disturbance they create, the easier and quicker the climb will be. Supervi-sors feel that they need more support from upper management. They are damned if they attempt to implement the policy to the letter, and damned if they allow the employees to function at a level that reduces production and increases costs to Brewmaster.

QUESTIONS

1. Should Brewmaster provide for the consumption of beer after work? If so, under what circumstances?

2. Evaluate the company's alcohol abuse program. Is it likely to be effective?

3. What went wrong in the John Groover incident? Who or what is (are) to blame?

4. What other measures can the company take to reduce alcohol abuse.

5. Is Brewmaster morally responsible for a worker's alcohol abuse to any extent? Give reasons for your answer.

Brooklyn's Dining

Brooklyn's Dining is a reputable chain of restaurants that offers a pleasant dining experience with over 105 menu items and is especially known for its tasty pizzas and pastas. This restaurant is ideal for families, sports teams, and groups of various ages because Brooklyn's Dining offers not only a restaurant experience, but also serves as a sports bar, providing large TVs showing various sports events. One of the franchised restaurants in the chain was recently purchased by a new owner, David Becker, who already owned two of the chain's restaurants in different locations.

The previous owner of that franchise had shown little interest in the day-to-day operations of the restaurant, preferring to leave it to the restaurant manager, Shirley, whom he had hired. Shirley tried to be on friendly terms with each employee and often consulted them on management issues. Shirley had seen to it that the employees she hired were competent, but she set no performance goals for food and bar sales or promptness of service. She seemed satisfied if the staff showed up for their shifts and appeared to be going about their jobs in a reasonable manner. She assigned the work for the servers, bartenders, and kitchen staff, but when the restaurant experienced sudden peaks in activity, as happened frequently, the staff were simply left to adjust their work allocations as best they could to help each other out. Shirley would join the employees and try to help out in the bar, dining room, or kitchen in various roles rather than reorganize or reallocate the tasks of the employees when the restaurant was extremely busy. Unfortunately, this method of coping with heavy workloads was often not efficient. Mistakes would sometimes be made in customers' orders, quality might suffer, and the service could be slow. Dissatisfied customers had to be given refunds when these problems occurred. In terms of profits the restaurant had been performing below the average of others in the chain.

David, the new owner, was determined to restructure the running of his new restaurant in order to increase its profits, as well as the quality of the dining experience for customers. He decided to replace Shirley with a new restaurant manager and to use the same organizational structure and policies that he had used in his

---

This case is based on original work by Kate Kononenko.

other two Brooklyn's restaurants. The entire current staff, ranging from cooks to mid-level supervisors to servers, was put on two months probation to determine who would adapt to the new rules and regulations and keep their jobs and who would be let go. This turned the atmosphere within the restaurant into one of anger and confusion, which was not helped by Kevin, the new restaurant manager. Kevin contributed to the growing dissatisfaction by not showing any friendly interest in the staff he was to supervise. Many of the staff members began to speak quietly, but openly, about the possibility of finding new employment.

Kevin had previously worked at another Brooklyn's Dining location and was apparently brought into this restaurant as a troubleshooter to "turn the business around". However, this restaurant was twice the size of the previous one, and that restaurant did not experience such high peaks in demand. As well, Kevin had to manage many more servers, hosts, and cooks than he had done before. Since he was reluctant to rely on the lower-level supervisors who had been put on probation, he had to supervise close to twenty people. David, the new owner, had confidence in Kevin. He had assured all the staff that Kevin was properly trained and would accommodate all of their needs and problems in a professional manner. "Working at Brooklyn's Dining," David said, "would become a much more enjoyable experience than ever before, as long as the new rules were followed and the staff followed Kevin's 'suggestions'." David told the staff that Kevin would monitor their job performance more closely than did the former manager in order to help the workers achieve the rates of efficiency and higher productivity that would raise profit levels. David informed them that each person should learn to work competently within his or her own job and would be evaluated accordingly. Kevin would make sure that the hosts were no longer helping the servers serve their food and that all staff would be restricted to their specifically assigned roles. Finally, Kevin was to monitor the employees' behaviour towards one another to minimize the amount of profane language that staff used so that everyone felt comfortable at the workplace. Anyone breaking these rules would be given a formal write-up.

On the first lunch shift that Kevin managed (with the new owner not present), the staff at Brooklyn's Diner were able to experience Kevin's approach to management first-hand. "You are all aware that I am your new head manager, and things will be run my way from now on. Whoever doesn't abide by the new rules will be let go. Don't forget you are all on probation." The staff was shocked to receive this kind of negative initial message from their new manager. Throughout that whole day, Kevin failed to establish any kind of a relationship with even one of his subordinates. Instead, he contributed to the already hostile and uncertain atmosphere. At dinnertime, he had not informed the servers of what reservations had been made, or how many people were expected that night when a Soccer Cup game would be showing on the big screens.

"You should all know what to do by now on big event nights, and I expect no less from you tonight. Just remember, I will be watching your work ethic very closely. Your mistakes will cost you money and perhaps even your job." Kevin was managing by threat instead of giving his staff any specific directions or assistance.

This announcement caused stress and uneasiness. Many employees began questioning the new owner and his intentions. "Why is Kevin trying to put all of us down when many of us have been working at Brooklyn's Dining for over five years? He treats us as if we're incompetent. He's waiting for us to make a mistake and get fired for it. If I knew this was the type of treatment I'd get, I would have quit on the spot and not have signed the probation form."

Later that night, as the dinner rush came rolling in and the Soccer Cup game was minutes from starting, Brooklyn's Dining had people lining up outside the restaurant to get a seat. The staff had seen a swarm of customers like this before and were prepared to take them on. However, they had traditionally got a lot of help from the manager on such a busy night, when the restaurant would usually earn the largest profit of the month. The staff knew it would be crucial for the new owner that tonight would provide high returns so that he could see the profit potential of his new restaurant.

One of the servers was initially overwhelmed with the number of tables she was assigned. She went to Kevin to ask for help in separating a bill for ten people so that she could serve her other six tables. When the server came to Kevin's office, the door was locked. He did not respond to her knocking, which came as a shock because of the open door policy followed by the previous manager on the instructions of the former owner. Kevin opened his door after fifteen minutes. When servers began running up to him to see what was going on and why no help was being provided to them, Kevin bluntly replied, "I had an important phone call — no more questions — get back to work — this place is getting out of hand. Do everything by the rules and get this place back in order. I'm here to supervise you and not to do your work for you." He closed his door again and was not seen for another forty-five minutes. When Kevin emerged and saw that the servers were unable to run all of their food to the tables on time, he finally and reluctantly instructed the hosts to help them. That help was too little and came too late. Many servers were already losing tip money and had to make refunds that would come, in part, from their own pockets. They believed this was because Kevin had been unable or unwilling to help. Customers were unhappy with the slow service. Many left before their orders arrived and swore they would never return to such a madhouse again. The staff were angry, not only at Kevin, but at David as well. They felt that the new rules were designed to fail them, not to help them.

At the end of the night, when the Soccer Cup was over and the kitchen was closing, the new owner, David, decided to drop in to Brooklyn's Dining to see how much sales revenue was received that night and to receive any feedback from Kevin on the employees' work. To his surprise, sales were actually less than they had been on other nights that were not as busy and were also less than sales for an equally busy night under the former management. After a talk with Kevin, David called a mandatory meeting with the employees of Brooklyn's Dining the next morning. "Kevin has told me that you people are extremely under-trained compared to other places he's managed. Most of you failed to follow the new rules and ended up wasting a lot of the restaurant's food on mistakes, causing us to not only lose money, but to lose customers." After the meeting, the servers expressed their frustration to David, one at a time. In different words, they all complained about Kevin's managerial style. Several servers were ready to quit immediately because they weren't prepared to be losing money night after night and to work in a hostile environment under Kevin's supervision. David later received several calls from the head office of the Brooklyn's Dining chain with complaints from customers about the terrible service they had received the night before.

QUESTIONS

1. Compare and contrast the motivational situation for the staff of the restaurant before and after the sale to the new owner.

2. What changes in job satisfaction occurred after the change in ownership? Identify the reasons for these changes.

3. Identify and assess the leadership styles of Shirley and Kevin.

4. In order to formulate a change to improve the restaurant's performance, what change **procedure** should be followed?

5. In your opinion, what changes need to be made, and why?

Central Prairie Hospital

Derek and Simone were Registered Nurses in a long-term care nursing unit in Central Prairie Hospital. The unit was staffed by 40 full-time and part-time Registered Nurses and Registered Practical Nurses. The Nursing Unit Manager, Naomi, was scheduled to take educational leave for four months at a university in a distant city. Derek and Simone, both registered nurses, were selected to share the role of Acting Manager while Naomi was on leave. They were to take turns on a weekly rotating schedule — a form of job sharing. On the days when both were present, one of them would therefore work as an ordinary staff member. Both Derek and Simone had expressed career interest in nursing administration, and saw this as a step in that direction. Simone had some previous experience in managing a unit on a temporary basis. Both had a Bachelor's degree, which was the minimum education required for nursing administration. Both Derek and Simone had participated in and chaired various committees within the hospital. This was one of the criteria that Naomi used when selecting them for this shared role. Naomi's own leadership style was typically people-oriented, but always firm when patient care was at stake. She was known as a capable administrator who dealt with staff fairly. Naomi had also arranged for Lee, a permanent manager in another nursing unit within the hospital, to act as an overall supervisor and resource person for Derek and Simone. Lee was only expected to manage areas that Derek and Simone were not allowed to deal with due to their union's collective bargaining agreement — such as hiring and reprimanding staff. Lee was also expected to continue managing her own unit. She was known around the hospital as a "hard-nosed" supervisor who required her subordinates to be obedient to her wishes. The rumour heard around the long-term care unit was that her authoritarian style was the reason she was chosen as the backup.

During the first two months of Naomi's leave, the unit ran smoothly. Simone and Derek were responsible for various unit activities including scheduling, ordering supplies, communicating information to staff and management, and investigating infrequent and non-serious patient and family complaints. These were solved by a quiet discussion with the nurse involved, usually over a coffee in the cafeteria. Lee

---

This case is based on original work by Karen Cowan.

checked in several times each day, and seemed relieved that her active involvement was not required.

Early in the third month a few more difficult problems began to surface. Family members and patients came to Simone and Derek with some substantial complaints of inadequate care. Both Derek and Simone investigated these situations. They discovered that much of it was due to some nurses who were arriving at work late. Certain of these staff members had been warned twice during the last year by Naomi for the same infraction. Initially, they were reluctant to involve Lee, although they couldn't discipline their colleagues on their own. Then, complaints became more frequent; possibly because the long-term patients sensed a growing lack of order in the unit. Derek and Simone now had no choice but to involve Lee with staff discipline. Lee reacted by deciding to move into the office on the unit, rather than work from her own office, in order to provide a more visible supervisory presence. Derek and Simone now shared the office with Lee to perform their managerial duties. In Lee's own unit an assistant manager was available to fill in, although Lee would check on her home unit often, since the assistant had little supervisory experience.

Lee's move onto the unit created more problems than it solved. Derek and Simone no longer had regular access to the scheduling and information files on the computer that Lee was using most of the time. As a result, schedules and assignments were drawn up late. Staff were no longer receiving directions from Derek and Simone in a timely manner. Supplies were not being ordered regularly. As a result of the disorder, Lee then tried to involve herself more heavily in the day-to-day functioning of the unit. However, due to her duties elsewhere, She could only do infrequent checks on the care the staff was providing, and could not follow up on her instructions to ensure they were being carried out.

Staff responded poorly to Lee's presence on the unit. Many refused to carry out instructions from Lee without speaking to Simone or Derek first. One staff member was disciplined by Lee, and some then refused to speak to her. Lee responded by not speaking to them either. Others refused Derek and Simone's directions without Lee's approval. Patient care now deteriorated rapidly, and complaints increased in number and intensity. Some staff members refused to attend weekly staff meetings held by Lee. Absenteeism, never previously a problem, threatened now to become one.

One day, after their shift was over, Derek and Simone tried to talk to Lee about the situation. They suggested that they were unable to manage the unit as a group of three, and that Lee should manage it on her own if she continued to occupy the unit's office. Lee said that she needed to occupy the office "to keep tabs" on the situation, but that her other duties prevented her from taking full charge of the unit. It would not be fair or even possible to manage two units on her own. She asked Derek and Simone to take of the administrative tasks and to help her monitor the level of patient care. Derek and Simone were to report all staff problems to Lee, and Lee would handle them. Lee indicated that present difficulties would improve with a stricter enforcement of discipline.

After their discussion with Lee, Derek and Simone began to talk to each other about looking for new staff positions on another unit within the hospital. They felt that leaving things as they were would cause medical and morale problems, and negatively affect their future promotion prospects. However, a few of their friends among the unit's nursing staff in whom they confided asked them to reconsider. They said things would only get worse if Simone and Derek left.

QUESTIONS

1. Trace the changes in the way leadership was exercised in the long-term care nursing unit from the beginning to the end of the case.

2. Evaluate the three-person leadership set up by Naomi. Was Lee a good choice for the backup supervisor?

3. Assess how the changes in the management of the unit affected the motivational levels and performance of the nursing staff.

4. Who is responsible for the deteriorating situation in the unit?

5. Is it possible for Simone, Derek, and Lee to supervise the unit together effectively? If yes, how could this be done? Develop job descriptions for these three people.

6. Assume that you are brought in as a consultant (as of the end of the case) to evaluate the problems of this nursing unit and make recommendations for solving them. What would your report say?

Chemplus Inc. (A)

Chemplus Inc. was a Canadian firm that provided sophisticated instrumentation and applications engineering assistance to research laboratories, chiefly in analytical chemistry and biology. The company, with annual sales of about $12 million in 1995, had its head office in Montreal and branch offices in Halifax, Ottawa-Hull, Toronto, Winnipeg, Edmonton, and Vancouver.

AN OVERVIEW OF CHEMPLUS (SEE FIGURE 1)

The head office took care of promotion, sales fulfilment, general administrative functions, and Montreal-region sales. The president, a sales force of two sales engineers, a repair department with a service manager and two technicians, and an administrative and warehouse staff of seven were located in a 600 square metre facility in a suburban industrial area. Except in Halifax, each branch office had two sales engineers (one of whom served as regional manager) and a secretarial staff of one. Toronto and Vancouver offices also had small repair departments, each staffed by one technician. The President, Harry Barlow, spent more than half of his time in direct sales activities with certain key accounts, which he alone served, and in supervising the two Montreal-based sales engineers.

The instrumentation that Chemplus sold was, for the most part, imported from foreign suppliers with which the firm had exclusive distribution arrangements for Canada. Most of the time, the equipment was simply shipped to the customer and set up in a researcher's laboratory by the responsible sales engineer. Occasionally, the technicians in the Montreal office would preassemble various pieces of equipment and perhaps add some part that they had fabricated in order to meet the customer's needs for instrumentation that was not available "off the shelf".

Virtually all the sales engineering staff had an educational background in science — usually in chemistry, physics, or in engineering itself. It was Harry Barlow's opinion that sales training could be learned, but that the technical education required to sell effectively in their market had to be of a level that would enable the sales engineer to converse intelligently with researchers about their work. In fact, two of the 13 sales engineers actually had doctorates. Service technicians, on the other hand were usually selected purely on their ability to repair diverse types of elec-

FIGURE 1   ORGANIZATIONAL CHART OF CHEMPLUS

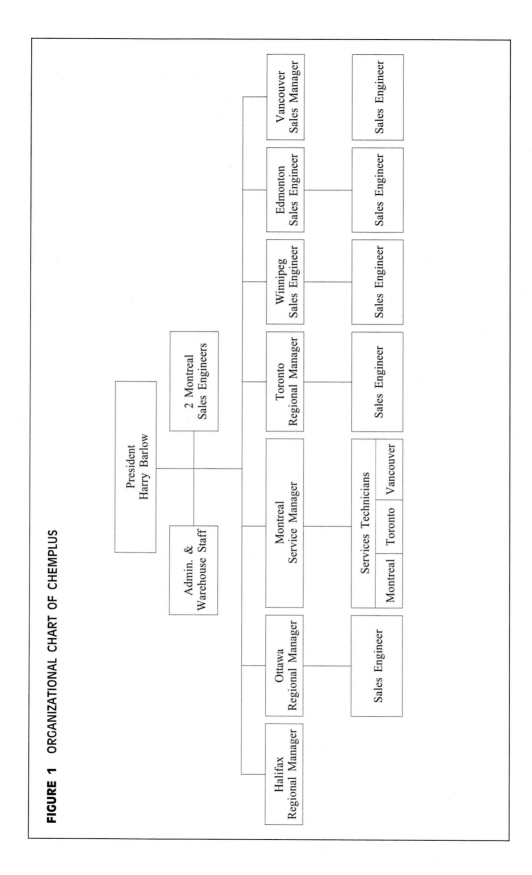

tronic equipment, and they had mixed formal qualifications — from a university degree to only completing high school and being self-taught beyond that. Although technicians and sales engineers were "laterally" related, with no formal reporting relationship from one to the other, the sales engineers enjoyed greater respect, better compensation, and more pleasant working conditions.

When Harry Barlow began Chemplus in 1980, he had just left a laboratory where he had been a junior researcher. He began his entrepreneurial life as a sales engineer, and hired the services of repair people as needed. He fondly remembered his days of travelling across Canada by car while his wife back in Montreal provided all the administrative support. Since the couple owned all the shares, profits had an immediate impact on their material well-being. Harry sometimes forgot that the incentive for his employees was not as strong. He paid salaries that were just within the top third of the industry and was reluctant to pay much higher, regardless of performance. Commission or bonuses for good sales performance was being talked about, but was not yet implemented. Often, he was annoyed when he called a branch office at 6:00 p.m. and found that everyone had already left. He routinely put in 12-hour days and six-and-a-half-day weeks. If he had a philosophy of success, it was that hard work could make up for any minor lack of ability, and work would always pay off. The existence of three other firms in Canada with similar product lines all competing for the same market strengthened his belief in these contentions. Although a pleasant person in personal relationships, it was often difficult to get him off the topic of business; and about business, he was always serious.

THE OTTAWA-HULL OFFICE

Located in Hull, because Harry Barlow thought that the rents would be cheaper there, this office was managed by Marie Benoit. She had a master's degree in Analytical Chemistry, and had previously served as a sales engineer in the Montreal head office for two-and-a-half years. There, she had impressed the president with her dedication and very satisfactory sales levels. When a resignation opened up the regional manager's job in Ottawa-Hull, she was an easy choice. Her appointment raised eyebrows and some resentment among more experienced staff in other offices who would have liked the promotion. She was the first woman hired for a sales engineering position, and it was clear that some of her peers felt that just being hired in the first place was "good for a woman".

While Marie herself had no doubts about deserving the promotion, she did wonder about her ability to manage an office, even though the staff complement was only one other sales engineer and a secretary. It was just that she had no managerial experience or training. She voiced these fears to her friends, who reassured her, but not within the company, where it might comfort those who envied her.

THE ALEX CLINTON SITUATION

Only days after her arrival in the Ottawa area, she was confronted by the resignation of the other sales engineer in the office, Carl St. Pierre, whom she was to supervise. He stated as reasons for leaving an excellent offer from a competitor and the prospect of working in their Vancouver office. In order to discuss the situation and the plans for hiring a replacement, she drove down to Montreal on a Saturday morning to meet with the president. On her arrival, she found out that he thought he had already solved the problem.

"This may surprise you, Marie, but I'm sending you Alex Clinton."

"For the sales job? He's a technician. I mean he is a great technician — probably our best. But a sales engineer . . . ?"

"Well frankly, Marie, he's been bugging me for about six months now. He wants to get into sales. I'm afraid if I don't try him this time, he'll leave. And with his abilities, I know the competition would love to get their hands on him."

"Gee, I don't know, Harry," she said, "He's not even really fluent in French."

"I've already thought of that, you can give him only English speaking accounts. Anyway, in your territory there's many more of them. Look, it's just something that we have to try. I'm only sorry that, with Carl quitting, there's no time to give him any sales training here at head office. You'll have to give him guidance on that. I know you can do it," Harry said, flashing a smile.

"Okay, I guess I'll have to make the best of it. But I'm going to be honest with you. I don't think it's a good idea. Alex is not really suitable. I've been with him on repair visits. The customers just love him because he can fix anything, and he just laps up the praise. It's not the same in sales. You've got to be tactful and empathetic. And you don't always get such a great reception when you arrive at the customer's office."

"Work on it with him, Marie. If anyone can turn him into a sales engineer, you can. By the way, he's arriving in ten days."

Marie drove back to Ottawa in a sombre mood. She understood Alex Clinton's desire to get out of the service shop. The service manager was a strict and humourless individual who felt superior to those he supervised because he had a university degree. Among repair personnel, only the technician in Vancouver shared that qualification. Alex himself actually had little formal postsecondary education, but had easily taught himself the repair of mechanical and electronic equipment. He had the reputation of being able to fix anything, an attribute that did not endear him to the service manager, who preferred to take credit personally. And although repair competence did endear him to the sales staff, it would never earn him equal status.

Marie was also somewhat discomfited by the prospect of a supervisory relationship with someone who had kept calling her "dear" and had often winked at her conspiratorially when she had worked in Montreal. Well, she thought to herself, that would be the first thing to get squared away between them.

As it happened, that issue never arose. Alex was obviously as surprised as Marie had been that he had actually succeeded in getting the position. During the first two weeks, when Marie introduced him around to the customers and during their discussions in the office, he was the model of attentiveness and obviously had a serious intention not to blow this opportunity. Marie was almost beginning to feel relieved. It was during the third week that misgivings began to surface once more. It was Marie's plan to now let Alex do the sales presentations. She would observe and go over his performance with him later. Alex was obviously ill at ease in that role. In the past, customers had always been delighted to see him, because he was there to repair some equipment that they badly needed. Now they appeared impatient as he haltingly went through a sales presentation for products that they had no present intention to purchase. It seemed to Alex that the customers were looking down upon him. Often, he would turn to Marie with a look of mild panic, and she would be forced to take over from him. Marie asked Alex in the office about these incidents. Away from the sales situation, however, he seemed more poised and confident. He would quickly brush aside her comments and questions with a statement that suggested that Marie's impressions were totally wrong. She decided to inform Harry Barlow of this problem by telephone.

"Harry, I'm worried about Alex. He's not doing well talking to customers. He's stumbling over his words, and I keep having to help him out. He doesn't know how to get the customer interested. I try to give him some pointers, and he does okay in the office. But when we get out there, he seems like a different person."

"How long has he been with you now, Marie, a few weeks? You know, you've been doing this for a few years and it's a lot easier for you. He's probably nervous about you being there watching him. Maybe it's time to let him out on his own a bit. I'd like to come down and help, but I'm not sure I could do anything that you're not doing. Anyway, Mike (the Halifax Sales Engineer) is in the hospital for a couple weeks and I've got to get down there and fill in for him. The best advice you can give Alex is to work hard at it. He's sure to improve. I gather he's bought a house now in Kanata (a suburb of Ottawa). If he doesn't work out in your office, we'll definitely lose him. And with what he knows about the technical problems with some of our products . . . I don't want to think about the consequences. Give him some room to breathe, Marie. Take some of your lower priority accounts and work up a week's schedule for him. He'll solve his problem."

"I don't think he believes that he's got a problem, Harry. But I'll try what you suggested."

After a week of letting Alex go out on his own, it seemed that Harry Barlow's suggestion might be succeeding. Every evening, Marie discussed the day's sales activities with Alex, and then went over his sales reports of visits with prospective customers. The initial discussions provided Marie with little useful information, but by the end of the week, the reports were showing that Alex was getting into more substantive product discussions. She decided to try another two weeks and, gratefully, began to concentrate more on her own sales responsibilities. During the second week, the reports continued to show evidence of improved sales presentations, and by the third week, definite expressions of interest in purchasing instrumentation began to appear. Alex's demeanour around the office seemed almost overly cheerful, but he still avoided any detailed discussion of his activities. Marie felt that it might take more time to develop a rapport between them, and decided to let him plan the next couple of weeks for her approval.

At this time, a quarterly sales forecast was due, and it was Marie's responsibility to submit it for her region. Alex was asked to provide an estimate for the customers he had visited so far, which he completed. Due to his inexperience, however, Marie felt that she should corroborate his data by checking with some of his key customers for whom he reported good sales prospects. As she knew most of them herself, she began to make some phone calls. The first few, from sales reports dating back to the second week that Alex was on his own, drew a puzzled response. The prospective purchasers seemed not to recall expressing any purchasing intentions. A few indicated that Alex had only been in to see them very briefly in order to drop off some sales literature. The next group of customers she called was from the next week of his sales reports, and Marie received much more startling responses to her inquiries. Alex had not been in to see them at all!

QUESTIONS

1. Why had Alex Clinton been falsifying call reports?

2. What communication, motivation, and leadership factors have contributed to this situation? Who is (are) responsible?

3. What should Marie do now?

4. (a) What steps should Harry Barlow take immediately?
   (b) What should he do so that this situation will not occur again? Include revised personnel selection procedures.

5. Is the organizational structure of Chemplus Inc. appropriate? Why or why not? Suggest any alterations that you feel would be beneficial.

Chemplus Inc. (B)

About six months after the events described in the (A) case, Harry Barlow was once again facing the possible defection of a senior sales representative to the competition. This time it was Gary Hill, the manager of the Vancouver office. Only after numerous telephone calls and, finally, a quick trip to the remote office was Harry able to negotiate an improved salary that convinced Gary to remain with Chemplus. While Gary got a nice raise, Harry Barlow reflected that it was very expensive to get into a bidding war with the competition. He also worried that a precedent would be set with the others.

"We're becoming a training school for sales engineers," Harry mused on the plane back to Montreal. Certainly, there was some truth in the statement. Although sales training was sporadic, Chemplus' technical training program was better than any similar firm in the industry. Extensive training sessions took place in Montreal periodically. Each sales engineer also attended several one-or two-week sessions per year in the United States at the offices of manufacturers represented by Chemplus. After three years of employment, the investment in each sales engineer was substantial — and so was the value put on Chemplus' personnel by competitive firms. Although the training was specific to the particular product line represented, most of the competitors handled equipment that was, on the whole, very similar. The technical aspects of the training were totally relevant for any of the firms, and a sales engineer acquired from Chemplus with detailed product knowledge would be very effective in then selling against his or her former employer. Some competitors seemed to have developed a strategy of hiring only experienced and knowledgeable sales engineers from competitors rather than hiring and training novices. The money they saved on training would help cover salaries that were just high enough to tempt valued personnel away from the firm that trained them. Harry could cut back on training and only hire more experienced people as well, but that wasn't his style. He liked the idea of fielding a competent sales force trained in the way he preferred.

A forthcoming general sales meeting gave Harry Barlow an opportunity to take action against "sales engineer piracy". The solution, he thought, was an employment contract. Its main provisions were to stipulate a salary (initially, the one already being received) and to prevent any sales engineer who voluntarily left the firm from accepting a job with a competitor for two years. The plan had its obvious attractions, but Harry Barlow was also a little worried. No other company in the market had such a contract. He wondered whether it might cause a general revolt if presented at the meeting without warning. To ease into it gradually, he sent a memo to all concerned across Canada that a discussion of an employment contract would be on the agenda of the meeting. He offered no information concerning its contents, but he stated that a benefits package, tied to the contract, would be introduced later.

This immediately provoked a frantic round of telephone calls among all the sales engineers. Since Harry had used one of the Montreal people as a sounding board, the details of the contract eventually leaked out. By the time everyone gathered for the meeting, it seemed that a consensus had formed to oppose it. Bob Elliott, manager of the Toronto office, was chosen to act as spokesperson.

The meeting began with a brief discussion of the agenda. Then the firm's accountant, Denise Lacroix, who was unknown to all present except Harry, started to discuss the need for a contract. Her pitch basically covered two points. The sales engineers would have their employment terms guaranteed (as long as performance was satisfactory), and the company would feel more secure in making a substantial investment in training. In the future, this might also lead to a company-supported pension plan and improved health benefits.

Denise read a simple two-page draft contract to the meeting and then paused for questions. Bob Elliott cleared his throat and stood up. "I guess I was picked to speak for the group. I'm afraid we're not interested. There's really nothing in it for us."

"Wait a minute, the intention is really to improve employment conditions in the near future," countered Denise. "You've got to . . ."

"I SAID WE ARE NOT INTERESTED," Bob interrupted loudly.

"HEY, CAN YOU LET ME . . .," Denise began with equal volume.

Harry Barlow, looking dismayed, stood up abruptly. "Okay, calm down everyone. Denise, I think we'd better delay this discussion of the contract. I'll speak with you later."

Exhaling noisily, Denise packed up her papers and left.

Harry sat down and announced that they would now take up the second item on the agenda, sales targets. For the remainder of that day's discussions, he stared grimly at his papers and generally avoided eye contact with the sales engineers. The next day, he seemed to be in a better frame of mind, but the contract was not mentioned again.

QUESTIONS

1. What are the positive and negative aspects of an employment contract for:
   (a) The sales engineers?
   (b) The company?

2. Was the employment contract an appropriate response to "sales engineer piracy"?

3. Critically assess the way in which it was communicated to the sales engineers.

4. What should Harry Barlow do as of the end of the case about the issues raised here?

Club Chaos

THE ORGANIZATION

Club Chaos is an exclusive, upscale, not-for-profit private organization that provides members with an array of facilities. The club includes a golf club (complete with a pro shop and instructors), indoor/outdoor tennis courts (with professional instructors), a curling rink, swimming pool, private meeting rooms, and extensive dining facilities (banquets, catered meetings, fine dining, sports lounge, a patio BBQ, a poolside BBQ/snack-bar, an in-house bakeshop, and catering outside the club for members). Club Chaos employs over 200 people, and has an extensive organizational structure. (See Exhibits 1 and 2 for organizational charts.)

The club's general manager is Antonio, a man with little formal education. Antonio can usually be found out on the golf course or playing tennis (usually in the company of his wife). He has recently created the position of clubhouse manager and promoted his friend Rocco, the former head of the maintenance department, to fill it. Rocco is also a self-taught individual, with limited formal education or business experience. Rocco ran a two-person home renovation company for a few years, the club's maintenance department for three, and now finds himself in charge of the majority of club operations. Rocco could often be seen in the lounge drinking with the club members for extended periods, and it was widely rumoured that Rocco was to be the "broom" in a "clean-sweep" of the organization.

THE CATERING DEPARTMENT

Cathy was the head of catering and was known for her efficiency in heading up the Food and Beverage operation, and her savvy in dealing with customers. Soon after Rocco's promotion, Cathy was told in a meeting with him that she was to dismiss her assistant Jan (her sister-in-law). The position of catering assistant was to be terminated, as the budget was being trimmed to boost revenue so that a new clubhouse could be built for the members. Cathy soon resigned as well, and the department fell into disarray. Rocco was playing an active role in the catering office, but new

This case is based on original work by Judson Bray.

EXHIBIT 1 CLUB CHAOS — ORGANIZATIONAL CHART

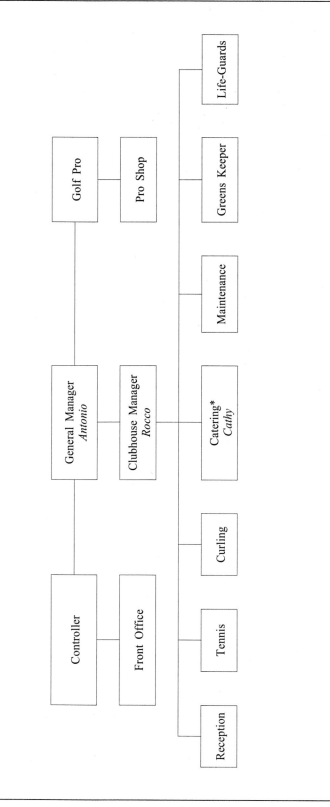

* See Exhibit 2 for the department chart.

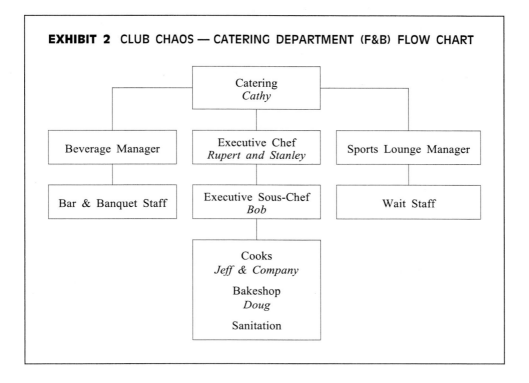

EXHIBIT 2 CLUB CHAOS — CATERING DEPARTMENT (F&B) FLOW CHART

people occupied and left the position of catering manager at the rate of one every three months. Contracts came in late, last minute changes were frequent and many details were left out of the function planning sheets. On one occasion, a contract for a wedding party of 160 people was overlooked until the morning of the event.

During this time, Rocco was also putting extreme pressure on the executive chef, Rupert. Demands were made to increase the kitchen's revenue, and the inconsistent quality of the food was a frequent criticism. On the other hand, Rupert was instructed to keep food and labour costs low and service levels high. Antonio and Rocco suspected that theft was the cause of high food costs lately. Rumours were circulating throughout the close-knit culinary group that Club Chaos was actively seeking a new executive chef, and phone calls by potential applicants were unwittingly forwarded directly to Rupert's office. Rupert soon resigned from his position, and Stanley was hired to replace him. Although Stanley had very odd behavioural quirks — he could be seen running through the kitchen on his hands and knees, barking like a dog and playfully biting his employees — he did create control systems that revealed what had been suspected. Large amounts of inventory were missing from the kitchen on a daily basis.

Rocco posted threatening notices in all staff common areas that said:

Whoever is stealing from the kitchen is in big trouble.
We're going to get you!

The chef took charge of the scheduling from the executive sous-chef, Bob, explaining that he wanted to phase out suspected thieves from the schedule and have them replaced. After three months only six original employees of 26 remained, most having been forced to quit, and one employee dismissed by the chef for a violent outburst. No formal training for new employees, performance evaluations or raises took place. Rocco explained to staff that there was no money in the budget for such activities. With the high rate of turnover, the rate of missing inventory slowed marginally at first, but soon picked up speed again, while the quality of the food the kitchen produced was still inconsistent at best.

THE INCIDENT

One day, executive sous-chef Bob was putting empty milk crates in the loading dock when he spotted something suspicious. Upon investigation, he found a heavily wrapped package that contained six pounds of ribs with all the trimmings. He left the evidence in place and consulted Stanley on the matter. Bob was ordered to keep an eye on the area, effectively setting a trap. Later that afternoon, Bob spotted two of the few remaining long-term, productive employees quietly leaving the facility through the loading dock, and he pursued. Bob not only found Jeff with the ribs, but the pastry chef, Doug, was pulling out a bag of assorted canned goods and a cake from under a pile of empty boxes.

QUESTIONS

1. Describe the management problems in Club Chaos.

2. What motivated the poor performance and stealing by employees? Identify the root causes.

3. Evaluate Rocco's measures to discourage stealing. Why were they not effective?

4. If you were hired as a consultant to change the organization, what would you do and how would you do it?

The Communication Taskforce

WestCoast Capital is a large corporation that provides full service investment advice to its clients. It is a subsidiary of the Bank of The Pacific. In recent years, the chartered banks in Canada have been allowed to offer many of the same financial services as provided by such other financial institutions as trust companies and brokerages. Prior to that change in the banking act, the banks were limited to the provision of traditional banking services such as loans and accounts. After some intense lobbying, the Bank Act was changed to permit the banks to provide a wider range of financial services. Most banks did this by buying out or merging with existing financial institutions. The Bank of The Pacific bought out WestCoast Capital, and made it a subsidiary of the bank.

The Bank of The Pacific is a large organization with many levels of management, and operates with a high degree of formality. WestCoast Capital is not as large as the bank, nor is it quite as rigid in its structure and policies. However, it is still a financial institution that is quite conservative in its orientation. WestCoast Capital is now integrated into The Bank of The Pacific, and WestCoast Capital employees can be found in most bank branches. Essentially, they sell WestCoast Capital financial products to the Bank's customers.

One branch of WestCoast Capital is unique. It is called the Personal Investment Manager Group. There is only one such office in the company located in Richmond, B.C. It is the only branch that hires Portfolio Managers to manage people's money. The branch provides a discretionary portfolio management service where contact with the client is not necessary to facilitate each trade in their account. Most of the Portfolio Managers are new employees to WestCoast and the Bank.

In a recent survey the employees rated the working conditions for this branch of WestCoast Capital as exceptional. The office is on the second floor of an impressive office building in Richmond, B.C. with easy access to public transportation. It is comfortable and the office furnishings are of high quality — almost luxurious. There are kitchen facilities provided, although there is no specific lunchroom. Boardrooms can be used by staff for meetings with clients and each other. The

---

This case is based on original work by Brenda Walker.

pleasant and prestigious working conditions of that branch are in some ways complemented by the human resource policies of The Bank of The Pacific, which are designed to encourage employee loyalty. There have never been any layoffs in this branch.

The branch itself has a formal structure, but one that seems to allow flexibility. There are two Branch Managers, eleven Portfolio Managers, a Branch Administrator and eight support staff. The two Branch Managers (who also work as Portfolio Managers) divide their responsibility geographically, with one looking after British Columbia and the other the rest of the country. The 11 Portfolio Managers are assigned to one or the other area Branch Manager. This geographical division is "soft", as clients will not change Portfolio Managers if they move across Canada. The Branch Administrator is responsible for the support staff, but only to the extent of a formal reporting relationship and with respect to administrative policies. The support staff report to the Portfolio Managers on a day-to-day basis. People in the branch generally have good relationships with co-workers, in part a benefit of being a rather small unit. People are friendly, share the occasional evening out and arrange seasonal parties, to which employees bring their spouses or partners.

The Portfolio Managers all have their own clients. The independence that this might provide is somewhat moderated, however, by the fact that they work for a corporation with policies and procedures to be followed. These, in turn, are largely influenced by the regulations of an Investment Retailers Association, a self-governing body designed to maintain high levels of integrity in the investment business. Within these boundaries, the Portfolio Managers can provide services to benefit their clients according to their own discretion.

The branch has developed a pattern of forming work teams. One such group consists of Portfolio Managers Bob and Brad along with two support staff members: Jane, who is designated an Investment Specialist, and Mary, who is an Administrative Assistant. Bob and Brad attempt to give everyone in the team a voice. Meetings are held every four days, and everyone's opinion matters. Changes are discussed and decisions are made at these meetings. Although the business they do is the responsibility of the Portfolio Managers, the ideas and knowledge of the Support Staff are considered valuable. These meetings are where various job tasks are assigned to an individual, or where discussions occur about things that are not working within the team.

Although each team member has specific duties to perform on a daily basis, there is also an overlap of duties. Bob and Brad are interchangeable in their service capabilities, and Jane can cover for the managers and the Administrative Assistant. Working together, they are able to provide seamless client service.

These practices make it seem that the branch is decentralized, but there are influences from the larger corporation. For example, incentive pay for the Support Staff is determined by their Portfolio Managers based on their net commissions. However, head office has recently determined that these incentive figures must also be signed off by the Branch Manager and by the Regional Manager. While these higher level managers have never exercised their authority to deny such payments to Support Staff, it does add an element of rigidity to the process.

Because the WestCoast business is fairly new to the Bank, there seems to be latitude for change and innovation. For instance, the group of Bob, Brad, Jane and Mary decided to add to their investment business by selling insurance and providing general financial planning. To this end, Jane completed a financial planning course and acquired her First Level Insurance Licence. Bob and Brad strongly supported these efforts by Jane to acquire the extra qualifications, as that allowed the group to expand its business. Jane took responsibility for designing, preparing and presenting financial planning summaries for the clients. In return, they added to Jane's authority by allowing her to take full responsibility for some clients' needs. In effect, she became the portfolio manager for some of the smaller clients. The portfolio managers also increased her incentive pay share.

The Branch Managers and the Portfolio Managers meet every morning to discuss, among other things, investment strategies, as well as tips and feelings about the stock market. This is also when they share important information about specific stocks that need attention. Jane has asked to attend these meetings. Her position was that since her current work as an Investment Associate included managing the portfolios of smaller clients, she needed access to the information that is shared at these morning meetings. Peter, her Branch Manager, denied her request on the grounds that if he let her into the meeting, then he would have to let all of the support staff in as well, and most of them would have little interest in the discussions that take place. Jane countered that she was different from other support workers in that she was an Investment Associate, the only one who managed portfolios, the only one with training in financial planning, and the only employee in the office with an insurance licence. She felt she held a unique position.

Peter decided that since Jane wanted the information from the morning meetings, this was a communication issue. His solution was to create a Communication Task Force to form an analysis and recommend a solution to the problem. He assigned Jane to the Task Force along with Brad, a Portfolio Manager from her group, and Sally, the Branch Administrator. He also asked Fred, the other Branch Manager, to round out the Task Force membership. He felt that Fred could be more impartial since he, Peter, had already taken a position on the matter. Peter was relatively new to WestCoast Capital, having been hired by the Bank from a previous position at a large, competitive financial institution. Fred was an experienced employee who had been with WestCoast since before the takeover by the Bank. He had served for many years as a financial advisor, but had never been promoted to management due to mediocre interpersonal skills. He had usually preferred to work alone. When the Bank took over WestCoast, all advisors were interviewed, and he was the surprising choice for a Branch Manager Position.

At the first meeting of the Task Force, Fred began by describing the structure of the branch, paying special attention to the important role of the Portfolio Managers. He said that the whole operation hinged on the skill and knowledge of these people. He then discussed the role of the support staff, giving special emphasis to the meaning of the word "support". Fred stated that he agreed with Peter's conclusion that this was only a communication problem and that, in his view, the solution would be found by effectively passing on information as to the decisions made at the managers' morning meetings.

Sally, the Branch Administrator, then stated her agreement with Fred's. Sally, like Fred, was a survivor of the takeover and who was then promoted by the Bank. She had no training or expertise in financial planning, and had recently come from a different branch of WestCoast. She offered her opinion that the solution would be to establish a clear channel of communication based on the authority and structure of the branch. Her view was that communication from management to the support staff should come through her office. In the course of her remarks she made it clear that she was not supportive of the idea of teams composed of Portfolio Managers and support staff working together. It seemed that she wanted more formality in the branch.

Jane was taken aback by these remarks but pressed ahead with her views anyway. She reiterated the position she originally took that she needed to attend the morning meeting to be informed about the stock market strategy being taken by the branch. She also expressed her view that management did not seem to realize the importance of the Investment Associates and, in particular, she did not feel they acknowledged the effort she had put into improving her qualifications. She revealed that she and one of her Portfolio Managers wanted to become Certified Financial Planners, and they planned to study together to prepare for the exam. She mentioned that she had previously applied to Peter for branch funding for this program, but was turned down even though the Bank approved of this form of certification. Peter had replied at the time that they didn't pay for these courses for other employees; he didn't want to set a precedent; the course wasn't applicable to her work; and they didn't have money in the budget. She now revealed that she had subsequently and inadvertently learned that the Portfolio Managers had been encouraged to take this program, and had been offered funding to cover their costs.

Brad did not say a word at this first meeting of the Communication Task Force. He sincerely wished he wasn't there.

QUESTIONS

1. Do you agree with Peter's contention that Jane's request amounted to a communications issue that needed to be resolved?

2. Evaluate Peter's decision to set up a Communication Task Force to resolve Jane's complaint. What motivated him to do so?

3. Would passing on a summary of the morning meeting effectively communicate what Jane needed to know? In what ways would it be less effective than actual attendance at the meeting?

4. Comment on the cultural fit between this WestCoast Branch and the Bank of The Pacific. How has this contributed to the issues that arose in the case?

5. Do you agree with what Jane has said and done? What should she do now, if there is no change in Peter's position on attendance at the meeting?

Company K

OVERVIEW

The K Group of Companies, based in Tokyo, Japan, is one of the leading manufacturers of elevators, escalators, and moving walkways in the world. Incorporated over 40 years ago, it started with a vision of one man, Mr. Tanaka, who dreamed of building the world's highest elevating systems through modern technology. At present, he serves as the Chairman of the entire global operations, divided into a geographically centred management structure, with over 70 Area Offices.

In line with its global strategy, the Group previously decided to enter the Canadian market, incorporating Company K in 1998. The President of the entire North American Region, and based in the United States, is Mr. Tanaka's American-educated eldest son, Gichin.

Start-up operations in Canada were ably handled by Mr. Ito (a university and personal friend of Gichin Tanaka), Head of the International Business Development Group, and now Vice President of the Canadian operation. Unfortunately, 1998 was one of the worst times to start a business in Canada, most particularly in Toronto, where new construction was almost at a standstill. Ito's strategy was to establish a strong presence as early as possible so that Company K would be well-entrenched when the economy started to improve. Challenges Mr. Ito faced ranged from established competitors sending a petition to the provincial government to ban his company from bidding on local projects due to lack of Canadian references; to the impact of the recently signed NAFTA on Canadian imported components from the United States; and the lack of influence with elevator consultants who are considered the key players in the industry, as they sway bid awards based on their recommendations to property owners.

Ito hired Mr. Bristol as General Manager from a competitor. Bristol had over 20 years of sales and marketing experience in the industry, and was well-connected with property owners and elevator consultants. With his help, they initiated an aggressive marketing campaign, culminating in a major installation contract in Vancouver with a contract price of over $68 million, after only 11 months of operation

---

This case is based on original work by Emelita Barbosa.

in Canada. They promptly opened a Vancouver office, and they received approval from the U.S. headquarters to hire an Administrative Assistant in Toronto to help them in daily administration. Lily, a newly landed Japanese immigrant, was hired due to her human resource and office administration experience and her ability to converse in Japanese. Two weeks later, due to personal problems, Mr. Ito abruptly returned to the United States, where his family was based. He was replaced by Mr. Azuma, former Manager of Field Administration and Cost Control in the United States, who spoke very little English. Married without children, it was rumoured that mobility, more than expertise, led to the President's choice of replacement.

Within two years, operations grew faster and larger than what Gichin and Ito had expected. Since the overall market had not improved, however, marketing became paramount, with little effort to develop internal controls and office procedures. The latter were delegated to Lily. By 2000, Company K in Canada had 29 ongoing projects, and personnel has grown to ten regular employees and 24 union employees. (See Exhibit 1 for an organizational chart.)

THE VANCOUVER AREA OFFICE

The business environment for construction in British Columbia was highly competitive but relatively attractive. Asian immigrants were moving to Richmond and Vancouver. This created the need for housing and more and better shopping and recreational facilities. Exploitation of this opportunity required aggressive identification of prospective projects and speed in the submission of bids. Also, since basic elevating systems are similar, a marketing edge was achieved by incorporating a more attractive service and maintenance package into the installation contracts. At Company K, although marketing activities were performed locally, bids were drawn up in the North American Regional Office in coordination with the Corporate Office in Toronto, and were subject to final scrutiny by Japan. To illustrate the complexity of the bid situation, the North American Regional Office provided prices based on quotations from U.S. vendors and suppliers in U.S. dollars. However, bid prices were always in Canadian funds. Thus, there was a heavy dependency on the exchange rate, which could change substantially during the months of contract negotiation. Bottom line figures were forecasted under the assumption that imported components from the United States would arrive duty-free under NAFTA, but no confirmation was given by Revenue Canada unless an import application was made pursuant to a contract being awarded.

ORGANIZATIONAL STRUCTURE

Global Operations Centre — Japan

The K Group of Companies was divided into a geographically centred management structure, where each part was named after the part of the world they represented — namely Japan, South Asia, East Asia, Europe and America. Company K sent all communications to Japan only through the Global Operations Centre (GOC), which in turn sent out replies based on information provided by any other concerned regions. While this procedure was well-ordered and systematic, problems arose when

EXHIBIT 1 COMPANY K — ORGANIZATIONAL CHART

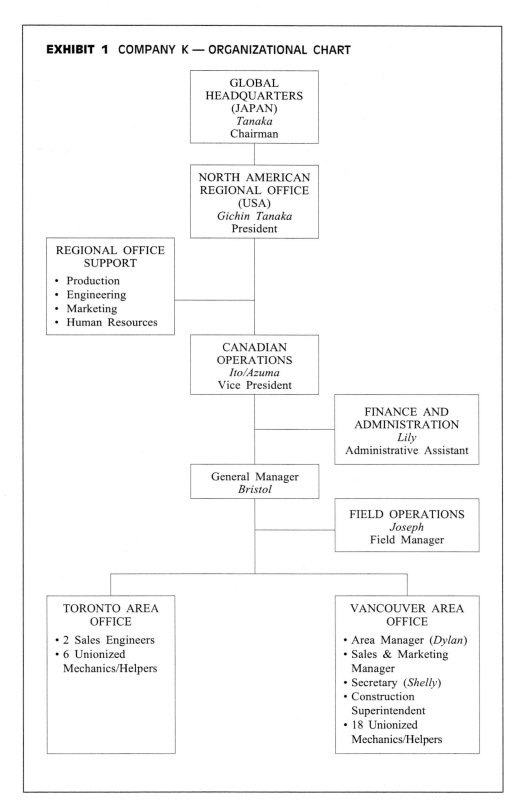

GLOBAL
HEADQUARTERS
(JAPAN)
Tanaka
Chairman

NORTH AMERICAN
REGIONAL OFFICE
(USA)
Gichin Tanaka
President

REGIONAL OFFICE
SUPPORT
- Production
- Engineering
- Marketing
- Human Resources

CANADIAN
OPERATIONS
Ito/Azuma
Vice President

FINANCE AND
ADMINISTRATION
Lily
Administrative Assistant

General Manager
Bristol

FIELD OPERATIONS
Joseph
Field Manager

TORONTO AREA
OFFICE
- 2 Sales Engineers
- 6 Unionized
  Mechanics/Helpers

VANCOUVER AREA
OFFICE
- Area Manager (*Dylan*)
- Sales & Marketing
  Manager
- Secretary (*Shelly*)
- Construction
  Superintendent
- 18 Unionized
  Mechanics/Helpers

immediate responses were required. The Canadian operation was dismayed when the response to an opportunity needing a rapid proposal was delayed by the cumbersome international communications.

The GOC had a stiff, vertical hierarchy employing a Department Manager, Group Manager, Subgroup Head, two Unit Heads and two supervisors, plus almost a dozen clerical staff, to coordinate worldwide operations. This structure ensured procedural consistency, but it also resulted in an assembly-line orientation, even for managerial staff at the GOC. For example, one supervisor was mainly in charge of ensuring that the fax coding system was followed to the letter. It was not unusual to receive a memo from the GOC stating that one had duplicated the use of a fax number or inquiring as to why the number of a fax was not in sequence. A GOC-issued Rules Manual included instructions on how to fill in colour-coded company forms and a step-by-step procedure on how to sew a logo patch on a mechanic's uniform. Inter-office correspondence was to be sent only to Mr. Azuma. As the document was routed, all managers in the loop were supposed to "stamp" their acknowledgement with GOC-provided personal seals. The size of the seal was dependent upon the rank of the manager. The GOC was definitely a highly centralized organization. In fact, all the Asian contracts require approval from the Chairman, and all area offices worldwide were required to submit regular sales forecasts and monthly sales reports to GOC.

One advantage of the rigid system at GOC was the uniform appraisal system. Appraisal forms were provided worldwide, with separate performance factors used for managerial, plant and clerical personnel. Self-appraisal occurred initially, before final ratings were given by the supervisor. One's chance of upward movement with excellent performance was very high. Although a typical Japanese company implemented re-assignments every three years without regard for personal choices, the K Group took family circumstances into consideration whenever possible.

The North American Regional Office — U.S.A.

It was not surprising that Gichin Tanaka's management style in this part of the globe was almost an exact replica of his father's. To his credit, Gichin had successfully walked the delicate line between centralization and efficiency. While maintaining strict adherence to policies, procedures and structures like the Regional Office Support Group, he had managed to trim down vertical layers by encouraging the training and development of specialists, and granting them some authority to act independently. To illustrate, the Regional Support Group in the United States and its departments were now given the additional task of supporting Company K in Canada. The personnel could coordinate directly with their Canadian counterparts — Joseph and Lily, respectively — as indicated in the organizational chart.

Company K — Canada

Corporate structure in Toronto was small, but complex, because reporting functions varied depending upon the function, department or individual. Mr. Azuma reported directly to the GOC in Japan and to the President in the United States. Joseph, the Field Manager in Toronto, and Lily, the Administrative Assistant, reported directly to the Regional Office VPs in the United States, as they conducted their daily responsibilities independent of the VP and GM in Canada. The rest of the employees then went through these two if they required any assistance from the United States.

The Vancouver Area Office was highly organic, bordering on "adhocracy". No job descriptions were provided, and reporting functions were unclear. Although the Construction Superintendent, a former union mechanic, reported to Dylan (the Area Manager), he coordinated directly with the Regional Office on construction detail, often without the involvement of Dylan. The only formal hierarchy was that the whole Area Office reported to Mr. Bristol in Toronto. However, informal relationships existed. With his former sales background, Dylan had a highly entrepreneurial perspective. Without the knowledge of Mr. Bristol, he consulted directly with the U.S. engineers concerning bids on projects. He once received a written warning, issued by Joseph on behalf of Mr. Bristol. Dylan had submitted a bid to a developer specifying maintenance services that turned out to be incompatible with the firm's engineering standards. The only supervisory relationship he had with the secretary, Shelly, was when she typed letters for him or asked him to initial accounts payable vouchers. Otherwise, Shelly relied on Lily in Toronto for procedures to be followed in doing her accounting, payroll and clerical functions. Although Dylan was officially Area Manager, he often felt he did not have the authority to go with the title.

MANAGEMENT STYLES AT COMPANY K

The Japanese Mr. Azuma and the Canadian Mr. Bristol were culturally different, and their management styles reflected this difference. Mr. Bristol was used to setting aggressive goals, and was aware of, but not averse to, the risks involved. Mr. Azuma, while agreeing that goal-setting is important, was risk averse. He took more time to analyze the merits and risks of a project, the latter being perceived very negatively. Although the Western culture seemed to favour swift decision-making, the Japanese tended to be more careful and to seek group consensus and approval from the top.

Mr. Bristol was considered to be "everyone's boss", as he was very relationship-oriented. He enjoyed the trust and respect of all subordinates, and encouraged everyone to consult him on problems, even if he rarely gave concrete solutions. Also, he personally selected all employees, rated them on their annual performance review, issued all commendation and reminder letters and signed all standard operating procedure memos prepared by Lily. Mr. Azuma, on the other hand, was more task-oriented, perhaps due to his cultural orientation and the reportorial demands of the GOC. Buried in paperwork, he rarely left his room and hardly ever had time to join informal discussions, sales briefings, or luncheon meetings with customers. The Toronto employees, with their generally good motivation at work, seemed to respond fairly well to the leadership of both the VP and the GM, particularly the sales and field personnel who were used to working independently. In Vancouver, however, the ambiguous job responsibilities and weak area management, which had caused workplace tensions, required stronger leadership from Corporate Office. Perhaps this should have been done from the start.

A CRITICAL INCIDENT

After the award of a major project in Vancouver, Joseph was designated the Project Manager because it was felt he would be better able to deal with the complexity of the design of the elevating systems required. Mr. Bristol issued a memo announcing Joseph's appointment. Copies were provided to the Regional Support Group and the Vancouver Area Office. In accordance with protocol, the U.S. office started sending the drawings to Joseph, who in turn was supposed to coordinate with Dylan. Company K did not want the project owners to think there was a problem in meeting specifications. For this reason, Dylan remained the contact person to deal with them. However, all official communications with the owners were to be cleared with Mr. Bristol. This was agreed upon in one of the biweekly conferences with the VP, GM and Joseph in attendance, and Dylan taking part via telephone. Towards the second month of the preparation of the final plan for the project, however, the Engineering Department in the United States informed Joseph that they had found a technical problem in the design of a hanging walkway that might not be up to their engineering standards. They agreed to send revised drawings in a week's time. The final blueprint would have to be approved in Japan, due to the critical exceptions.

Joseph informed Dylan as soon as possible about the revisions and the week's delay in the issuance of final drawings. He scribbled the note right on the transmittal cover of a fax of the old drawings. The fax was sent to Dylan, and the confirmation sheet showed that the transmission was successful. There is no doubt that the message was received, as the fax code system at the Canadian operation was an exact duplicate of the Japanese system. All faxes were properly numbered and logged in an incoming fax record book. In a few minutes, Dylan knew of the delay. He was perturbed that the owners had to wait another week, since he had personally promised them prompt action on documentation so that groundbreaking for construction would occur soon. He immediately called Mr. Bristol, who, having been briefed on the matter by Joseph, instructed him to wait a few more days and then inform the owners of the delay.

GOC faxed a message to Mr. Azuma that final drawings would be couriered from Japan the next day. They would reach Toronto two days later, and would take another day to reach Vancouver. Hearing this, the impulsive Dylan decided that, since the drawings were being shipped almost immediately, he could submit his revised, detailed contract to the owners with a note that the drawings would follow. He did not bother to inform Mr. Bristol or Joseph, and had a personal reason for this breach of protocol. He never spoke of it to anyone, but he was not happy with the fact that Joseph in Toronto was overseeing his Vancouver operations. In fact, he had told the client that the project was under his control. He perceived Joseph's fax concerning the delay as interference. Knowing that the final drawings were being sent, he threw caution to the winds. He had decided to interpret the requirement for revised drawings as a mere formality that would not change the overall design in a significant way.

However, a day after he had sent out the package to the owners with the final costing, GOC faxed another message to Mr. Azuma informing him that, upon further review, an entire portion of a specific assembly did not fit the Group's components. Discussions with the owners on significant design revisions were required, and there would be some minor additional cost. It took Mr. Bristol two trips to Vancouver, within seven days and two weeks of negotiation to deal with the situation. It was most difficult to explain to the owners why a final proposal that had been sent was being revised only a day after submission, and at a somewhat higher cost. In the end, some of the cost adjustment had to be swallowed by Company K to save the contract.

Following this incident, Dylan was re-assigned to be the Sales and Marketing Manager in Vancouver, and a seasoned Operations Manager from a competitor was hired as the new Area Manager.

QUESTIONS

1. Describe the structure and organizational type of the worldwide Company K, including its Canadian operation.

2. Is the structure well suited to the needs of doing business in Canada? Explain your answer, identifying functional and dysfunctional aspects at the local and global levels.

3. What are the benefits and drawbacks of the Group's rigid communications system?

4. How does the multicultural environment influence the Group's structures and policies?

5. How is it possible that a local office such as Vancouver, with such loose job descriptions and informal practices, could exist within the overall organization?

6. Who is/are mostly responsible for the "critical incident", and why?

7. What organizational changes would make the operation of the company more effective and minimize the possibility of more incidents such as the one described?

ConAccFin

ConAccFin is an Ottawa-based software company that offers financial solutions for the construction industry. Most of its clients and prospects are construction companies in the United States.

There is a prescribed procedure to follow during the sales process at ConAccFin. It requires the efforts and co-operation of two departments: the Sales Department, which actively searches for prospects; and the Solutions Department, which performs product demonstrations for prospects. A Vice-President of Solutions, Bob, and a Vice-President of Sales, John, together, manage the various parts of the sales process. (See Exhibit 1.)

Stage one of the sales process is to initiate contact with a prospect via cold calling, a recommendation from existing clients, or meeting at networking events. An interest and discovery document is then sent to the prospect to determine who their key decision-makers are (those who will be involved in all future discussions); what are their financial and accounting needs and procedures, and how they currently fulfill them; and what modules of the ConAccFin software system they are interested in. After this assessment is made, a Web conference is arranged to present the prospect with ConAccFin company information and a brief overview of the specific ConAccFin system that best applies to the prospect's interests and needs.

The second stage of the sales process consists of the introduction of the Solutions Team members, who are sent, along with the salesperson, to the prospect's head office for an in-depth product demonstration over the course of two days. Following this, the prospect is given the opportunity to sample the system in a demonstration under the supervision of a Solutions Team member. If all of the above is successful, contract and licensing discussions are the final steps of the sales process, which then leads to the acquisition of a new client for ConAccFin.

The coordination of the participation of Solutions Team members in this process is conducted by Denise, the Solutions Coordinator. She is contacted by the salesperson and assigns the appropriate Solutions Team member, based on his or her skill and availability.

This case is based on original work by Dana Tal.

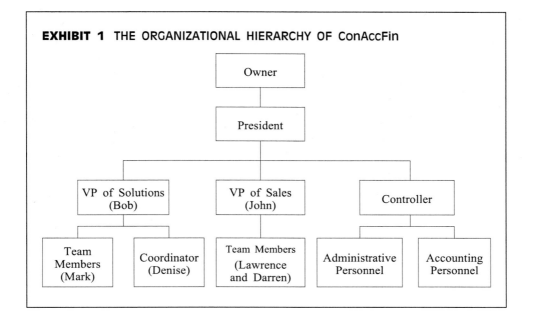

EXHIBIT 1 THE ORGANIZATIONAL HIERARCHY OF ConAccFin

Each salesperson is responsible for an assigned geographical territory. A colour-coded map of the United States representing the states that are part of each salesperson's territory is available on the firm's intranet. ConAccFin's marketing activities include many trade shows and conferences that take place throughout the United States. These events often bring construction companies from all over the country to one city and are a highly effective way to connect with prospects. If a salesperson makes contact with a prospect outside his or her jurisdiction, the policy is that the prospect is to be referred to the proper ConAccFin sales representative.

The sales team is paid strictly on commission, and this creates a high-pressure environment. There have been only a few disputes among the sales team over the years, but two sales members, Lawrence and Darren, seem to have ongoing problems. Lawrence's territory includes the northeastern states, such as Massachusetts and Pennsylvania, while Darren's territory includes the southeastern states, such as Georgia and Florida. Although there had been no previous disputes between them involving territory, Darren complained that Lawrence was always insisting that his request for resources be given priority and was never willing to assist other members of the sales group. Lawrence answered that he was there to obtain new clients in his territory and that he didn't have the time to spend on activities that did not directly relate to his sales.

While attending a major trade show in Philadelphia, Lawrence met a prospect who worked at a branch of a construction firm headquartered in Miami. Even though he knew that this prospect should be handed over to Darren, as the headquarters location determined whose territory the prospect falls into, Lawrence proceeded to contact this prospect's key decision-makers in Miami and continue with the sales process without informing anyone else at ConAccFin. He felt that this potential client was an excellent prospect that would generate a substantial commission; if he turned it over to Darren, he would receive nothing for his efforts. In fact, no one was aware of the existence of this prospect until after a Web conference was completed by Lawrence on his own.

Lawrence's next step was to move to the second phase of the sales process. Ignoring Denise, the Solutions Coordinator, he promptly emailed Mark, his Solutions Team Member of choice, to reserve him for this engagement. When Mark informed Lawrence that he had a previous engagement already booked for the same day for another sales member, Lawrence assured him that his previous commitment had already been turned over to another Solutions Team member, freeing Mark for the Miami prospect. Without stating it directly, Lawrence gave Mark the impression that Denise was already on board with this arrangement.

Mark had worked reasonably well with Lawrence in the past, but the lack of any notification from Denise, and the fact that she had not been copied on the email from Lawrence, made him a little suspicious. In his reply to Lawrence, Mark included Denise as a bcc recipient. When Denise saw the full correspondence included in the email, she felt undermined by Lawrence. His circumvention of the organization's strict territory protocol left her with the difficult task of reorganizing the allocation of Solutions Team members. This was not the first time this had happened. Allocating resources for the now-chaotic schedule of sales engagements would be difficult. Denise notified Mark that none of what Lawrence said had any merit and promptly informed Bob (Vice-President of Solutions) about the dispute. Bob was enraged to discover Lawrence's behaviour and his disregard for ConAccFin protocol. While he didn't have authority over the sales team, Bob was able to intervene in the issue concerning Mark, promptly re-assigning him to his original commitment.

This quickly became a public issue within the Solutions and Sales departments. When Darren found out about Lawrence's tactics to steal a prospect in his territory, he confronted Lawrence. There was a loud and vulgar exchange of words in the office. Then John (Vice-President of Sales), faced with the question of whether to re-assign the prospect to Darren, decided to allow Lawrence to proceed with the prospect. Although it was an unusual departure from company policy, it was not a great surprise to most people. John was well known for his preference for aggressive and competitive behaviour among his sales people. He justified this decision by saying that Lawrence had already established a relationship with the key decision-makers at the prospect and that Darren had invested no time or effort in the process. Sales people made their living from their commission and had to be rewarded for the work they put in. When Bob confronted him about Lawrence circumventing Denise, John shrugged and said that wasn't his department. He said that his responsibility was sales, and he needed to reward those who performed. Bob was infuriated with John's refusal to discipline Lawrence for his failure to follow ConAccFin protocol.

Lawrence followed through with the sales process and signed on the Miami prospect as a ConAccFin client without any negative consequences for his actions during the sales process. This incident created a degree of distrust and hostility in the ConAccFin Sales Department in general, as it was sensed that the territorial divisions might not be honoured in the future. The previously strained relationship between Lawrence and Darren was now one of open conflict. Each referred to the other in very derogatory terms. Most of the other members of the Sales Department supported Darren and treated Lawrence in a manner that showed their dislike for him.

A couple of months after the incident, Darren left the firm to work for a company providing a similar type of software to small-scale manufacturers. Lawrence successfully acquired two more clients, both within his territory. However, he left ConAccFin soon after Darren had to take a position in sales management. In an executive meeting, Bob pointed out to John that the strained atmosphere in the Sales Department was costing them personnel. John said that didn't matter. He could replace them and, in the meantime, ConAccFin sales were very satisfactory.

QUESTIONS

1. What are the ethical issues in this case (if any)?

2. What are the implications for corporate culture in this case?

3. What are the motivational effects on Lawrence, and on Darren, of the decision to allow Lawrence to work with the prospective account?

4. What would have been the motivational effects on Lawrence, Darren, and other members of the sales team if the decision had been to prevent Lawrence from working on the prospective account?

5. Assess the way in which the decision was made to allow Lawrence to work exclusively on the prospective account. What would have been a better decision-making process?

6. Overall, did ConAccFin benefit or lose from the events in the case? Why or why not?

Conavia "H"

At the end of 2002, Stanley Jackson, an experienced aviation consultant, had risen to become Senior Vice-President, Economics and Finance, of Conavia Canada Ltd., a Vancouver-based consulting firm specializing in avionics. He reported directly to George Markov, the President and surviving founder of the firm. Although there was a parallel Vice-President, Projects and Facilities, the position had remained unfilled for more than two years since the untimely death of its incumbent, Ron Gilbert. Stanley was, in fact, the number two executive with the company, which had nine employees.

Since 1996, when control of the company was restructured following the death of George Markov's founding partner Samuel Kahn, the firm's equity was distributed as follows:

	Shares	Percent
George Markov	3,100	52
Stanley Jackson	1,500	25
Paul Frees	750	12
Other employees	650	11

Share transfer was restricted by a shareholder's agreement requiring all shareholders to be employees of the company. In the event of termination of employment for whatever reason, outstanding shares were to be repurchased by the other shareholders, if they wished, or otherwise by the company on a fixed formula basis related to the previous year's financial statement. At the end of 2002, the formula value of the shares was determined to be equal to $27.22. This valued the entire company at $163,000, which was not unusual considering that it rarely did more than break even financially.

The three-person board of directors was composed of Markov, his wife Eleanor, and Marvin Kaplansky, the company's attorney. The full board met rarely, with most activity taking place within the fiction of the company's books. Although Stanley was excluded from the board he was not disturbed by it, and believed that, as

This case was written by Richard Fisher.

Conavia was effectively Markov's creation, he had the right to operate it as he saw fit. As most of Stanley's remuneration was in the form of salary, he did not believe that his elevation to the board would change his remuneration potential.

In early 2003, while at an airline operators' conference in San Juan, Puerto Rico, George Markov took Stanley aside, and, to his surprise, told him that he would be stepping down, at least temporarily.

"As you know," he said, "Jet BC have been losing a lot of good people during this latest ownership scramble, and they need help badly. To make a long story short, they've made me an offer I can't refuse, and it looks as if I'm going to take it." Jet BC was Canada's largest (and only) manufacturer of light business jets, producing a line competitive with the Cessna Citation series. They were based on Vancouver Island, and had recently been divested by the federal government after a five-year stint as a Crown Corporation. An equity issue had been floated successfully.

Stanley, who had received no advance warning of the situation, was aghast: "I don't know what to say."

"You don't have to say anything," continued George, "because nothing is going to change. I'd like you to take over the leadership of Conavia, at least on a tempo-rary basis, as Executive Vice-President. I'm certain that you'll do a fine job. While the company can't afford an immediate raise, I can promise you a substantially revised compensation package when you come up for review next year."

"Who do you have in mind for a new president?" asked Stanley.

"At the moment, nobody," replied George. "I'm certain that you can handle the responsibilities yourself. Meanwhile, I'll always be at the other end of a phone, or a fax machine, or even the ferry. In fact," he continued, "from what I've seen, Jet BC could use a lot of sales engineering assistance. Who better to help out than Conavia?"

"Isn't that an obvious conflict of interest?" Stanley suggested.

"It's been discussed," George answered. "My Conavia shares will be placed in a trust to be voted by Marvin. Meanwhile, I'll continue to serve as an outside direc-tor. And as long as Conavia can provide consulting services on a competitive basis, why should they be discriminated against?" He smiled enigmatically.

For the first time in several years, Stanley was forced to re-examine his rela-tionship to the company. He had always worked in the shadow of George Markov, who, in addition to a demonstrated record of success, was also an extremely strong personality. Stanley had always deferred to George in matters of corporate strategy and had generally consulted him prior to proceeding with his own projects. The new organizational structure would clearly require more responsibility from Stanley, and he was uncertain how he would respond to it. Nonetheless, after considerable reflec-tion, Stanley decided to accept the challenge. "Hell," he thought, "I've been more or less running my half of the business for five years anyway. There's no reason why I can't pick up the other half as well."

For the first six months, events proceeded smoothly. Although George moved to Sidney, BC, he was generally in Vancouver once a week, and always stopped in to discuss business with Stanley. Stanley considered his advice useful, and generally accepted George's suggestions.

The composition of Conavia's business, however, began to change. With 30 years of senior experience in the Canadian aerospace environment, George was welcome in the highest echelons of both Victoria and Ottawa. Conavia had received a substantial volume of sole source work in the strategic consulting area, including a major, two-year study with DIST (the federal Department of Industry, Science and Technology) regarding the future direction of Canada's aerospace industry. Stanley soon found, however, that while deputy ministers might respond to George, they rarely returned his calls, and the company's backlog of projects began to shrink. To compensate, Stanley began to develop business in areas where he was stronger, namely, the more technical (or at least project-specific) aspects of aviation that did not require as much input at the political level.

One immediate side-effect was lower rates. Whereas DIST showed no qualms about rates in the region of $1,200 per day ("Hell," said George, "that's dirt cheap compared to what Booz Allen or SRI would charge"), both Transport Canada and CIDA (Canadian International Development Agency), Conavia's next largest clients, balked at rates that were much in excess of $700. In fact, CIDA tried to adhere to a $500 maximum limitation.

"We can't make money at $500," said George, during one of his periodic visits. "You've got to get the rates up, Stanley."

"Actually we can," countered Stanley. "We're running a much lower overhead shop. No offence, but your costs in particular were always high, what with you charging off to Ottawa every second week, lunches at the Rideau Club, entertainment, and all that jazz. Don't get me wrong, it worked well for you, because you were always able to get the high-rated business to cover it, but I can't do it that way. If you check the six month P&L, you'll find that our net is about the same as always."

In fact, Stanley was very proud of the way he had managed to control expenses. He believed that if the company was to remain profitable under his stewardship, costs would have to drop, because he was not certain he could maintain Markov's level of revenue generation.

"Sure the net is the same," replied George, "for two basic reasons. One is that we're still charging against the last of the old DIST contracts. Two is that I've brought you a quarter of a million dollar's worth of business from Jet BC. That's what's keeping the company alive."

Although revenues and costs both dropped under Stanley's stewardship, the volume of business, as measured by chargeable man-hours, remained high. Stanley had particular success in obtaining business from CIDA, including a half-million dollar aerospace industrial offset project in Southeast Asia. Stanley was personally involved with it from mid-2003 until well into the spring of 2004, and much of his time was spent overseas. Conavia was staffed with seasoned veterans, however, and little direct administration was required.

In fact, this was a source of great pride to Stanley. Although gross revenues had dropped, he had managed to maintain the company's business volume at stable levels with no drop in the company's profits. He was also pleased with his success in moving the company into new business areas. The contracts Conavia had succeeded in obtaining were now strictly the results of Stanley's efforts, so he believed, rather than of George's.

The weekly meetings with George became less frequent because Stanley was out of the country more and more. However, this did not stop George from visiting Conavia and talking to Paul Frees, the next senior man, or his former secretary. Following some of these visits, Stanley would occasionally receive a fax from George the next day. Most dwelt on the rate situation.

"We can't continue like this," read one, in September 2003. "Business at $500 is killing us, and you're not able to make the rounds in Ottawa and Victoria while you're sitting in a hotel room in Manila. Our backlog is down, and our revenues are down. You're going to have to spend more time getting higher quality business." Stanley was furious, and counted to ten before replying that one paragraph faxes sent halfway around the world were not the proper medium in which to develop a sound business strategy.

Stanley returned home for a month in early October and immediately phoned George. "When do you want to meet?" he asked.

"It's a busy month," answered George. "Jet BC's agreement for federal funding is up for renewal, and I'll be east most of the month."

"What about the fax? Do you want a formal reply? George, we're making good money here, and it's not being done with mirrors. Under CIDA rules, I can charge for seven-day weeks while our staff is on overseas assignment. The time budget allows for it, and CIDA condones it. That's an effective 40% surcharge off the top. Check the project budget sheets: we're making money."

"I wouldn't worry about it, Stanley. It's not necessary to waste any more time on this. Just try and do your best."

While Stanley was upset by George's attitude, he chalked it up to personal idiosyncrasies and continued to manage the company as he saw fit, knowing full well that in the event of a confrontation with George, he would be supported by very positive financial results.

Stanley was correct. The profit and loss statements, although unaudited, were available from the computerized accounting system in early January, and indicated that profit levels in 2003 were the highest in five years. The comparative results were as follows:

	Net Profit
1999	$ 90,000
2000	(123,000)
2001	17,000
2002	2,000

In relation to 2002, revenues had dropped by $110,000, but costs had been reduced by $147,000.

Although Stanley knew approximately how the year would look, he did not see the figures immediately because he was in Kuala Lumpur at the time presiding over the completion of the CIDA job. When he returned in late January 2004, he discovered that Conavia had a new president.

"You could have told me," he said to George, as soon as they could meet. "I don't object to a new president, that's your prerogative anyway, but you could have at least let me know in advance. Who the hell is Dennis Wilson, anyway?"

"You said you didn't like faxes in remote places," replied George, "and the whole thing came up suddenly, anyway. Dennis is an experienced executive with close ties to the federal Tories. He's responsible, among other things, for fund-raising in the lower mainland, and he's very close to the highest levels in Ottawa. He's exactly the man we need. He'll complement your skills. I still expect you to continue with the day-to-day running of the company: Dennis can't possibly do that, anyway. What he can do is get us some badly needed high-rated business in Ottawa."

"At what price? We're successful now due as much to cost control as to revenues."

"It'll be pay-as-you-go. No fixed salary. Is that OK by you?"

"I guess so," said Stanley.

If Stanley maintained his composure with George, he was fuming internally. In the course of his year's stewardship, he had succeeded in restructuring the company so that it could operate profitably in George's absence. He had maintained the company's size and profitability in the face of reduced revenues by stringent cost control. Now that the transition year had passed, he was looking forward to the firm growing, both in terms of size and profitability. Yet, he thought to himself, George had rewarded his outstanding performance by saddling him with a "politician" who had no experience in either aviation or, for that matter, business. In Stanley's vocabulary, "politician" was not a compliment.

In the event, Dennis turned out to be a personable, if not brilliant, president. He was rarely in the office, and Stanley maintained effective control over Conavia. It was not until March that Stanley received his first surprise, an invoice from Dennis' holding company for an advance against commissions of $12,000.

"But we don't pay advances against commissions," said Stanley the following week, when he finally managed to meet with Dennis. "We don't even pay commissions ourselves. We work on the basis of chargeable time: if you charge time to a project, you get paid for it. I can't authorize this."

"Presidents don't come cheap," explained Dennis. "I've given up a lot to take this job, at no salary whatever. I have to spend time in Ottawa, prepare proposals, meet people. This is just a bridge to cover expenses until the jobs start to come in."

"I didn't realize you were writing proposals," said Stanley. "I haven't seen anything cross my desk."

"Oh, nothing written. You can take care of the details after the fact. But I can tell you that I had some very promising discussions with a certain minister when he was in town last week. I'll let you know as soon as I need some back-up."

"I still can't authorize payment on this," said Stanley, stubbornly, waving the invoice. "Not without some indication that remunerative work has been done, some-how, somewhere."

"Then I'll have to get it authorized elsewhere," said Dennis, softly. "We'll talk about it later, Stanley."

If Stanley was upset when Dennis had been appointed, he was now starting to become frightened as well. The key to Conavia's success, he believed, had been his tight cost controls. Now, he was faced with a new president who apparently wanted to develop business in George's old style but without any demonstrated ability to bring in the compensating high-yield contracts. If costs were to increase without a new source of revenues, he was suddenly worried that he might be blamed for the overall results.

Following this latest conversation with Dennis, Stanley immediately tried to reach George, but discovered he was out of town and unavailable. He left messages at several locations, but his call was not returned. Six days later, he received an information copy of a director's resolution stating that, with immediate effect, Stanley's check-signing authority was to be transferred to Dennis Wilson.

Stanley's first urge was to dash off a letter of resignation in protest; in fact, he drafted one. A few hours of reflection after work, however, led him to the conclusion that, other than these recent management developments at Conavia, he really enjoyed his job. It was unlikely that the same degree of personal autonomy and the fascinating array of challenging projects in exotic locations would be available in another firm. Still, he could not ignore a problem that was causing frequent, severe headaches and chronic fatigue due to many sleepless nights.

QUESTIONS

1. Critically assess George Markov's leadership. What are his strong and weak points?

2. What mistakes were made by Stanley Jackson in dealing with George Markov?

3. (a) From a motivational point of view, why did Stanley Jackson react so strongly to the new president and his practices?

   (b) Answer the same question with respect to George Markov's reaction to Stanley's activities.

4. How should George Markov have introduced Dennis Wilson to Stanley Jackson?

5. Recommend, in detail, a course of action for Stanley Jackson.

Cross-cultural Connections

INTRODUCTION

As more and more organizations go global, foreign governments are increasingly recognizing the importance of teaching English, the international language of business, in the early grades in public schools. The following events took place in the English Division of the Office of the Ministry of Education (O.M.E) in a metropolitan area in Asia.

BACKGROUND INFORMATION

The O.M.E. is organized and run by Dr. V, Chief Superintendent, who manages five divisions. The division responsible for English instruction in local public schools is overseen by Ms. W, a supervisor with a long history in education and fluency in English, but with no experience of teaching English as a foreign language. There are 12 districts in the area, and supervisors change positions every six months. As of 2008, the O.M.E. supervised over 2,400 public schools with over 1.8 million students and more than 78,000 local teachers. Since 2005, over 350 native-speaking English teachers (NSET) from Canada, the United States, Australia, England, Ireland, Scotland, and South Africa were placed in local public schools.

In 2006, the O.M.E. hired 160 NSET. Ideally, qualified teachers were selected, but since the demand for NSET around the world is high, not all hired NSET held teaching certificates from their home countries. Candidates' personality traits such as flexibility and adaptability were also part of the selection criteria. Although contracts stipulated that NSET were to "assist" local teachers in and out of the classroom, they were, in reality, expected to plan, prepare, and lead the lessons. This fiction was necessary because local laws barred the employment of foreigners under the title of "teacher". Salaries were based on qualifications and years of experience. Health insurance, accommodation, return flight reimbursements, and end-of-year bonuses were also provided upon completion of contracts.

This case is based on original work by Nicole Cloutier.

The organizatio chart in Figure 1 illustrates the O.M.E.'s management structure. Chloe, an NSET from Canada, was hired and sent to teach at M School, the second-poorest school in the city. With over 10 years of overseas teaching experience, including six years of teacher-training experience and three years of school-administration experience, Chloe was the most experienced NSET recruited that year. She was assigned to work for Principal X, an ambitious person who had previously been a supervisor at the O.M.E. Principal X hoped to build a good reputation for his school in the economically depressed area, and it was his hope that it would become recognized as the leading school of English education in his district. He hoped this would provide him with additional points towards an upcoming promotion that he was hoping for.

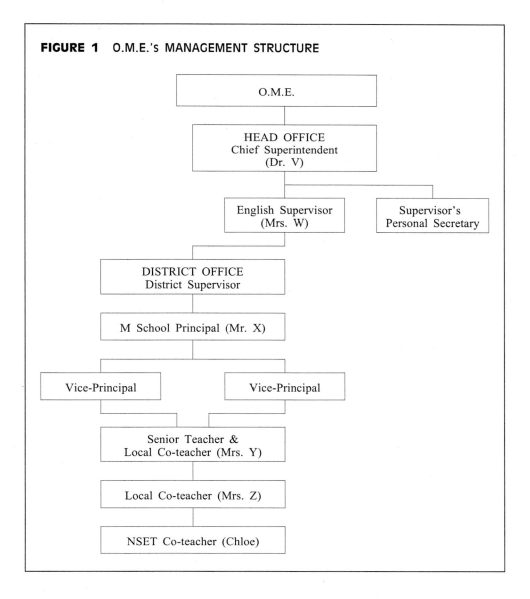

FIGURE 1 O.M.E.'s MANAGEMENT STRUCTURE

Upon arrival, all NSET attended a compulsory, paid orientation/cross-cultural training session lasting one week. Seminars on the region's culture and cuisine, transportation systems, travel, sensitivity training, and a survival course on the local language were provided. Cultural differences were focused on early in the training sessions. The Western work philosophy was branded as goal-oriented and direct, while local Asian principles were more relationship-centred and indirect. In addition, trainers called attention to the fact that local culture and customs put emphasis on formality, which was reflected in speech used to address people of different ages and ranks; for example, individuals of higher age or rank were treated with more deference than younger or more junior individuals.

During the orientation session, trainees were told that while most procedures and regulations, pay, and performance appraisals were controlled at the O.M.E., authority over NSET's schedules and holidays were managed by the local public schools. All matters regarding housing, remuneration, travel reimbursement, training, and contract renewals, etc., were governed by Ms. W at the O.M.E. All of the NSET's queries and complaints were to be reported directly through local co-teachers. These would then be reported to the vice-principals and make their way up the chain of command until they finally reached Ms. W, who would look into them. Most school principals and vice-principals did not speak much English. Therefore, local co-teachers (who possessed varying degrees of English proficiency) would act as translators for the NSET, who were not expected to speak the local language. Chloe was content with the information provided. Her previous overseas experience in Europe, the Middle East, and Asia contributed to her positive outlook and self-assurance.

The following day, Chloe set off for M School, which employed 60 full-time local teachers. She met her colleagues and superiors: Principal X (who spoke no English); two vice-principals with very limited English abilities; and her two co-teachers, Ms. Y and Ms. Z (both with advanced levels of English proficiency).

THE SITUATION

The first month went by quickly. Staff were exceptionally welcoming and accommodating. Although Chloe was dependent on her co-teachers for regular translation, she felt fortunate to have been sent to M School. Teaching economically disadvantaged students brought her tremendous fulfillment as she became aware that the skills she brought to the classroom could make a positive impact on her students' English skills and, ultimately, on their future prospects. She was very passionate about her work.

News of her strong work ethic, coupled with her innovative teaching methods, spread quickly across the school. The Principal and vice-principals observed her classes often. Chloe focused on communicative activities and presented them in a dynamic and motivating fashion. Her students were engaged and grew to love her classes, and her co-teachers witnessed marked improvements in students' abilities early on. This led to Chloe gaining respect and trust, which afforded her considerable freedom as to how she taught her classes and she spent her time outside of lessons. Given Chloe's limited ability to speak the local language, Principal X exempted her from attending weekly teachers' meetings and permitted her to use this time as she saw fit. Chloe used this time to devise teaching materials, lesson plans, displays, handouts, and games, and went further by creating and implementing after-school clubs, a resource centre for teachers, and activity days during the year. Undoubtedly, Chloe could see the impact of her teaching in her classes. Previously unsure, struggling students rapidly became self-assured, functional speakers of English. To everyone's delight, M School's results on national English exams far exceeded expectations. All of these things combined to give Chloe great satisfaction.

By the end of her second month, Chloe was hosting open classes for district and M School teachers who observed and talked to her about her methods. Although this required extra time and effort for Chloe, she happily accepted both because she thoroughly enjoyed teacher training. These open classes were successful, but true to local fashion, the requests to hold them were made with very little warning, causing stress and frustration on her part. As time went on, these last-minute requests fuelled negative feelings for Chloe, who regarded the lack of notice as both disorganized and showing disregard for her. Chloe asked her co-teachers if they could give her more notice in the future, but Ms. Y explained that this was the local way and was out of her control, since the requests came from higher up. Chloe gradually became more aggravated and began volunteering less and less for supplementary projects. Once, she even declined an offer by head office to be televised and interviewed about her teaching for fear of more undue stress and irritation.

The leadership at M School created problems for Chloe, who often found herself caught in the middle between her co-teachers. According to head office, Ms. Z was directly responsible for Chloe. Thus, all communication with head office was to be done through her. However, Chloe shared an office with Ms. Y, while Ms. Z's office was in a separate building. Chloe also taught 90% of her classes with Ms. Y. Hence, she had fewer opportunities to communicate with Ms. Z. When Chloe needed things for her classroom, she would invariably speak to Ms. Y, who was highly regarded by the principal and vice-principals. In addition, the situation between both local co-teachers was a tricky one. One day, Ms. Y explained: "Ms. Z is older than I am. So, even though I'm her superior, according to local custom, I should treat her with more respect. Sometimes, I'm afraid to tell her what to do because I know she doesn't like it. Then things get very uncomfortable." Matters were certainly complicated. Once, when Ms. Y had to conduct a performance evaluation, Ms. Z became defensive upon hearing criticisms about her teaching methods. Moreover, because Ms. Y had established a good relationship with head office (she had been a well-known and respected teacher trainer for the past 10 years), she was often given information off the record that even the District Head or the Principal were not privy to. Sometimes she passed details on to Chloe, whom she regarded as her Western confidante.

One Monday morning, Ms. Y approached Chloe and told her that an upcoming district training day had been scheduled and that Chloe and Ms. Z's classes would be cancelled. Ms. Y insisted that Chloe not say anything to Ms. Z, since the information had not yet made its way down the chain of command. This made matters very awkward for Chloe, who had to plan her lessons with Ms. Z. Chloe felt frustrated and irked for having to work on a task that she knew would be fruitless. This was by no means an isolated incident. On another occasion, Ms. Y told Chloe, long before Ms. Z, that there would be major changes to the English curriculum. Chloe felt trapped because these changes would have implications for her lesson planning with both her co-teachers. In a later meeting with Ms. Z, Chloe accidentally made a comment about information that had been made privy to her. Ms. Z was stunned and asked her how she had come across this information. Not wanting to lie, Chloe told her that Ms. Y had told her. Ms. Z was annoyed and asked Chloe why she had not been informed. Chloe responded that she did not know and later apologized to Ms. Y about the slip-up.

QUESTIONS

1. What issues of ethnic and cultural diversity arise in this case?

2. Is Chloe's adverse reaction to being called upon for extra work without much notice reasonable under the circumstances? Why or why not?

3. How should Chloe have handled the relationship between Ms. Y and Ms. Z?

4. Would you recommend alterations in the orientation of the NSET to avoid the situations that were disturbing to Chloe?

DataSil Inc.

DataSil Inc. is a fairly large distribution firm that specializes in the sale of computer equipment and electronic components in Canada. The company was recently bought by a major U.S. electronics firm whose goal was to expand into the Canadian computer and electronics market via acquisition of an existing firm, rather than by establishing a new subsidiary.

Employee morale and motivation were extremely high leading up to the takeover when it was announced that DataSil would be restructured to include more autonomy for all employees and coordination of activities by lateral communications instead of relying only on top-down policies. There would also be employee salary increases as soon as all the legal technicalities of the takeover were finalized. Employees were very enthusiastic about the new management style when they were told about the plans the U.S. firm had for the company. They were really looking forward to participating in the parent company's smooth integration into the Canadian market because they hadn't had enriched job descriptions with the old company. They felt that they had been treated poorly in the past, because the company's former top management saw them as just workers and not as valued employees who could contribute information and ideas to the organization. They had been hired with many promises of a rewarding and interesting career, but found themselves instead in very routinized jobs with little room for autonomous decision making.

During the first three months of the takeover, the organization seemed to be operating well. The company ran much as it had previously, but the new top management (both in the U.S. head office as well as the newly hired Canadian operations manager, Bill Weekes — see Figure 1) actively solicited the views and opinions of employees and encouraged meetings to resolve any problems. Employees were also happy with their new location in a prestigious location. The office was exceptionally well decorated with wall-to-wall carpeting and state-of-the-art office furniture. Actually, some employees compared the office to home because it was so comfortable and relaxing. There was even an informal cocktail party that allowed

---

This case is based on original work by Carron Brome.

EXHIBIT 1 DataSil Inc. Organization Chart

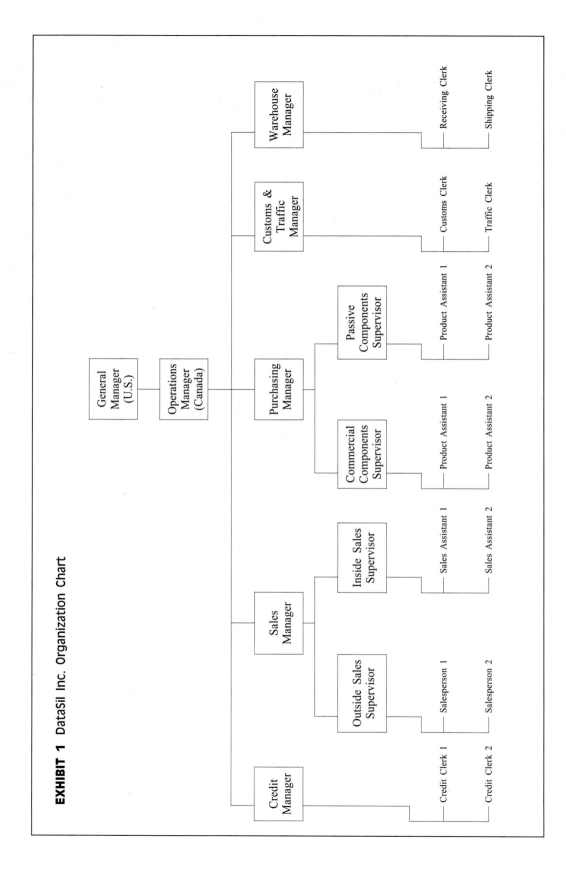

the employees the opportunity to mingle with members of local and head office management who were visiting from the U.S.

Two weeks after the party it was announced that each branch employee was to receive an upgraded workstation because the company would be going on-line with the head office. All orders would be forwarded to the U.S. distribution centre and the processing would be done there. Most of the shipments would originate from a central U.S. warehouse instead of being sent from the Canadian facility. Although the Canadian warehouse would still exist and would sometimes make the final ship-ment to their customers, it would contain much less stock than previously. Some orders would arrive at the Canadian warehouse from the U.S. and then be shipped to the customer; others would be shipped directly from the U.S. distribution centre and a few could still be filled directly from existing Canadian stock.

Many key employees attended a number of training sessions in the U.S. to familiarize themselves with the rules and procedures of the U.S. organization and its departments. It was mandatory that at least one person from each Canadian depart-ment attend. At the end of the training sessions, there was a noticeable change in the employees' attitude to the jobs. Many of them said that they were not satisfied with the new procedures, because their customers would be extremely upset when additional charges for freight and handling were billed to them. In addition, it would almost always take longer for customers to get the product.

About four weeks after the new procedures were implemented, the Canadian operations manager sent an e-mail to all the department managers in Canada asking them to attend a staff meeting to discuss the numerous customer complaints. The departments represented at this meeting included purchasing, sales, credit, customs & traffic, and warehousing. Mr. Weekes started the meeting by saying that he received a call from the controller at the U.S. head office stating that the Canadian branch was losing sales. He would like to know the reason why, and what was being done about it. He also stated that he received about five calls from disgrun-tled customers who were unhappy because their product was taking at least two weeks to be delivered to them. Customers were threatening to go to the competitors, who were offering them a delivery time of three days. Something had to be done.

"Any suggestions?" asked Mr. Weekes.

Mr. Barker, who was the manager of the purchasing department replied, "Yes, why doesn't the customs & traffic department look for a more efficient carrier? It seems that this is the problem."

"How would you know what the problem is?" asked Ms. Wood, the manager of the customs & traffic department. "Our department always has to take the blame for the other departments' errors."

"I agree to a certain extent with Mr. Barker," said Ms. Bowe, the manager of the sales department. "We place an order with the distribution centre — today, for example — and the shipment doesn't arrive at the customer's location until two weeks later. The carrier must have some control over when it will be arriving, and if that is the case, then it must be responsible for the long lead time. Moreover, when the shipment is not made directly to the customer from the U.S. and it comes into our warehouse first, it sits for a couple of days because of the complex ware-house procedures that the receiving area now has to follow. It really is becoming an urgent matter. My employees are very unhappy because the customers are calling them and expressing their anger. One of my best employees has threatened to quit because she is frustrated that she has to constantly placate irate customers. In addition, she has to expedite shipments, which is not included in her sales job responsibilities."

"I am truly sorry to hear that," said Ms. Wood, "but we have told the U.S. distribution centre repeatedly that we have to find a more efficient carrier. Furthermore, those direct shipments to the customers are beyond our control. It is the responsibility of the person keying in the order to show that the goods are to be shipped by a premium carrier offering a two-day delivery service maximum. If the correct carrier code is not keyed into the system at the time the order is entered, then the correct carrier will not be used. Bill, is it okay to issue a general e-mail detailing the codes and the related carriers as well as the lead times to the destinations within Canada?"

"Yes, Kay, we can try that route and see what happens. However, the employees in the purchasing and sales departments have to ensure that the orders are entered into the system correctly. Is everyone agreed on this?" asked Mr. Weekes. Everyone nodded in agreement, but without much enthusiasm.

"I have another issue that needs to be addressed," said Ms. Wood. "We, the employees in the customs & traffic department, would like to know why the other departments do not approach us regarding customs matters, particularly duty rates, countries of origin, and the preferred choice of carriers that need to be clarified. I was very upset the other day when a salesperson approached me for a duty rate for power supplies from an Asian supplier. It seemed that they were inquiring about the same power supplies that the supervisor of passive components in the purchasing department had requested only two days before. I particularly asked him at that time whether these products were for special use and if he had consulted someone in the sales department. He said that they were not for special use. Now, Bill in sales is telling me that he needs a duty rate so that he can quote a price to his customer. However, he said these power supplies are not for general use and should be given a special duty rate. My response to him was that he should speak with the passive components supervisor and between the two of them provide me with documentation from the customer indicating this. How are we supposed to do our job effectively if we have no co-operation from the other departments regarding correct product information? No wonder we are losing sales! No doubt we are probably using the wrong duty rates."

"Well, I was not aware of this, but you can be sure that I will investigate this matter," Mr. Weekes said. "Mr. Barker, we need to speak with the supervisors in the purchasing department. Arrange a meeting for tomorrow. Well, I believe that we have addressed the main issues regarding the customers' dissatisfaction with the delivery time. How can we work around the extra billing charges?"

"I think that we should just build it into the selling price the way we did before," said Ms. Nordy, the manager of the credit department. "The customer will see only one figure on his invoice, and it will eliminate the idea that he has incurred additional charges. However, I must say that, like the sales department, I am disturbed because customers are more than a little upset regarding the changes implemented in the credit department. They want to know why they are being billed in U.S. dollars and why the terms of payment have changed. I am trying my best to appease them, but if the complaints continue we are going to have to implement new procedures to rectify the situation."

"Okay, I will bring these matters to the general manager's attention. This meeting is adjourned unless there is something else that someone would like to add," said Mr. Weekes. "Ms. Wood, would you please stay a moment."

Ms. Wood waited until the other managers had left the room and then she turned to Mr. Weekes and asked, "What can I do for you?"

"I understand that the employees in your department are very unhappy. Is that true?" Mr. Weekes asked.

"Yes, it is," Ms. Wood replied. "My co-workers and I believe that we are in a no-win situation. I know we have specific rules and procedures, which we try to follow, but we have had situations time and time again where managers have demanded that we alter the rules because top management is aware of how crucial it is to maintain the account. The excuse given is often that we are going to lose the account, and we should do whatever it takes to correct the situation. However, when the bills resulting from the special treatment of these shipments come in for payment, we are advised that we should have used alternative methods because the shipping costs were too high for the customer to accept and we should have found a cheaper means of shipping the goods. So, first we are told to get the goods delivered at all costs and then we are blamed for the unreasonable shipping expense. Before we were taken over, all decisions concerning critical situations had to be made by top management and that was often frustrating. Now, we are supposed to resolve our problems by collaboration both within our areas and among departments, but there seems to be many more issues and it's hard to find solutions. I really like working in the customs & traffic field, but now I don't know whether this job is worth all the aggravation."

QUESTIONS

1. Identify the main problems in this case and specify their root causes.

2. To what extent is the organizational structure at fault for the problems that occurred?

3. Identify the reasons for the declining levels of motivation among the DataSil staff.

4. What are the communications issues in this case?

5. What are the decision-making issues in this case?

6. Assess the effectiveness of the meeting for solving the problems.

7. Assess the change process undertaken by the new parent company. What were its positive and negative aspects?

DeskPal Ltd.

DeskPal Ltd. was an innovative manufacturer in the office furniture industry. Through market research, upper management had recently found that the company was not meeting its goal to "delight customers by providing the **best** workplace solutions". The company had also reached a standstill in market share growth. In response, management implemented several organizational changes.

The most significant change was made immediately in the Customer Service Area. Edna Wills was promoted from Manager of Customer Service where, it was believed, she had been an effective manager, to Vice President of Customer Quality. Several functional departments were combined into one beneath her: Customer Service, Order Processing, and Custom Engineering. The resulting Customer Quality Department now consisted of an integrated team of 52 people. The intent of the change was essentially to streamline and coordinate all order management activities, thereby making the service faster, more effective, and more pleasant for customers. General Management wanted to implement the change as quickly as possible in order to regain growth in market share. Edna Wills had been a perfectionist in her approach to the details of customer service and General Management hoped that she could impose her high standards on this whole new Customer Quality area. Edna was a very intense and controlling leader. Delegating authority to her subordinates was not one of her strengths or preferences. She liked to have "a finger in every pie". This large department would prove to be a challenge for her to release some of her authority and empower her subordinates to make some of their own decisions. Her direct subordinates were called Team Leaders. There were three Regional teams (Atlantic, Pacific and Central), one Export team and the Core Support team. The Team Leader positions were not simply given to the former managers of the functional departments; they were open to anyone within the company who wished to apply. It was felt that the former managers of Order Processing and Custom Engineering had not been sufficiently effective in their jobs, and they were not given priority for the new roles. The key criterion for gaining the new team leadership positions seemed to be good performance ratings in previous placements.

This case is based on original work by Lisa Rowsell.

The regional teams and the export team comprised Customer Service, Order Processing, and Custom Engineering staff members who were expected to work together to support their region or international customers. The Core Support Team included several different functions that could not be divided regionally, and these individuals worked in support of all the other four teams. Although some members of General Management had wished also to include salespersons in these teams, others were reluctant. There was concern expressed that the more "individualistic" salespersons might be hampered by being "buried" in a team.

The Pacific Team Leader position was given to Lila, who was formerly a hard-working, but not very popular, co-worker of the employees she would now be supervising. Lila soon experienced problems with her employees arriving late and an increase in the amount of sick leave within her group. The team members often complained that they were being overworked and could not finish what was required of them, despite the fact that sales had not increased. The problem seemed to be that team members in the functional areas of Customer Service, Order Processing, and Custom Engineering were not coordinating their activities well. This led to both duplication of efforts and errors in order specifications, deliveries, and repair jobs. Lila spent much of her time trying do the difficult work and less time supervising. Frequently, Edna would roll up her sleeves and try to sort out the more serious problems herself. During these situations, Edna would appear pressured and would not talk to staff except to ask for documents or information, and to criticize their errors. Lila would then usually stand silently behind Edna, looking worried but not contributing much. Non-work-related discussion among team members often ceased when Lila entered the room.

The Atlantic Team Leader position was given to Claude, who was formerly a successful salesperson and sales manager within the company, but had little experience in customer service. Some negative feelings existed between Customer Service and Sales in general. Due to a lack of training for the salespeople, Customer reps were often left to "clean up" installation problems that occurred due to improper specification of the furniture by the salesperson. One employee said that the salespeople "get all the perks", and that service are always "saving their butts" and are expected to "work harder" than sales. Unfortunately this perception was held by some of Claude's workers, who resented his new position above them. Although Claude did have significant prior experience and success in a sales management role, his subordinates possessed greater knowledge of the work procedures in the department. As a result, they rarely consulted him on major decisions with Customer Warranty issues, etc. Claude's area was also displaying an increase in absenteeism. Edna put Claude in charge of arranging training sessions for all the teams with various consulting groups, and many of his employees sarcastically commented that he was the one in need of training, not them. Claude's response to that attitude was to be very dictatorial and to "show them who's boss". The team members then tried to ignore him and, as they were generally able to resolve their problems before they became crises, Edna did not interact much with this team.

The less significant Core Support Team Leader position was given to Sam. Sam was the former manager for the Order Processing and Scheduling Department. Significant frustrations had been experienced between Sam and Edna. The two were formerly peers on a management level, and now Sam was reporting to Edna. It was a small group, and Edna overstepped Sam to work directly with his subordinates to resolve issues, instead of allowing Sam to exert his authority. Sam's reaction was to feel resentment and to back off completely. He felt that he had no authority with his workers.

A second survey indicated that DeskPal Customers were a little happier with the services they were receiving than they were previously, but their responses were still in the "satisfied" category overall, instead of the "delighted" category that the company was striving for. In particular, and despite the multifunctional orientation of the teams, coordination of the various aspects of the customer relationship still seemed to be a problem.

QUESTIONS

1. Sketch the organizational structure of DeskPal before and after the change. What is the impact of the different structure on the way the firm operates?

2. Critically analyze the way change was carried out at DeskPal. Given that the goal was improved customer satisfaction leading to a larger market share, what problems in achieving this goal occurred due to the design and implementation of the change?

3. What were the positive and negative aspects of the placement of Edna Wills as the Vice-President of Customer Quality? Why do you suppose she performed better within the old Customer Service Department?

4. How should people have been selected for the positions of team leader? What criteria would have been appropriate? What training would have been required?

5. What would you do now to improve the functioning of the Customer Quality Department and benefit company performance?

Dimitri's Baked Goods Inc.

BACKGROUND

Dimitri's Baked Goods is a Windsor-based bakery specializing in Macedonian pastries, "zelnik" and "vielnik", sweet and regular bread, and traditional Christmas and Easter cakes. The company employs four sales representatives, two secretaries, and a production staff that varies between 24 and 32 people. The firm also employs a small sales staff of three at its only retail outlet. The pastry, bread, and cakes are distributed all over Ontario and western Canada. Distribution channels in eastern Canada are in the process of being established.

Dimitri Leakos started this business in a small shop over 30 years ago. Leakos was not self-employed when he first settled in Canada from the Macedonian region of Greece. Macedonians are proud of their heritage, although they are not well-recognized as a distinct ethnic group. The Canadian census did not even list Macedonians or the Macedonian language until 1981. This neglect is the result of the fact that historic Macedonia falls today within three Balkan countries: Bulgaria, Greece, and Yugoslavia. Throughout its recent history, Macedonia has been subjected to external and sometimes divisive control. The first significant immigration to Canada probably came as a result of uprisings against the Ottoman Empire in the early years of the 20th century. Both world wars led to further waves of immigration. Most Macedonians live in the Toronto-Hamilton area, but a group from one Macedonian village settled in Windsor.

It was important to Leakos that he became established in a Macedonian community, and Windsor provided that for him. At first he was an employee in a bakery owned by others in order to learn the business and to learn to read and write English. But he always had the need to control his own environment, and was motivated more by this need than by any ideas of greater wealth.

Dimitri's Baked Goods began as a small bakery near the tunnel to Detroit. It was close to the downtown area of Windsor and in the heart of the local Macedonian area. He still maintains this original location as a retail sales outlet, although he has had to move his production and distribution to a suburban area where larger

---

This case is based on original work by Steven Zullo and John Tannis.

quarters were available. Leakos expanded his business to a 3,000 square metre facility on Dougall Avenue.

Dimitri's growth was based on two factors. The first was the growing demand from the Macedonian community for commercially produced versions of ethnic food that were originally produced at home. While many first generation Macedonians still do their own baking, the next generation is more inclined to buy it. The second factor was his success in broadening his market beyond its original Macedonian base. This is by far the most important cause of his growth. His enthusiastic marketing to non-Macedonians has been enormously successful.

Leakos is the stereotypical workaholic small businessperson. He is the owner, plant manager, production manager, sales supervisor, marketing manager, product development supervisor, and also one of the line workers at Dimitri. These duties force him to work between 12 and 17 hours a day, seven days a week, but he allows himself to take three-week-long vacations spread throughout the year. He is a moderate risk taker who does not undertake new ventures without a great deal of research to prove to himself it will be successful. Once he starts a task, he remains committed to it until it is accomplished. He prefers tasks that provide immediate feedback to those with only long-term prospects. For example, when any of his sophisticated machinery breaks down and engineers are flown in from the manufacturers in Europe, he will spend as much time as possible with them in order to learn how to perform the repairs.

STRUCTURE

Decision making is extremely centralized at Dimitri's Baked Goods. Leakos has total control over his business. He has been running it this way for three decades with great success and, until recently, he has seen no reason to change. He feels centralization makes his business more flexible because he can act without delay when problems arise.

The structure at Dimitri's is quite informal. Leakos deals with all of his employees on an individual basis. The production roles in the bakery vary at different times. Workers are not forced to specialize in one skill. Their work might rotate among packaging, shipping, and maintenance. Only the bakers are somewhat specialized, but they too "help to get the goods delivered". The hierarchy is extremely flat and has very little horizontal differentiation. There is a production department, a sales department, two office workers, plus the retail outlet. Leakos handles all the staff functions of personnel, planning, and budgeting. Every employee at Dimitri's reports to Leakos. Dimitri has followed this functional structure since the business was first developed.

LEADERSHIP STYLE

Because Leakos is the only supervisor at Dimitri's, his practices have defined the supervisory style. He seems to practise an employee-oriented leadership. He helps his people with personal problems, treats them as equals, and avoids punitive actions. Leakos seldom refuses to compromise, nor does he insist things be done his way. His style is unobtrusive, leading by example rather than by threats. Everyone admires his personal effort on the production floor every day. He is more concerned with results than methods.

Leakos's supervisory methods have developed very high employee morale. As a result of this, there are few grievances and a low turnover rate. Many employees have been with the company for 10–15 years. His main problem comes during peak seasons such as Christmas and Easter, when production cannot keep up with demand. At those times, Leakos is forced to hire seasonal staff, and many employees have to work overtime and weekends. Then, Leakos becomes more authoritarian, and grievances increase. These holiday work schedules conflict with family and social festivities. Because of his excellent personal relationships with his employees, he is able to keep turnover low, even though these problems arise.

Motivation is often a problem in assembly line work, and may result in high absenteeism and employee turnover. Leakos uses a strategy of job rotation and job enlargement. This strategy grew naturally from the expansion of the business over the years rather than from any deliberate policy on his part. He has avoided job specialization, only because it was not natural for him to have it. Leakos also understands the need for rewarding desirable behaviour. At Christmas and Easter, when he needs employees to come in on weekends, he rewards them with praise, free coffee and doughnuts, packages of pastry, and legs of lamb to take home to their families. He also has a Christmas bonus program that he uses to reward those who are willing to work overtime. He schedules a one-week vacation period after the peak Christmas and Easter seasons, and again during the first week in August. Leakos is fairly generous with pay and benefits. The production employees are paid about twice the legal minimum wage, and get time-and-a-half for overtime. They have all statutory holidays off or are paid overtime for working them. There are three weeks of paid vacation. He provides personal time off with pay for family emergencies and illnesses, and is also understanding of the needs of his workers to fulfil family duties. Leakos is very generous when his employees have a wedding or Christening in the family.

Almost all of the workers at Dimitri's are from the Macedonian community in Windsor and speak Macedonian. Most of them are housewives earning a second income. They are unskilled and have little formal education. At Dimitri's, employees find themselves in a comfortable environment where they can speak their own language and affiliate with others with similar cultural background and interests. Since the Macedonian community in Windsor is well organized, the employees know each other from outside and see each other on their own time. They all know about upcoming weddings and planned outings to the Boufsko Cello, the Macedonian community park on Lake Erie. Whenever a new position becomes available, the employees are encouraged to spread the word to others in their circle who might be interested.

EXPANSION PRESSURES

Sales are now escalating so quickly that production facilities are unable to keep up with demand. Leakos has had to delay his plans to expand into the US market even though he knows his products are popular in Detroit. The customs officers at the

Windsor/Detroit Tunnel tell him they see his cakes and pastry every day (bought in Windsor and carried over the border). Some of his pastries are served in the Greek restaurants in downtown Detroit. The recent Free Trade Agreement with the US has led him to think that now is the time for a major marketing move into the US.

Another development is that his two children will be graduating this spring, and he hopes that they will join the business on a full-time basis. They have always worked at Dimitri's during vacations and when needed during the busy seasons. His son is graduating with a diploma in business administration from St. Clair College. His daughter is graduating from the dietician program at the University of Windsor. Both of his children have talked about finding work elsewhere, but Leakos believes that if he can come up with the right incentives, he can convince them to join the family business. He particularly thinks that they would be interested in his ideas for expansion. His plan is to get them together this Sunday afternoon to discuss the expansion and their roles in the future of Dimitri's Baked Goods Inc. If all goes well, Leakos can look forward to a very bright future, and maybe even think about retirement.

QUESTIONS

1. (a)   Draw the existing organization chart for Dimitri's Baked Goods Inc.
   (b)   Develop an alternate organizational design complete with job descriptions and reporting relationships for Leakos and his two children. Describe any required changes in the functionally-oriented structure. Since the plan is to expand, include contingency measures to accommodate growth.

2. Major expansion would probably mean that many non-Macedonians would have to be recruited into the plant. Discuss the implications of altering the monocultural work environment.

3. Describe the current employee benefits and discuss whether they need to be formalized.

4. Is the company ready to undertake geographical expansion?

Easy-Money
Department (A)

The organization involved in this case is a revenue-producing department of a government ministry. Its head office in Ottawa provides staff support to the field offices of its production section. The department has 500 employees throughout Ontario, and the payroll accounts for 30% of the department's expenditures.

The organizational structure of the Easy-Money department is divided into various functions. Recently, management has attempted to geographically decentralize. However, this attempt was restricted to the Production section, where the degree of decentralization is apparent in the organization chart (See "B" case). However, all decision making is still centralized at head office. The reorganization has resulted in confusion as to who has the responsibility for decisions: the territory managers, or the production head office managers?

The department is proactive in its environmental relations: various programs are designed to initiate contact with the private sector concerning the Taxation Statutes. These programs are designed to increase the department's visibility and act as an incentive for taxpayers to comply with the Statutes.

The department uses a three-pronged approach to achieve its objectives:

1. Liaising with the public — to inform and educate the general public, businesses, and professional associations;
2. Collections — to collect outstanding accounts receivable;
3. Audits — to administer and encourage compliance with the statutes.

The three functions are the responsibility of the Production section which spends 75% of the department's budget. The field offices of the section report to territorial managers, who in turn report to the production head. Each office performs the three functions to obtain revenue.

In the operations of the Easy-Money department, the Administration, Legislation, and Systems and Planning sections are used in a consultative capacity. These sections, although operating independently, must ensure that the needs of the Production section are met, since Production is the revenue-producing area. There is always a substantial percentage of businesses and taxpayers complying with the Statutes. As a result, there is a general complacency that permeates the organization — "All you need to do to maintain the system is to oil it now and again." New program initiatives are designed to give the department high visibility to senior ministry officials — "Emphasis on giving back money instead of hard-nose tactics like audits and collections." Such programs are usually very diluted in effect by the time they reach the field office level.

THE MAIDSTONE FIELD OFFICE (PRODUCTION SECTION)

The Maidstone Field Office is one of the larger offices of Easy-Money Department. There are approximately 70 employees, who are evenly distributed among the four functions:

1. **Administration**
   Responsible for typing, petty cash, equipment, etc.

2. **Collections**
   Responsible for collecting outstanding accounts receivable.

3. **Public Relations**
   Providing services to the public — answering interpretation calls, conducting seminars, liaising with professional organizations.

4. **Audit**
   Responsible for examining books of accounts and levying assessments where non-compliance of the taxing statute is uncovered.

Decision-making is centralized at head office. Policies are sent to the field offices as directives through the chain of command.

Mr. Fred Jones was promoted to the position of Field Office Manager three years ago. His prior position was at head office, where he conducted research on developments of audit techniques and approaches. Mr. Jones is aware that the audit area is encountering problems: staff turnover is very high — approximately 60% of the audit staff has less than one year of experience; absenteeism is high — the average is eight days per year per employee.

The audit area is directly supervised by Mr. John Smith and indirectly by Mr. Fred Jones. Both of the supervisors are middle-aged, and qualified accountants. Mr. Jones is aware that the quality of work from the audit area is well below average, because he personally reviews all of the completed audits. Mr. Jones knows the audit supervisors fairly well because they were all working in the same section at head office. He also heard through the "grapevine" that Mr. John Smith was the latest "Hot Shot", and was sent by head office to keep an eye on Mr. Jones because the Maidstone office was performing poorly.

Because of the high turnover, Mr. Jones was frequently forced to recruit from universities and colleges to fill the vacancies. A year ago Mr. Ray Bourke applied for the audit trainee position, and was successful. Ray was a recent business graduate from a rural college, and was happy that he had won the position. Ray was given an intensive training course that lasted four weeks and covered the audit program, audit techniques, interviewing skills, the Taxing Statutes, and administrative matters (how to complete forms, etc.). On the first day, Mr. Jones addressed the new group of audit trainees — "I want you all to know that this group should do well in the Easy-Money department and will significantly contribute to my efforts in making the Maidstone Field Office the no. 1 office in the department. I have an open-door policy and welcome you to discuss anything on your mind. However, please make an appointment with my secretary when you wish to see me."

After the training period was over, Ray felt that his knowledge of the Statutes was inadequate, and he conveyed his concern to the training supervisor. This person said that the Act is complex, and Ray should not worry about the inadequacy of his legislative knowledge because it takes time to develop close familiarity with its many provisions.

Ray was assigned to a regular audit group supervised by Mr. Smith. A few days before his assignment began, he spoke to one of the auditors in Mr. Smith's group.

Ray: How do you like working for Mr. Smith?

Auditor: Well Ray, there are a couple of things that you should know about Mr. Smith. He is a former member of the military, and he has a tendency to extend his military habits to the work environment. Smith is performance oriented; he is very conscious of the number of completed audits, revenue per audit, and especially the number of audits with no assessments.

Ray: I don't think there will be a problem with performance. But is he helpful? Is he easy to get along with?

Auditor: If you have a problem with the Statute, forget it. Smith does not know the Act, so it is no use asking him to solve your problem. He does not trust his auditors — he always questions nil assessments. Occasionally, he phones the auditor at the taxpayer's place of business just before quitting time to find out if he left. One more thing, you have to be careful when Mr. Jones (Field Office Manager) is around. He has a habit of listening to your conversations while pretending that he is looking for a file in the cabinets.

After the conversation with the auditor, Ray was apprehensive about being assigned to Mr. Smith's group. Ray also gathered from the conversation that the auditors did not have a good rapport with Mr. Smith because of his suspicious and unsupportive nature. Ray could not believe the auditor's comment on Mr. Jones because it seemed to be a sneaky way of gathering information on auditors.

Mr. Smith requested a meeting with Ray to familiarize him with the rules that must be followed in his section.

Mr. Smith: Welcome to my section, Ray. There are a couple of things that you should be aware of when working here:
  (1) time reports must be submitted on time, and each hour worked must be recorded on the time sheet, and
  (2) Any problems that you have must be channelled through me.

Ray: Sure thing. The training section taught me to complete the time sheets. Do I have to contact you on interpretation problems?

Mr. Smith: Yes Ray, all problems. I should also remind you that you are still on probation, and an employee appraisal will be prepared within the next three months. The level of performance indicated on the appraisal will form the basis for increments, and also your being classified as permanent staff.

After the meeting, Ray realized that the high staff turnover could be attributed to the management/staff relationship. Managers like Mr. Smith are traditional — performance oriented, employing close supervision, and suspicious. Ray felt that his relationship with Mr. Smith would not be too smooth.

Ray's first audit was of a manufacturer of canned food products. Ray was comfortable with the audit procedures because the audit program was specific and easy to follow. However, after examining a piece of manufacturing equipment, Ray was unsure whether the item was taxable or not. He consulted his interpretation guide, and was unable to resolve the problem. Finally, he decided to call Mr. Smith for assistance:

Ray: Mr. Smith, I am having some difficulty in establishing whether an item attracts tax or not.

Mr. Smith: Did you check your guide for assistance?

Ray: Yes, and I am inclined to believe that it is not taxable.

Mr. Smith: You have to be careful when classifying an item as exempt of tax. However, you are in the field and would be in the best position to determine the status of the item. You should try to make your own decisions and use the knowledge gained during training sessions.

The next time Ray encountered an interpretation problem, he spoke to one of the auditors in Mr. Smith's section. Unfortunately, Mr. Jones was conducting one of his eavesdropping sessions and overheard Ray's conversation. Mr. Jones decided to speak to Mr. Smith regarding the matter.

Mr. Jones: I heard one of your auditors discussing an interpretation matter with another auditor.

Mr. Smith: Oh, which one of the auditors?

Mr. Jones: One of the new auditors, Ray Bourke.

Mr. Smith: I told that guy when he joined the section about the protocol to be followed if a problem is encountered.

Mr. Jones: I would suggest that you remind him of the procedures. You know, I don't understand these auditors. They should feel lucky to have a secure job when there are millions of unemployed out in the marketplace.

Mr. Smith: I will speak to Ray about his procedures.

Mr. Smith felt that Mr. Jones was criticizing his section too much; this was the third incident of a similar nature that Mr. Jones brought to his attention. All Mr. Jones was concerned about was making the Maidstone Office no. 1 so that he would look good. However, Mr. Smith knew he had to reprimand Ray in any event.

Mr. Smith: I was advised that you were consulting someone on an interpretation problem.

Ray: I was, because I was unsure of the status of the item. Who advised you of my conversation?

Mr. Smith: Mr. Jones. You should be reminded that all problems have to be channelled through me. In addition, you have been spending too much time on your audits which has resulted in a low revenue per hour.

After the meeting Ray was upset and concerned. He wondered what effect the incident would have on his employee appraisal and increment.

QUESTIONS

1. In the Maidstone office, how do the interpersonal relations and attitudes of Messrs. Jones and Smith affect the task and work environment for new auditors like Ray Bourke? What is likely to be the motivational effect?

2. Comment on the leadership styles and modes of communication of the two supervisors.

3. Present a more appropriate set of policies and procedures to better serve the needs of new auditors.

Easy-Money Department (B)

SYSTEM AND PLANNING SECTION

The Systems and Planning section within the department contains a section head, two managers, and a mixture of junior and senior planning specialists. The structure of the section resembles a matrix where planning specialists report to a specific manager depending upon the type of project.

The previous department head had emphasized the importance of the section because he viewed planning as the most important ingredient for operating a successful organization. However, the current department head feels that production alone is crucial. This has resulted in the reduction of the Systems and Planning section's staff by 50%, the majority of whom were transferred to the Production section.

Mr. Karl Darmody is a junior planning specialist who began his career in one of the department's field offices (Production section) and was promoted to his current position four years ago. Karl's job responsibilities include research projects and development of computer-based manual systems. He has developed a good rapport with his fellow workers and is satisfied with his salary. The job is structured and there are manuals that stipulate the methods of conducting projects. However, objectives and user requirements are difficult to define. Karl's current manager is Mr. Wallace, who has a pleasant personality and is easy to deal with. However, it is difficult to obtain decisions from Mr. Wallace, and he does not follow up on assignments given to his staff. In addition, there is no feedback from Mr. Wallace regarding completed projects. Therefore, the staff is unaware of whether their performance is satisfactory or not. Decisions and policies are made by the managers, and in many cases the impact of their decisions on the employee is never considered. A month ago, Karl was summoned to a meeting with all the managers:

Mr. Cameron (Systems and Planning): Karl, we (the managers) have decided that you will be taken off your current project — you know, the project that will develop tools to aid managers with their planning process.

Karl: Why? The project team has the right mix of skills to complete the project successfully. We have a good team spirit, and why change the team after only six months?

FIGURE 1 ORGANIZATION CHART OF THE EASY-MONEY DEPARTMENT

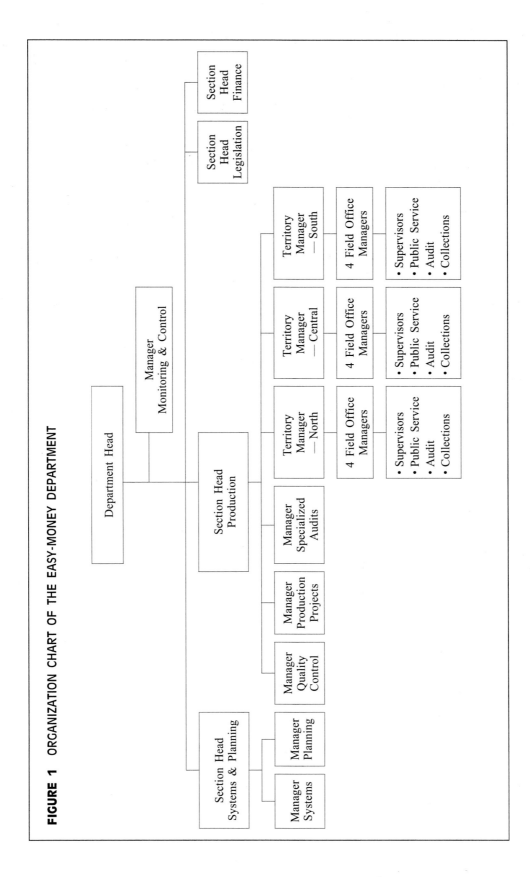

Mr. Wallace (Manager): This change will be good for you, Karl. Consider it to be a career-development change. You will be exposed to other projects.

After the meeting, Karl was furious and frustrated. The Planning Project was the first major project in Corporate Planning, and he had enjoyed working on it. The others are "fire fighting" projects — "fix this, fix that" — that are boring and repetitive. Karl thought that the phrase "career development" was a joke because the Systems and Planning section was small and promotional opportunities were low. He did not want to go back to the Production section because management there is dictatorial, employees are treated poorly, and the environment is unstable — "One day you could be working at head office, and the next day you are in a field office in Thunder Bay". Karl remembered Mr. Persaud, who was switched from office to office — six field offices in two years. Mr. Persaud's social life suffered and his marriage almost ended in a divorce. Karl was always a little nervous when Mr. O'Keefe (Production Head) spoke to Mr. Cameron (Systems & Planning Head), because Karl was afraid that he might be asked to go back to the Production section. Mr. O'Keefe has a habit of raiding the section for good employees.

Once such a request was made, Karl would be able to do nothing. If he did not go, he would be labelled as an employee with a "negative attitude". The Systems and Planning management is powerless in dealing with the Production section management, since the department head always emphasizes the importance of the latter. Work done in the Systems and Planning section is either unknown to the other areas of the branch or regarded as having little importance.

Within the last 18 months, Karl has observed an additional decline in the status of his section. Two recent committees were formed to foster horizontal communication among the various sections in the Easy-Money department and to resolve policy issues that operating units encounter in performing their tasks. However, the Systems and Planning section was excluded from these committees. Karl felt that this omission truly reflected the lack of regard for Systems and Planning in the department.

One of the objectives of the section is "to monitor and adapt to the changing technological environment". The staff feel that the objective is facetious because one of the recent technological developments — microcomputers — is absent from the section. Other departments are using microcomputers regularly, but budgetary requests for this equipment from Systems and Planning have so far been denied.

During the last section's staff meeting, the relationship between Systems and Planning and the Production section was discussed.

Mr. Rose (Senior Specialist): And why is it so difficult and frustrating when dealing with the Production section staff?

Karl: I worked in Production before. Those guys take a dim view of us and basically have no respect for our section. They always complain that we are too slow and cautious.

Mr. Rose: I get the same feeling too. The Production managers feel that their request should be treated as top priority.

Mr. Bond (Junior Planning Specialist): Those guys in Production never communicate with each other, and when there is a foul-up, we get the blame. Remember the request that Production made to change Report 40. Well, Mr. Wallace and I had a meeting with the manager in Production to discuss the changes that he wanted. We went ahead and made the change. However, after the new Report 40 was printed, one of the manager's local supervisors came running to me and asked, "Who authorized you to change Report 40?" I told him to see his boss. I never heard from them again.

Mr. Wallace: From now on, when they want a change, they have to put it in writing; no more verbal agreements.

There is hardly any socializing among the various sections, and staff members tend to think in terms of their area of specialization and not from a departmental perspective. Each section isolates itself from the others because they are comfortable within their own sphere of influence. Even within sections this problem often occurs. This low level of communication has resulted in a lack of coordination among the sections and a suspicious atmosphere within the Easy-Money department. The situation is illustrated by the following examples:

1. One section purchased three expensive word-processing machines because the central word-processing service was accused of being slow. In reality, the extra equipment was unnecessary.

2. A taxpayer phoned four different field offices for an interpretation of the Act and got four different answers.

Office politics is an accepted norm within the Easy-Money department. Each section views the others suspiciously, and memoranda are filtered for hidden motives and innuendoes which cause the information contained in the memo to be distorted. Recently, a production staff member was caught searching and reading letters on a planning officer's desk.

The Systems and Planning managers feel that their staff are treated fairly, are well paid, and their basic needs are met. The managers feel that their ability to change procedures, work environment, etc., is restricted because of the high degree of bureaucratization of the organization. Too much of their time is devoted to fighting their counterparts in the Production section, which prevents them from dealing with their own internal problems. The Systems and Planning managers recently conducted a survey to determine job attitudes experienced by their employees. The results indicated that there is a need for employee recognition, incentive to work is low, and feedback is almost non-existent.

SURVEY

From a scale of 1 (low) to 10 (high) rate the following dimensions in your current job.

			AVERAGE SCORE
1. *Variety of skill*	What is the degree of use of different skills, abilities, and talents?		7
2. *Identity of tasks*	Do you do a job from beginning to end with a visible outcome?		3
3. *Significance of the task*	Does your job have a significant impact on others internal and external to the section?		2
4. *Autonomy*	Do you have freedom, independence, and discretion in determining how to do your job?		4
5. *Feedback*	Are you provided with clear and direct information about job outcomes and performance?		1

QUESTIONS

1. Why are the coordination and communication problems within the branch felt more acutely in the Systems and Planning section than in Production?

2. Evaluate the motivational state of Karl Darmody, and specify how the bureaucratic structure and the style of leadership influenced it.

3. What changes in the department generally, and in the Systems and Planning section specifically, would improve the latter's operation and benefit the productivity of its employees?

The Email Manager

I am Alicia, a senior accountant working in a mid-sized accounting firm located in Winnipeg. I have been working for this firm since my graduation from university.

I started with this firm as a temp, helping out in the tax season, and was ultimately offered a full-time position. At the time, the job market was very depressed. In particular, there were very few junior staff accountant positions available. I have always appreciated the opportunity given to me by this firm.

During the five years that followed, I obtained both my Canadian and U.S. accounting certifications. As an immigrant from a non-English speaking country, I understand that success in public practice in a foreign country relies not only on professional certificates, but perhaps more on hard work. My work ethic has always been very strong. I also keep a positive attitude towards mainstream Canadian culture, since proficiency in communication is largely based on a reasonable level of comprehension of the prevailing culture and its people.

Over the past few years, the firm and I have gone through several significant challenges.

THE NEW SOFTWARE

When I started with this firm, our clients' financial statements were first drafted by staff making pencil corrections on the prior financial statements, which were then typed out in a Word document by a secretary.

About three years ago, the partnership decided to adopt new software that could generate financial statements automatically from the accounting data. It was predicted that, in the long run, automation would save 80% of staff's time in drafting, typing, and formatting documents. However, the benefit would not likely be seen in the first year, since staff would first be required to load the initial set of financial statements into the new program and type out notes in a format conforming to the standard. The task was challenging, especially for those who had little knowledge of computing and programming, and it was definitely time-

---

This case is based on original work by Jie Lian.

consuming. Ideally, the launch of the new software should have taken place during the times of lighter workloads, such as summer or early fall, so that there would be sufficient time for staff to learn and practise. When the partnership announced the introduction and adoption of the software, it was already mid-January, the beginning of the firm's busiest season. Staff were told that from then on all financial statements had to be generated and produced by the new software. It was clear that there would be no time savings in the first year. On the contrary, it would take more time to draft a set of financial statements than by using the traditional method. To make matters worse, no additional time was allocated to staff to work on each client's files to allow for the initial set-up. This increased pressure on the staff, creating considerable resistance to the change. Some staff complained to the partners of the firm, asking why the implementation was taking place during the busiest period rather than a few months later, during the summer.

The partners seemed to believe that introducing the software during a busy period would ensure a rapid changeover in the systems. Therefore, they pressed on with introducing the new system, regardless of staff complaints. Only after one year did the firm begin to realize the time saved by the automation.

THE AUDIT

It is a common understanding that after three to four years of working as a certified Chartered Accountant, a staff accountant should be promoted to a managerial position. If the promotion is not offered by that time, the person is considered to have very little potential for moving up a level in the organization, not to mention the distant goal of joining the partnership. After being with the firm for five years, my title was still senior accountant.

Last summer, the firm assigned me to lead a new audit engagement responsible for auditing the year-end financial position of a group of three companies. Two staff members were assigned to the team: one intermediate accountant, Lucy, and one junior accountant, Frank. Lucy had joined the firm a few months before, in May. She had previously worked for three years in the Toronto office of one of the "Big Four" public accounting firms. Given Lucy's experience, the partner in charge of the audit assigned her to look after the year-end for one company from the group of three. As usual, the engagement turned out to have more issues than we expected. Consequently, the completion deadline was delayed several times. Due to the complexity of the account, working overtime was the only choice we had. I worked until 11 p.m. almost every weekday, as well as Saturdays and Sundays during that period. In addition to completing my part of the engagement, I also had to supervise and review Lucy's and Frank's work. I provided review notes to them for deficiencies in their working papers. One day, just after lunch, I gave Lucy my review notes on her file. I told her that I expected the corrections to be done by the end of the day. She said she would do it right away. However, at the end of the day, she came to me and said, "It is now 5 o'clock, I have not had a chance to work on the corrections, and I am leaving. Can I give it to you tomorrow?" I wanted her to stay to finish the work, but I realized that as I was only a senior accountant, I did not have the authority to require staff to work overtime. Reluctantly, I said yes to her request. After several similar incidents, which were becoming unpleasant, I stopped giving her review notes for correction. Instead, I stayed even later, correcting her work to avoid further delays.

At the end of November, Michael, the partner in charge, wanted to know the status of the account. I said "Michael, I worked very hard on my part of the job. However, I could not get Lucy to complete her file. I gave her review notes last Thursday and asked her to clear them by the end of the day. I have not received anything from her. It seems that she just won't stay overtime. Every time I try to call her extension after 5 p.m., she is already gone." Michael asked, "Why don't you just tell her to stay overtime?" I replied, "Michael, I am just a senior accountant. I don't think I have any authority to ask staff to stay overtime." Michael said, "Next time this type of incident happens, let me know. I will tell her to stay until she finishes her work."

It was a nice offer, but impractical. I could imagine the resentment that would be caused if I went running off to a partner to force someone on my team to stay after hours. I had to work with them every day, and they certainly didn't feel that I was entitled to give orders. Calling a partner in to order them to work would just poison our relationship. Instead, I continued to work more overtime to finish off Lucy's file and avoided further delays.

THE PAPERLESS ENVIRONMENT

Last year, the firm decided to adopt a paperless environment, meaning that all files would be prepared and saved in an electronic format, including source documents. As a result, new document management software was introduced in mid-February. Several training seminars were offered to staff. Many questions were raised about the details of the software and its implementation, but only vague answers were provided by management. Frustration and confusion permeated the workplace. An immediate impact was on the preparation of working papers for personal tax return.

Typical questions from staff included "Why do we always have to deal with new procedures or tools in the middle of the busy tax season? ... We are already very busy and don't have time to learn new methods and procedures ... It will take more time to prepare working papers electronically than to use paper. Can we wait until we are not so busy? ... How am I supposed to organize these documents? I'm not sure how to use the software, even after the training."

One major reason for the resistance was time pressure. It appeared that more time was required on each file, especially for those whose computer knowledge was considered relatively weak, and consequently needed more time. But the majority of the staff just wouldn't stay overtime.

A meeting was held immediately by the Paperless Committee, and I was invited to attend. At the meeting, Michael, the Tax Partner, said, "Staff are complaining about the paperless process, and it seems that it takes more time to complete a file. My concern is that if each file takes a little more time under the new process, will we be able to complete all the personal tax returns that are due April 30?"

Muriel, the partner who oversaw the project, said, "Paperless is the future and has been successfully adopted by many firms. We met with one of these firms, and it seems that time commitment was an issue at the initial stage but the long-term benefits outweighed the costs. If we postpone implementation to the summer, we will not be able to convert to paperless for another year. Staff reaction is more from uncertainty. If we can come up with a sample file and provide more guidance for them, we should be able to ease the stress and speed up the work process." Muriel was the only female partner in the firm. It was widely felt among staff that being a relative of one of the male partners was a big factor in Muriel's promotion.

I was of the opinion that the firm should have adopted paperless documentation a long time ago and, at the meeting, said that we should definitely proceed with it now. After the meeting, I sent an email to Muriel further expressing my support. She suggested that perhaps I could prepare a sample file with detailed instructions for staff to follow. The meeting was held on Saturday. I spent Sunday in the office, compiling the sample file, including instructions. On Monday morning, I showed Muriel my work. She said, "It looks fine to me. Could you please send an email to all staff notifying them of the availability of the sample file and instructions? And also tell them that they should speak to you if they are still not clear about the procedures."

Two months after that meeting, at about 9:30 p.m. on Tuesday night, I was still working at my desk, while most of the staff had left earlier. Muriel came over and said to me, "Do you have some time for a quick conversation?" I said, "Sure." We sat in a small meeting room. Muriel then asked my opinion about the performance of several junior and intermediate accountants and their potential future with the firm. It seemed to me that the firm was reviewing the effectiveness of the existing accounting team, possibly because people would be on the list to be let go. Immediately, I thought about my long wait for promotion.

I told Muriel my impression of the staff I had worked with. I then said, "Despite having been with the firm for so long, in my present position, I have difficulty giving my team members work orders and requesting their compliance with the deadlines that I set. They consider me a peer, not a supervisor. My goal is to move up to the managerial level so that I can do more for the firm."

Muriel smiled and said, "I can understand that perfectly. But I am afraid a promotion is not possible just yet. We feel that moving you up the ladder now might cause some resentment among our longer-term and equally productive staff, and these days we need their morale and efficiency to be at the highest level. We do want you take on more managerial responsibility, but informally. Work with your team and suggest how they can improve. If you have problems, we'll back you up. I can assure you that you have a good future with this firm. You are important to us (partners). Even if we lay off some staff, you won't be included."

Having heard similar comments several times before at my annual performance reviews, I walked out of the meeting with no clue as to what type of position I would get. The only thing I was sure of was that my job was secure and for now I would continue to manage without real authority. Perhaps the partners and managers were happy for me to continue to send email suggestions to staff and then do the work myself if those emails were ignored.

Soon after the implementation of the paperless project, the recession hit North America. One day, I received a phone call from our secretary, "Robert wants to know whether you are available this Saturday at 2 p.m. for a meeting." Robert is our managing partner. Since he had called me for a meeting by special invitation, I felt it must be very important.

When I walked in the boardroom on that Saturday, I noticed that I was the only non-managerial staff member attending the meeting. Everyone else was either a partner or a manager. The meeting involved planning the firm's workload, not the type of meeting a staff accountant would normally attend. At the meeting it was clear from the planned allocation of work that the firm would be reducing its professional staff in anticipation of reduced revenues during the recession.

After the meeting, one of the managers whispered to me that I could be the next on the roll to be promoted to a managerial position. Having received this type of vague hint for three years, I did not take it seriously. Although I was not very happy with the lack of a promotion, the pay was always good. Every year I received a greater raise than I expected. Also, the clients I worked with seemed very happy with my attention to detail and how I responded to their concerns, which made me feel that my work was valued.

APPENDIX: ORGANIZATIONAL STRUCTURE AND ISSUES

In this firm, the positions and organizational structure are as follows:

- At the top level, there are three senior partners who provide overall supervision to all staff. They also have ultimate responsibility for certain large audit projects. (The partners mentioned in the case were both Senior Partners.)
- At the next level, there are four general partners who are ultimately responsible for any projects that the senior partners are not leading.
- Next, there are two accounting managers. These are certified accountants who were promoted to this position. They have authority to organize the work of the staff accountants on the projects to ensure that the schedule is met. They will report to either the senior or general partners, depending on which partner has the ultimate responsibility for the project.
- There also three tax managers who will provide a final review on any tax-related work carried out by staff accountants. They report to the tax partner, who is one of the senior partners. They typically do not exert any direct supervision over accounting staff.
- Four senior accountants work on key audit projects and will either work under the guidance of an accounting manager or directly with a partner. In the latter case, the senior accountant often has to be personally responsible for organizing the work, since the partner involved may not exert much hands-on supervision until the final review of the work. When it occurs, this lack of supervision is sometimes a source of friction and conflict among staff, especially when the review is not positive and staff are required to correct their work extensively.

- Three intermediate and two junior accountants are supposed to work on projects under the supervision of an Accounting Manager. Exceptions occur, such as the incident with Alicia. When intermediate and junior accountants are working on projects with senior accountants, instead of an Accounting Manager, the relationship between the senior accountants and the other accountants is ambiguous and sometimes tense.
- An IT manager is responsible for all of the firm's computers, networks, website, software, etc., and reports to a Senior Partner. This is a source of frustration when the IT needs of staff accountants are not being met. The staff accountants have very little influence over the IT Manager, and they are reluctant to go over his head to the Senior Partner.
- A Human Resources manager, who reports to a senior partner, performs support functions, such as payroll administration, but has no supervisory role.
- Four secretaries report to both the general and senior partners. They handle all secretarial tasks for staff accountants, managers, and partners. Staff accountants and managers sometimes find it difficult to request work from this group who may "drag their feet" on such requests. However, they respond well to the senior and general partners.

Partly because clients are often slow to respond to requests for information, auditing projects and the clients' corporate tax returns for clients frequently run up against tight deadlines. A prevalent pattern in this firm is that the responsible partner (often along with a manager) actively intervenes when the deadline is approaching to insist that the relevant team work overtime until the job is done. Accounting staff find this frustrating and disruptive to their personal lives. Frequently, the accounting staff finish the bulk of their work on time and submit it for final review. The partner (and sometimes the manager) then leaves the file sitting for several days, reviews it at the last minute, and finds areas that to be corrected or change. Then, the staff accountants, who have been waiting for the review, have to work long hours to meet a deadline they thought they had already met. Late nights were common for staff accountants and often for managers, but rarely for Partners.

QUESTIONS

1. Describe Alicia's level of job satisfaction and the factors that contribute to it.

2. Why is Alicia motivated to work longer hours than other non-managerial professionals in the firm?

3. Does the firm's reluctance to promote Alicia raise any issues of ethics or justice? If so, what are they? If not, why not?

4. Describe the structure of this organization and identify any issues that may be caused or worsened by it.

5. Do the structure of the firm and the issues identified in the appendix help to explain the conflicts that occurred with the introduction of the new software and the paperless environment?

6. What changes in the organization's structure would help to create a more productive firm, lessen the problems with workflow, and create better attitudes among all groups of employees?

7. What should Alicia do with respect to her position and role within the firm at the end of the case?

Federal Airlines

Federal Airlines, founded prior to World War II, employed just over 15,000 persons in the early 1990s and operated a large modern fleet of aircraft.

Although the 19th largest airline in the world, the company recently found itself in a highly competitive situation. Routes once monopolized by the company now had several other airlines competing for a market share. However, the company was confident that it could retain and improve its market share as long as it undertook an aggressive $4 billion program to upgrade facilities and equipment over the next ten years.

One of the programs that management planned to undertake was a new Work Improvement Program (WIP) for employees working at the airport maintenance hangar. A highly respected industrial psychologist, Jack Miller, was hired to help implement the program. During previous contracts with the numerous firms, he had often been able to increase labour productivity and morale and decrease absenteeism and employee turnover. After six months of work with senior management staff and the union, the program was implemented with excellent results.

During Miller's WIP implementation at the airport Maintenance base, other unions carefully watched and weighed the results. They quickly noticed the benefits in terms of employee morale that were surfacing from the program. One union in particular saw an immediate need for his services. The Canadian Airline Employees' Association (CALEA), which represents 3,000 reservation and passenger service agents, was in contract negotiations with the company. One of the concessions won by CALEA was that the next department to implement WIP would be the Reservations department.

Word of the agreement reached by the company and the union spread swiftly throughout the union ranks. The company took advantage of this mood by proclaiming that this program would be the greatest example yet of "the quality of work philosophy". The program would strip away the daily drudgery and routine associated with the job. Agents were to become human beings once more, and not mindless attachments to computers.

By Anwar Rashid. © L & S Management Publications.

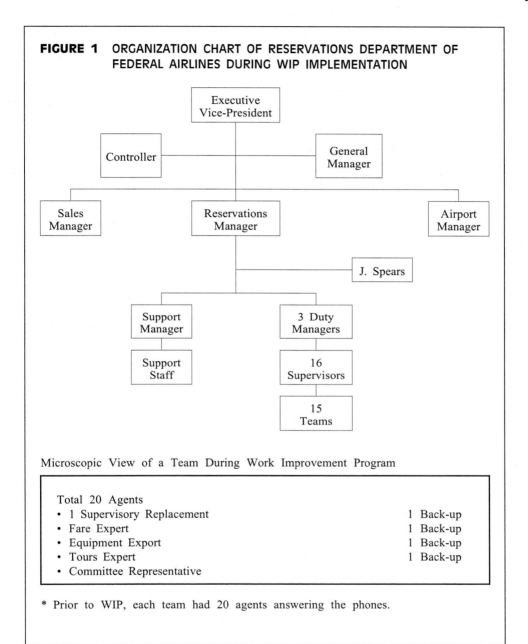

FIGURE 1 ORGANIZATION CHART OF RESERVATIONS DEPARTMENT OF FEDERAL AIRLINES DURING WIP IMPLEMENTATION

Microscopic View of a Team During Work Improvement Program

Total 20 Agents
- 1 Supervisory Replacement   1 Back-up
- Fare Expert   1 Back-up
- Equipment Export   1 Back-up
- Tours Expert   1 Back-up
- Committee Representative

* Prior to WIP, each team had 20 agents answering the phones.

Newspaper reporters and TV crews suddenly appeared on the reservation floor, shooting thousands of feet of film, snapping pictures, and interviewing managers, supervisors, and agents. This wave of interest swept over everyone involved and only reinforced what the company had said and what the agents wanted to feel. However, no one had bothered to ask the question: "How will WIP actually change my daily job?"

THE PROBLEM

The Reservations department employed over 300 agents along with 16 supervisors, three duty managers, one support manager and staff, and the reservations manager.

Results of a behavioural test written earlier in the year by every employee of CALEA indicated that morale was at an extremely low level. The results also indicated that only those individuals working in the Group, Charter and Tour sections of the Reservations department enjoyed their work. This was mainly because the section had little supervision, individuals were able to prioritize their work, no time clock was used, and if an individual wanted to be transferred to the section, he or she had to be recognized as a high potential candidate.

Jack Miller felt that the results indicated that work should start immediately with the reservation teams and that Group, Charter, and Tour should be the last, rather than the first, section to introduce WIP.

The mandate of the reservations manager was to achieve a Promptness of Service (POS) factor of 80% at the end of a month. This factor would be achieved by answering 80% of all calls within 20 seconds of the first ring. Agents were responsible for keeping plugged-in for calls for at least 80% of their total working day. The average team had 20 agents, with an agent taking approximately 115 calls per shift. Over a period of two months, the Reservations department received over 1.25 million calls.

Miller faced a department with generally low morale, high absenteeism, and poor productivity and in which the POS mandate of 80% was underachieved and performance was stalled at 65%.

The first step taken by the WIP committee (Miller; Elford, a senior training instructor; and Smith, a supervisor with a BA in Philosophy) was to take the job performed by the agent, break it down into its many different aspects, and then organize the agents into teams of "experts". Normally an agent worked with a VDT, answered calls through a headset, booked flights, cars and hotels, and quoted fares. Miller felt that each team should be a self-reliant entity; therefore, each team would have (a) a VDT and headphone expert responsible for answering questions regarding equipment; (b) a tours expert; (c) a rates expert who could sort out the complicated and often confusing tariffs; (d) an individual who would take over the team in the absence of the supervisor; and (e) the right to elect a member to represent the team when new policies and procedures were being studied.

However, once WIP was introduced, problems soon started to be noticed. Teams were carrying WIP one step further by electing backups to the experts. Experts were being pulled out of line for long periods of time to help fellow agents, and if the expert on the team was busy, agents would go to the backup agent and pull that agent out of line. Every expert on the team belonged to a committee that met at least once a month. The Promptness of Service factor dropped dramatically to below 50%. Supervisors had been assigned the role of observers with little authority to eradicate abuses by agents. Prior to WIP it was unusual to see three or four agents standing or walking through the office unless they were on a break. During WIP, it was the exception to see just four agents out of line. Everyone seemed to be standing and talking to each other or walking through the office.

Eight months after the official start of WIP, a corporate directive was sent to CALEA headquarters notifying the union of the termination of the project.

Within weeks, the team experts were once again telephone agents, and supervisors were given carte blanche to discipline any individual not meeting the office standards. New information systems were purchased to compile reservation statistics on every agent as they worked. The system kept track of the number of calls taken, agent in time, agent out of time, fatigue factor, and duration of the average call. This information was accumulated per agent, team, and office for a timeframe of an hour, day, month, and year.

Federal Airlines, or rather its management, intended to make sure that the performance of its agents, supervisors, and managers was once again monitored by computers. It looked as if no vague concepts such as job enrichment, job enlargement, or quality of work life would ever be seriously considered again.

Finally, six months after the termination of WIP, the office Promptness of Service had risen to a satisfactory 83%.

QUESTIONS

1. Identify and discuss the key reasons WIP was a failure with the Reservations department. Refer to issues in:
   (a)   motivation
   (b)   status and role
   (c)   communication
   (d)   informal group behaviour

2. Do you feel that job enrichment is still appropriate for the Reservations department? Give your rationale.

3. What are the general prospects for job enrichment in the Reservations department?

4. If you were executive vice-president of the company, would you continue to keep Miller as a consultant? Answer with particular reference to the role of a consultant in organizational development programs.

Flexible Packaging Inc.

Flexible Packaging Inc. is a company that specializes in providing a variety of packaging products to a wide array of companies across Canada. Flexible's clients range from magazines to beverage companies. The competition in the packaging industry is fairly intense, with a large base of competing firms. Flexible is considered to be a moderately strong competitor. It directly employs approximately 44 full-time people who make up the accounts receivable department, sales department, transport department and warehouse department. Its warehouse is approximately 10,000 square metres and the company has sales in excess of $9 million annually. Flexible is recognized throughout the packaging industry for its high quality packaging goods and services at moderately high prices. Its outstanding customer service counter-balances its prices and continues to attract new clientele.

The coordinator of the warehouse is Renzo Garcia, who is responsible for 12 subordinates, who all work within the warehouse. The warehouse contains packaging machines, as well as materials and products that are stockpiled either for inventory or for direct shipment to the customer. The efficiency of Renzo and his staff is essential for customer satisfaction.

Renzo arrived at work Monday morning at 8:00 a.m.. He settled in his office to gather the work orders for the day. After he organized the warehouse tasks, he went to the warehouse lounge where he briefed his staff on the day's activities. He assigned tasks to groups of four (which the subordinates formed on their own) and explained that it was imperative that all orders were successfully filled. He then proceeded to explain that he would be absent from the warehouse since he was going to be attending a planning meeting all day. (Recently, these meetings were occupying much of his time.) The groups dispersed with their fill orders for the day. Once their supervisor had left for his meetings, Todd Ballard and his group were reluctant to work. Todd loudly expressed his group's dissatisfaction, which was that Renzo gave them the "dirt" orders to fill. Just to spite him, he would work in a leisurely manner. Todd also complained that the guys in the warehouse who operated the packaging machines were receiving higher wages for work that was easier than what

---

This case is based on original work by David Rosen.

he was doing. So he felt there was no reason for him to work any harder. He also disagreed with the majority of Flexible's employee policies, which he said favoured the managers and discriminated against the ordinary workers. Ellen Shimano, an informal leader of another work group, was getting frustrated as the day progressed with Todd's "slack" behaviour, and found that she had to work harder to fill some of the orders that Todd neglected. Ellen was a diligent worker with strong leadership qualities. However, her patience soon grew thin, and she finally told Todd to "get off your butt and do something!" Todd angrily responded by saying, "You're no manager, so why don't you take your employee of the month attitude and shove it!" The day came to an end with many uncompleted orders still in the warehouse. Ellen was proud of the immense amount of work she and her group had accomplished, but she was frustrated with Todd's pathetic attitude, and was upset that Renzo's orders were not all filled. That evening, upon his return from his meeting after the warehouse groups had left, Renzo found a mysterious and unsigned memo on his desk:

> *"The unsuccessful completion of the fill orders was a result of certain warehouse persons' uncooperative and negative attitudes. It might be a good idea to find those individuals to encourage a change in their behaviour and acquaint them with their job descriptions!"*

Renzo was quite sure he knew who was complaining, and which person and group she was complaining about. When it came to bad-mouthing the company, Todd was the natural leader. Under normal circumstances, he would have called Todd and his group in for a talk the next morning and spent some time sorting out this problem. However, corporate planning meetings were being held every day for the next three days, and he would have only enough time to do the usual morning task assignment meeting. He felt that the best approach, in the interim, would be to post a notice in the lounge reminding everyone of the need to "put in a full day's work and complete their assigned tasks". When he printed out the notice, however, it looked weak; so he changed it to the following:

> *"I would like to remind all of you in the Order Fulfilment Groups that your continued employment is totally dependent upon your performance. Our company is known for customer service, and management insists that all of you do your best to maintain it at the highest possible level. Those who are unable or unwilling to do so have no place in Flexible Packaging Inc."*

He thought that by not singling Todd and his group out for a reprimand, they might take the hint without losing "face". But, when he returned to his office at the end of the next day, there were an even larger number of unfilled orders, and the notice had been torn off the wall. He also noticed that the memo he had received on the previous day, which he had put in an unlocked desk drawer, had disappeared. Finally, by the large piles of packaged products awaiting allocation to orders, he realized that the packaging machine operators had been, for some reason, highly productive that day.

QUESTIONS

1. Discuss all the reasons Renzo's notice was ineffective as an organizational communication. Refer to the medium of communication he employed, the content of his notice, and its likely effect on all those who saw it.

2. What are the equity issues in this case? How would they likely affect the behaviour of the various warehouse employees?

3. In terms of informal group behaviour, what changes would likely take place as a result of the events that took place? Would Todd's and Ellen's informal leadership of their groups be strengthened or weakened?

4. Given that Renzo's notice was ineffective and that he did not have time to meet with Todd and his group for the next few days, what should he have done instead?

5. What should Renzo do now?

The Georgian Rescue Squad

During the mid-1990s a rescue squad emerged in Georgian County. This development was partly in response to a few dramatic highway accidents that featured media stories of victims trapped in vehicles for prolonged periods of time. A multi-vehicle accident on the major divided highway in the county, during a winter storm, resulting in several deaths and provided a particular stimulus.

A secondary stimulus for the squad came from the development by fire equipment manufacturers of rescue tools such as the Jaws of Life which use hydraulic power to open crushed vehicles. This development replaced the previous reliance on acetylene cutting torches, axes, pry bars, etc., which had been the tools of choice.

Georgian County is a large (population 500,000) rural (urban proportion less than 20%) county located north of Toronto. It consists of eight townships, two of them quite large, and a small city. The city does not participate in the county government structure. The county is in the heart of a four-season vacation region and straddles the major highway arteries connecting southern Ontario with northern Ontario and western Canada. In the southern parts of the county there are major bedroom communities for Toronto workers. Various studies have estimated that approximately 20% of county breadwinners are daily commuters. The highway traffic in the county is extremely heavy.

Basically, the squad was a group of volunteers who maintained a truck loaded with rescue equipment. Most of their time was actually spent training, which was done at car wrecking yards. The truck did not have a permanent home, and was moved amongst the members on a rotating basis. When called by police, fire, tow trucks, ambulance, witnesses, or others, they would rush to the accident scene to help out. They also monitored emergency radio frequencies. When the need arose, a call would go out to the volunteers to respond. The member with the truck would proceed directly to the accident, and the others would arrive when possible. Telephones and radio pagers were used for this call-up. The squad was not paid for the service they rendered, nor were the squad members compensated financially, although they were all strongly motivated by the other rewards of the service.

Money was a problem. The trucks and especially the equipment were very expensive. The squad began with one vehicle for the whole county, and later added another to provide separate northern and southern squads. Plans were under way for another expansion in the more heavily developed area in the southern part of the county. There were fund-raising campaigns at each stage of the expansion. At first the money was raised by private donations from individuals and service clubs. When the equipment bills increased, the squad approached various townships in the county for grants for the purchase of particular pieces of equipment. The squad began presenting itself as a new county service even though its existence had never been approved by the county or any township.

Small townships in the county had little use for the service. Residents simply did not expect much from their municipality, and would never expect it to provide a sophisticated service such as this. Two larger townships gained some benefit. They both had major highways running through them, and their fire departments were regularly called upon to render what service they could in highway accidents. Supporting the Georgian Rescue Squad was cheaper than equipping their own fire departments and training their staff. Furthermore, many of the Rescue Squad members were volunteers in their own fire departments. They had made grants in the past and could be expected to contribute in the future. The city did not participate. Their own fire department was fully equipped for rescue work. Calls for the Georgian Rescue Squad from the city were rare, and only initiated by private citizens.

The Georgian Rescue Squad was a media favourite. The aftermath of a highway traffic accident was always a good photo opportunity. The "uncrushing" of a vehicle and the rescue of a victim made good TV coverage. Technical descriptions of the rescue were readily available from the volunteers. Media crews were rarely far behind the Rescue Squad when the call for help went out.

In Georgian County the related emergency services were organized as follows:

1. **Police:** The provincial police patrolled the major highways and policed most townships. The two larger townships and the city had their own police departments.

2. **Fire Fighting:** Each township and the city provided their own fire fighting services. Only the city had a large full-time fire fighting department. The others were part-time "paid" volunteers headed up by a municipal employee who had other duties, such as building inspector, etc. A mutual aid agreement existed in Georgian County whereby townships could call on the fire fighting resources of their neighbours. An annual reckoning balanced out costs and benefits. The hourly rates were high enough to discourage frivolous calls.

3. **Ambulance Service:** Ambulance services were provided by the provincial Ministry of Health, and were centralized in Georgian County at the regional hospital in the city.

4. **Tow Trucks:** Emergency towing was under the control of the police, and the different forces followed their own policy as to who to call. The Provincial police used a rotating list system to spread out the work. The city police used a selected contractor. The township police called local businesses as available.

5. **Road Maintenance:** Roads were maintained by the province, the townships and the city. The county coordinated road projects.

6. **Medical Services:** All emergency medical services in Georgian County were organized through the hospital in the city. Municipal governments played only a small role in this function.

RE-ORGANIZING THE RESCUE SQUAD

Last January, the County council elected its new Warden. Sheila Woodley was well prepared for the job. She was a reeve of the smallest township in the county, but had managed to impress her county colleagues with her political skills. She had been particularly adept at implementing new programs and services in her township. She viewed the Georgian Rescue Squad with less enthusiasm. The squad was now keen to expand again, and was beginning to push forward suggestions that it ought to become a formal service of the county. The head of the squad would dearly love to make it a full-time job and be able to divert his energy from fund raising to rescue work.

Woodley wanted none of it. As far as she was concerned the squad should have a fire fighting function, and should not be a county-wide service. She also had a problem with the image of the squad. Many county politicians shared her view that this group seemed to have developed an inflated opinion of itself. Another politician had applied the old epithet, "The bigger the boys, the more expensive the toys" at the last budget request by the squad.

As she saw it, all she had to do was organize the political forces needed to dismantle the "volunteer" county squad, transfer the function and the squad equipment to the townships, and leave the county unburdened by this uninvited and unwelcome new service.

QUESTIONS

Conduct a Lewin Force Field analysis of this proposed change.

1. Identify the forces supporting the change, the forces opposing the change, and the currently neutral forces that might be tipped one way or another once the change process has begun.

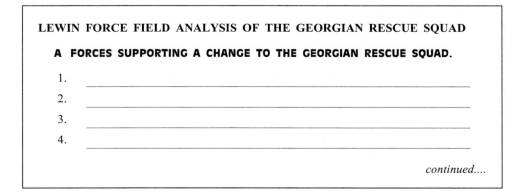

LEWIN FORCE FIELD ANALYSIS OF THE GEORGIAN RESCUE SQUAD

A FORCES SUPPORTING A CHANGE TO THE GEORGIAN RESCUE SQUAD.

1. _____

2. _____

3. _____

4. _____

continued....

LEWIN FORCE FIELD ANALYSIS OF THE GEORGIAN RESCUE SQUAD
(Continued)

5. _____

6. _____

7. _____

8. _____

B   FORCES OPPOSING A CHANGE TO THE GEORGIAN RESCUE SQUAD.

1. _____

2. _____

3. _____

4. _____

5. _____

6. _____

7. _____

8. _____

**C   FORCES NEUTRAL TO A CHANGE TO THE GEORGIAN RESCUE SQUAD
BUT THAT MIGHT BE TIPPED ONCE THE CHANGE PROCESS HAS BEGUN.**

1. _____

2. _____

3. _____

4. _____

5. _____

6. _____

7. _____

8. _____

**D   STRATEGY FOR "UNFREEZING" THE STATUS QUO TO
BEGIN THE CHANGE PROCESS.**

1. _____

2. _____

3. _____

4. _____

5. _____

6. _____

continued....

LEWIN FORCE FIELD ANALYSIS OF THE GEORGIAN RESCUE SQUAD
(Continued)

7. _____

8. _____

E CHANGE STRATEGY, INCLUDING CONTINGENCY PLANNING.

1. _____

2. _____

3. _____

4. _____

5. _____

6. _____

7. _____

8. _____

F STRATEGY FOR "REFREEZING" THE NEW STATUS QUO AT THE END OF THE CHANGE PROCESS.

1. _____

2. _____

3. _____

4. _____

5. _____

6. _____

7. _____

8. _____

2. Develop a change strategy that is based on strengthening the forces in favour of change, weakening the forces opposing change, and covers the contingencies arising from the tipping of currently neutral forces.

3. Develop a strategy for "unfreezing" the status quo so as to begin the change process.

Greig's Supermarket

This supermarket, located in an urban area, has been in operation for over 25 years. The store employs approximately 150 employees, of whom about 40% work on a part-time basis. Employee turnover is quite high, particularly among the part-time workers. Many of these are students who quit because of school graduation pressures.

The hierarchical structure of the organization is quite simple, being of a purely "line" nature. The store manager, who is changed every two or three years, is the pinnacle of authority in the store. Under the store manager is an assistant manager (changed slightly less often, about every four to five years), followed by six managers of equal authority: the head cashier, grocery manager, meat manager, produce manager, general merchandise and snack bar manager, and the bakery manager.

The head cashier is responsible for approximately 40 cashiers (20 part-time students working nights and ten part-time and full-time older women working the day shifts). She is also responsible for two full-time and ten part-time "packers" who run the parcel pick-up and assist cashiers and patrons at the checkouts.

The organization generally follows the "authoritarian" model, where orders come down from the store manager or the department managers, and employees comply without questioning. Socializing is strongly discouraged. Few suggestions, if any, to improve the operation are made by employees, mainly because there are no rewards offered in return.

For some time, there have been rumours among the cashiers that the store was going to switch over to computerized cash registers that automatically updated inventories. Suddenly, near the end of August, employees were formally informed of the imminent change. Cashiers were approached individually by the head cashier, and told that a schedule for training on the new cash registers was being set up. The training would take place at another Greig's store some miles away. Each cashier was required to attend training at this store for a period of 16 hours, spread over four sessions, each of four hours. The cashiers would be paid their regular hourly wages for the time spent in training. However, no transportation would be provided

By Anwar Rashid. © L & S Management Publications.

or paid for, nor would the time spent in travel to and from the training site (well over half an hour in each direction) be compensated for by the company.

One week after the training of all the cashiers was completed, the new cash registers were installed. This was accomplished outside of store hours in only one weekend. As of the following Monday morning, all cashiers were required to operate the new registers in actual, real transactions. No further training was allowed for anyone. The complete change-over, including training and installation, took place in a period of only three to four weeks.

Fourteen new registers were installed. All were hooked up to a main computer located in the office that overlooked the store. Cashiers would ring in groceries using a coding system that would identify the various products (e.g., a cashier punches in #728, and the register tape shows one bag, 2% milk, and the price). Initially, a set of 300 codes was put into use through this system. One year later, however, the old codes were abandoned and a new set, consisting of over 700 codes, was implemented. This set is still in use today.

A booklet containing all the codes and the procedure for ringing in transactions is attached to each register. However, it is impossible for a cashier to maintain any type of speed and efficiency without memorizing approximately 80% of the codes. Also, the design of the new, accompanying checkout counter is such that the cashier is now required to ring groceries in with one hand while simultaneously packing the groceries with the other. Previously, this was a two-step process, whereby the cashier rang groceries in first before packing the bags with both hands. The old method also provided for the assistance of a packer who packed the groceries into bags while the cashier rang the items in. The new system was specifically designed to eliminate the need for this assistance.

The new registers were also capable of recording the level of performance achieved by each operator. Several aspects of individual performance, in fact, were analyzed and recorded by management, and a comparison of cashiers constantly took place. This had not been possible before the introduction of the new registers. Supervision, then, became much stricter. Standards of performance were arbitrarily set by management (employees were given no say in the matter), and feedback was provided to individual cashiers. While direct threats were not imposed, employees were urged to "try harder".

Curiosity and excitement were the first reactions to the rumours of the impending change. However, when faced with the actuality of training and adjustment, the cashiers were, in general, both fearful and angry. They resented the fact that the training schedule had been arranged without first consulting them. They also resented the fact that the training took place at only one strange and very distant location, which had to be reached by their own means. The older women resented being trained by strangers who were younger than themselves. In addition, some cashiers felt that the training time was insufficient, whereas others complained it was too long and repetitive.

Once the system was implemented, the cashiers were eager to receive feedback on their performances, both individual and relative to the others. The assessment of performance revealed that the older cashiers who worked the day shift performed at a much lower rate than did the younger cashiers. Many of the former groups had been employed at the store for over ten years, and it was generally felt that, due to their resentment at being required to change after such a long period of time, they intentionally kept their speed down. They appeared to be very set in their ways and determined to hold things up. They spoke of being confused about the necessity of the change, and voiced annoyance at having to memorize all the new codes and procedures.

The younger cashiers, on the other hand, seemed to enjoy the challenge, and often spoke of the new registers initially as being similar to computer games.

All the cashiers felt, however, that they could not pack the bags as well with only one hand as they used to do with two. It was harder to grasp and manipulate products and more difficult to arrange things so that more goods would fit into one bag and fit snugly. They also missed the opportunity of socializing with the packers. This form of socialization was considered very important to many cashiers, who claimed it helped to reduce the boredom often experienced on the job.

As the new registers led to increased efficiency and time saving, both the cashiers and the packers (who were now given odd jobs) feared both reduced hours of work and layoffs. As it turned out, their fears, at least in part, were justified. The hours per cashier and packer were reduced by 15 to 20 percent, and, for a few months, former packers who quit were not replaced.

QUESTIONS

1. Why did each group (experienced cashiers and younger students) react to the introduction of the new equipment in the way they did? Answer from the point of view of (a) motivation, (b) communication, (c) leadership, and (d) quality of work life issues.

2. Identify ways in which this organizational change was badly designed and implemented.

3. Suggest how this change could have been brought about with better results and a greater degree of employee satisfaction.

Harassment in
the Ministry

Rebecca Cheung, a female supervisor of a team of cleaners with a federal ministry, was sexually harassed by her foreman, Alphonse Legault, on several occasions. There were numerous conversations of a sexual nature, and several physical encounters including attempted sexual intercourse. All of these incidents, except the last, took place while Rebecca was on probation for her job. Rebecca testified that she was afraid and intimidated. She continually told Alphonse to stop and that his advances were unwelcome.

Alphonse made comments to Rebecca such as, "If you don't have my support, you'll fall flat on your face", and, "I am your boss and I'll charge you with disobedience". He used this authority to persuade her to agree to acts to which she would not otherwise have agreed.

The Canadian Human Rights Tribunal that first heard the case identified three characteristics of sexual harassment:

- The encounters must be unsolicited by the complainant, unwelcome to the complainant and expressly or implicitly known by the respondent to be unwelcome;
- the conduct must either continue despite the complainant's protests or, if the conduct stops, the complainant's protests must have led to negative employment consequences; and
- the complainant's cooperation must be due to employment-related threats or promises.

The Ministry was held responsible for Alphonse's acts. When it appealed, the Supreme Court of Canada stated in its decision that an employer has a responsibility to provide a work environment free of harassment. It added that "only an employer can remedy undesirable effects (of discrimination); only an employer can provide the most important remedy — a healthy work environment". Holding employers responsible for all acts of their employees that are "in some way related or associated with employment" places "responsibility for an organization on those who con-

---

This case was written by Peter Kells.

trol it and are in a position to take effective remedial action to remove undesirable conditions".

Rebecca and the Ministry agreed to an "out of court" settlement. However, the settlement did not make any provision for an apology to Rebecca from the Ministry, or any compensation for hurt feelings. A review tribunal found that the remedies provided for in the Canadian Human Rights Act were designed for two purposes — to compensate for private, personal harm, and to serve the public interest by acting as a deterrent to future harassers and/or as a means of education. Compensation for pain and suffering and an apology are in the public interest. Since they were not provided for in the settlement, the review tribunal ordered that they be provided in addition. The Ministry was therefore ordered to pay Rebecca $5,000 for pain and suffering, the maximum amount available for this purpose under the Act. The Ministry was also ordered to formally apologize and post the written apology in all its facilities.

QUESTIONS

1. Comment on the appropriateness of the three identified characteristics of sexual harassment.

2. Describe other characteristics which might generally define sexual harassment.

3. Is it appropriate that an employer be held responsible for all employment-related acts of its people?

4. Were the penalties imposed sufficient? Would you prescribe different penalties?

Harbour General Hospital

Harbour General Hospital is a medium-sized hospital located in the Maritime provinces. It is an amalgamation of two previously separate hospitals: the General and the Harbour. They were merged in a recent provincial government push for greater efficiency in province-wide health care delivery. The Harbour Hospital was originally established and funded by a religious order, while the General had been owned and operated by the municipality. Both buildings were maintained and are located about 5 km from each other. The original Harbour Hospital was much smaller than the General Hospital, so the merger seemed more like a takeover.

After the merger, each site maintained its own complete Health Records Department. However, this department was one of those slated for rationalization once the merger was completed. Three sections within the Health Records Department are presented in this case study: the clerical section, the coding section, and the utilization analysts.

The clerical section is by far the largest and busiest and has staff located at each of the hospital sites reporting to the Health Records Supervisor. Its duty is to process the patient charts, which it gathers and files after physicians complete the records. The section works 24/7, so clear schedules for work and performance expectations are required. As the "keeper" of a patient's chart, health records departments are governed in part by a provincial Act that governs public hospitals and in accordance with the guidelines of the Canadian Health Records Association, a professional body that accredits those working in this profession. The records still typically begin as actual paper charts filled in by the physicians, but their output is electronic. The switch-over to having physicians fill in the data electronically and then reviewed and assembled by the clerks is slowly being implemented. Strict adherence to record practices is a necessity. The clerical job can be very repetitive, so providing a social environment for the staff becomes important.

The coding section has the key role of seeing that the hospital is paid by the provincial government for its activity on behalf of patients. The coding staff (or the coders) use the output of the clerks as their data input. There are less staff than in

This work is based on original research by Cindy Shipmaker.

the clerical section, and the personnel are divided between both sites. Staff work a regular day shift. They assign each discharged patient a series of codes based on the diagnosis, procedures, and medical activity generated on behalf of that patient. These codes are entered into a database and submitted monthly to the government department for reimbursement. Coders are different from the clerical staff, since they have received certification and are registered with the Canadian College of Health Records Administrators. They are therefore members of a recognized profession. Coding is considered part art and part science. Two coders may code a chart slightly differently, depending on their interpretation. Developmental leadership is helpful to ensure that the best practice is determined and quality is maintained. It is common for a supervisor to hold informal "clinics" where interesting charts are analyzed with a group of coders in an effort to bring a consensus to coding practices. This is also important because feedback to coders is limited and therefore has to be artificially created through audits.

The coders report to the coding supervisor, who tries to lead the two groups with a democratic style. This is more successful at the General site, where the supervisor's office is located. A common belief, shared by this supervisor, is that Harbour's coders need more "hand-holding."

Finally, there are only two utilization analysts and both are located at the General site. These analysts use data from the coding and cost databases to produce reports for use by internal and external clients of the Health Records Department. They report to the Director of Health Records and Patient Registration and usually handle requests from other departments on their own, without supervisory input. These reports are a key part of the efficiency and quality-control studies that are critical to the operation of the hospital.

COMMUNICATIONS ACROSS THE HOSPITAL

A hospital is a large organization that operates 24 hour a day, 7 days a week, so it has always been difficult to ensure timely communications of important matters to all shifts in all departments over both sites of the merged institution.

The communication strategy employs the following methods: email, voice mail, paper mail, a weekly newsletter, the President's Forum and a variety of notice boards. An initial problem existed because the email systems of the two sites operated differently. The Harbour site had always operated a proprietary system of email using their health care computer system, which was only accessible from within the hospital. The General site had used PC-based email using popular industry-wide software. The industry-wide software was installed at the Harbour site to ensure that the Harbour and General staff had a system they could both use. Most staff members at the Harbour site now use two email systems, with the emphasis still on their internal system. They feel that this system, which is unavailable to anyone outside their site, helps to maintain their identity and sense of community. A similar compatibility problem existed with voice mail, with the General's voice mail being imposed on the Harbour site. Traditional mail boxes are found around both sites, and paper mail is delivered daily.

The hospital prints its own weekly newsletter, which is delivered to each department and is available free of charge in the cafeterias and via a PDF file on the hospital's intranet. Everyone has a chance to pick up the newsletter from one of these sources during the week, but this communication is not guaranteed to reach everyone at the same time and cannot be used for urgent matters.

The President's Forum is used frequently throughout the year. The President will hold a forum in the cafeteria where all staff members are invited to come and hear the latest news and ask questions. Most members of senior management attend to answer questions. A bulletin highlighting the discussion is published on the intranet. Of course, not everyone can attend, and the Harbour site does not have its own forum. Instead, the hospital has a video hookup to allow the President to deliver his message simultaneously to each site. Timing can be difficult if the President wants to address a controversial or urgent issue. Times of "crisis", when her message is most important, are also the times when she has the most time constraints that force her to put off the forum. Many staff members have stopped attending, as there is a perception that the President will "not really say anything".

COMMUNICATIONS BARRIERS BETWEEN THE TWO SITES

Because the Harbour site was originally founded by a religious order, it has its own unique culture that influences informal information sharing. The Harbour site has numerous long-term employees; many employees are related, and, of course, a large number of them belong to the same religious affiliation. This means that there are some things that they seem to know by learning from their common external community. For instance, employees in departments that generally would not speak to one another in the course of business may communicate along social or familial lines. This has created a very tight "family" feel. This site also benefits from being a physically smaller facility.

In contrast, the General site had specific rules of how many related employees may work in the facility at the same time (no more than two and none in the same department). The background of the employees of the General site tends to be more diverse. Employees in different departments of the General site might rarely interact if it is not required as part of their work.

Due to cultural differences, communication differences, and the physical isolation of both sites, each site's grapevine (informal communication network) is isolated from the other. This has probably helped to diminish the spread of rumours across the entire hospital, but it has also prevented an overall sense of community and shared interest.

COMMUNICATIONS IN HEALTH RECORDS

Among the staff of the clerical section, those who work at the General site are expected to receive most information via email, which staff members check regularly, and this is also how they receive instructions from the previous shift or supervisor. The Harbour site has had to get used to using email for this purpose. Before the merger, face-to-face communication was more commonplace, and much of their non-urgent information came by paper mail. Now, the Harbour staff have a supervisor who is physically located at another site, so they need to use the General's email system to send and receive supervisory communications. For communications among themselves, they revert to their old system.

The coders work during the day, Monday to Friday, so these staff members are in daily face-to-face contact with their Supervisor. Those at the General site see their supervisor more regularly than their counterparts at the Harbour site. Since coders at both sites share a supervisor, they have had to adjust their expectations as to how often they can meet. The Supervisor's office is located at the General site. Because coding is complex work, written memos and emails are not enough to clarify instructions properly, and face-to-face communication is frequently required.

The utilization analysts report directly to the Director and are accustomed to receiving details via email or, more commonly, voice mail. They also receive many direct requests for data from senior levels of management, who seem to prefer voice mail. Due to the nature of the requests, it can take more than one communication to ensure that the request is understood. In some cases, face-to-face contact is necessary. Because utilization analysis has its own jargon, it can be difficult to ensure that the requester of the information has really asked for what they need. The standard joke is, "Do I give him what he wants or what he asked for"? There are only two analysts, and they work closely together at the General site on the same shift.

THE MERGER

The General Hospital had nearly three times as many beds as the Harbour Hospital. This imbalance was reflected in nearly every aspect of the merger to the extent that the merger was regarded by many staff members on both sites as a takeover. The merger proceeded from the top down, with a new board created out of the previous two boards. The former General Hospital board dominated the new board. In fact, the only former General Board members who were not appointed to the new board were members whose term was expiring and who did not seek re-appointment. The same could not be said of former Harbour Hospital board members. The President of the Harbour Hospital saw the handwriting on the wall and negotiated a comfortable exit. The President of the General Hospital took over the control of the new Harbour General Hospital. The merger followed this pattern throughout the organizations of both hospitals.

Harbour Hospital had always operated with a fairly authoritarian managerial style, in that neither decentralization of decision-making nor participatory management was practised. However, the attitude towards all employees was benevolent. Employee needs were always deemed important, as long as management was not asked to give them more power over their jobs. Perhaps, this was because of its roots as a hospital founded by a religious order, which had historically exercised strict control. Harbour people had always expected and received a fair amount of detailed direction about their work.

The General Hospital was newer, municipally built, and managed by reasonably progressive hospital administrators who employed a more consultative leadership style. However, it was also a more impersonal organization. Catering to individual employee needs was only done to the extent that standard policies allowed.

The Health Records Department was created as a merged operatoin headed by the Director of Health Records from the General Hospital. He created two new supervisory positions, one for the clerks and one for the coders. Both came from the General Hospital staff. The Director of Health Records from the Harbour Hospital retired. Prior to the merger, neither hospital had supervisors responsible for the clerks and the coders. Further, the Harbour Hospital had never had separate utilization analyst positions, preferring instead to assign the work to their coders on an ad hoc basis. The General Hospital had one utilization analyst, and another coder was promoted to fill the other position when the merger took place. While these various promotions required job postings and competitions, none of the staff at the Harbour filled the new positions.

THE PROBLEM

The Hospital's auditors were the first to alert the Board that the Harbour General Hospital was losing money and that the source of the financial trouble was the Harbour site. The Harbour Hospital had always been very efficient in the past, so the current situation had developed after the merger. Unfortunately, the rumour that spread at the General site was that the Harbour site was performing inefficiently and affecting the performance of the whole organization. For the duration of the financial crisis and even long afterward, this particular false belief would surface at hospital gatherings, usually accompanied by knowing nods among the General site staff members, who felt superior.

The President called on the accountants to pinpoint the problem, but, after two months of searching, they could only state that the Harbour Site was underutilized. The medical staff scoffed at that finding and claimed that the site was operating at full capacity as it had always done. The President then set up a task force to look into the matter, making sure that all the key players were involved, including the Director of Health Records.

Ultimately, the utilization analysts serving on the task force discovered the problem. Between the clerks and the coders at the Harbour site, charts were being missed. It turned out that when charts for some cases were entered by the clerks, the coders would not find those charts in the database that they regularly accessed for their processing. Further investigation revealed what seemed to be small errors on the part of the clerks and the coders that together caused these charts to be overlooked. When questioned, both groups at the Harbour site claimed that they were simply following instructions. This turned out to be correct. It was the instructions themselves that were at fault. At the Harbour site, the labelling of data records according to the instructions created these errors for about 6% of the charts. For the General site, a small difference in the way data was entered there meant the problem would never occur. Naturally, the Harbour site Health Records employees blamed the imposition of procedures from the former General Hospital. The General site staff felt that the problem should have been picked up long ago by the Harbour site's clerks and coders. "Don't you talk to each other and think about what you are doing? Over here, we check our work." was one comment from the General site's coders. The clerks and coders at the Harbour site were united in insisting that the problem was simply not their fault.

With the recovering of the missing chart data, the hospital would receive the lost revenue from the provincial government, so there would be no permanent financial penalty. However, claiming payment later for services that were missed earlier would alert government inspectors, bring unwanted attention to Harbour General, and possibly affect its reputation. The President also wondered whether there were other, similar issues that might arise in the future between the two sites, and how these might be prevented.

QUESTIONS

1. What issues of justice and fairness arise in this case?

2. What are the cultural differences between the two sites of Harbour General Hospital?

3. What actions and policies during and after the merger maintained and reinforced the cultural differences between the two sites?

4. How did the different cultures and policies of the two sites and the overall policies of the Harbour General Hospital contribute to the problem of the missing chart data?

5. Was it reasonable to expect the Health Records staff at the Harbour site to have spotted the problem in advance?

6. What recommendations would you make to the President concerning changes to the practices and/or structure of the hospital, and why?

The Hiring Process

There was a requirement to fill a vacant Clerical/Financial Services Officer position with a federal government department in Ottawa. Jennifer Logan-Smith, an executive-level manager, requested the advisory services of a Staffing Officer from the Personnel Department to assist her in filling this position. It had historically been staffed by open competition.

In accordance with federal government regulations, the Public Service Commission referred the candidates for the competition, and the Staffing Officer sent the candidates' resumes to Logan-Smith. She in turn was required to convene a Screening Board. However, despite the requirement for a board, Logan Smith, with one other Board member, proceeded to interview only three of the seven candidates. They assessed the third candidate, a Mr. John Groats, as entirely suitable for the position, told him that he had been successful, and informed the Staffing Officer of their decision. The remaining four candidates were not contacted, and were not interviewed. Mr. Groats commenced his new position two days later.

The Staffing Officer advised Logan-Smith that the Public Service Employment Act had been contravened in that all seven candidates should have been assessed to determine that the successful candidate was, in fact, the most qualified person. Logan-Smith thanked the Staffing Officer for his advice, but insisted that "the Board was completely satisfied with its decision and intended to validate the appointment of Mr. Groats, and that should other vacancies occur, which regularly happened, the other candidates would then be assessed." She added that her supervisors supported the Board's decision, and insisted that the Staffing Officer complete the necessary paperwork confirming Groats' appointment as soon as possible.

This response troubled the Staffing Officer. His advice had been ignored, and the fundamental "raisons d'etre" of a validated and reliable staffing system had been called into question. Although the Staffing Officer's involvement with the Screening Board was of an advisory nature, he also held, by delegation, the ultimate authority to make the staffing appointment on behalf of the Federal Government, in accor-

---

This case was written by Peter Kells.

dance with the Public Service Employment Act and its regulations, selection standards and orders.

The Staffing Officer felt uneasy about signing the appointment documents, knowing that the screening process was flawed and that any subsequent audit or review of this process would impact negatively on his reputation. On the other hand, it is his duty to assist Logan-Smith to achieve her staffing objectives and to ensure client satisfaction with the staffing outcome. Significantly, his supervisor encourages actions that lead to client satisfaction. That approach is preferred to the more procedurally controlled approach to staffing.

QUESTIONS

1. What issues in personnel selection are involved in this case?

2. Could proper procedures, as well as Jennifer Logan-Smith's preferences, be satisfied? If so, how?

3. As the Staffing Officer in this case, what action(s) would you take? Explain why.

Hi Style Inc.

Hi Style Inc. is an international company in the sportswear distribution industry with its head office in North America. The head office has 141 employees, divided into 85 administrative and clerical personnel and 55 warehouse personnel. The warehouse personnel consist of six supervisory positions, four non-union clerical positions and 45 union positions. The Quality Assurance Department accounts for about one-half of the warehouse employees.

Within the firm the official communication flows are governed by its highly bureaucratized structure. The dominance of downward communication and centralized decision-making results in a slightly dysfunctional work environment within the Quality Assurance Department. Feelings of low morale, alienation and job dissatisfaction sometimes occur among the personnel working there.

THE QUALITY ASSURANCE DEPARTMENT

The Quality Assurance Department employs 26 of the 55 warehouse personnel. The function of the department is to inspect all merchandise for conformity to the purchase order, to apply price ticket information, and to ensure the quality of the merchandise and packaging prior to shipment. The 26 employees include:

- 1 Director
- 1 Accessory Supervisor
- 1 Apparel Supervisor
- 1 Nonunion Clerical Ticketing Operator
- 2 Lead Hand/Section Heads
- 20 Classified Union positions

The Director of the Quality Assurance department is Frank Larkin, a 59-year-old with many years of experience in quality assurance, the last eight as the Director of QA at Hi Style Inc. Frank Larkin demonstrates a lack of leadership skills that would normally be considered essential for a dynamic and positive work environ-

---

This case is based on original work by Karyn Mallette.

ment. He has a tendency to procrastinate and put off critical decisions. His style is excessively formal and non-interactive. He appears to be very resistant to change. Frank's communications are almost totally limited to supervisory personnel. He often hides behind closed doors and is not aware of the daily practices in his department. He seems completely satisfied with his "closed door" policy, as long as deadlines and standards are met.

The Accessory Supervisor of the Quality Assurance Department is Doris Chong, a 35-year-old of Asian descent. She was transferred from the Hong Kong office, bringing with her several years of experience in apparel manufacturing and quality inspection. Her supervisory skills, however, are limited, with almost no training in management theory or practice. Her strong personal work ethic developed in Hong Kong was, unfortunately, not easily transferred into the operational practices at the North American office. She is accustomed to working in a very structured task environment with little deviation from her job classification. She experiences frustration when challenged with day-to-day decision-making and problem-solving in the very dynamic and constantly changing work environment. Due to limited communication from Doris to the front-line workers, the personnel who report to her are often left with feelings of resentment and without a clear perception of their goals. Doris often delegates her supervisory responsibilities to other employees and demands immediate completion.

The Apparel Supervisor of the Quality Assurance Department is Groda Walesa — a 55-year-old woman of European descent. Groda came from a labour intensive background in the garment industry. She worked for many years in a small apparel manufacturing company in downtown Montreal. Frank Larkin hired Groda in 1994 as the Apparel Supervisor. Groda has a tendency to alienate her staff, and yet demands respect. She pushes her staff for high productivity, but offers them little support, understanding or concern for their well-being. She lacks the educational background of her subordinates, and has never received any formal supervisory training. This puts her at a disadvantage when it comes to interpersonal skills and social relations.

The nonunion Clerk of the Quality Assurance Department is Brenda Clark — a 22-year-old, colleges graduate from some fashion arts managements program. Brenda is a very ambitious and dedicated employee with career plans to grow within the company. Ultimately she would like to work her way into a management position. She continually looks for ways to enhance the productivity and efficiency of the department. Brenda's position, called Ticketing Officer, is responsible for providing support functions to the Quality Assurance department and the American stores. She reports to the Accessory Supervisor, Doris Chong. In addition, Brenda responds to all inquiries from the buyers of major clients. Her functions also include: data entry of product and pricing information; printing of Universal Price Codes (UPC); collection of quality control reports for internal distribution; preparation and distribution of UPC reports to major customers; processing of data for statistical cost reporting and the processing of employee time and attendance records for the entire Quality Assurance Department.

Brenda had been in the above position as Ticketing Operator for three months when Doris left on maternity leave for approximately seven months. Brenda was then required to report directly to the Director of Quality Assurance, Frank Larkin. Doris' temporary replacement, Steven Tyler, had little knowledge or experience for this position. Steve relied on Brenda's knowledge of the department to assist him in procedures and in any difficulties he encountered. The department was functioning smoothly: all deadlines were being met, and any pending problems were immediately solved by Brenda and Steve. Brenda implemented many new procedures to save time and money, and experienced a sense of achievement due to the informal job enrichment. Brenda felt she now had greater control over her work, and was motivated by her accomplishments. The only real problem she encountered was with Groda Walesa. Groda would not consider any of Brenda's suggestions unless they were sent "through channels". This meant that Steven had to formally propose them to Frank Larkin, who would then approve them and instruct Groda to follow the new procedures.

Doris Chong returned to her position as the Accessory Supervisor after her maternity leave, and Brenda was immediately directed to re-assume her old job description and practices. Doris had difficulty accepting the new procedures that were implemented while she was away. She perceived that she had lost control of her area, and continually grumbled about how these procedures were inconvenient or ineffective. Piece by piece, Doris was undoing all of the changes. Brenda lost her opportunities for creativity and decision-making, and experienced a decline in her desire to do a good job. She had originally expected praise from her supervisor for the improvements she had made. As Brenda's sense of satisfaction over her job deteriorated, serious conflict began to develop between her and Doris.

This turned out to be not only Doris' and Brenda's predicament. The entire department was, ultimately, to get involved in the warfare between the Ticketing Officer and the Accessory Supervisor. On Brenda's side (at least, before he knew there was a conflict) was Frank Larkin. He was grateful that he did not have to become a more active leader when Doris was away. Frank was appreciative that Brenda and Steve had handled the situation, although he knew few details about how resourceful Brenda really had been. During a rare appearance among the warehouse staff upon Doris' return, he had publicly thanked them. Supporting Doris vocally was Groda Walesa, who thought that Brenda had exceeded her authority and had meddled in supervisory matters during Doris' absence. With Doris having the support of the unpopular Groda, most of the unionized employees went to Brenda's side. It usually took very little persuasion to convince the unionized staff to take up an anti-supervisor position.

As the conflict developed, Doris, with the encouragement of Groda, seemed intent on preventing Brenda from being able to carry out her statistical and reporting responsibilities competently. Doris withdrew or delayed her cooperation, and gave Brenda low priority tasks to accomplish when her more important work had to be done. Groda always seemed to be looking at the time sheets that Brenda needed. On her part, Brenda began to object publicly that Doris was being petty and mean. Frank Larkin, who was always attentive to the timeliness of these reports, became alarmed when they were delayed. His reaction was to call Doris in for a discussion of the problem, since she was Brenda's immediate supervisor. He had little idea of how much bitterness really existed between Doris and Brenda.

Through the grapevine, Brenda found out about this impending meeting, and that Frank Larkin was upset about the drop in performance. She decided to try to go over Doris' head and request her own meeting. Brenda felt that Doris would tell Frank that it was her fault that her work was falling behind. She believed that the firm's strict reliance on the chain of command could now cause her to lose her job without a fair hearing. She also realized that, given the usual way that formal communication took place at Hi Style, she would be lucky to be granted a meeting with Frank Larkin. While she was waiting for a reply to her request, the sympathetic union steward told her that, although she was not part of the bargaining unit, the union local was quite sympathetic to her plight, and might be willing to take some informal action on her behalf. Brenda realized that the steward could be using her as a lever to put pressure on the unpopular supervisors through Frank Larkin, but she also thought that Frank might be swayed by a hint of union action — formal or informal. She would also enjoy regaining a little power in this situation.

QUESTIONS

1. Performance in the Quality Assurance Department at Hi Style has suffered due to the events in this case. Who are to blame, and what is the extent of each person's responsibility?

2. What are the issues of power and influence?

3. To what extent are the firm's policies and practices (including communications) to blame for the deteriorating situation? What common causes are there for both Brenda's dissatisfaction and the general level of poor morale among the employees?

4. How could Frank Larkin have better provided for replacing Doris' functions during her leave of absence?

5. How should Frank Larkin handle the upcoming meeting with Doris? Should he also meet with Brenda and, if so, how should he handle that meeting?

6. Do you think that Brenda should suggest to Frank Larkin that there will be "union trouble" if she is punished or fired? What are the advantages and disadvantages of using this strategy? Do you think it is right for her to do so?

7. How could this situation be resolved without dismissing Brenda? Suggest both short term measures to defuse the conflict and long-term measures to deal with root causes.

HK Handbags

Linda's last confrontation with Ruby, her Store Manager, was the final straw. Once again, Linda felt she was being punished for no valid reason. Now she was being isolated from her social group in addition to being threatened with dismissal. Linda felt she couldn't tolerate the situation anymore. Something had to be done. Even though she was still in school and needed the part time employment, she had reached the conclusion that nothing could compensate for such bad treatment from Ruby. One of the options Linda had was to talk to Jeff, the owner, but she decided that even if he then had a talk with Ruby, and things were fixed for a time, she would not be happy working there. Ruby would continue to dislike her, and more problems would ensue. The next day, Linda handed her resignation letter to Ruby.

HK Handbags was a small handbag business in Hong Kong. It was opened by a rich and retired man named Jeff, who opened the store to "kill time". Nine people were employed, including one store manager, Karen, two assistant managers — Ruby and Vivian, and six sales people.

- Jeff was 66 years old. He was married with no children. His wife was a few years younger, and working as a bank manager. Since his wife was still working, he opened HK Handbags, but Jeff did not like to be tied down to the business. He liked to spend time playing golf with his friends. That was why he hired his neighbour's daughter, Karen, to manage most of the firm's operations.

- Karen was the store manager. She was 27 years old and had graduated from the University of Hong Kong with a degree in Business and a certificate in Accounting. Karen had previously worked as a salesperson and as an assistant manager at a shoe store for four years. There, she had developed the leadership skills that would help her at HK Handbags during the two years since it had opened. Karen was an only child who had always been given many things by her parents, who didn't spend much time with her when she was growing up. Karen's hobby was frequent shopping for expensive items. Even though she had a full time job, was paid the equivalent of $60,000 (Canadian) per year, and lived at home, she spent

---

This case is based on original work by Christina Chow.

all her money quickly and even asked her parents for additional spending money. Away from the store, her main source of happiness seemed to be acquiring new, expensive personal items.

- Ruby was one of the assistant managers. She was 40 years old and had been working in the retail industry as a sales person for 15 years. She was in a commercial college for three years and graduated with a diploma in business. Within the last fifteen years, she had left sales positions at over 20 different retail stores because she couldn't seem to get along with some of the employees at each job. She especially resented those younger than she, which over time became the majority of co-workers. Sometimes, her departure from a job was due to an outburst at a co-worker following the promotion of someone else. Ruby had a brother, who had emigrated and lost contact with the family. She now provided the sole support for her elderly parents. She had been briefly married about 15 years previously, but was now divorced. HK Handbags was her fist job with supervisory responsibilities.

- Linda was a new sales person at the store who had been working for only four months. An 18-year-old, this was her first year in university, and she needed some spending money. When Linda put her mind to do something important, she did her best. She was open to learning new things, enjoyed socializing, and got along with most people because she was a very tolerant person.

All working schedules made by the store manager had to be checked over and formalized by Jeff because he felt that a good working schedule was necessary to prevent turnover rates and stress among the employees. The sales staff was asked to write down their job availability each month because they were part-time workers. Then the store manager scheduled them according to their availability. Once the work schedule was checked over and formalized by Jeff, no one was allowed to change it. Other than the work schedule, Jeff was not concerned with any other aspects of the store's operations. He delegated everything else to his manager.

Therefore, Karen, the store manager, had the authority to make all rules and procedures, create job descriptions and deal with any problems that arose. Karen kept those rules and procedures at a minimum because she wanted more autonomy for the sales staff. She believed that this would result in better work performance from everyone. The rules and procedures included some of the following: lateness was not tolerated; any customer concerns or complaints were to be reported to the store manager; sales staff were to write down their availability, and everyone was to work hard and have fun. The two assistant managers were to handle complaints from employees to ensure that the sales staff were doing work-related activities, and to help the store manager whenever needed. The sales staff's job was to ensure that the display of the handbags was organized and presentable, to clean the store after closing, and to assist customers. At the end of every month, Karen would have a meeting with the two assistant managers to ensure that there were no ongoing problems in the store. Whenever Karen added a new rule or procedure, she would notify Jeff of the change, but he did not pay much attention to these matters. Jeff even gave Karen the bookkeeping responsibility, since he trusted her and she had a certificate in accounting.

At the end of every month, Karen would calculate the company's profit. Karen would then take out 8% of the profit and put it in another company's savings account. Every three months, Karen would take the money out and all HK Handbag's staff (including Jeff) would go for dinner. The three months' profit would be split equally among everyone. If a person's dinner came out to be a little more than each person's dinner budget, then that individual would have to pay the difference. If someone decided not to go for dinner, then that person's dinner budget would be equally divided among the others who would attend the dinner. This was done to compensate the firm's staff for their hard work. If there was money left over after the dinner, the money was put back into the savings account and added into the next dinner's budget. For Christmas, the staff would play Secret Santa and Karen would also organize a potluck party. After the party, they would get to choose either to go bowling, watch a movie, take part in karaoke or whatever else they wanted to do. Jeff would pay for the evening.

HK Handbags was doing well, and profits were increasing. Karen especially admired Linda's job performance. Ever since Linda was hired, revenue had increased by 25% compared to the previous period. However, the Assistant Manager, Ruby, was often dissatisfied with Linda's work, and talked to Linda about it on many occasions when Karen was not present. For example, when Linda arranged the display of the handbags, Ruby would tell Linda to change the display around because she said that Linda's displays were not "eye catching" enough. Ruby's dissatisfaction seemed mainly aimed at Linda. Except for this friction with the Assistant manager, Linda was happy working at HK Handbags. She felt that Karen's leadership style made for a great working environment. Karen was concerned with each of her employees' performance, but she was also concerned with their well-being and with the social atmosphere in the company. Karen related well to everyone and tried to ensure that all employees got along. To enhance the social atmosphere, Karen would organize a special event once a month. Jeff encouraged the staff to attend by offering to pay for half of the event's expense. For example, the event could be bowling, golfing, going to an amusement park, etc. All the staff looked forward to the day of the event.

Karen was also concerned with getting tasks accomplished efficiently. For example, every two months, a new shipment of goods arrived. This meant that inventory would have to be changed around in the store to accommodate the new arrivals. New posters were mounted and the displays of the handbags were changed. Everyone would be scheduled to help with this work, which was usually done after store hours. They would be paid for six hours work to accomplish this task, but could leave earlier if the work was finished faster and it usually was. Karen would consult the employees about work-related matters, which included promotions, store-wide sales, monthly quotas, etc. They would come up with a decision that they were all satisfied with. This was easy to accomplish, because there were only nine staff members. Karen also treated everyone equally. Karen would not use her authority to force other employees to do certain jobs. For example, Karen would offer to wash the employee washroom while a sales staff looked after the store.

As time went by, Karen seemed to increase her shopping and spending. Everything she now bought seems to have an exclusive brand name. She asked her parents for more spending money, but they became alarmed. They thought that her behaviour was extreme, and actually started to cut back her allowance. Then, Karen saw this very pretty, high quality diamond bracelet by Louis Vuitton that cost $12,000 (Canadian). She didn't have enough money to buy it, and became increasingly upset. One morning, she was sitting in her office, and she just couldn't concentrate on her work. She felt frustrated and was afraid the bracelet would be bought by someone else. However, she was also under pressure from the amount of work she had to do. It was at that moment when Karen first began to believe that she wasn't being paid a fair salary. She felt that she was doing two jobs — Store Manager and Accountant. She believed that if she "borrowed" the money from the company, it would okay. She was planning to replace the $8,000 she needed as soon as her parents agreed to help her out, or she could save it over a few months. She also thought that no one would find out because Jeff never checked the books of accounts. Unfortunately for her, Karen was caught. She went to the bank to withdraw the money at the same time that Jeff was there to withdraw money from his personal account. Karen was so eager to get the money out that she didn't notice Jeff at the bank. Jeff overheard Karen instructing the teller to withdraw $8000 from the company's account. When Jeff confronted her and she had no satisfactory explanation, she was fired on the spot.

Jeff had a meeting with the remaining eight staff members to decide on the appointment of a new store manager. Since Linda was still new to the company, despite her misgivings she went along with the other six sales people, who decided that Ruby should be the store manager. Ruby clearly had the most experience and had worked closely with Karen. Also, Jeff felt the company didn't need two assistant managers. The decision didn't bother Vivian because she didn't want the responsibilities of store manager. After Ruby's promotion, everything went well for a while. Ruby's leadership style was similar to Karen's and Linda didn't feel that she was being singled out for criticism as much as before. Three months later, however, it was clear that Ruby was not doing as well as Karen in some of the administrative work, especially bookkeeping. (Jeff had arranged for an accountant to review the books at the end of each month, but he did not involve himself in the store any more than he did before.) Ruby began to appear nervous and ill at ease in the store. Again, Ruby started to treat Linda adversely, complaining about her work in front of other staff and, sometimes, customers. Once again, Linda felt she was being singled out unfairly.

Their relationship reached a crisis one month before Christmas, when a lot of new stock arrived. All staff had to work to change the inventory and arrange the displays. Everyone arrived at work on time hoping to finish early. Ruby assigned Linda to work with her, which made Linda apprehensive. They were to bring out the new handbags and display them along the shelf closest to the door, so that the customers would see the new arrivals as they stepped into the store. Linda was to take out the new inventory from the stock room and put it in the display area for Ruby to arrange. Linda brought out three boxes of handbags. When Ruby checked one of the boxes, she realized that those handbags were not from the new stock.

Ruby immediately turned to Linda and yelled at her for bringing out the wrong handbags. Ruby said that Linda was wasting her time, and sent her home right away. This mistake was commonly made by all staff members, because it was dark in the stockroom and it was hard to tell which ones were new arrivals and which ones were not. These outbursts had been happening with increasing frequency of late, and Linda was almost always the target, although she was performing as competently as ever. Everyone felt bad for Linda, but they lacked the courage to defend her, as they felt they could be next.

A week later, there was a sales meeting to be held Saturday morning. Unfortunately, Linda's great-grandmother had passed away and the funeral was to be held on the same day as the meeting. Linda told Ruby that she would not be able to attend the meeting because she had to go to her great-grandmother's funeral. Ruby said that it was okay and that she would tell her what happened at the meeting later. However, at the end of the meeting, Ruby told everyone not to talk to Linda because she did not attend the meeting. Ruby said that going to a funeral was not a good excuse to miss a meeting. Ruby said that if she saw anyone talking to Linda, that person would be fired. The next day Linda came into work and Ruby took her into her office. Ruby told Linda everything that was talked about at the meeting, except for what Ruby had said at the end of the meeting about Linda. There were two other employees working that day. Linda approached them and asked how they were doing. They both ignored her and walked away. Later in the day, Ruby and another sales person left early and only Linda and one other employee, Ivy, remained in the store. Ivy told Linda about what Ruby had said. She said that she felt bad for ignoring her, but she had no choice because she didn't want to lose her job. Before Ruby had left, however, she had hidden a small recorder in the store to monitor conversations. The next day, Ruby took the tape home and heard Ivy's conversation with Linda. The following morning Ruby fired Ivy. Ruby called Linda at home to notify her that Ivy was fired, but gave no reason for her dismissal.

There was now one week left until Christmas. As part of the Secret Santa tradition at the store, everyone had already been given a name for whom to purchase a gift. Ruby called everyone else to inform them that Ivy had been fired because she was caught telling Linda about what she said at the end of the meeting. Since Ivy was fired, Ruby gave out the names for Secret Santa again. This time Ruby excluded Linda from the tradition. When Linda came in to work her shift, she asked for a name, but Ruby told her that she wasn't going to get one. When Linda asked her why, Ruby just said that she didn't deserve to play Secret Santa. Linda asked Ruby a second time to give her a reason, but Ruby answered that if she asked one more time, she would also be fired.

QUESTIONS

1. Explain how Karen's leadership style and the internal environment motivated the employees to perform well.

2. How is it possible that Karen's dysfunctional personal behaviour could co-exist with her effective leadership style?

3. Should Ivy have told Linda about the meeting? Why or why not?

4. Describe Ruby's leadership style and explain how it is dysfunctional.

5. Who is responsible for the situation at the end of the case?

6. What should Linda do now?

The Honourable Head-Hunter

PART I

Bob Marshall finally knew it was wrong when George Baker bluntly told him, "Don't send me any black applicants." That forthright statement by his client rang the bell. The problem was, what should he do about it?

Bob worked as a head-hunter for the Adanac Employment agency in the City of Winnipeg. He had been on the job for about a year. Before that he had worked in sales. But as the economy grew sluggish, he found it opportune to move into this new kind of sales career. For reasons he was only now understanding it was a growth industry when the rest of the economy was weakening.

The business was fairly straightforward. A local business would hire Adanac to refer candidates to them for jobs they had open. Small- and medium-sized businesses found this to be easier than maintaining their own personnel departments. The client would send over a job description with a list of the qualifications they were looking for. The head-hunter would look through Adanac's pool of applicants to find suitable matches and arrange interviews. A fair amount of time was spent with these job applicants, making sure the information about them was complete, accurate, and up to date.

Adanac earned a fee when a client selected one of its candidates. The head-hunter earned a commission on the same basis as if the match had been a sale. When Bob first joined Adanac he was assured it was a sales job like any other: "Just give the employer what he wants." Bob learned it was a different sales job in one important way . . . the money could be terrific. To a guy such as him, who was accustomed to the hustle of the sales world, it was like putting a fox in charge of the chicken coop. None of the other head-hunters at Adanac had a sales background. Mostly they had been office workers or, in a few cases, blue collar people. He quickly realized that he could climb to the top, and that could mean salary and commission approaching $100,000 per year.

The problem was "giving the employer what he wants". As long as he stuck to the application form and the job qualifications, it seemed easy enough. The reality was different. He would send over a perfect match only to have him or her rejected.

Naturally Bob would follow up, eager to close the sale and wanting to know how to improve his product. The employer would just say, "The applicant had a bad attitude." When he would ask for particulars, none would be forthcoming.

Another common response from the employers when rejecting an applicant would be that, "The chemistry just wasn't right." "Chemistry" seemed to be as obscure a concept as "attitude". He asked one of the other consultants about this, and one of them suggested that he was not looking at the right aspect of attitude or chemistry. Maybe he had better look at the offices of the clients and see if his candidates would fit in ethnically or racially. Bob checked it out. He made certain that the next candidate he forwarded to the employer was a suitably white Anglo-Saxon even though her formal qualifications for the job were actually a poor fit.

She got the job. In a post hiring interview with the employer, he was advised that the job as a receptionist was highly visible, and looks mattered more than anything else.

Bob realized that to find the person the client wants, including the right attitude and chemistry, was going to mean a supplementary set of job qualifications. And even more important, it meant a supplementary set of candidates' qualifications. The problem with both of these tasks was that it was frowned on by the Human Rights Commission. Modern "approved" application forms and job postings are remarkably sterile documents. All they tell you about the job is what skills, knowledge, experience, etc. is required. The same with the candidate's resume. It tells what they can do and have done. Neither has a word to offer about "attitude" or "chemistry".

Bob learned to get around this problem by making his own shorthand notes on the forms about these off-the-record attributes and requirements. He even learned there was a sort of office code in use: "Mary" meant Jamaican, a paper clip identified an Oriental, an asterisk marked a disabled applicant and a reference under working conditions stating that this job was "in public view" meant, "Send over white applicants only." One unexpected observation he made was that these "marked" candidates seemed to be exceptionally well qualified. Whenever an employer did not refer to attitude or chemistry, they ended up with a very suitable employee.

The other thing he learned was how to justify all this subterfuge. The head-hunters had their conventional wisdom about the job. "Our business is to find the person the client wants. We get paid to find the right attitude." "If a client wants to discriminate in hiring, that's their look out. Me, I don't hire anyone." "Why should I waste everyone's time sending over a candidate I know isn't going to get the job?" "The client doesn't hire me to teach him about the law. If he wants to know the law, he'll hire a lawyer."

Over a period of months Bob came to realize that one of the reasons for the growth of the employment agency business even as the economy slowed was that the agencies had taken on a whole new role. They were serving as a route around the Human Rights Act. Employers were very leery of running afoul of the act, especially after there had been a recent, high profile and costly settlement against an electronics retailer for overtly discriminating against non-white applicants. Smaller firms were prepared to pay experts to cover for them.

Despite these nagging concerns, Bob managed to convince himself that while what he was doing may not be righteous, at least it was OK. His rationalizations were in place. He knew that if he did not do the job, someone else would. And the money was becoming very wonderful.

George Baker rang the bell good and loud. By bluntly directing Bob to not send any black applicants, he had pushed things over the edge. Up until then his relationship with the employers had maintained the subterfuge of discreet, even polite, discrimination, if such was possible. The cover was now off, and Bob could feel his helpful justifications falling away. If he undertook a direct contract to discriminate against blacks in the hiring process for George Baker, then he was Baker's agent, and he would clearly be breaking the law. He might even be implicating Adanac and its owner Harvey McGill in the offence, since he was following the policy of "meeting their clients' needs".

It was late enough on Friday afternoon for him to leave and take the weekend to decide what to do.

QUESTION

Help Bob with his weekend. Summarize the issues and concerns he faces. What are his options? What contingencies exist with the different options? Draw up a plan for him to follow to deal with the conflict he now feels.

PART II

Bob's strategy was simple. If he was going to break the law, he was not going to do it alone and without his employer's knowledge and consent. In other words, he wanted Harvey McGill on board and backing him all the way. His major concern was being isolated on this problem.

He had every reason to expect Harvey's support with this problem. Harvey had singled him out for praise and recognition several times and was quite interested in his sales skills in filling their clients' needs. Their interpersonal relationship was also quite solid. Bob had even been invited to join Harvey and a couple of the old timers for an after work happy hour on a couple of occasions.

He arranged to see Harvey first thing Monday morning. At their meeting Bob laid it all out. If he was going to comply with George Baker's request, then Bob expected Harvey to back him up. The back-up would consist of a written statement from Harvey that Adanac expected its head-hunters to comply with all of the clients' requests.

Harvey was cagey. It was quickly apparent to Bob that he was not going to get a written directive. Harvey correctly pointed out that such a document would be damning evidence in any case that resulted. Furthermore, Harvey stated, he did not condone any subterfuge carried out by his employees aimed at circumventing the Human Rights Act. He did acknowledge that he was aware that a few isolated liberties were occasionally taken, but that these were the exception, not the rule.

Bob was stunned by all this. He challenged Harvey's plea of ignorance about the usual office practices, and pointed out that Harvey had to be aware of this powerful drive behind the current growth of his business. Bob also pointed out that the whole structure of the business, with head-hunters heavily reliant on commissions to earn a decent living, clearly indicated management support for the practices they were following.

The meeting ended unsatisfactorily. Bob did not get his cover as he had hoped, and he was even more confused than ever by what was going on.

Later that afternoon Harvey stopped by Bob's office and invited him out for a friendly drink. Just the two of them. After they got settled into a quiet corner of a nearby lounge, Harvey began by saying that this was just a friendly off-the-record chat. Harvey said he did not want Bob to be confused as a result of their official meeting this morning. He explained that he knew exactly how his business operated, and that he realized the nature of the requests his head-hunters were sometimes called upon to fill. He was aware of the dodges they used to hide their true work. But, he explained, it was important to maintain the formal cover of compliance with the law. That meant learning how to accommodate the George Bakers and their blunt requests. He went on to say that he saw all this as a transitional phase with some remaining old style business people who had not recognized the changing colour of the community and the workforce. He commented that eventually everyone would realize that discrimination cut you off from too large of a pool of talent and that nobody would care if your image had a little variety in it. He added that he saw all this current scrambles to circumvent the Human Rights Act as a backlash against employment equity programs espoused by governments.

He concluded his remarks by assuring Bob that he greatly valued his work and that Bob would be receiving a memo the next morning informing him that he would receive a raise in his commission rate. Bob felt he had little choice but to thank Harvey for this background information and for the raise. This off-the-record support was better than the deceit of the morning. He now knew exactly where each of them stood.

QUESTION

Exactly where do Bob and Harvey stand? What does Bob do now? Have his concerns been resolved enough to allow him to continue with his job? Do Harvey's rationalizations help smooth things over?

PART III

After mulling things over for the rest of the week, Bob realized that there was some truth in what Harvey had said about the changing nature of the community and about the workforce. He also agreed that this might be the last backlash of a fading majority, not yet ready to welcome the future. He also suspected that Harvey, like his clients, was one step behind the times.

He reviewed his files of applicants to confirm his earlier feeling about how well qualified these "marked" applicants were. His suspicions were correct. In almost any job category, if you requested white-only or some such restriction, you invariably lowered what you could get for the other job-related attributes. The pool of well-qualified WASPs was getting dry.

He also checked out the employment equity programs, and quickly realized the enormous pressure that recruiters for these programs were under. But he saw this as a trend that business would eventually have to follow. New government legislation ensured this trend. A few phone calls confirmed that this was indeed a significant market niche.

His business plan began to take shape. He would help companies meet their employment equity targets. Maybe he could set up a subsidiary to help prepare employment equity plans. There were many possibilities.

Bob decided to cut his association with Adanac and launch his new business with one stroke. He blew the whistle on Adanac and its illegal and unethical practices. He contacted a reporter for a major daily paper that he knew to have a progressive editorial policy, and he told all.

The reporter covered the story with additional material from rights groups and a representative of an employment agencies association, as well as the usual politicians. The big play was from the Human Rights Commission, which announced an immediate investigation.

As a footnote, the reporter announced Bob's plan for a new employment service of minority head-hunting.

QUESTION

Evaluate Bob's business plan, and develop improvements.

PART IV

Bob's business got off to a roaring good start. He soon had a large pool of very well qualified job applicants. The jobs were a little harder to find, but they were coming in. He has had a problem getting government agencies to use his services. They are not accustomed to using a head-hunter.

Bob is now worried that he has acted precipitously. He wonders if the whistle blowing strategy was injudicious. He certainly received a lot of negative feedback to the newspaper story.

Harvey sent him a very brief note. It said, "Nobody, but nobody, likes a Whistle Blower."

QUESTION

Discuss whistle blowing as employee behaviour. What are the ethical and practical considerations involved?

PART V

Six months later, the following story appeared in the same newspaper.

JOB AGENCY SHOWED BIAS, RIGHTS BODY CONCLUDES

The Human Rights Commission has concluded that some staff from Adanac, a metro area employment agency, did comply with employer requests to discriminate when sending them job candidates. But the commission did conclude that Harvey McGill, the owner of the company, did not create, ratify, authorize, sanction or condone a deliberate discriminatory policy. The commission did order the company to draw up a comprehensive employment equity program which the commission will oversee. The program will include better staff training. A commission official stated that this was an extremely stern step for it to take and set a new standard of employment practice.

QUESTION

Evaluate this solution by the Human Rights Commission.

The Human Resource Strategies Branch

HUMAN RESOURCE (HR) PROGRAM

The Human Resources Program is a division of the Federal Government. Its mission is to "provide support and advice to the federal employer in promoting the renewal and revitalization of the federal workforce to achieve the key outcome of dynamic and innovative people delivering quality public service." The Division supports ministries through policies and programs. It establishes a Human Resources (HR) policy framework and labour relations environment designed to promote organizational flexibility, which supports the business planning objectives of the federal public service. The Division is both a catalyst and a facilitator for change, improvement and learning. The Division attempts to foster positive working relations among employees, managers, bargaining agents and the employer, and is committed to promoting a healthy and safe working environment. However, it is not involved in processing any specific human resource issues. That is left to the individual ministry's HR departments to manage.

HR STRATEGIES BRANCH

The HR Strategies Branch is one of three branches housed in the HR Program. The Branch leads the development of the human resources policies to support the business objectives of the government. It develops policies and programs regarding planning, recruitment, learning and development, health and safety, and compensation issues for all non-bargaining employee groups, other than the senior management group, thus providing the strategic framework and tools to support business outcomes. The Branch also manages the federal Internship Program, which hires recent graduates into occupational areas where skill shortages are anticipated. It develops and implements the HR Plan for Managers, an ongoing project to address HR issues facing Management level employees.

This case is based on original work by Rosanna Delgrosso.

SITUATION

The whole Public Service was affected by political change and, over the last few years, there have been a number of restructuring and downsizing exercises. As a result, some government bodies have been either eliminated or amalgamated into remaining ministries or agencies to meet the political commitments. In addition to streamlining the organization, the present government mandated that each ministry must provide total quality service to its customers. Each ministry and program is expected to provide quality customer service with existing resources.

The HR Strategies Branch has had a history of low morale and a high turnover rate in comparison to the rest of the Division. Over the last two years, the branch has been able to hire on additional staff. However, the heavy workload still required staff to work 12–15-hour days. Regardless of their position, staff generally felt overworked and underpaid. They also perceived a double standard within the branch. Although they were the ones who developed the HR policies, that did not necessarily mean they were able to follow them. Frequently, new projects with a high profile would suddenly arrive, and staff would be expected to work on them in addition to their normal workload, which was already very demanding. It seemed that the branch had to do any work that did not directly fit into the mandate of the client ministries or the other Branches.

Staff would be asked by the Director to take on special projects depending upon whether their knowledge, experience and position enabled them to handle the assignment. These assignments were usually high profile and often not part of the yearly operational plan. The Director used a type of matrix structure when pulling together a team to handle these high profile issues. This helped to streamline the work, but still kept the chain of command intact. Staff remained in their functional roles, reported to the Director (who would serve as the project manager) to work on special assignments, and reported to their Manager or Team Leader for their regular duties. This form of matrix led to confusion for the staff. It encouraged the staff to think that the organization is flatter and more organic than it really is. By working with the Director for the special projects, staff tended to have a false sense of direct access to the Director. Potentially, if staff members are not satisfied with a response by their manager, they may feel that they have the option to by-pass the manager and proceed to the Director for a definitive answer. This caused frustration for both the manager and the staff member. Some managers would deal very formally or defensively with a staff member who they felt might have the ear of the director.

Staff also experienced frustration in their work of formulating HR policies and gaining acceptance for them among the client ministries. They would hold focus groups, and report their recommendations, sometimes all the way up to a Deputy Minister. Additional approval would be required if Cabinet was involved. The process could take months and sometimes years. On the other hand, political considerations would often create the "policy of the month" that would have to be formulated very quickly without due regard for potential problems. Many times, staff would be directed to discontinue a project that was no longer in favour, only to return to it years later with the same issues still not resolved. On other occasions, their carefully crafted policies would be changed without their input, and what was intended to move in one direction would veer off in a totally different direction that they had not intended or contemplated. Despite all these impediments, the Branch had an official commitment to Total Quality Management (TQM), as did the entire Human Resources Program.

ISSUE

Samantha is a professional with university training in HRM, backed up by the attainment of national certification as a Human Resources Professional. Samantha reports to Jack, her Manager, in the Youth Initiative Unit. Since returning from maternity leave, she had requested many times to be placed on a condensed work week (CWW) schedule. This would reduce the number of her two-hour commutes to and from work each day, and give her a weekday to spend with her new baby. It would mean more work hours during the other work days, so that her total hours would not change. Before returning from leave, she had spoken to Jack over the phone about CWW. Jack refused her request because the Youth Initiative Program dealt with newly hired interns, who called into the program on a daily basis. Samantha would personally deal with Interns in several client ministries. He was concerned that if Samantha was not available to address clients in a timely manner, then the Unit would not be able to maintain the level of quality service the program has reached in the past, and this would compromise TQM. At every opportunity, Samantha spoke to Jack about CWW, and even provided him with options of others filling in to address his concerns. Jack continued to refuse her request, finally saying that CWW had not been officially adopted by the Branch (although the policy had been formulated by the Branch). She then went to the Director, who said she would look into it on her behalf. During one of the Director's weekly meetings with Jack, she asked about Samantha's request. Jack, annoyed with Samantha for going over his head, explained that given the TQM mandate, the request was impossible to accommodate. If she were not on the job five days each week, it could compromise the handling of the interns and the advising of the ministry managers who were hosting the interns during their rotation. Again, Samantha's request was denied — this time, by the Director.

One day, as Samantha was taking a break for her daily cup of coffee, she met Amy. Amy reported to Rose in the Policy and Planning Unit. Amy was not a HR professional, but had advanced to Administrative Assistant from previous secretarial positions. Her current job had recently been converted from part-time to full-time. She provided administrative support to 11 policy advisors, and did not deal directly with any ministry clients.

Samantha was curious about how Amy was handling the additional work hours.

Samantha: "So, how is it going being back full-time?"

Amy: "Oh! It's great! Rose has been really wonderful about it."

Samantha: "How so?"

Amy: "Well, I'm on CWW. So, I can still have a day off during the week."

Samantha: "But I thought the Branch didn't take part in the program."

Amy: "It doesn't. I'm on small 'cww', not capital 'CWW'."

Samantha: "What's the difference?"

Amy: "Well, I only report my condensed work week to Rose. Higher-ups and even the Personnel people don't know about it. That way there's no paper trail. All I have to do is keep a record of my time during the week. Whenever I have reached my 36 ¼ hours, I give Rose my time sheet and then take the next working day off. So far there have been no problems. I usually end up taking off Monday."

Samantha: "Yeah, but what about the others in your unit? Don't they need you around?"

Amy: "Why, so they can ask me to do their photocopying? No way! They type up their own stuff, and everything is e-mailed. The time the staff do need me is when there is mass work to be done, like mail-outs. I'm never involved on urgent stuff. Plus, they know I'm on 'cww'. So if there is anything they need, they know to get it to me as soon as they find out about it."

After this discussion with Amy, Samantha was upset. It seemed unfair that the higher-rated position she occupied had less perks! She knew that it was pointless to go back to Jack or the Director with the information. They still would not allow her CWW. Also, she did not want to get Amy into trouble or cause her to lose out on her current situation. She began to resent her situation all the more, and thought about applying for other positions.

QUESTIONS

1. How does the role of the HR Strategies Branch within the Public Service contribute to the problems described in this case?

2. Critically assess the form of "matrix" structure employed by the Director.

3. What are the sources of job satisfaction and dissatisfaction for Samantha?

4. Does the dual reporting relationship (to her Manager and Director) worsen or improve Samantha's situation?

5. Is her resentment justified? Should she be entitled to CWW?

6. What should be done, if anything, by the Manager or Director about Samantha's request?

The John Highfield Company

The John Highfield Company is a large department store that has been in existence for many years. The company's main store and head office are located in the downtown area of one of Canada's largest cities, but the company also operates a number of branch stores in the surrounding suburbs as well as in a number of other cities. The particular branch being discussed in this case is located in a suburban area and has been operating successfully for close to ten years.

The store is divided into 20 different departments headed by three store managers who have joint responsibility for running the entire store. Figure 1 indicates the rough organizational structure of each department. As can be seen, the employees in each department report to their respective superiors in the hierarchy, but they may also receive instructions from any of the higher managerial levels. Consequently they may at times report directly to any one or more of the four higher levels of supervision. The employees have grown accustomed to this system or at least have not expressed much concern about the overlap. The section head reports to the assistant manager as well as to the department manager while the assistant manager reports only to the department manager. It has been established by tradition that the department manager is the only person from each department to report directly to the store managers. Basically, each department operates as a single unit competing with other departments for profitability and budget purposes.

The Furniture and Appliances department of this store had always maintained a good sales record and was generally regarded as a very profitable unit. The employees of this department were recognized as "high performers" and the department came to be regarded as the "ideal" department to work in. Mr. Guthrie, the previous department manager, was an amiable person and an effective boss who was highly respected not only by his own employees but also by the other employees throughout the store. The employees enjoyed working for him and they seemed to derive a great deal of satisfaction from their work. Unfortunately, during the last few months, major changes have taken place in the management of this department. All the existing managers or superiors were either promoted or transferred to other newly estab-

---

By Anwar Rashid. © L & S Management Publications.

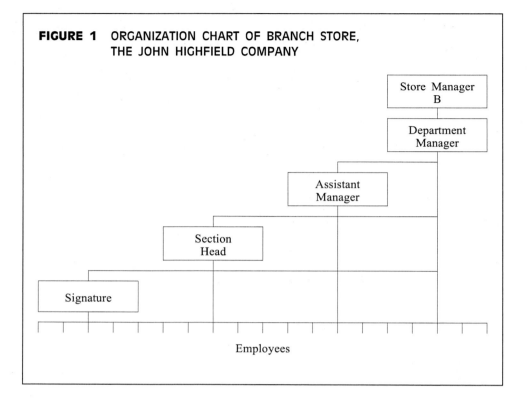

FIGURE 1 ORGANIZATION CHART OF BRANCH STORE, THE JOHN HIGHFIELD COMPANY

lished departments, and a whole new set of managerial staff have taken over the vacant positions. Mr. Guthrie was replaced by Mr. Broadbent as the department manager.

Mr. Broadbent is 30 years old. He has been with the company for seven years and has worked himself up from the position of salesman in the hardware department to the department manager of Furniture and Appliances. Before coming to work at John Highfield, Mr. Broadbent was studying for a degree in Psychology, which he did not complete. Originally, it was his ambition to become the personnel manager of this company. However, he relinquished this goal because of his failure to obtain his psychology degree which he believed, rightly or wrongly, was an essential prerequisite for the job.

The Furniture and Appliances department is no longer viewed by the employees as an "ideal" department to work in. They now refer to it as "the prison" with Mr. Broadbent as the "prison guard". In fact, his favourite position seems to resemble that of a prison guard — standing at the far end of the department with his arms folded, watching over his employees. As a result of his extremely close supervision, the employees in the department have become uptight and apprehensive, always wondering whether they are doing the right thing according to his expectations. Furthermore, Mr. Broadbent does not converse with any of his employees, and it is a rare privilege to get a "good morning" or "good night" out of him. If an employee greets him, it is very unlikely that he will get any response. The only persons that he treats in a normal way are the three supervisors below him in the department. However, he seems to be more than willing to "tell them off" if he is not pleased with their work. One of the company's policies is that employees must not talk to the store manager under any circumstances. They may speak if they are spoken to but they must not initiate the communication. If an employee violates this unwritten policy, he is severely reprimanded by his or her department manager.

Mr. Broadbent has an unusual way of running his department. He actually said to a newly hired employee, "Within three months, I intend to have you all fully trained so that you people can run this department without any help from me." At the same time, however, he also said to him that he must not do any work without checking with him first. No employee is to do work on his own initiative except serving the customers and tidying the area. Furthermore, if any work is done for any of the other supervisors without Mr. Broadbent's prior approval, then the employee concerned will be penalized. An employee will also be penalized for receiving personal phone calls each day, but he considers that his position entitles him to this privilege.

Lately, the employees have been expressing more and more dissatisfaction with the present state of affairs. Working simultaneously with the four levels of supervision, an employee may be instructed to perform several different tasks at the same time, each task assigned by a superior who has his own notion regarding the importance of the work he wants to get done. A problem of this nature arose three weeks ago when an employee by the name of Derek Matthews was told to do two different jobs by two different bosses. Mr. Broadbent had asked him to check the arrangement of some merchandise, which had in fact already been done that morning by another employee. However, the assistant manager approached Derek and asked him to do an important stock requisition that had to be sent out right away. This being a priority job, Derek dropped his merchandise-checking work and proceeded to compete the stock requisition. When Mr. Broadbent later saw Derek filling the requisition, he told him that he had no business undertaking the assignment given by the assistant manager when he had already been told to do something else by himself.

Occasionally, although very rarely, Mr. Broadbent will seek an employee's opinion on something related to departmental work. However, the employees have learned not to volunteer any opinion because Mr. Broadbent will criticize the idea from every possible angle simply to prove that he is always right. A general feeling of "worthlessness" now prevails among the employees of this department. They have developed the "couldn't care less" or "who cares" type of an attitude. Mr. Broadbent constantly gives them meaningless or unnecessary tasks just to keep them busy while he watches over them and cuts them down to size whenever a mistake is made. The employees believe that Mr. Broadbent has no feelings for his employees. Since all the other supervisory staff in the department are also relatively new, the employees do not really know how they stand in relation to these new bosses. A couple of weeks ago, Mr. Broadbent yelled at a female employee in front of customers and other employees, causing her to end up in tears in the stock room. The assistant manager went to comfort her and then approached Mr. Broadbent about the incident. Mr. Broadbent laughed it off by saying, "I really can't see why she was so upset. Don't worry, she'll get over it. And she probably won't make the same mistake again."

Another development worth mentioning is the high incidence of employees calling in sick ever since the change-over took place in the management of this department. The total number of persons employed is ten plus four members of the supervisory staff. On an average, three to four people report sick each week as opposed to an average of one every two weeks in the previous set-up under Mr. Guthrie. Several employees have said privately that they don't really care if they show up for work or not. They have neither the desire to help the company nor any sympathy with the department's management staff. In fact, they don't think twice now about calling in sick at the shortest possible notice. Even some of the students employed in the department began to stay home and study rather than go to work there, which shows how bad the situation was. As a result, when employees do show up for work, they generally do not do any more work than the bare minimum. They also tend to take longer breaks and lunches than are allowed. With Mr. Guthrie this was never as problem. Employees went to lunch on time and returned on time. However, it is now becoming a major issue in the department. People leave early and return late. This upsets the whole department's schedule. Because of this problem, Mr. Broadbent recently posted a sign reading "Break and Lunch: 15 minutes and one hour: Return on Time and Leave on Time." In response to this sign, employees now leave even earlier and arrive back even later, giving all manner of excuses when caught.

Unfortunately, many employees who previously enjoyed their job now dread it. One particular employee would really like to keep her job because she enjoys this type of work. However, she cannot tolerate the "prison" any longer. The only solution, other than quitting altogether, is to apply to head office for a transfer to Mr. Guthrie's new department. However, any such transfer would first have to be approved by Mr. Broadbent who has already stated that "if any employee seeks a transfer from this department, he will try to have him or her fired before he grants permission." Therefore, an employee who applies for a transfer really has only the choice of quitting the firm or staying in the same department with Mr. Broadbent and facing some retaliatory action.

The general employee dissatisfaction within the department and the dislike for Mr. Broadbent are becoming painfully apparent. It is so bad right now that four employees (four of the ten who have been there the longest and know the most about the department and its merchandise) have decided to quit. However, that is not all. They are all going to quit at the same time and plan on doing so the week before Christmas. As a result, the "prison" and Mr. Broadbent would be left high and dry in the busy season. Before they quit, the employees intend to go as a group to the store manager and have a discussion with him about the present circumstances. Although the pay and the discount privileges are good, they are not enough to compensate for the environment in which they work.

QUESTIONS

1. Identify and critically analyze Mr. Broadbent's leadership style.

2. Why have the employees become demotivated?

3. Have the organizational structure and policies contributed to the problem?

4. What should the store manager say when the group of quitting employees arrive for a discussion?

LiveLife Health Care

LiveLife Health Care Inc. owns and operates medical centres all over Alberta. At the top level, the company has two senior partners–owners: Bobby Baron, who is the CEO, and Justin Cole, who is responsible for business development and marketing. Vice-President of Operations Kelly Henderson reports to the senior partners and has three territory managers and the human resources manager report to her.

Shirley Adler is a territory manager of three branch offices. Due to recent restructuring, her territory was expanded to include an additional branch office in Pickering, where Jeannie Sparrow is the branch manager.

Shirley has been with the company for over six years, joining as Branch Manager and moving up to territory manager — managing two offices initially and now four offices. She is known for her expertise in operations and for having an in-depth knowledge of the organization's software systems. She won last year's "Territory Manager of the Year Award," a recognition based mostly upon the financial performance of the offices under her control. Although a warm-hearted person, Shirley has a strong personality and comes across as abrasive and abrupt when carrying out managerial duties. People who know and understand her attribute her shortcomings to her background, which included a tough, deprived childhood. Her supervisors have routinely indicated in her performance reviews that her communication skills need to be improved. She has been sent to courses on coaching and training in people-management skills, the most recent session being completed in the past year. She is hesitant to accept criticism, but has been known to make comments on her progress in managing and communicating with people, which indicates her awareness of her weaknesses. A recent project that Shirley coordinated was unsuccessful. The vendor she was liaising with became very upset and disappointed. The project required considerable coordination, and the vendor's lack of knowledge hadn't helped Shirley, who had become irritated with the vendor's contact person. Shirley's reaction to the incident was to advise management that the project was lost from the start due to unclear guidelines and a client that was difficult to deal with.

This case is based on original work by Rathika Jayasinghe.

Jeannie has been with the company for seven years, starting as a clerical employee, moving up to supervisor and then to branch manager. The dynamics of the Lethbridge branch location that Jeannie manages is unlike any other branch in the company. Jeannie has had to cope with the temperamental personalities of several of the medical service providers. Although her superiors have occasionally stepped in to assist her, she has ably managed the day-to-day operations of the branch, despite the difficult, demanding personalities of these doctors. She has at times departed from standard policies and procedures, but senior management has ignored these shortcomings due to her overall performance. Senior managers believe her headstrong and forthright style is necessary to manage this branch. The office staff knows that she will support them in disputes with the medical staff, when the latter are being unreasonable. Knowledgeable in all operational aspects, she strives to ensure that budgets are met on a weekly and monthly basis so that her team can receive a quarterly and annual bonus. Of late, however, her team has not been able to meet revenue figures, and top management has provided her with several options involving reducing numbers of staff and compensation. The implementation has been left to her discretion, as management felt she had the skills to turn around the situation in the branch.

Shirley took over as territory manager of Jeannie's branch office in April of last year. As the company's fiscal year ended in June, Shirley was responsible for completing Jeannie's performance review. Shirley indicated in the review that Jeannie was only "satisfactory" and still "developing" in areas such as "planning and organizing", "policy and image compliance", and "accuracy and attention to detail". Jeannie was shocked at her review and questioned it. Shirley provided examples of incidents where the lack of these skills was evident because the branch operations had departed from company standards. Although Jeannie believed otherwise, she grudgingly accepted the review. Then, at a recent branch team meeting that Jeannie was to facilitate, Shirley took over the meeting giving instructions on how the branch team must achieve its goals. Her attitude was high-handed and controlling, while Jeannie was left in the role of an observer.

Subsequently, Jeannie approached the vice-president of operations, Kelly Henderson, to request that she act as her own territory manager. She explained to Kelly that she didn't believe that she could continue to function effectively under her present manager. Jeannie provided several instances where Shirley's strong personality had been detrimental to her and her team.

Kelly had been involved in the hiring of Shirley and Jeannie. She had noticed Shirley's failure to improve her people-management skills and believed that a frank and open session between Jeannie and Shirley might help. Kelly advised Jeannie that it was a firm policy for every branch to report to a territory manager, and she should sort out matters with Shirley. Kelly suggested that a lunch meeting with Shirley might be helpful. Jeannie agreed to set up the meeting on the condition that Kelly would convey the reasons for the meeting to Shirley. Kelly told Shirley about the meeting, and advised Shirley that it would be best to be a listener at the meeting and hear Jeannie out.

The meeting did not go well. Jeannie indicated disappointment with Shirley and the lack of her support as a territory manager. She gave examples where Shirley had interfered with the management of her team, going around Jeannie and providing contradictory instructions. Jeannie vehemently expressed that Shirley's aggressive nature sent the wrong message to staff and that she should conduct herself in a calmer manner. Jeannie's outburst noticeably shocked Shirley, who remained almost totally silent. Jeannie indicated that she had been advised by Kelly that Shirley should not be shocked, as similar comments had been brought to her attention several times before. Jeannie's non-stop attack left Shirley upset to the point of tears, but she did not visibly react or answer Jeannie's complaints.

Kelly spoke to Shirley afterward and realized that Shirley was still reeling from the outburst. Jeannie was also left feeling discouraged that she had voiced her concerns and had received no response from Shirley. Kelly felt the need for a different approach to Shirley to help her understand what went wrong during the meeting. Kelly requested owner and CEO Bobby Baron to meet with Shirley to discuss the issues of her leadership.

Shirley was still visibly upset as she began the meeting with Bobby, who asked her what she thought of the meeting with Jeannie.

Shirley said, "Well, it was a verbal bashing session."

"So, what did you do to manage it and make it a more productive one?" asked Bobby.

"I was told that Jeannie was voicing some of her concerns and my job was to sit and listen and not to react," replied Shirley. "I proceeded to do just that."

"So, as Jeannie's manager, you feel your lack of action was justified?" asked Bobby.

"Completely," replied Shirley. "I was instructed by my boss not to respond, and since Jeannie obviously felt that I had wronged her in so many ways, I didn't want to add fuel to the fire."

"Yes," agreed Bobby. "However, was there no opportunity to use the skills from your coaching and mentoring sessions? I know it must not have been easy to sit and listen to Jeannie. Perhaps you needed to stop her and guide the conversation in a more productive direction."

"I understand what you are saying, Bobby," responded Shirley. "But you must understand my situation. Here I am sent like a lamb to the slaughter, without any advance notice about what will be discussed, and then my subordinate verbally lashes out at me without a worry in the world, simply because she had the approval of my boss. How can I even possibly begin to react to the situation?"

QUESTIONS

1. Do you agree that Shirley's review of Jeannie was likely unfair?

2. Should Shirley have been more active during her meeting with Jeannie and, if so, how?

3. Evaluate the meeting between Shirley and Bobby. Do you think it will have positive results?

4. From the information in the case, assess Shirley's leadership style, and contrast it with an optimal style for that situation.

5. What should be done to improve Shirley's leadership performance?

Machined Solutions Inc.

The firm is an eastern Canadian machining company manufacturing precision components principally for the agriculture, transportation, medical, mining, and aerospace industries. Primary markets have been developed in North America, and there is a minority of overseas sales. Currently, Machined Solutions has 50 employees.

A BRIEF HISTORY OF MACHINED SOLUTIONS

Smith had established a highly respected reputation for his engineering and manufacturing excellence within the manufacturing community. Previously, he had worked for a large, specialty machining shop in the Pacific region of Canada for 15 years. Seeing an untapped niche for high quality, precision machining, Smith was beginning to be frustrated within the larger company and developed a business plan to start his own company. Smith quit his job, refined his business plan, and approached a number of individuals and venture capital companies to finance the start-up of Machined Solutions. The individuals and companies Smith approached for financing required control of the company, and/or the cost of capital was extremely high. Smith was unprepared to enter into an arrangement whereby he lost control of Machined Solutions.

Close to depleting his savings used to support his family in the year since he had quit his job, Smith approached a long time friend, Gitano, who was also the president of a private holding company in Quebec, referred to in this case as "Holdco". Holdco invested primarily in real estate, but had a desire to diversify into other ventures to offset the cyclical nature of real estate. After discussions of the proposal and analysis of the business plan by Holdco's Vice President, Levesque, an ownership structure was agreed upon whereby Gitano and Holdco would each own 50% of the common shares in Machined Solutions. This ownership structure was a departure from Holdco's normal pattern of controlling companies within its group. It reflected the long time friendship of Smith and Gitano. Gitano would be able to help his friend realize a dream of running his own company and, at the same time,

---

This case is based on original work by D. Paul Graham.

acquire a company to meet Holdco's objective of diversification within its risk/ return preferences. Holdco agreed to invest $150,000 in Machined Solutions to purchase two machining centres to be acquired from Japan.

Machined Solutions's shareholder's agreement reflected the respective responsibilities of each party. In essence, Smith was to be responsible for all day-to-day operations of Machined Solutions, and Holdco would be responsible for all financial, banking, legal, and other such decisions affecting Machined Solutions. Smith's engineering and manufacturing brilliance and Holdco's financial sophistication and business acumen would be an effective combination with which to start the company. Machined Solutions was incorporated in the fall of 2001, and commenced actual manufacturing in January 2002.

Six months after startup, an opportunity arose for Machined Solutions to acquire a local competitor that would quadruple its manufacturing capacity. In order to finance the acquisition, it was necessary for Holdco to guarantee bank loans. Holdco perceived an increase in the level of risk for their investment in Machined Solutions as a result of these guarantees. Smith was offered the option of maintaining the original growth plans, as detailed by his previous business plan, and keep his ownership position at 50%; or he could decrease his ownership position to 30% (bringing Holdco's ownership position to 70%) and acquire the competitor. Smith desired greatly to see the company grow as quickly as possible, and agreed to the minority ownership position. He therefore relinquished control of the company to Holdco. Despite the change in control, the respective responsibilities remained the same as previously stipulated in the shareholder's agreement.

In addition to contending with problems inherent with such rapid growth, Machined Solutions was confronted with an economic downturn throughout North America. Machined Solutions failed to reach its financial objectives, and started to lose money. However, both shareholders were committed to investing in new technology for the firm and the development of a quality system that exceeded customer expectations. Holdco funded the operational losses and maintained working capital for Machined Solutions. But the first quarter of fiscal year 2003 ended with severe losses. In fact, Machined Solutions was the poorest performer of the Holdco group of companies. Levesque was sent to the plant to review operations and labour costs in an attempt to reverse this cash drain. Smith, however, still felt strongly about expanding the company through technology acquisitions despite the poor financial performance. Gitano had invested substantially more money than was originally planned, and was vocal in his expectation for Machined Solutions to show breakeven performance in the short run and quick achievement of projected profit levels. No further capital acquisitions would be allowed by Holdco until such time as costs were controlled. Smith was upset by this, and voiced his displeasure many times with Gitano and Levesque about the ownership structure. In one meeting in particular, Smith stated that he felt taken advantage of, and said that he had been out-negotiated by Holdco in the ownership restructuring. Gitano very clearly indicated that as the risk increased with the acquisitions, so should have the ownership position. If Smith didn't like this, he should not have gone after the acquisition. Smith stated that he felt that he didn't have a choice in the matter. He said that unless Machined Solutions could become the foremost firm in its field, "he would not be achieving his personal goals."

Despite the poor financial performance, Machined Solutions continued to be recognized as a high quality machining plant. A large contract was won with a major agricultural machinery producer. More machining capacity was required to fulfil orders, but banks were hesitant to lend further capital to Machined Solutions because of its history of losses and the general economic climate of the early 2000s. Holdco arranged external financing for new machinery to meet production requirements, and capped its investment in Machined Solutions at the current level of $750,000.

Smith continued to want to expand Machined Solutions by capital investment in technology. Attempts were made, unsuccessfully, to raise additional capital to acquire more machinery. Holdco was unprepared to increase its risk profile in Machined Solutions, and Smith was becoming increasingly impatient with what he saw as foregone revenue and market share opportunities due to limited production capacity. Smith began to openly express his desire to buy out Holdco, but could not afford to finance such a move. Holdco was willing to sell, but insisted on a price that would give it a decent return for its investment. Gitano and Smith were barely on speaking terms, but neither could see a clear way out of their increasingly unpleasant relationship.

QUESTIONS

1. Would you judge that Smith's or Holdco's plans were the best for the present and future of Machined Solutions, and why?

2. What do the behaviour of Smith and the events in this case tell you about the motivation and values of entrepreneurs? What rewards was Smith seeking, and how did they compare with the rewards that Holdco wished to obtain?

3. Research into the "entrepreneurial personality" reveals that a strong need for control over the business is nearly always present. Why do you suppose Smith was willing to give up his control over Machined Solutions at the time of the takeover?

4. Do you believe that the positions of Smith and Holdco are reconcilable, and why?

5. You are a consultant called in by Holdco to recommend a solution. Present the executive summary of your report, and provide full reasons for your recommendations.

Mason Electric

Professor William R. Mason's original "call" system was simple. It electrically sig-nalled the furnace room when a classroom needed more heat or had too much. Intrigued by the idea but dissatisfied with the device, Professor Mason went on to invent the first all-electric room thermostat. In 1885 he left the teaching profession and founded the Mason Electric Service Company.

The successor, Mason Electric, is a multinational corporation employing over 23,000 people in six divisions. This includes 113 branch offices in Canada and the United States, and manufacturing facilities in 29 locations (11 countries) throughout the world.

The Canadian division, Mason Electric (Canada) Ltd., includes 14 branch offices from coast to coast and head office operations (administrative, research, design, and manufacturing) in Toronto. All accounting and personnel functions for Canada are handled by the head office in Toronto without much interference from the corporate head office in the United States.

During the years in which the events described in this case took place, the Canadian operation showed increased profits: 17.5% for 1977 over 1976 (Figure 1) and 34.2% for 1978 over 1977 (Figure 2). The company's forecast for 1979 was for a 20% increase over 1978, but this had yet to materialize (Figure 3).

Employee morale at the branch level is very high, and this probably accounts for the continued sales activity. Unlike the "open door" type of atmosphere at the branch, the employee situation at head office seems tense and unsettled. Over the last two years, there has in fact been a steady exodus of employees from head office to the branches and other companies.

During 1978, the corporate head office in the United States was alerted to a potential employee problem when two managers (each with over ten years' service) resigned. Further investigation revealed that the overall turnover rate was increasing drastically, and the profit/loss picture was trending to less satisfactory levels. The corporate heads reacted by appointing a new Canadian president.

The new president was renowned for his successful managerial practices in other areas of the company. Within four months of his appointment, the executive committee had four new faces. Most of these new faces came in the form of suc-

FIGURE 1

MASON ELECTRIC (CANADA) LTD.
Profit & Loss Statement
for the 12 Months Ended December 31, 1977
(in thousands of dollars)

	Year-to-Date		
	ACTUAL	**PLAN**	**LAST YEAR**
Gross Sales	28,642	29,278	22,616
Cost of Sales	19,826	19,703	15,234
Gross Profit	8,816	9,575	7,382
% to Sales	*30.8*	*32.7*	*32.6*
Selling-Adm. Exp.	6,158	6,319	5,175
Operating Profit	2,658	3,256	2,207
Other Income (expense)	80	80	124
Pre-tax Income	2,738	3,346	2,331
% to Sales	*9.6*	*11.4*	*10.3*

FIGURE 2

MASON ELECTRIC (CANADA) LTD.
Profit & Loss Statement
for the 12 Months Ended December 31, 1978
(in thousands of dollars)

	Year-to-Date		
	ACTUAL	**PLAN**	**LAST YEAR**
Gross Sales	32,979	34,164	28,642
Cost of Sales	22,773	23,353	19,793
Gross Profit	10,206	10,611	8,849
% to Sales	*30.9*	*31.1*	*30.9*
Factory Profit Realized	567	659	680
Manufacturing Variances	(471)	(499)	(713)
Gross Profit	10,302	10,771	8,816
% to Sales	*31.2*	*31.5*	*30.8*
Selling-Adm. Exp.	6,964	6,989	6,158
Operating Profit	3,338	3,782	2,658
% to Sales	*10.1*	*11.1*	*9.3*
Other Income (expense)	336	(115)	80
Pre-Tax Income	3,674	3,667	2,738
% to Sales	*11.1*	*10.7*	*9.6*

FIGURE 3

MASON ELECTRIC (CANADA) LTD.
Profit & Loss Statement
for the 10 Months Ended October 31, 1979
(in thousands of dollars)

	Year-to-Date		
	ACTUAL	**PLAN**	**LAST YEAR**
Gross Sales	21,593	25,755	22,762
Cost of Sales	15,262	17,640	15,881
Gross Profit	6,331	8,115	6,881
% to Sales	*29.3*	*31.5*	*30.2*
Factory Profit Realized	447	560	329
Manufacturing Variances	(306)	(545)	(523)
Gross Profit	6,472	8,130	6,687
% to Sales	30.0	31.6	29.4
Selling-Adm. Exp.	6,217	6,620	5,503
Operating Profit	255	1,510	1,184
% to Sales	*1.2*	*5.9*	*5.2*
Other Income (expense)	206	(180)	386
Pre-Tax Income	461	1,330	1,570
% to Sales	*2.1*	*5.2*	*6.9*

cessful former branch managers, whose newly vacated positions were, in turn, filled by the displaced members of the executive committee.

The Toronto head office consists of 155 employees. Of these, 48 are production workers and another 107 are in engineering, design, accounting, etc. (See Figure 4.) There have been 22 terminations and two transfers from the production floor (approx. 45%). From the 107, there were 24 terminations (approx. 22%) and 12 transfers. During 1979, a staggering number of head office employees left for greener pastures.

The chief problem that faced the new top management in mid-1978 was the disorganization caused by employees leaving their positions. In some departments the turnover rate was so high that people never had time to adjust. This was creating problems with the branches, which require quick and accurate product information if they are to remain competitive.

The president realized that it would take time to get to the heart of the turnover problem. Meanwhile he must change the structure of his departments so that, if any department member left the company, his or her job functions could easily be taken over by someone else.

FIGURE 4 FORMAL ORGANIZATIONAL CHART OF THE TORONTO HEAD OFFICE OF MASON ELECTRIC (CANADA) LTD.

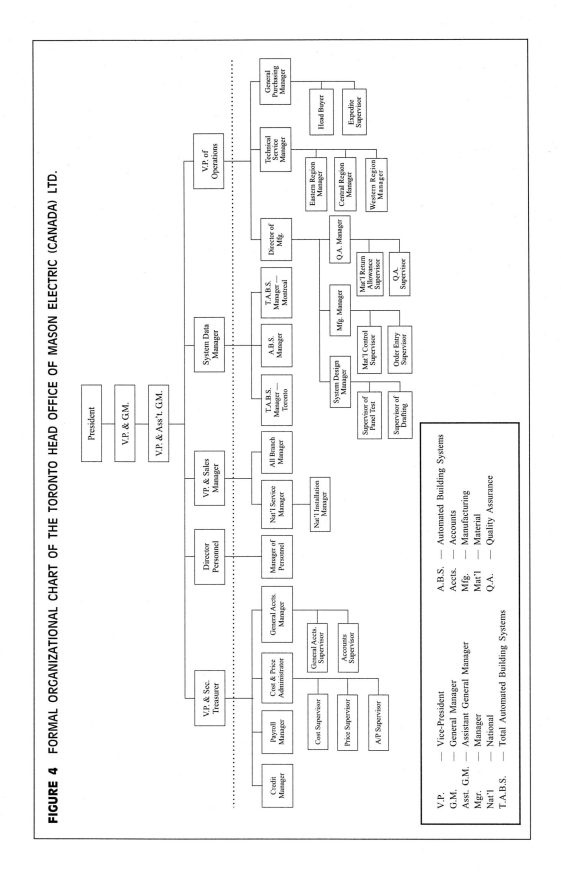

Department heads were then given specific instructions, and they in turn passed down specific task directives to their subordinates. "Standard Practice Instructions" manuals were developed, and specific job functions established throughout each department. Now, if someone left, there would at least be detailed standard written instructions of his or her job function within the organization.

This procedure did decrease the disruption caused by the high level of employee turnover, slightly improving the overall efficiency of the departments. However, it also tended to make the employees' roles quite rigid. The program was supposedly a temporary measure to buy some time to tackle the root problem. While the middle managers and supervisors were busy implementing this new approach, top management was busy sending out "feelers".

One step taken by top management in an endeavour to locate the cause of the high rate of employee turnover was to request that all terminating employees fill out a questionnaire. Basically it asked, "What made you dissatisfied with your job?" and, "What changes would you recommend?"

At first, the completed questionnaires were not taken seriously because some of the comments written for the latter question were apparently quite facetious. However, a distinct pattern started to emerge from the answers to the former question. (See Figure 5.) The results indicated a communication problem with regard to the evaluation of an employee's performance. The upward communication link was

---

FIGURE 5

INTER-OFFICE CORRESPONDENCE

DATE	October 19, 1979
SUBJECT	Performance Appraisals
FROM	D.A. Bigler — Toronto
TO	Branch/Department Managers, Department Heads

Further to my letter of June 4, 1979, we wish to remind you that a copy of performance appraisal form #6101 must be submitted for each employee who is being considered for a salary increase associated with our 1980 general salary review.

These forms are to be received by the Personnel Department by November 1, 1979.

During a recent study concerning exit interviews with terminating employees, it was learned that one of the main dissatisfiers was that the employees were never afforded the opportunity to discuss their performance with their supervisor.

Please do not let this happen to us!

DAB:dm

suspect. Therefore, policies were considered to establish closer links between subordinates and their supervisors.

These conclusions took many months to form. During this time, the downward communication channel was becoming well established. Job descriptions in the form of specific task directives were flowing downward, along with information on organizational practices and procedures. Rigid instructions became the measure of the day. Meanwhile, the employee exodus continued.

FIGURE 6

Employee Self-Evaluation

NAME

JOB TITLE

BRANCH

NO. OF YEARS IN PRESENT POSITION

DATE

1. Do you basically agree with your job title?
2. In what areas are you satisfied with your performance and growth this past year?
3. What do you feel are your strengths?
4. In what areas are you not satisfied with your growth and performance this past year?
5. What do you feel are your weaknesses?
6. What personal goals were achieved this past year?
7. What personal goals were not fulfilled?
8. What are your goals for the year ahead?
9. What are your long range goals?
10. What obstacles do you see that might keep you from achieving your goals?
11. How do you feel your department can become more effective and efficient in the year ahead?
12. Do you know what the objectives of your department are for the year ahead?
13. Are you happy in your present position? If not, why?
14. Please describe briefly how you feel the department performed this past year, outlining strengths and weaknesses.
15. What are your expectations for the performance of the department for the year ahead?
16. Do you feel you are being adequately trained?
17. Do you have any responsibilities outside the department office that affect or contribute to your position at MEL?
18. Are there any other items you feel need to be discussed at this time?

(Answer questions on separate sheet)

FIGURE 7 SUMMARY PERFORMANCE APPRAISAL FORM

Employee Name		Social Security No.
Location Name		Location No.
Position Title	Payroll (Check One)	☐ 2 = Weekly ☐ 3 = Monthly ☐ 4 = Part Time
Appraisal Covers Time Period:	From	To

☐ **Annual Appraisal** — years in current job _____

Complete this section if this is an Annual Appraisal (for employees who have completed their probationary period):

Overall Performance

Review the entire performance appraisal and judge the employees' overall performance in current job. Place the appropriate number of the rating in the box to the left.

	OUTSTANDING	HIGH	COMPETENT	NEEDS IMPROVEMENT	UNSATISFACTORY
☐	1 Far exceeds overall standards for this job	2 Exceeds overall standards for this job	3 Meets overall standards for this job	4 Needs improvement to meet standards for this job	5 Fails to meet standards for this job

FIGURE 7 SUMMARY PERFORMANCE APPRAISAL FORM (Continued)

Overall Potential

Judge the employee's capacity and ambition for future advancement, both within the current department or branch and within MEL. Place the appropriate number of the rating in the box to the left.

| | 1 | Outstanding candidate for future development. Could be expected to go far | 2 | Capable of developing beyond current position | 3 | Has probably reached most suitable level of work | 4 | Uncertain at this time |

☐ **Probationary Appraisal**

Complete this section if this is a Probationary Appraisal (for employees currently in or completing their probationary period, including new employees and recent transfers or promotions).

Overall Performance

Review the employee's overall performance since starting work. Judge performance against standards for a trainee. Place the appropriate number of the rating in the box to the left.

| | 1 | Performance has been adequate or better than expected for a trainee END PROBATION | 2 | Performance has been only minimally adequate for a trainee. Certain areas need improvement EXTEND PROBATION | 3 | Performance has been less than satisfactory TERMINATE or DEMOTE and EXTEND PROBATION |

FIGURE 7 SUMMARY PERFORMANCE APPRAISAL FORM (Continued)

Complete this section for all employees:

1. What are the employee's major strengths?

2. What areas need improvement? What actions are being taken to rectify the situation?

3. General Remarks: Indicate any comments to further clarify this evaluation.

To the employee — Please sign below to indicate that you have seen this appraisal.

Employee's Signature _____ Date _____

Supervisor's Signature _____ Date _____

Branch Manager's Signature _____ Date _____

Regional Manager's Signature _____ Date _____
(If different from Supervisor)

Three programs were developed almost simultaneously by three department heads (accounting, personnel, and manufacturing) to foster upward communication: an employee self-evaluation questionnaire (Figure 6) for use by supervisors and their superiors; a job appraisal form (Figure 7) that a supervisor used to rate an employee's performance; and last but not least, a committee called ICC (Interdepartmental Communication Committee) was formed.

These attempts to institutionalize the feedback had, to the latter part of 1979, failed miserably. The self-evaluation form was to be handed to an employee's immediate supervisor. Many employees, especially those that had not been with the company long, were very intimidated by the questions asked. As a result, they were reluctant to write what they actually felt for fear of recrimination or reprisal. The information collected from this type of census becomes what employees feel their bosses want to hear. There were not too many people who wished to discuss their weaknesses (question 5 of Figure 6) or how they feel their department performed this past year (question 14). The latter question hints at an assessment of the competency of department heads or supervisors.

Another weakness with this evaluation was the insistence on determining the employees' personal goals (nearly one-third of the questions pertain to this). If an employee was planning to quit the company within the next year, the chances were nil that he would have highlighted this as his future goal.

The job appraisal form was a summary of an employee's performance. It placed numbers (one is outstanding and five is unsatisfactory) on a person's performance, and this rating was completed by an employee's immediate supervisor. The supervisor then allowed his subordinate to see the appraisal, and sign that he has seen it. This tended to place supervisors in a vulnerable position and, in some cases, has caused outward hostility by an employee toward his supervisor.

The Interdepartmental Communication Committee was established as a back up to the other programs. Its function was to supply verification for the self-evaluation form and to hear the needs of the employees. Unlike the other institutionalized programs (self-evaluation and job-appraisal), the ICC idea could potentially supply a more personalized form of communication with the potential to establish a natural upward flow. The shortcomings of this committee are twofold. First, the committee had as its chairman the payroll manager, who answers directly to a member of the executive committee (vice-president and secretary-treasurer). Second, top management has (by November 1979) yet to interpret the information collected by the ICC in a serious manner. Many managers actually condemn the idea of the committee. They feel they are being talked about, and declare that the committee meetings (once a month for two hours) cut into valuable working time.

The committee was to have voluntary membership, with a limit of one representative from each department. Members were not to be appointed by department heads, but picked by their peers to act as representatives. Since the committee was not taken very seriously, it was not seriously supervised by top management. As a result, committee members were appointed by their department heads. This was the very situation that the committee was trying to avoid (usually, the appointee was one in favour with his/her supervisor).

Some departments did, however, choose their representative by the democratic process. In some of those cases, the manager or supervisor was chosen. However, other managers and supervisors tended to shun those elected by their subordinates.

The format of the committee is fairly simple. One week prior to a meeting, departmental representatives submit topics for review (these topics should stem from discussions by employees and the ICC representatives in individual departments). The chairman then publishes an agenda with the topics in a priority ranking. His bias, of course, determines the ranking. Since meetings to date have lasted only two hours, the lower priority items were usually postponed to future meetings. This set up some hostility among certain departmental representatives. The downfall of the committee was becoming more evident with every new meeting. In December 1979, just 16 months after its first meeting, there are only six departments remaining with representation (out of 13). For this reason, there is a lot of destructive criticism regarding the committee's future function.

The chief cause of the committee's downfall began last year when there were rumours within the company that a new benefits package was being considered for 1980. The ICC felt that this would be an excellent opportunity to show how effective it could be. Permission was eventually granted for the committee to carry out an independent survey on certain benefit proposals. The following is a description of the meeting that proposed the survey.

Since all departments were concerned about the benefit package, it obtained a high priority on the upcoming ICC meeting scheduled for May. The idea of the survey was first introduced by a member of the cost accounting department. Her motion was seconded, and accepted by a majority (nearly unanimous) vote.

The existing benefits package was discussed and, from certain ICC observations, preliminary questions were prepared. They took the form of a questionnaire (Figure 8) that would be handed out with the pay cheques and collected by means of a suggestion box. (The committee actually killed two birds with one stone; the company never had a suggestion box prior to this survey.)

The company's existing benefits included two weeks' vacation for service up to seven years. After seven years' service the employee would receive three weeks; after ten years, four weeks; and after 15, six weeks. Medical insurance would be paid for by the company after one year's service, but there was no dental plan. There was a salary continuation program for which each employee paid a weekly amount. Hours of work were 37.5 a week for administration, and 40 for the production group.

The results of the benefits questionnaire were summarized and submitted with recommendations to the personnel director. The majority of workers were not in favour of a shared cost dental plan. About 30% were in favour of a profit-sharing plan in the form of an RRSP, based upon the company matching an employee's donation from company profits (if over 20% for the past year). The topic that raised the most concern was the vacation allowance. An overwhelming majority was in favour of three weeks after three years and four weeks after seven. The ICC felt it had contributed effectively to the needs of the majority of employees, and hoped that the top brass would treat their recommendations and findings seriously.

FIGURE 8

Employee Survey

The employee is asked to fill out, with his benefit in mind, the following questionnaire.

No names are to be given and try to give comments where instructed. It is in your best interest to give accurate and honest answers.

Please print all comments.

Thank you.

1. Are you satisfied with the company's present program?

   ☐ Yes   ☐ No

   Comments:

2. Were you satisfied with your last pay increase?

   ☐ Yes   ☐ No (if no, give reasons)

   Comments:

3. Are you in favour of a dental plan?

   ☐ Yes   ☐ No (if no, give reasons)

   Comments:

4. Are you satisfied with the vacation schedule?

   ☐ Yes   ☐ No (if no, give reasons)

   Comments:

5. Do you understand the profit-sharing concept?

   ☐ Yes   ☐ No (if no, please consult your supervisor)

   Comments:

6. Would you be in favour of investing in a profit-sharing program (similar to an RRSP) with the company?

   ☐ Yes   ☐ No (if no, give reasons)

   Comments:

7. What is your main complaint with the present benefit program?

   ☐ None   ☐ Other (if other, give explanation)

   Comments:

The new benefits package was presented to the employees in four groups on four different days. Expectation was high until word got out after the first group had received the presentation. The vacation schedule would remain the same; a dental program would be established providing there was 40% membership; and the company was offering the new profit-sharing program.

After the deadlines for enrolment into the different programs had passed, a newsletter was sent out to all employees. There would be no dental plan (only about 28% enrolment), and the profit-sharing plan only interested 18% of the employees (down from about 30% when the survey was taken). The disastrous profit-sharing plan (the committee feels) was the result of retaliation for the insensitive decisions of top management. The ICC lost most of its integrity that day.

From then on, membership in the committee fell, and general morale dropped to an all time low. In fact, the committee was to have only one small victory. For years the company parking lot had not been paved, and in winter many cars would get bogged down in the snow. Two months ago, the lot was paved after an ICC recommendation.

The committee's recommendations for combined break and lunch hours, summer hours (working extra time each day for one Friday off a month), a bowling league, and a social club have been ignored. Proposals to remove names from evaluation forms and to have an outside chairman for the committee have fallen on deaf ears. In fact, most people have come to the conclusion that the committee is a waste of time and soon will be dismantled.

Office personnel are still encouraged to take their breaks and even lunch at their desks. There are three different breaks and lunch periods, as well as two starting and quitting times. No socializing between departments is allowed without good reasons, and socialization at lunch (bowling at nearby lanes) is discouraged, with punctuality as the main reason.

The ICC comprised secretaries, clerks, supervisors, foremen, and a manager. Even with this cross section, they could not influence top management. The most recent proposal was for a reward (in the form of cash bonuses) for developments or innovations that benefit the company. Again, the committee was shocked at a refusal based on, "People would be going off on all kinds of tangents."

The "temporary" rigid job descriptions now seem to be here to stay, and they are creating alienation. More and more, there is a race for the door when quitting time comes around, and people are generally doing only what is required to get by. The relationships between roles and employees have become more formalized. As a result, the organization is becoming less dependent on the services of particular individuals. The system, as it now stands, is barely coping with a high turnover, and has become only partially successful as a coping mechanism rather than as a preventive check.

At the next ICC meeting on December 7th, the committee, will put forward the following suggestions:

1. That every department be represented by a nominated employee.
2. That an outside neutral party be hired to chair the committee and that he or she will report to the president.

3. That the committee meet on a regular basis.

4. That top management take turns (when the need arises) in attending the committee meetings.

5. That management consult the ICC regarding any planned changes in company policy concerning benefits, job descriptions, and working conditions.

6. That an employee's identification on self-evaluative or opinion forms becomes optional, or that the forms be eliminated.

7. That employees be encouraged to use the suggestion box through a system in which innovative employees are formally recognized or rewarded.

QUESTIONS

1. (a) What are the problems faced by Mason Electric (Canada) Ltd.?
   (b) What are the root causes of the problems you have identified?
   (c) If these problems and root causes were solved, what would be the **first** indicators of this change?

2. Assess the function of the Interdepartmental Communications Committee, highlighting the factors that are necessary for its success.

3. What levels of management would be most threatened by an effective ICC?

4. Evaluate the policies put into effect to deal with high turnover.

5. Will the suggestions proposed in the December 7th meeting, if adopted, significantly improve the situation at Mason Electric?

6. If you were the president of the company, what would you do?

Metropolitan General Insurance

This case depicts events at an Oshawa, Ontario, branch office of a large international insurance company, Metropolitan General Insurance Co. It is one of the top 15 general insurance companies in Canada, with annual premium income of almost $200 million. Although its head office is located in Toronto, the company transacts business through independent insurance agents and brokers right across Canada through 20 branches.

Metropolitan General is committed to a decentralized operating structure, with the various branches having autonomy for their daily operations, including types of business written, agents to deal with, selection and utilization of staff, and a full branch operating budget. Head office is used as a resource centre in the financial area (investment planning and control), and also provides technical expertise (e.g., the various product line managers provide guidance and knowledge to the branch staff). The company has out-performed the industry over the past five years in the areas of underwriting profit and premium income growth. Ultimately, this was not the case at the Oshawa branch.

THE OSHAWA BRANCH

This branch employs 30 people, including the branch manager and the various department managers (see Figure 1 for the organization chart). The branch was opened seven years ago to take advantage of the growth opportunities that were developing east of Toronto in the areas of personal insurance and commercial insurance (i.e., fire, liability, and casualty insurance for commercial enterprises).

The staff complement of 30 is made up as follows:

1	branch manager
3	department managers
1	personnel supervisor
3	senior underwriters/examiners
7	intermediate underwriters/examiners
5	junior underwriters/examiners
10	clerical staff

FIGURE 1 ORGANIZATIONAL CHART OF THE OSHAWA BRANCH OF METROPOLITAN GENERAL INSURANCE

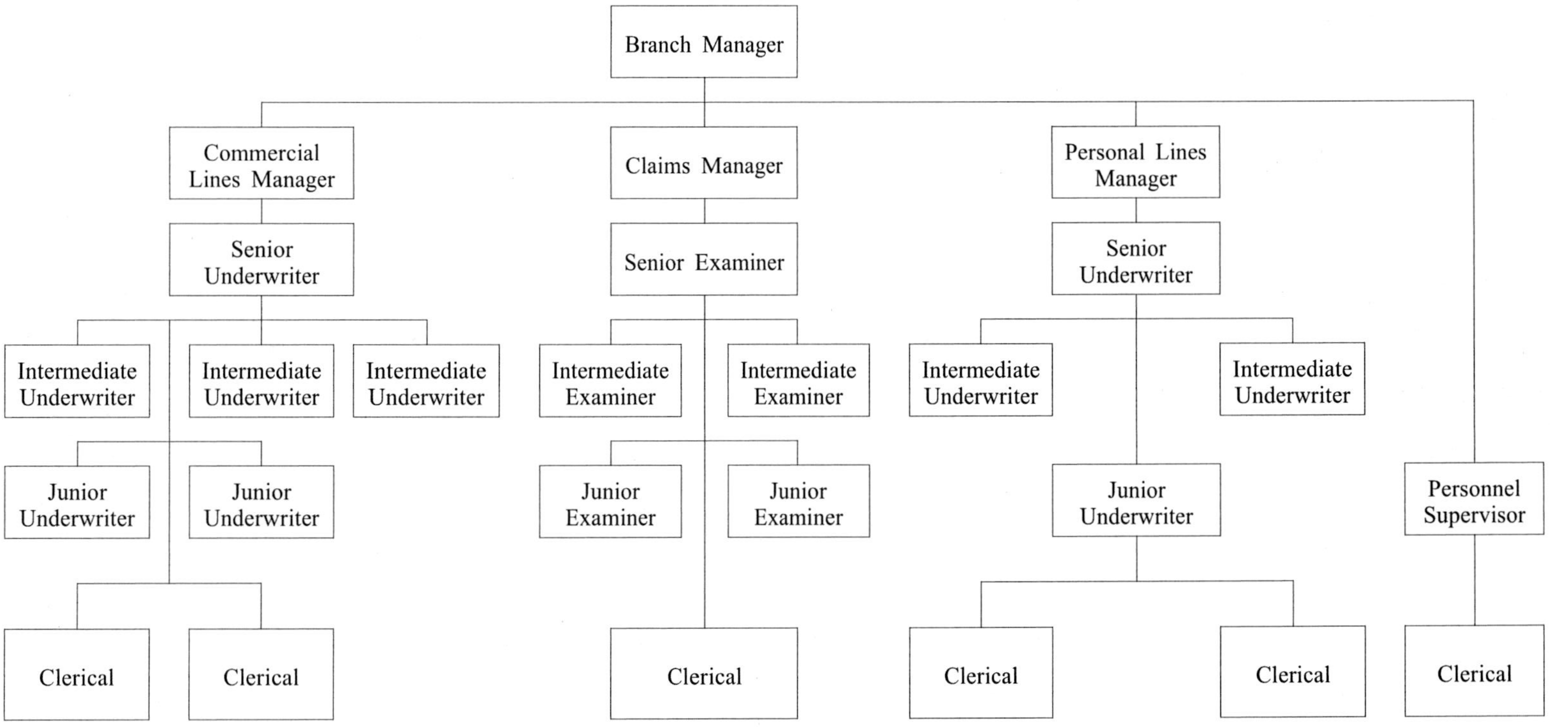

The staff are divided into four departments in order to facilitate the overall branch operation. These departments and their staff complements are as follows:

Management/Administration	7 staff
Commercial Lines department	9 staff
Personal Lines department	7 staff
Claims department	7 staff

The various departments operate almost independently of each other. Coordinating them is the responsibility of the branch manager and the personnel supervisor.

The branch transacts business through an independent agency network consisting of 152 brokers located throughout its five territories (running east of Toronto to Kingston, as well as recently acquired territory north of Toronto to Barrie). The branch had premium income at the end of last year of $8.5 million, and an underwriting loss (excess of claims paid out over premiums paid in) of $1.1 million. Its projected premium income for this year is $7.6 million, and it hopes to "break even" with respect to underwriting profit/loss.

Following is a brief description of the managers and other key staff members within the Oshawa branch:

Branch Manager — Larry Gelbart   Larry is 43 years old, and has been a branch manager for ten years. He has been with Metropolitan General for over 25 years, and has worked his way up through the ranks to the branch manager position. Gelbart was given the job of opening the Oshawa branch. (He had previously been manager of a smaller branch in another province.) The position was awarded on the understanding that significant growth and profit would enable him to progress further up the corporate ladder to the executive level at head office. He is considered to be a close friend of the company president, having worked with him as a department manager. However, he is not well liked by many of the other senior executives in the firm because they consider him "pushy". Branch employees, on the other hand, feel that they hardly know him.

Commercial Lines Manager — Sadie Tompkins   Tompkins is 29 years old, and has held this position for approximately one year. Prior to being appointed Commercial Lines Manager in the Oshawa branch, she had been an assistant to one of the head office line managers for two years. There she dealt very effectively with the paper flow, but rarely with people. Tompkins has been with Metropolitan General for almost eight years and had worked, prior to her most recent appointment, purely in a technical underwriting capacity. Her staff see her as quite demanding — sometimes unreasonable.

Claims Manager — Harry Higman   Harry is 55 years old, and has been in the insurance business for over 35 years (the last 11 with Metropolitan General). Prior to becoming Claims Manager in Oshawa, Harry had been a senior examiner in a larger branch in Ontario. His appointment to department manager was somewhat of a surprise to the others. He had not previously exhibited any management ambitions. Higman is considered to be technically competent by the line managers he deals with in head office. However, he considers that the head office is interfering in his department whenever they query anything. Problems among his staff make him feel uncomfortable.

Personal Lines Manager — Connie Burns   Connie is 27 years old, and has held her present position for only two months. She was appointed from within the Oshawa branch to replace an incumbent, Bob Hood, who had been promoted to the position of senior underwriter within the branch. Previously, she had spent one year in the Oshawa branch as a commercial lines underwriter, and five years in other branches in the Personal Lines area. She is well regarded in the head office, particularly for her "people skills". Her appointment as a manager in Oshawa was looked upon very favourably by the rest of the staff.

Personnel Supervisor — Ruth Burkholtz   Ruth is 34 years old, and has held her present position since the opening of the Oshawa branch, when she was hired by Metropolitan General. She had no previous experience in personnel, but has learned well on the job. She is a close confidant of the branch manager, Larry Gelbart, and he relies upon her input in his decision making. She has tended to be jealously protective of Gelbart. She occasionally restricts input and access to him by other staff, including managers.

Senior Underwriter, Personal Lines — Helen Whiteface   Helen is 54 years old, and has been with Metropolitan General for 28 years (seven years in her present position with the Oshawa branch and 21 years in a similar position in another branch). She is considered to be very technically sound and she enjoys the confidence of Gelbart, who had worked with her in another branch. He specifically requested her for Oshawa. She is seen by some of the junior staff as a benign matriarch. That is a perception that pleases her, and she does nothing to discourage it. She views herself as the expert in Personal Lines and the anchor for the department over the past seven years. She is often the focal point of small groups of staff during lunch time and coffee breaks.

Senior Underwriter, Commercial Lines — Bob Hood   Bob is 41 years old, and has been in the insurance business for 17 years. He was hired by Metropolitan General three years ago to fill his present position in the Oshawa branch. Hood is considered technically expert in his line, but is seen as somewhat reluctant to make decisions and often appears disorganized. He had been promoted briefly by Gelbart to Commercial Lines Manager. However, he was quickly and quietly demoted when he encountered problems and complaints from some brokers. Hood has become somewhat resentful of both Gelbart and the company.

THE PROBLEM

The branch has been realizing less premium income for the past five years. The following is a breakdown of annual premium income:

Year 1	$7.6 million
Year 2	$7.2 million
Year 3	$6.3 million
Year 4	$5.1 million
Last year	$8.3 million*

* growth last year is the result of the transfer of the territories north of Toronto to the Oshawa branch. The total volume transferred with these territories was $3.5 million.

The projected volume for the end of this year is $7.5 million, including the new territories, and this projection may be difficult to achieve in the currently competitive market.

The staff turnover in the branch has been in excess of 20% each year for the past three years. Recently, one intermediate underwriter and one junior examiner resigned. Another junior underwriter was fired after 16 months in the branch. As well, the recent changes in the Personal Lines manager's position (with the incumbent being demoted to a senior underwriter's position within the branch) has created some resentment among the staff in general.

Productivity levels have dropped significantly, and this has adversely affected the level of service and the attitude of the branch's independent brokers. When Larry Gelbart held a marketing meeting recently for his senior staff, his response to the question of broker alienation was, "They are going to regret treating us this way. If they don't want to do things our way — then to hell with them!"

The quality of underwriting in the branch has also deteriorated, resulting in the acceptance of substandard risks. Because of this, the branch has lost money in each of the past three years. This unprofitability has been of great concern to the corporate head office. Also, in light of the loss in premium income, the viability of maintaining this branch has been under examination.

At a recent meeting of the branch management and senior staff held to discuss branch problems, the following series of exchanges took place.

Larry Gelbart: I know why we keep losing business. The territories we service are the most competitive in Canada, and head office won't give us competitive price on our products.

Connie Burns: But our brokers say that we're competitive, at least in some products. It's a case of us not providing the service and backup that they need. They tell me that when they phone in for a quotation, the staff doesn't really seem interested in handling their requests.

Helen Whiteface: You haven't been here long enough, dear, to realize that we've done everything we can for these brokers. You can't expect us to work 24 hours a day just to satisfy them! I'm sure that our people are doing their best. And I should know by now.

Larry Gelbart: That's right, we run this branch, not those brokers. If we could give them better service with the staff we have, we would. We sure pay them enough. And didn't we just move you into your job in an effort to improve things, Connie? Anyway, I'm not aware of anyone acting like that.

Harry Higman: Besides, there's only so much that we can do. We have to satisfy head office all the time, and they're even more difficult to deal with than the brokers. If we try to change too many things, head office will be on our backs again looking for information and asking questions. I say: Let sleeping dogs lie!

Sadie Tompkins: I'd have no problem giving these brokers the service they want, if only I had some time to do some underwriting. Every time I sit down to move some paper my staff keeps interrupting me with their problems! How am I supposed to get anything done in that situation?

Ruth Burkholtz: I know what you mean Sadie, Larry faces the same problem every day. Fortunately I've been able to reduce the interruptions somewhat, and this allows him to get on with the work.

Larry Gelbart: I appreciate your efforts, Ruth. The problem for you, Sadie, may be solved if you had someone to run interference for you in your department. Perhaps Bob here could act as your screening mechanism to give you time to get some real work done.

Bob Hood: I could do that if you want. Of course I'd need a little help in determining which items or people should be passed on to Sadie and which items should be dealt with elsewhere. And I assume that this would mean some relief from my more routine work — not just more work added on. You know, the usual policy is to load it all on "Old Bob". Anyway, I could check this out with you later, and we can decide something then.

Sadie Tompkins: Fine Bob, then maybe I can give some of these brokers the service that Connie was talking about!

Larry Gelbart: Well, I'm not too sure that we can do much in that area myself; not with the pricing structure head office has saddled us with. However, see what you can do, and let me know. I appreciate that feedback, Connie. But I also think Helen and Harry may be right.

Helen Whiteface: It's just those damn brokers! If they weren't so demanding with their "I need this quote yesterday" stuff, we could organize our workload and get things done in an orderly way.

Ruth Burkholtz: You can say that again. You should hear the way they talk to me when they have some complaint and are trying to get hold of Larry. It's all I can do to convince them to deal with the right person instead of screaming in Larry's ear.

Larry Gelbart: Maybe I should let you people in on a rumour I've heard — that head office is sending down a 'troubleshooter'. I understand that he's either going to help us turn around the profitability of the branch or maybe even decide to shut us down. I guess there is not a hell of a lot we can do about it except work as best we can. What a situation! Well, I suppose that's all for now . . .

Connie Burns (looking alarmed): Wait a minute, people. We can't just do nothing and watch our jobs go down the tube!

Sadie Tompkins: Gee, I didn't know things were that serious. I better start leaning on my staff to work harder.

Harry Higman: Oh, calm down ladies. It's just the usual sort of nonsense handed out by head office to keep us off balance. Right, Larry?

Bob Hood: Yeah, don't worry. We all know who the 'fall guy' is going to be — AGAIN.

QUESTIONS

1. Under the headings of motivation, communication, and leadership, discuss the root causes of the performance problem at the Oshawa branch office.

2. To what extent are interpersonal relationships and branch office structure responsible for the branch's problems?

3. In what ways is the branch office "culture" preventing an improvement in performance.

4. What should Connie Burns say next? (The meeting may be continued with the roles being played by participants in the case discussion.)

5. As the "troubleshooter" from head office, what recommendations would you make to Larry Gelbart if the situation did not improve? What recommendations would you make to head office?

Millennium Presence Advertising

Millennium Presence is a major Canadian advertising firm that has been in existence for 40 years (under a different name for the first 37 years), with a national clientele and consistent profits that began to slip a few years ago. Eighteen months ago, the firm began to question its profile in the industry and re-evaluate its operations. This was mainly due to environmental factors, such as new entrants into the advertising market and globalization pressures. Larger U.S. firms were seen as a threat in the home market. In response to these pressures, Millennium Presence decided to merge with an organization of about the same size headquartered in Chicago and with offices in several American and Canadian cities. The partners of each firm believed that together they would be a stronger force, with increased market leverage, and with a better chance at tapping a global market. The resultant firm would have approximately 460 employees and eight regional offices, at least before any cuts were made.

As the official merger date approached, the decisions regarding rationalization of resources were being made at the "top of the house" and communicated downward for implementation. Decisions about resource redeployment for some functional groups, such as account executives, were easy to make. In the short run, all would be retained by the merged firm, giving clients continuity in their relationships. However, decisions regarding shareable resources, such as graphic artists, human resources and accounting were much more challenging. Some of these would now be more closely analyzed under a new resource value microscope. Recently, it was announced that cuts were required to the Human Resource Department to help achieve organizational goals. A flurry of activity ensued, with numerous "emergency" budget meetings attended by partners and managers.

Within the Human Resource (HR) Department of Millennium, Dan, a very capable, quality performer working in the compensation and incentives area, heard about the budget challenges and began to wonder if he would still have a job when all these discussions were finished. Although Dan had heard many of the needed savings were going to be realized through early retirement and attrition, he was

This case is based on original work by Deborah Slade.

really concerned. Dan was in his early 50s and didn't want to have to find a new job with a new company, even if Millennium suggested early retirement to him. In addition, Dan also was upset because promotional opportunities, which used to be filled in an equitable manner with successful candidates chosen based on their performance, wouldn't be available for a long time. He wondered if this would turn into a dead end job. Dan responded by becoming quiet, withdrawn and much less productive. Every person in the training department reacted to these budget cuts in a different way. Some of Dan's peers became hostile, some sad, and a few, like Lori, did not appear affected at all.

Lori's performance was above average, as it had been before, although she did begin looking outside the firm for some new volunteer activities to help keep her mind busy. Lori was so confident in the long-term outlook for the firm that she even began mentoring and discussing the benefits of the merger with her peers. Lori kept herself informed by reading all of the published information regarding the cost cutting exercise and the advantages for the merging firms. She knew the challenges and that they were going to impact the people she worked with. She even understood that while some of her colleagues would be let go, luckily, most of the cuts would be realized through normal attrition.

The personnel in the HR Department, who had operated in a highly policy- and procedure-oriented environment, with confidence in their continued employment, no longer had that assurance. With year-end performance ratings due shortly, people began to wonder if their bonuses and annual salary increases would also be in jeopardy. Dan found this very difficult to think about, because he had already made plans for his bonus. He was a team player with many years of service to his credit. He had worked for many people: some good, and some not so good. Over the past several years, Dan had enjoyed an exceptionally good relationship with his boss, Helen. He knew his job well, was given a lot of freedom, and often carried on activities for a couple of days before "checking in" with Helen. Even with this strong historical relationship, Dan now distrusted Helen. She seemed less communicative, cooler to all her subordinates, and was called into frequent meetings that caused Dan some anxiety. Helen had previously made herself freely available, but over the past three weeks Dan couldn't even catch her eye, let alone get information from her regarding the decisions that were being made! She only seemed to have enough time to tell Dan what to do each morning and then run into the next meeting.

Lori also reported to Helen, but she seemed to be totally unconcerned by the change in her behaviour. She assured Dan that Helen would advise them of any changes as soon as she could. Lori reminded Dan of how compassionate and fair Helen had been when dealing with the performance problems of one of their peers only a few months ago. Helen often had fought for things the team had needed, and consistently looked out for their interests. She had always been an excellent coach and mentor. Unfortunately, she was now struggling to cope with the pace of change and the difficulties associated with making strategic staffing decisions.

Dan said that he agreed with Lori, but noted that she was about 20 years younger, with much less to worry about. He just can't bear it any longer. The rumour mill is rampant. He's feeling isolated, and is getting headaches from all the stress. He has to do something!

QUESTIONS

1. Other than the difference in their ages and alternative job prospects, what other factors might explain the differences in attitude and motivation between Dan and Lori?

2. Do you believe that Dan's anxiety is reasonable, given the circumstances? What should he do?

3. Would it be better for Helen to interact with her staff more intensively, even if she has no positive news to report?

4. What measures can firms take to minimize the negative effects of mergers and acquisitions that are described in the case?

Motivation in the Boiler Room

You can call me Tom. These days everyone complains about the way telemarketers interfere in their lives. People complain about how they always seem to phone just when it is the least convenient and that they are pushy and aggressive on the phone. The telemarketing that most people complain about is those phone calls that begin with a few seconds of silence when you answer the phone, followed by the polite voice of a young person who tries to get you to take on a new credit card or buy insurance for your mortgage or purchase some product or service from a national organization.

These calls originate from large call centres located in parts of the country with an ample supply of cheap labour and with a government willing to install the telecommunications infrastructure necessary to support the industry. Increasingly, these call centres are being located offshore, where labour is even cheaper. The calls are dialled centrally by computer, and when the phone is answered by a human, the call is switched to a telemarketer, who goes into the pitch. There have been efforts to curtail this telephone sales activity by legislating rights to privacy. The reality is that telemarketing has been around as long as the telephone.

I'm from the old school and there are plenty like me around. I don't sell products or services over the phone. My customers are sales people who buy lists of prospects from me and then sell those people products or services that they don't have.

Here's how it works. I call up someone and tell them I'm conducting market research on consumer goods and services. I assure them I'm not selling anything and that this questionnaire will only take a few minutes of their time. Let's say I'm working with someone who is selling vacuum cleaners. I ask the person a variety of questions, but all I really want to know is whether they have a built-in vacuum cleaner and whether they have a credit card. The name, address and phone number of someone who does not have a built-in vacuum cleaner and does have a credit card is worth money to a vacuum cleaner salesperson. These people will follow up with a strong pitch to get an appointment to demonstrate their expensive product in

---

This case is based on original work by Laura Tannis.

the home. Usually they offer an incentive, because if they can get in the door a sale is very likely. The sales commission can run to hundreds of dollars for a single evening of work.

This is all done on a local basis. I work with sales people from my area who buy my lists of prospects. Sometimes, we work out of the same location, such as a back room in the warehouse district. We don't need a storefront location. The reason they will pay me for the list of prospects is that it takes time to find people who meet the qualifications of a sales prospect. The vacuum cleaner sales people are better off spending their time in customers' homes trying to close deals on vacuum cleaners, rather than spending time on the phone trying to find prospects. They only want to talk to customers who are "qualified" to buy a vacuum cleaner.

Obviously, I can do things to improve the likelihood of a sale by finding out other things such as whether they have recently bought a vacuum cleaner, whether they have a high enough limit on their credit card for a costly purchase, whether they have carpet, etc. These enhancements to the information on a list of prospects make it a hotter property, and in my business my reputation is made by the quality of the prospects we find.

I run my operation in direct conjunction with a team of sales people who are pushing a particular product, such as vacuum cleaners, and I am part of the team. Nonetheless, I am still independent, and have found ways to get the most income out of my prospect list. When I am gathering information about prospective customers, I usually ask them about all of their household appliances and, as a result, have valuable information for other sales operations. I can sell my list to several other clients.

However, there is no way I can do all of the phoning myself and still earn what I consider a decent income. It can take a dozen or more calls to find one person who will talk to me. So I hire people to do the phoning for me at minimum wages. I hire them to come in for a few hours each evening, usually 5:00 p.m. to 9:00 p.m., to make calls. I write a script for them to follow that I feel will give the best results. At my level of operation I don't use fancy automatic dialling equipment. My telemarketers just sit at a table with a phone, photocopied pages from a phone book, the script and an information sheet to be filled out on each prospect. This workplace is called a boiler room.

For my employees, it is not very desirable work. What they do is phone people who don't want to hear from them, try convincing people to answer their questions about their household and their finances, and prevent these people from hanging up before they get enough information to know if they are "qualified" to buy the product. Generally, the location of boiler rooms is not convenient for after hours work, and the work environment is not particularly comfortable.

Usually, my operation is "off the books", and I pay in cash. This allows me to recruit people who would not otherwise be willing to take the work. I get a lot of single mothers on welfare, students with student loans, people on disability pensions, people in bankruptcy and moonlighting workers of all sorts. My requirement for workers can fluctuate wildly, and my workforce is very transient. We can be very busy for a month, and then shut down for a few weeks while the sales people catch up on the prospects we have provided.

Typically, there is a brief training period where we work with new employees to help them catch on to the process. We give them tips about the patter to use, how to answer common questions, and how to modify the tone of their voice to assure the people that it's okay to answer the questions. Later, they will learn tricks of the trade about how to deviate from the script to improve responses. For example, we offer only a vague identification of who we are. We never give a name that is in the phone book, and we regularly change the business name. If the customer thinks we are from a well-known polling organization or Statistics Canada, well so be it. Our relationship with them will end in a couple of minutes, and no real harm has been done. We play things pretty close to the edge; but if we didn't do it, others would.

So here I am with a dozen or so irregular employees. People often don't show up for work. They call in at the last moment to say they can't make it because their kid is sick or their child care arrangement fell through, or they do show up, but they're drunk. And sometimes they show up and just sit there like a lump, expecting to be paid for doing as little as possible. My main motivational strategy is to fire anyone who doesn't meet their quota. I monitor the phone calls to see how they're doing and to be able to validate their report sheets. They learn it doesn't pay to fake their results. Usually, I pay them cash at the end of each week, and if they want to be paid, they had better do their job. This works, to a certain extent. I get rid of the slackers who do very little, but it doesn't seem to do much to motivate my best employees. If I spend a shift on the phones, I can easily get twice as many "qualified" prospects as my best employee. I know they can do better, but I can't seem to get them to do more than the minimum required to keep their job.

I need some better motivational strategies in the boiler room.

QUESTIONS

1. Using a theoretical approach in communication to explain your answer, how do the callers successfully obtain personal information?

2. Why is Tom unable to motivate his best employees?

3. Develop strategies in their job design to improve the motivation of the best employees.

4. Evaluate the business ethics at work in the boiler room.

CASE 46 ---

Multi-Bake Corporation

With annual sales exceeding $100 million, Waterloo, Ontario-based Multi-Bake Corporation ranks as a strong competitor in the bakery sector of the Canadian food industry. Its subsidiaries manufacture and market a variety of goods, ranging from frozen foods to specialty bakery products such as Christmas cakes and sweet goods. Recently, the company expanded beyond Ontario and into Québec when it acquired the controlling interest in a number of French-Canadian bakeries. Multi-Bake now has five production plants: three in Kitchener-Waterloo, and one each in London and Ottawa. Each of these plants supports numerous sales areas. The company's Ottawa operation was expanded by the addition last year of the B.I.T. Buns Company. This acquisition increased Multi-Bake's share of the Ottawa market, but also added to the company's headaches. In addition, the company now has the recently-acquired Québec bakeries.

ORGANIZATIONAL DETAILS

The organization chart shown in Figure 1 sets out for Multi-Bake the top management structure and the reporting relationships in the area of finance and accounting, from the accountants up to the president.

About a year and a half ago, John Stone was promoted to the position of Corporate Controller reporting to Don Keyes, the Vice-President of Finance and Information Systems. Stone's background in the auditing field with a large retailer had brought him to Multi-Bake some years ago to fill the position of Manager of Internal Audit, whose incumbent also reported to Don Keyes. John Stone had been able to learn about the various facets of the bakery business through his various auditing activities. His easy-going manner and friendly disposition had also gained him many friends, not only in the sales and marketing groups, but also in the production and distribution areas. In the relatively short time that he had been Controller, John had gained respect from his staff and was well regarded by his peers. John's political savvy in the organization and his shrewd manoeuvres made him a valuable ally. When the workload slackened, John was often found with the accountants discussing the football pool and hockey standings. Aside from his suit and age, there was very little to distinguish this boss from his subordinates. The camaraderie that

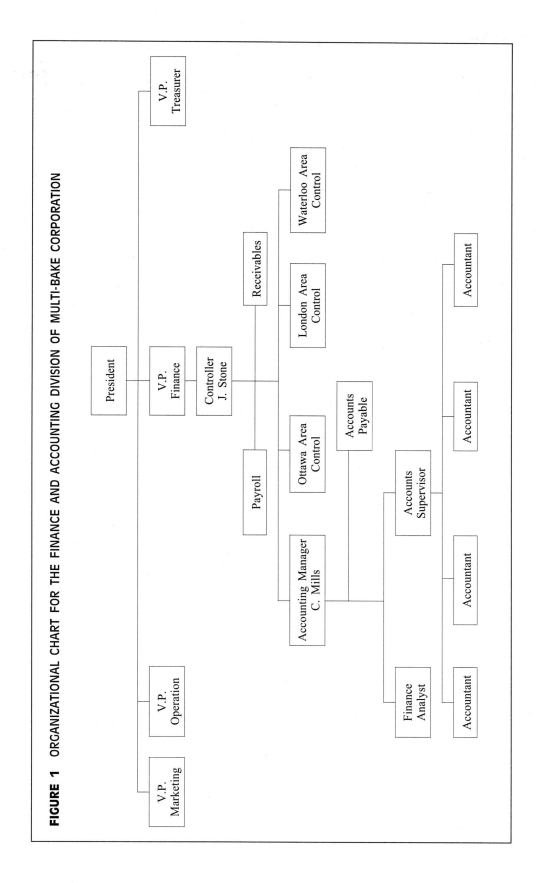

FIGURE 1 ORGANIZATIONAL CHART FOR THE FINANCE AND ACCOUNTING DIVISION OF MULTI-BAKE CORPORATION

existed bound the group together. And it was very useful when upper management pressured him for some fast analysis and when individuals at the branch level demanded financial explanations.

Explanations and analysis were a routine part of the accountants' workload. However, in recent years, the increased amounts of information that needed to be processed, coupled with human error, had resulted in more and more reports that were incorrect in amounts or late in preparation. For example, the sales route accounting system developed for the company many years ago had been adequately designed for the recording of sales, discounts, and receivables information. However, as the company had grown, the system needed to be upgraded. In fact, what had happened was a series of band-aid solutions that were only to cause many more problems in the future.

Under the system that had originally been designed, each sales area was divided into various routes serviced by a company route salesman. Each route consisted of many customers. At the beginning of each day, the salesman picked up his daily standing orders for delivery, and his route number was charged with the sales amount of products that was loaded for the day's deliveries. At the end of the day, the route was credited with the amount of sales and products returned. The information was then totalled for all the routes in a sales area, and a consolidated route accounting report prepared. Originally, the route statement for a sales area allowed for a maximum of $999,999.00 in sales, both cash and receivables. For anything over $1 million, the computer dropped the seventh digit. This caused many problems for the accounting department when various sales areas started to record sales of over $1 million — only one of the many problems that lack of foresight had caused.

THE PROBLEM

From the first day that John had become Corporate Controller, he had been saddled with the problems arising from the B.I.T. Buns Company acquisition. No one had stayed in the position of Area Controller for the company's Ottawa area for more than nine months. John's most recent recruit, Jerry Farrell, gave John a month and a half's notice, which should have been sufficient to find a replacement. In the following weeks, John Stone and Cecil Mills, the Corporate Accounting Manager, had many discussions about finding a replacement for the area controllership position.

During this same time, there was a change in John's reporting relationship. Don Keyes, whose reputation preceded him wherever he went, contributed to his own demotion through his lack of social graces, his lack of tact, and moreover his incompetence in his area of responsibility. The area of finance was removed from his jurisdiction. John was to report directly to the president. It was speculated that John Stone would be made vice-president of Finance at the next general meeting of the shareholders. By that time, many hoped that Don Keyes would have left the company, and that the area of Information Systems would also be given to John Stone. This would facilitate better co-operation between the Data Processing department and the Accounting department.

John's philosophy was not to be overly optimistic; he would wait and see. Cecil Mills, the Accounting Manager, knew full well that should John become vice-president and move upstairs to the executive row, his chances of getting the corporate controllership position would be greatly improved. Company history had shown that the average tenure of a controller was about a year and a half. In the five years that Cecil had worked in the Accounting department, three different controllers had occupied the office with the door, the third being John Stone. Cecil's experience and ambitions had now placed him one step away from the controllership position he had wanted for so long. He had been overlooked three times because, so he believed, he was not close enough in his education to a professional designation. Yet his long experience in the department had made him invaluable to each new controller in his or her initial months.

During the last two years, Cecil's work had centred on the mass conversion of an older accounting system to a newly acquired computer system. His involvement in this particular project made him almost irreplaceable. No other person in the company had such an extensive knowledge of the new accounting software system. This advantage would be a bargaining point for Cecil during reviews. Because his position in the company was not a highly visible one, Cecil's accomplishments in this area had gone largely unnoticed, which had made him feel even more frustrated.

"If only they knew what I could do . . . with one instruction I could scramble the entire system . . . but they really don't know," Cecil confided to a close friend. Cecil's frustrations came to the surface in occasional bouts of depression and temper. However, this behaviour served to reinforce John's feelings that Cecil belonged where he was. At least there, his outbursts would be confined to the department and would not jeopardize relationships with upper management or other departments.

With Don Keyes' demotion, John became more accountable for the Ottawa problems. These were problems that had arisen from poorly trained staff, lack of continuity of management, and ill feelings between the formerly B.I.T. Buns Company employees and the Multi-Bake Ottawa employees. In the last year or so, efforts to amalgamate both companies' operations had been hampered by a lack of accurate information. A main contributor to this problem was the reluctance of the B.I.T. Buns Company employees to conform to Multi-Bake's reporting procedures. The problem was further compounded by the fact that there had been no area controller in Ottawa to see the problems through to a solution.

Jerry Farrell's replacement would have to commit himself or herself to seeing those same problems through. Choosing a replacement was not an easy task. John felt that the replacement should come from within the organization. There was no lack of qualified people in his department, but there was lack of desire on the part of any of them to go to Ottawa for a lengthy period of time.

The Ottawa controllership position provided front-line training that would have given the person appointed an opportunity to see operations at the depot level and to see the information being amalgamated into a comprehensive reporting package. The primary responsibility of an area controller was to ensure that the information transmitted to head office was accurate. How that controller arrived at that goal was up to the individual. Each controller had favourite methods of scrutinizing and controlling the flow of information. For the ambitious, this position would have offered invaluable training for a more challenging management position at head office.

"We are running out of alternatives, John," Cecil pointed out, "Joyce and Patrick won't consider this assignment without some guarantee that they will be brought back to Waterloo within a year and a half. You know, as well as I do, that it may take years in Ottawa to straighten out the mess that we bought."

"We can offer it to Hilary, Cecil. She would take it without any strings attached. Besides, the change would do her good."

"You must be joking, John. Hilary might do more damage than you think. You know she's not discreet about anything, least of all her personal life."

"I don't understand what you mean, Cecil. Her personal life has no bearing on her work. The facts are she has no family, therefore, she would have no qualms about working late; she has worked in receivables for months now in a position of relative authority; she's been a good supervisor; and her experience in data processing would be an asset. Hilary would not find another position comparable to this anywhere else. It's time we addressed the problem of turnover in that position."

"Alright, John, if that's what you want, I'll speak with her in the morning. But I advise against it," Cecil said flatly.

"It will work out fine. Besides, if it doesn't, you'll make it right," John chuckled.

Hilary Oates was 40 years old, divorced, and had no children. She had been with the company seven years in various capacities: in the marketing department, data processing, and most recently held the position of accounts receivable supervisor. Her performance was quite satisfactory. It was her lack of formal training that prevented her from going much further in the company. On John's insistence, Cecil offered the position to Hilary the following morning. The offer was promptly accepted and, two weeks later, Hilary was on her way to Ottawa.

From the first day onward, it was an uphill fight to gain acceptance and respect. On the first day, Hilary held a general meeting for all the staff at the Ottawa office. After the initial introductions, she began: "When I accepted this position, I knew, as the entire company knows, that this office and this entire area of the company has been running haphazardly. Mistakes that result from carelessness are inexcusable. We are responsible adults, and from this day onward your work will reflect this attitude. We are paid to do a job, and I have a big job ahead of me. With or without your cooperation, this operation is going to be cleaned up. Tardiness and absenteeism will stop. Those guilty will be dealt with promptly. Needless to say, your cooperation in this matter will make things easier for everyone concerned. If there are no further questions . . . we will return to work."

From that point onward, the staff knew that what was ahead of them was not going to be easy for anyone concerned. In the following months, Hilary's attempts to resolve some of the Ottawa problems seemed only to increase them. The atmosphere of the office was tense and hostile. The staff were always on the defensive, wary of her every move and question. They were uncooperative and suspicious of her intentions.

"She's constantly breathing down your neck . . . questions, questions, and more questions about everything I do or don't do. She's probably looking to replace me, you know; I feel it in the way she treats me . . . If you ask me, I think she's going to replace all of us," one woman complained.

"She doesn't leave for her two-hour luncheon dates until we've all returned from our half-hour breaks. She must think we're blind. I have heard all about her meetings at lunch, and let me assure you that I could write a book on her exploits," gossiped another.

"Wouldn't it figure that head office would send a woman to do a man's job. She doesn't know much . . . she's created more work for me than I can handle. I don't have time to explain everything I do to her. She's got more nerve than brains. I don't know how much more I can take of her and her condescending ways. 'Do this and do that,' as she's peering down the end of her nose at you."

Such comments and complaints were commonplace in the Ottawa office, and the situation was not improving. Also, positive results were not coming as quickly as some of the executives had hoped. Suggestions were being made at head office that John did not have a handle on the Ottawa situation, and this placed even more pressure on him to show results. Hilary was made aware that the situation had to change and quickly.

Hilary believed that the staff did not take her threats seriously enough in order for her methods to be constructive. The following day provided her with an opportunity to show that she meant what she said. Hilary and the sales manager worked late that day reviewing sales data. They had used the terminals to access the information. In order for them both to view the screen properly, the equipment was somewhat rearranged. The equipment was left until the next morning when Leah Goldman, the terminal operator, arrived at work. Leah was an established member of the Ottawa staff. With her experience and seniority, many people turned to her for direction and guidance in procedures. Even though her expertise was limited, her intentions were good. She organized the children's Christmas parties, the social events, and the hockey pools, etc. She was generous with her time as well as her criticisms. Leah's tongue was sharp, but her temper was short-lived.

On that particular morning, Leah was upset that the equipment had been moved around and not returned to its proper position after being used. Upon further investigation, Leah learned that it was Hilary and Johnson, the sales manager, who had been using the equipment. Leah had had enough of Hilary by then, and commented sharply: "Common courtesy would have made me move the equipment back to the place I found it. I don't have time to rearrange everything after anyone who uses it . . . least of all people who don't even ask for my approval to use the equipment I'm responsible for!"

"Your approval, Miss Goldman?" Hilary sneered, "You seem to forget that you work for me. I don't need your approval or anyone else's approval to get some work done in this office. I would strongly suggest you change your tone of voice when speaking with me. You may find yourself short of a job. Everyone is dispensable . . . even you."

"You're wrong, Miss Oates . . . I used to work for you! I quit!"

"Correction . . . You're fired!" Hilary had found her example. Surely, the staff would cooperate now. Unfortunately, her firing of Leah only served to bind the staff together more firmly against her. Rumours of her iron hand and the resulting discontent filtered through to head office. John began to have serious doubts about the entire situation. Perhaps, Hilary was not the right person for the Ottawa area. He decided to send Cecil to Ottawa to investigate the situation and provide some recommendations on how to resolve it. Cecil's knowledge of the reporting systems would enable him to pinpoint the sources of the inaccurate reporting. Moreover, it would give him an opportunity to show that he could deal with interpersonal problems as well.

When first approached, Cecil had chosen to decline the assignment. The Ottawa situation was not one of the easiest to deal with. But top management was impatient for results and were carefully watching any new developments. Using a different approach, John tried once again to encourage Cecil to take up the challenge.

"Cecil, you know that the spring annual meeting is not that far away. If all goes well, I may be on the 12th floor and my office will be unoccupied. Your assistance in resolving this problem can be a great selling point when I go to bat for you. You know how highly visible this problem is ... It will give you the kind of exposure you need. Show me results, Cecil, and you could well have my office in the spring."

Knowing that he was seriously being considered for the corporate controllership position, Cecil finally decided to give the Ottawa crisis a try. Cecil already knew what the problem was. After all, he had tried to tell John from the very beginning that Hilary was not the right person for the job. Cecil left for Ottawa two days later.

His arrival in Ottawa was perceived by Hilary as a reinforcement sent from head office to help her in her crusade against insubordination. It was quite obvious that the atmosphere in the office was uncomfortable. Hilary seemed to try to discourage Cecil from having any prolonged contact with any of the employees. Consequently, Cecil soon realized that to get any feedback from the staff, he would have to approach them informally after work. So he invited a few of the staff up to his room after work for a few get-acquainted drinks. Before long, he was receiving an earful of complaints and comments.

"Let's not be naive, Cecil, everyone knew that the only reason Hilary got the job in the first place is because she slept her way here. It's common knowledge that John Stone and Hilary Oates have been having an affair for years. It's no wonder she gets away with everything."

"I can't understand her attitude. She's always so condescending — as if we weren't even people," another offered.

"I gather then, that you would want her out of your lives?" Cecil asked. "Have you considered that she may really be trying to do her job?"

"Do her job? She doesn't arrive until 10:00 A.M., but she'll be the first to point it out if you are late. She takes lunch from 12:30–2:30 P.M., but if we're late coming back, even five lousy minutes, she'll be calling you in for a 'talk'. She's got everyone running around doing things that have already been done. Creating work for you even if it serves no purpose ... You call that doing a job?"

Cecil felt that with the ill-feelings that existed, Hilary would never be able to gain acceptance. Her recent move in firing Leah Goldman, so it seemed, had permanently alienated her. There seemed to be few options left. If action was not taken immediately, the company would be faced with the possibility of losing the entire Ottawa office staff. On the same afternoon that Cecil returned from Ottawa, a petition arrived addressed to the president of the company, with copies to the Director of Employee Relations and to John Stone. It was a petition demanding that Hilary Oates be removed from the Ottawa office and that the situation in Ottawa be given greater attention. It charged that John Stone was ultimately responsible for the problem. It was signed by almost all of the Ottawa staff. That same afternoon, two resignations arrived from two key members of the Ottawa staff.

CONCLUSION

Early in the afternoon, Cecil submitted his recommendations to John, which were as follows:

1. Hilary Oates should be removed from the position of area controller for the Ottawa area.
2. The London area controller should be given the assignment to clean up the operation in Ottawa with the full cooperation and support of the head office personnel. (The London area ran like clockwork, and had become the standard by which all areas were compared and measured.)
3. The position of area controller for the Ottawa area should be filled by a replacement from outside the company, preferably from the Ottawa-Hull area.

At 4:00 p.m. that same afternoon, the first of Cecil's recommendations became unnecessary. Hilary Oates submitted her resignation.

QUESTIONS

1. Under the headings:
   (a) leadership
   (b) motivation
   (c) bureaucratic structure
   discuss why Hilary Oates failed to be a successful supervisor.

2. Was Hilary a victim of sexual stereotyping? If she had been a man and behaved similarly, do you think the results would have been as bad?

3. Discuss the organizational problems that exist at this stage of Multi-Bake's expansion. Identify problems unique to mergers.

4. Comment on the behaviour and performance of John Stone and Cecil Mills as managers, indicating the various forces that govern their relationships and decision-making roles.

5. Would you consider that John Stone's and Cecil Mills' actions were optimal concerning the Ottawa situation? What would you have done differently from the beginning up until Hilary's resignation, and why?

Multi-Store's Imaging Department

Multi-Store, one of the largest organizations in the country, was highly successful. Its success was based on innovations. One of those innovations was the creation of the Multi-Store Credit Corporation in 1998. This was followed by the formation of a new department, the Imaging Department.

Image processing is the ability to replace paper documents with an electronic likeness, and then store, retrieve, display, process, distribute, and print the information. Image processing is accomplished by feeding a paper document into a scanner that digitizes and captures an electronic image of the document. This image contains all the information that appears on the original document. Images can also be created from faxed-in forms. The effect is to eliminate paper files.

The Imaging Department consisted of nine full-time workers and 15 part-time workers. They had originally been located in the New Accounts Department where they were Credit Assessors who evaluated customer applications. There they had enjoyed their responsibilities until the company decided to divide the department functionally. The chosen, decision-making people remained in the New Accounts Department, while the others were relocated into the Imaging Department as Imaging Operators or Verifiers. They lost their decision-making function and concentrated solely on imaging and checking the credit applications.

The basic functions of a Credit Assessor had been to verify and evaluate credit card account applications. To qualify for such a position, applicants had to possess good communication skills, pleasant telephone manners, keyboard and typing skills. At the start of their employment with the company, they were enthusiastic as they perceived their new positions to be a challenge and a situation where they would be able to gain valuable experience. Then, electronic imaging was introduced and about 60% of the Credit Assessors were shifted to relatively structured jobs with no customer contact or decision-making opportunities. Comments from these seemingly downgraded employees were as follows.

This case is based on original work by Dennis Woo.

Fawzia: Imaging Operator "I think the tasks given to us are a waste of time. Why don't they teach us to do the whole functions? We're supposed to be Credit Assessors. We should be credit assessing. Before, the quality of our work was important. Now, it's the quantity. I think maybe they think we are not competent enough to do the whole job. They even brought someone in from another department and gave him the customer contact responsibilities. It seems unfair. We are the ones who have more experience in the department. It doesn't make sense. He had to learn from scratch. I'm not really motivated at work. I know I'll be doing the same thing every day. The job's OK — better than being on the streets — but no future. There's not much room for advancement in the company. Once you are given the job, that's it. If I stay here for 20 years, I'll probably still be in the same position as I am now. I'd like to see employees have more say. Management decides something, and then they impose it on us. That's all. It's like being treated like a machine."

Wilson: New Accounts Clerk (Verification) "Even though they assign you specific tasks, they are not really saving time. Work gets passed on to someone else and, if it needs more looking into, it gets passed on to another person, which is a long process. I think that they should give people more responsibilities, have more faith in their employees. I was first hired as a Credit Assessor. Two months down the line, I was thrown into doing only verification. No one asked me what I thought about it. There were other people here, and they could have chosen them. Initially, I didn't mind because it was better than imaging. Verification is not that bad. There's a bit more decision-making on approval of applications. It has a bit more variation, less boring. But I'm still dissatisfied. It's not really that challenging. To me, anyone can do this. Anyone can sit down and phone and verify employment or bank records. All you need to know is how to write and speak English. I can't see any challenge in this type of work unless you are in the upper management level."

Sylvie: Imaging Operator "It's not a bad job, but it's not one for me. I like to use my mind when I'm working. This job doesn't require thinking, but it is a job somebody has to do, and it just happens to be me. A lot of time they hire you for a particular job and that's what they hire you for. Why should you do something different? I'm not really motivated at work. When I wake up for work, I don't feel like going. I always look forward to the weekends."

More recently, even those who retained the credit assessment function were affected by technological change. Artificial intelligence had taken over human decisions. Previously, the computer's function was to trace the involved applicant's credit history. The assessor would then base her/his decision on the information given. However, the computer system has now been modified to a point where the computer, itself, can assess the data put in and make the decision. This upgrading of the software downgraded the jobs.

The Multi-Store Credit Corporation had spent over a year and many dollars in the development of the new imaging system. But, after all this effort, it was still very much in doubt whether the concept of imaging was valid; whether the new system could gain the market that had been anticipated for it; and whether it was reliable. Errors had been made in the credit approval process that seemed to stem from "bugs" in the software. But, as one of the Directors of the Corporation indicated: "The rate of change is accelerating, only adaptable companies will be the ones who survive. We must recognize the need to change, be receptive. Changes in the service sector must be accompanied by technology." Hence, the reason for imaging.

QUESTIONS

1. What were the motivational and attitudinal differences among the three employees who were quoted in the case?

2. For Credit Assessors who become Image Operators or Verifiers, in what ways did the extrinsic and intrinsic factors of the job change?

3. In what ways was the introduction of imaging mismanaged by Multi-Store? Suggest a different change process.

4. Must automation of this nature always lessen the challenge in jobs? Why or why not?

The New Sales Commission

The Amalgamated Transportation Company was originally formed by a merger among a traditional truck freight business, a leading courier service and a customs broker. The new company quickly became known as Amtransport, and adopted that name. It also grew rapidly as it moved into new services such as overnight air delivery, formed international partnerships, and provided solutions to shipping challenges in the expanding international trade market.

By the year 2000, Amtransport had approximately 5,000 employees across Canada with headquarters in Winnipeg, Manitoba. Amtransport held about 50% of the overnight air market and was dominant in most of the other markets it served. The exception was with ground services, where they were weaker than a number of competitors. Amtransport executives decided that to dominate this market they should take over one of their strong competitors. They did so and re-branded it as Amtransport Ground.

While the services they provided were quite independent in their operations, Amtransport had a centralized structure for many of its staff operations, such as personnel, finance, corporate relations, legal, billing, marketing and, significantly, sales. With the takeover they acquired a number of new account executives, and senior management took this opportunity to restructure the sales department and its commission system.

Amtransport has a sales force of about 150 full-time account executives. Each account executive is responsible for a specific territory defined by postal code. The executive is responsible for maintaining existing accounts as well as for achieving sales growth in the territory. Revenue goals are set prior to the beginning of each fiscal year, and then allocated for each quarter. The executive is paid a base salary plus a quarterly bonus based upon achievement of the revenue goals they have been assigned. The base salary for the account executives is well below the industry standard, but the bonuses are very generous. Above average performers can do very well working at Amtransport.

This case is based on original work by Pauline Da Silva.

The bonus is separated according to the three core products offered by Amtransport: International Transportation, Overnight Domestic Transportation and Amtransport Ground, the newly revamped product that included the acquired firm. Under the old system an account executive had to obtain 96% of the revenue goal in a category to receive a bonus. The bonus was then based on performance above 96% in each category.

Senior management decided that, since they had three strong products, they wanted to change the bonus system to encourage the account executives to promote all three, especially the newly expanded ground service. Some senior managers strongly believed that the existing account executives were not doing an effective job in identifying opportunities for all the products that Amtransport had to offer. They believed that the account executives pushed the products they were familiar with rather than all the products Amtransport had to offer. Management had found it extremely difficult to get their account executives to move beyond this comfort zone.

A second, related issue was a concern that the existing Amtransport executives would ignore the newly expanded ground service, while the executives brought over from the new company would favour the ground service to the detriment of the other products. They worried that this would result in an imbalance of sales efforts since the sales force was organized geographically and not by product.

Senior management at Amtransport knew that their account executives were a very achievement oriented group, and they decided to modify the bonus plan accordingly. The new bonus plan would require them to achieve a minimum of 80% of goals in each product area before they would earn a commission in any one area. The payout began at 96%. They referred to the 80% threshold as a gate. It didn't earn a bonus in itself, but was a requirement for the bonus plan to come into effect.

Amtransport had a tradition of strong downward communication with little effort made to gain feedback of any type. Not surprisingly, the new commission system was communicated by letter at the beginning of the next new fiscal year, only two months after the merger and revamping of the ground transport business.

The account executives did not support this new bonus plan. Nevertheless, those who had been with Amtransport for some years weren't terribly surprised by this substantial change to their compensation formula, as they had rarely, if ever, been consulted about previous alterations to policies or procedures. They quickly began to develop strategies to alter their work to cash in on the new sales commission program. One immediate strategy was to share their strengths and help each other out with sales approaches.

However, of the 150 executives, about 25 were from the former ground transport company taken over by Amtransport. Their reactions were totally different. Their former company had provided them with a substantial base salary and a modest commission system and a corporate culture existed that emphasized collegiality, cooperation and consultation. They were barely adapting to the new Amtransport environment when this change landed on them. Many quickly realized that they were at a disadvantage with respect to the existing Amtransport account executives, since they only had experience with one product. The 80% threshold was going to be a challenge for them, with products they had never sold before, many in an unfamiliar territory and working for a new company.

At the end of the first quarter, most of the 125 original Amtransport account executives earned a commission, while only three of the new executives made a commission. Their problem was the 80% gate. Six resigned and there was a lot of muttering among the rest. Most were actively job hunting.

Senior management reviewed their new sales commission program and declared it to be a success.

QUESTIONS

1. Was the new plan a success? Give full reasons for your answer and list all the pros and cons for the plan.

2. Describe and assess the impact of the new threshold on the motivation of the long-term account executives and on those from the firm that was recently acquired, taking into account their previous compensation plans.

3. Evaluate the implementation plan for this change to the sales commission.

4. Since the goal of the takeover was to expand the ground transport business, the loss of account executives from that business could be considered a problem. Develop a plan that would have prevented this situation from occurring.

Newton College

BACKGROUND INFORMATION

Newton College of Applied Arts and Technology is a multicampus educational institution serving Toronto and surrounding regional municipalities. Founded in 1970, the college first operated out of various rented facilities with an initial enrolment of 852 full-time postsecondary students and 1,067 part-time registrants. Enrolment figures for 1991 show 9,500 full-time and 28,540 part-time students.

In its relatively short 20-year history the college has had a host of program offerings. The college now offers a wide range of educational opportunities: from Business Studies to Early Childhood Education, from studies in Technology to Recreational Programming, and from Liberal Studies to Law Enforcement. The studies include both full-time day diploma programs for graduating high school students and a multitude of continuing education programs for the community at large.

To service student requirements for 1991, Newton employs 1,500 people: 700 faculty members (professors) who are directly responsible for teaching, 600 support staff (clerks, typists, maintenance) who respond to faculty and administrative needs, and 150 administrators (chairpersons, deans) who oversee the whole operation. This compares to 1970 employment figures of 100 faculty, 80 support staff, and 20 administrators.

ORGANIZATIONAL CULTURE

Newton's raison d'être is summarized in its 1988 Mission Statement.

> "Newton College stands committed to training and education that will enhance effectiveness in the workplace and quality of life for all. In this continuing endeavour, the college shall ensure excellence in teaching and learning for its communities. Students will participate in programs dedicated to relevance, social responsibility and lifelong learning."

This case was written by Peter Kells.

To achieve this mission, the college in that year also established primary objectives that emphasized quality education, student achievement, and employee development.

The stated objectives were:

- To offer academic programs that are excellent and relevant to the needs of the communities that Newton College serves.
- To improve the quality of student life, in co-curricular and extracurricular activities.
- To enhance current relationships and develop new relationships with the many communities that the college serves in order to: ensure greater understanding of college issues and greater awareness of college programs, courses, activities, and services; and to address current issues and local needs as perceived by these communities.
- To contribute to student achievement through the provision of effective counselling, recruitment, admissions, and placement services.
- To ensure the continued support and development of all employees and the enhancement of the quality of employee life in an environment conducive to growth and well-being.
- To contribute to the achievement of academic excellence through providing appropriate and well-maintained physical resources and appropriate administrative support services for all programs and service divisions.

EMPLOYEE RELATIONS

The second decade of Newton's existence has been turbulent to say the least.

A number of indicators lead one to believe that the quality of working life of faculty members at the college — as indexed by job satisfaction — is in decline: a first strike (1984) in the college's history, which lasted almost one month and resulted in faculty being legislated back to work; the large number of faculty grievances that have increased annually to their formation of divisional associations independent of the union to press for workplace changes; poor faculty response in applying for positions of promotion; faculty "self-actualizing" outside of their work place; poor after-work-hours relations with the college; poor volunteer rate for college committees, graduation ceremonies, and external liaisons (high schools, student employers); and disrespect for management in the form of open letters of criticism to the public and press constitute a few of the more measurable examples of dissatisfaction. Feelings of distrust, mistrust, hopelessness, and anger exist also, and, while more subjective, these feelings are no less important as indicators of a degraded quality of work-life situation.

The issues of job dissatisfaction in the college, however, are not as clear cut as they appear at first reading, since certain ambiguities and paradoxes cloud the situation; for example, there have been relatively few resignations among tenured staff, who enjoy a high degree of job security, an excellent paid vacation and holiday schedule, a complete benefits package, and a very competitive (with industry) salary. Furthermore, the union that represents faculty members has in place a system of automatic dues deduction, membership in several college decision-making labour-management committees, an input into staff layoffs, and a well-established grievance procedure. While these **basic** quality of work-life arrangements appear to have been implemented early in the life of the college and have perpetuated, an examination of the current situation reveals a second strike in November 1989, continued bitterness, frustration, and increasing anxiety among many of the organization's members.

EMPLOYEE ATTITUDE SURVEY

In April 1990, a survey questionnaire was distributed to the three major employee groups at Newton, asking them to provide input with respect to their attitudes towards the college in several areas: e.g., as an employer, issues of career development, and attitudes towards jobs, etc. Table 1 details a summary of responses to that survey.

TABLE 1 SUMMARY OF RESPONSES TO THE SURVEY QUESTIONS

	SUPPORT	FACULTY	ADMIN.
	(percentages)		
Newton is better than it was three years ago.	10	12	13
Newton does a good job in planning.	23	14	17
Newton is well managed.	27	15	25
Newton provides adequate facilities.	43	22	31
I would attend more social functions at Newton.	51	23	41
My Dept./Div. is above average compared to others at Newton.	33	43	71
My Dept./Div. is better than it was three years ago.	17	23	35
I think my Dept./Div. is Excellent/Above average in terms of:			
• management	35	34	64
• reputation in the community	38	58	61
• planning	29	29	39
• interest in employees' ideas and opinions	32	36	67
• attitude toward students	39	58	54
• providing working hours that are convenient for me	56	71	60
• having enough people to do the work in my area	21	21	15
My job makes good use of my skills and abilities.	72	86	81
My work makes a contribution to the educational process.	70	81	77
I agree that extra work and exceptional job performance lead to advancement.	30	21	48
I know what is expected of me in my job.	88	79	80
I am adequately informed about the college's policies and procedures.	60	50	75
I have opportunities for career development within Newton College.	52	36	54
The people I work with cooperate to get the job done.	73	72	90
The machinery and equipment I need to do my job are available.	68	43	64
I feel I have job security at Newton.	76	59	60
The promotional system rewards the best qualified.	16	9	23
I am informed about salary and benefits.	90	82	85

TABLE 1   SUMMARY OF RESPONSES TO THE SURVEY QUESTION
(Continued)

	SUPPORT	FACULTY	ADMIN.
	(percentages)		
I am satisfied with:			
• the recognition I receive for the work I do	55	49	60
• the people I work with	78	77	91
• the work I do on the job	82	95	87
• the pay and fringe benefits	49	72	69
I am satisfied or very satisfied with:			
• working conditions	59	50	74
• my job as a whole	70	81	84
• life in general	89	97	87
There is another job at Newton I would prefer.	54	22	42
Supervisor is Excellent/Above Average in:			
• knowing his/her job	60	48	74
• giving regular feedback	38	27	44
• giving me the information I need to do my job	39	33	55
• listening to what I have to say	?	?	?
• informing me of college policies/procedures	36	33	57
• solving problems	38	36	66
• appraisal of my job performance	41	26	48
• developing teamwork	31	25	51
Supervisor is Excellent/Above Average in:			
• providing information on opportunities within Newton	22	18	35
• being available to discuss a problem	54	53	57
Advertised positions are truly available.	18	14	27
The college has a great deal of interest in my career.	7	7	12
My Dept./Div. has a great deal of interest in my career.	19	17	28
The most important factor that would influence my decision to go through a training/development program:			
• to get a new position	25	7	14
• self satisfaction	41	64	61
• to get a pay increase	16	5	5
The factor that counts the most in getting a promotion:			
• education	11	6	4
• work experience	11	3	8

Of the 729 respondents, 260 were support staff, 344 were faculty, 85 were administration, and 40 employees who answered the survey did not state their employee group.

The percentages given in this summary table are column percentages. For example, 10% of support staff felt that Newton is better than it was three years ago, while 23 percent of support staff felt that Newton does a good job in planning.

PRESIDENT'S SUMMARY REPORT

The President of Newton College, A. R. MacDonald, communicated his response to the Employee Attitude Survey in a Summary Report:

"I am pleased to forward to you an Executive Summary Report and to indicate that copies of the full report will be forwarded to each College Resource Centre, as well as each divisional office, in the event that you wish to review the report in its entirety.

Attitudes are usually based on perceptions. While perceptions are not in themselves either right or wrong, they are real. If perceptions are built on lack of information, misinformation, or worse still, rumours, then it is important that better communication efforts be put in place if one wishes to have people perceive things as they really exist.

For example, much of the time of the college's senior management has been spent **addressing** both short- and long-range planning, as well as the current issues facing all Newtonians. However, if, as is indicated in the survey responses, people perceive that no planning is under way, then this indicates a breakdown in communication with respect to the information flow from top to bottom and, conversely, from bottom to top. This is only one of the areas identified by this survey that can be addressed immediately.

The Committee working on this study met last week and looked at several things that could be done immediately to respond to the findings of this survey. They are as follows:

1. **The introduction of 'Newtonians Update':** This internal document will be distributed to all Newtonians and will cover, in capsule form, the myriad of activities taking place within the college on a daily basis.

2. **Management training:** In response to the request for and the perceived need for additional management training, the Professional Development department has been asked to identify a "core program" that will be mandatory for all administrative personnel. With the exception of a few seminars, in the past two years most administrative staff professional development has been self-directed. This core program will ensure that we are all working from a common base.

3. **Excellence Awards:** Consistent with the recommendations that are now approved by the Board of Governors for the establishment of Excellence Awards, the college will proceed immediately to form the local structures that were recommended to address issues that enhance and/or restrict the achievement of excellence at each of our campus locations.

4. **Communications:** The survey produced some surprises for those of us who have tried to work diligently to ensure that policies and procedures are in place to address many of the areas questioned in the survey. As stated earlier, it became very evident that information is not flowing up or down within our organization as we would hope. Many of the written comments indicated that people did not know where to turn or how to convey their feelings if they had what they thought was a good suggestion and/or concern about current issues of their work environment.

    The Committee has recommended the establishment of a method of communicating your concerns and/or questions to the appropriate source. Therefore, the following is to be put into effect immediately:

    A "hot line" telephone, local ext. 0001, has been established in my office that will be monitored daily, and your questions or suggestions will be forwarded promptly to the appropriate person.

The Professional Development department is committed to conducting a second survey within the next two years to see what changes have taken place.

To those who participated by filling out the questionnaire in order to help with this project and to those who worked to prepare and collect the data, may I say thank you on behalf of the college. This type of information is meaningful only if you act upon it. As someone once wrote — and I quote loosely — it is not where you stand on an issue, but more important is the direction in which you are moving!"

QUESTIONS

1. Provide a summary report detailing problems **you** feel currently exist at Newton.

2. Comment on President MacDonald's proposed solutions: are they appropriate and sufficient?

3. Will the attitudes of Newton's employees impact on the organization's stated objectives? How, and to what degree?

4. A second survey will be conducted within the next two years. What changes would you expect to see in employee attitudes, and how would they be reflected in the Summary of Results?

The People's Insurance Company of Canada

BACKGROUND TO THE CANADIAN BANKING INDUSTRY

All banks operating in Canada are chartered banks governed under the federal legislation of the Canadian Bank Act. Historically, the Canadian financial sector was divided into what are known as the four pillars: namely, banking, trust, insurance, and securities, with each institution being prohibited from servicing more than one pillar. It had been speculated in the late 1980s that the Bank Act would be revised to provide for in-branch sales of insurance. But in 1992, that idea was put aside. Provisions were made, however, to allow banks to engage in expanded bank activities both within and without the financial sector. As a result, banks could buy insurance companies and establish them as separate entities. Through discussions with the government, the banking industry came to anticipate that full deregulation of insurance would occur by 1997, giving the banks further opportunities.

THE PEOPLE'S BANK

The People's Bank (PB), located in Ottawa, saw a great opportunity to get involved in a new venture that would complement its wealth management strategy. An insurance company would make sense, given that deregulation seemed to be just around the corner, and it would be a natural extension of the services sold by the bank. The insurance company would operate at arms' length in compliance with government regulations, establishing and managing its own operations. The bank had a traditional hierarchy, with a Chairman, Presidents of four divisions reporting to the Chairman, the Board of Directors, and Senior Vice-Presidents below that level. A key division was the Personal and Commercial Banking Section, which sold life insurance policies for mortgages and personal loans. This was viewed as a stepping stone to getting the insurance company started, because of the existing business in

The preparation of this case was funded under SSHRC Grant Number 561170 and was jointly prepared by Deborah M. Zinni, McMaster University and Monica Belcourt, York University.

the same field. A search for a Vice-President to head up the insurance company resulted in hiring David Dunnigan.

DAVID DUNNIGAN

David Dunnigan came to the People's Insurance Company of Canada (PICC) in early 1990. He almost did not, as he argued that being hired as Senior Vice-President to head up a major insurance company was inappropriate given the task at hand. After much negotiation, the bank agreed that he would become the CEO of PICC. His first priority was to hire four senior team members, including Mary Thorne, VP, Human Resources, Lorna March, VP, Finance, Neil Gordon, COO of General Insurance (Personal and Commercial, also referred to as P&C), and finally Gary Evans, COO of Life Insurance. The entire senior team had experience in insurance, except for Thorne, and were all considered to be extremely well qualified for their roles. They were very impressed by Dunnigan's vision of a company that was customer-focused and selling insurance direct to the market. There would be no need for traditional insurance agents. Team members had to be marketers first and insurance people second. Employees had to be customer-focused, empowered, innovative, possess good interpersonal and team building skills, and had to be strategically competent. They had to be prepared to live in an open office environment, and they would not have reserved parking spots. Dunnigan wanted an open, honest, non-bureaucratic and non-hierarchical organization. He envisioned an inverted pyramid structure for the insurance organization. The team was excited to hear that the bank would provide them with enough funds to get their businesses started, and would allow them at least five years to become profitable before the bank would get directly involved in the insurance business. Mary Thorne was particularly excited by the opportunity to be able to grow the HR department from scratch. The team worked closely and saw Dunnigan as a great communicator and strategic planner who always tried to include his team in decision-making.

THE SITUATION

Because the bank had previously been involved in life insurance and had existing business, the customer base would be transferred to the life insurance department of PICC. The two insurance departments would initially operate as two departments, and then eventually be integrated. The goal was to be the number one direct writer of insurance, which would be unique in the Canadian insurance industry. However, when PICC approached the bank for the necessary funding promised, they found that the amount was drastically reduced. This left insufficient funding for P&C insurance, and the senior team agreed by consensus to delay the start of P&C and turn the funds over to Life Insurance. The bank anticipated that the existing base of customers that it had turned over to PICC would generate some of the needed funding.

PICC operated out of the bank's head office until they outgrew the space and were forced to find suitable facilities away from the parent. Thorne added responsibility for facilities to her HR activities. Facilities were located near Kanata in a setting described as a "campus environment." A total open concept was developed. The hallways were given street names, and the subsidized cafeteria was named the "Hard Rock Café". Employees were given street addresses for mailing purposes. The cafeteria became an issue from the bank's perspective, since theirs had recently been closed down. A fitness centre was also made available to PICC employees; but, again, with reluctance from the bank. The fight was won on the premise that such benefits were required to instil a sense that PICC was different, and as a means to increase morale and, ultimately, productivity.

Parking assignments were allocated to the senior team, and Dunnigan was given a private office. Thorne was not happy about having a parking spot, and wanted to give it up to a pregnant employee. The senior team overrode her, saying that it would set a bad example. The employees were concerned about confidentiality, and approached Dunnigan, saying that an open concept was inappropriate for Thorne's position. Therefore, she too was given an office. Within six months of moving to the new location, PICC had again reached capacity. Space was available within the building, but at an additional cost. Growth was occurring much faster than had ever been anticipated.

Other facility management issues were troublesome to Thorne. Dunnigan would sign off on purchases, such as the telephone system, but signatures had to be obtained from several layers of bank management in order to obtain additional approvals. Thorne was frustrated, since she considered that Dunnigan should have the proper authority to sign off on such purchases.

Recruitment and selection were onerous. It became apparent that the bank expected the insurance company to absorb displaced bank employees. Thorne had difficulty explaining that some positions required specialized skills, and felt compelled to accept the transfers. Insurance experience was not always necessary, but employees had to have the right attitude and approach to dealing with customers. A major concern was technology. Having an appropriate key person to head up technology was necessary for insurance, and having a bank person would not be appropriate, since the skill sets were different. However, Thorne and Dunnigan felt compelled to agree to a transfer from the bank for the key technology position. Unfortunately, this position remained unstable for a number of years, with personnel transferring from the bank to the insurance company and then back to the bank, where their loyalties remained.

PICC needed to adopt HR policies and procedures that were conducive to an insurance environment. The policies of the bank would not necessarily fit the internal environment the insurance company was trying to achieve. This was an issue that was more troublesome at the senior levels within the bank. For example, the titles assigned to the senior PICC team appeared higher than comparable levels at the bank, and there were similar discrepancies in pay levels. Thorne justified her salary decisions by pointing out the importance of attracting people with the necessary skills from the insurance industry. This issue spilled over into the benefits area where, for example, senior levels within the insurance company were getting company cars while comparable executives within the bank were not receiving similar benefits. The bank reluctantly accepted some of the differences.

Training was very important to the success of the insurance company, particularly in regard to the call centre. Since the policy was to be customer-focused, the direct sales call centre was essential to fulfilling this aspect of the strategy. Dunnigan also ensured that the senior team received ample training, so that relationships and trust could be fostered among them. Orientation training for new employees included meeting Dunnigan, so that he could sell his vision and describe the type of empowered team environment he was encouraging. Honest, open communication was constantly encouraged among employees at all levels.

Dunnigan found himself in constant competition for funds. Whenever he met with his senior counterparts from the bank, he found himself in direct conflict over this matter. His peers viewed him as selfish and as not understanding that the insurance company was part of the bank. Resources in the bank were tight, and every division was required to justify its requests for funds. Naturally, it was difficult for others in the bank to understand the financial needs of PICC. The insurance company had incurred a lot of expenses. They had to buy new equipment and had new offices, whereas personnel at the bank worked with older, outdated equipment and facilities.

Things began to change a couple of years after the start-up. Dunnigan spent considerable time away from the office, selling the direct insurance concept externally. When he wasn't making speeches, he could be found on the golf course. Social contact was important. As CEO, Dunnigan saw a responsibility to be in the public light. Some of the senior team became concerned about his absences. They felt that he had forgotten this was a start-up company that required more of his time in the office. Dunnigan was no longer meeting with new hires because of his schedule, and regular meetings with employees were no longer taking place.

QUESTIONS

1. Describe the intended culture and the emergent culture of PICC.

2. The intention was that PICC would have an organic structure. Would you classify its present structure as organic or mechanistic, and why?

3. What problems have resulted from PICC being owned by PB? What effect will they have on PICC's mission?

4. Predict the state of affairs at PICC a year or two after the time of the case. How could the problems you foresee be avoided?

Portrait of a Canadian Advisor

Results of this study provide a revealing portrait of the Canadians who work as advisors on CIDA-sponsored projects. From interviews with advisors, spouses, colleagues, and national counterparts the following profile emerges of a typical Canadian advisor.

The typical Canadian advisor is a male between the age of 40 and 50. He was born in Canada, where he has lived at least five years of his life. His mother tongue is English (47%) or French (44%) and he is well educated, having at least one university degree. He is married and is accompanied on this assignment by his spouse.

Our advisor is a professional working for a private Canadian firm that is under contract to CIDA. No stranger to the developing world, he has had at least one previous overseas posting, and has spent at least two years working in developing countries. On this assignment, he is working in an urban setting as part of a team. He will be working directly with a counterpart from the country of assignment in a management capacity. He sees his role as an advisory one involving training and the transfer of skills and knowledge.

Our advisor approaches this assignment with confidence. His interest in the host country is high, and he is not worried about his ability to adapt. He is confident that he will do well on the assignment and that he can make a significant contribution to development efforts in the country. He feels he has better than average interpersonal and communication skills. And although he considers himself to have a high sense of adventure and altruism, he is concerned about his security and places a high value on upward mobility.

A desire to give and/or learn lies behind our advisor's acceptance of the overseas assignment. His attitudes on development are fairly conservative, and he views the transfer of technology as the key to improving economic prosperity in the developing countries and to narrowing the gap between rich and poor nations. He sees no need for the developed world to limit its standard of living and supports Canada's

Daniel J. Kealey, "Cross-Cultural Effectiveness — A Study of Canadian Technical Advisors Overseas", 1990, pp. 32–33. Published by Canadian International Development Agency. Reproduced by permission of CIDA Briefing Centre, Hull QC and Daniel J. Kealey.

policy of tied aid, which requires that the majority of our development dollars be spent on the purchase of Canadian goods and services.

On assignment, our advisor expresses a great deal of satisfaction in his personal, family, and professional life, and experiences a high degree of involvement in the local culture. In his mind, the process of adaptation has been a smooth one involving little culture shock, and he feels more satisfaction with his life overseas than he did previously in Canada.

On the job, he feels that his terms of reference are well defined and understood and that both he and his colleagues have been highly effective in the task of transferring skills and knowledge to their national counterparts. Although status differences exist between himself and his counterpart, he does not see this inhibiting their working relationship. And while he feels that his living conditions are generally less comfortable than those in Canada, he does not see this as an impediment to his assignment.

DIFFERING REALITIES

The views and attitudes expressed above are the advisor's perceptions of himself. A different and less optimistic portrait emerges, however, from field interviews with spouses, colleagues, and counterparts, as well as observations made by field researchers. As seen by others, our advisor has minimal involvement with the local culture, preferring instead to spend his leisure and social time in the company of other Canadians and expatriates. He has made little effort to learn the local language, and is likely to spend little time outside the job with his counterpart or other nationals. Although he is able to accurately identify the key factors that promote success on a development assignment, he is less able to actually demonstrate the required skills and interest in his own behaviour. What people say and what they do are often inconsistent. How an individual sees and assesses himself often bears little resemblance to how he is seen and assessed by others.

QUESTIONS

1. Why is the gap between the typical Canadian advisor's self-perception and the perceptions by others likely to be greater in a foreign environment? Would similar gaps exist in a domestic environment?

2. How is this gap likely to affect the advisor's performance?

3. What measures would you recommend to improve the accuracy of the advisor's self-perception and performance?

Puck Stop

In 1987, after ten years of stardom as a goaltender with the Toronto Maple Leafs, George Athlone retired from professional sports, and returned to his native Ottawa, where he had also played junior hockey with the Sixty-Sevens. With a relatively small capital investment, he opened a small pub, called Puck Stop, in a slightly run-down area near the University of Ottawa. It quickly caught on with the students, and by 1990 was making a regular profit.

In that year, he sold his majority interest to CanServe, a food service conglomerate specializing in regional franchises. With their financial backing, additional Puck Stops were quickly opened in neighbouring suburbs. By 1994, there were five units in Ottawa-Carleton, and one in Hull (l'Arrêt-Rondelle). By 2004, the chain had expanded nationally, with approximately 65 locations across Canada, and, with the exception of a few specific locations, had lost its university orientation. The decor was similar at all locations, with sports memorabilia covering the walls. A large bar area with adequate standing room stood to one side of the entrance, while an informal restaurant stood across from it. The menu was limited, specializing in chicken and ribs. Each pub was fitted with at least ten television sets hooked up to a satellite receiver. Wall-sized screens were located in both the bar and restaurant areas, while others were scattered throughout the location. It was not unusual to telecast three or four sports events simultaneously on a given evening. In 1993, CanServe established Sports Action facilities at all of its Puck Stops.

Sports Action was incorporated in Detroit in 1992. They had a very simple premise: to capitalize on the substantial, mostly male, market for professional sports by using the latest in communications technology to develop an interactive system for wagering on events. Using satellite communications and networking technology, they provided a sophisticated video game system to participating bars. Patrons were given portable terminals, with which they could predict the result of individual at bats during simultaneously televised baseball games (strikeout, walk, or hit; fly ball or grounder; right, left or centre; etc.). A control centre in Detroit transmitted the actual result within seconds of the event, and correct choices were rewarded with

---

This case was written by Richard S. Fisher.

scoring points. A special video display in each bar kept track of all patrons' scores. At the conclusion of a game, each bar was ranked against all others playing that particular game throughout North America, as were all individual players. All Puck Stop locations subscribed to Sports Action.

On Tuesday evenings, a time of generally low bar patronage, Sports Action ran a lengthy (two-hour) continent-wide version of its trivia game, called Brainiac. Brainiac rapidly became a fad at a few locations, generally those located near universities. Although Puck Stop teams occasionally achieved national ranking, the emotional level of the competition was decidedly local. Most Puck Stops offered a free drink to the person with the highest Brainiac score in the bar.

In 2003, a Puck Stop was opened in Forest Hill Village, the commercial centre of an upscale enclave of Toronto, where the demographics showed income levels well above those of their typical locations. Jack Stanley, an experienced Puck Stop troubleshooter from Ottawa, was brought in to develop it. It was assumed that once the location had become profitable, Jack would hand the job over to local management and return to Ottawa. Within a year, despite problems relating to local opposition to a liquor licence and outdoor patio seating, the location had developed a regular clientele, and was becoming marginally profitable. Jack attributed his success to scrupulous control over general cleanliness and food quality. While prices were kept reasonable, Jack believed that his specific market was not particularly price-sensitive.

In early 2004, in an effort to improve mid-week business, Puck Stop management decided to hold a system-wide trivia contest on Tuesday nights. While they would utilize the Brainiac game and scoring system, the contest was for Puck Stop locations only. With only 65 participating pubs, the chances of winning the Puck Stop game would be greatly improved over the national system, which by 2004 boasted over 3,500 participating bars. A preliminary round was to run for eight consecutive weeks, with the eight highest scores qualifying for three rounds of single-game playoffs during the following three weeks. The rules stressed team participation, with each pub's total based on the sum of each of its five highest individual scores. Equipment was generally available for up to 20 participants at each bar.

Jack estimated that prior to the contest, there were about five people playing Brainiac at 9:00 p.m. on Tuesdays, out of about 30 bar patrons overall. In order to ensure that patrons knew about the contest, Jack had posters displayed throughout the pub, and added promotional text to the CanServe TV feed advertising the event.

Before the Brainiac game on the Tuesday prior to the start of the contest, Hannah Kurtzman, a regular player, made the rounds of the bar and suggested to the other regulars that they play cooperatively, and see how well they did. By mutual agreement, five players crowded into an end booth designed for four, and shared their answers. Although the pub finished twelfth out of the 65 contenders, Hannah thought they might be able to improve with time. "All we need are more people," she suggested. "As only the top five player scores count, more players means more margin for error."

Mike Colangelo, one of the other regulars, had his doubts. Mike estimated that he had suggested answers for at least 45 of the 50 questions in the game, while the other four players had contributed only one or two. He believed that in order to win, they required not just some more warm bodies, but additional people with knowledge in areas where he was weak, notably the arts in general and the hard sciences. However, rather than offend Hannah, he simply suggested that both of them try and recruit some more players for the team.

For the first week of the contest, Hannah brought in two additional friends, while Mike added an English professor from the University of Toronto named Bob Carstairs. With eight people playing, the pub finished eighth, putting them in contention for the playoffs, if they could maintain their momentum. "Did you notice, however," said Bob to Mike, after they had left, "that we were the only ones answering questions? Don't the others have anything to say?" "It doesn't matter," answered Mike. "All they have to do is listen to us, push the right buttons, and not think for themselves and get a wrong answer."

By the fourth week of the contest, the team had grown to about 15 players: about ten like Hannah, who did not suggest answers, and five like Mike, who did. As the team outgrew their booth, Jack reserved a segregated section for them towards the rear, and disconnected the jukebox for the duration of Brainiac. Mike's group tended to stay together on one side, discuss the answers among themselves, and then announce it to the rest of the team. More often than not they were right: occasionally, they were wrong. However, the team continued to rise in the standings, and were now generally ranking among the top three locations. "We still need more manpower," commented Mike. "We'll make the playoffs, but we're not yet good enough to be a favourite.

The team was also spending more time in the bar. They now tended to congregate by about seven, eat dinner, discuss the previous week's game and standings, and practise on other trivia games that preceded Brainiac. Although Brainiac ended at ten, the post game discussions often continued for an additional hour.

The team continued to grow during weeks five through seven, and now generally commanded the full complement of 20 boards. However, although their scoring averages improved, their relative standings did not. About five other Sports Action locations were also taking the game seriously, and expanding and honing their teams as well.

For week eight, Bob brought in an engineering colleague of his, who he identified only by the pseudonym "Wombat." "He's great," said Bob, while introducing him around. "He plays this game a lot up at another bar, but got fed up with how they were treating him. He was really carrying their team." With Wombat's help, the team was doing quite well going into the final question, which was worth up to 50% of their collective score to date. The screen flashed, "What was the last country in Europe to give women the vote?" "Switzerland!" yelled Wombat. "Without a doubt!" "Are you certain?" asked Bob. "I thought it was one of the old southern Catholic dictatorships; Portugal, or maybe Spain or Italy." Wombat stood up. "Switzerland!" he roared, and then sat down again. Twenty fingers pressed the Switzerland button.

The 30 second time allowance ticked slowly, and when Portugal was revealed as the correct answer, Bob slammed his terminal on the table in disgust, and stalked off towards the men's room. "They're . . . wrong!" yelled Wombat, "and I'll prove it. I'll call them as soon as they're open, tomorrow morning." With a few more expletives, he grabbed his coat and stalked out.

Despite their poor showing in week eight, the team still qualified for the quarterfinals, and Mike walked in about seven. "They were right," he said. "Switzerland in 1971, but Portugal in 1976. Where's Wombat?" "I dunno," shrugged Bob. "Maybe he's too embarrassed to show up again." Despite Wombat's absence, the team still commanded 20 terminals, and squeaked through to a narrow win. During the post-mortem, however, Hannah was upset. "You know," she said to Mike, "the five of you congregate in your little corner, and we can't always hear you. We're losing points because our answers are often late. You should mix in with the rest of us." "If you'd come up with an answer once or twice, maybe we would," Bob interjected, and without saying another word, stalked out.

The team (minus Wombat) seemed to put their differences behind them for the semifinals, and once again managed to beat their opponents by a small margin. No one stayed to savour the victory, however. Hannah left immediately after the results were displayed with a curt, "See you next week," and Bob and Mike departed shortly thereafter.

On the night of the finals, Jack offered the players a round of drinks on the house, as he was satisfied with the results of the contest. The pub had netted about 15 new customers, who were both eating and drinking over the course of several hours, and the nightly gross sales had increased by about $500. Unfortunately, the game itself proved to be an anticlimax. The team made a few errors early, and never recovered. They were soundly beaten. "That's it!" yelled Bob. "That's the last time I play as part of a team. I do better on my own!" "Maybe that's your problem," countered Hannah, before turning her back and talking to one of her friends.

The first Tuesday following the contest, Mike dropped in to the Puck Stop as usual, about 8:30, to play Brainiac, breathing a sigh of relief that the contest had finally finished. When the game began, he was surprised to find himself the only one playing. The following week, the situation was the same; none of the team members had returned.

For the remainder of the summer, Mike saw none of the former Brainiac regulars, and Jack saw his trend of increasing sales turn into a net decrease by September. In October, Puck Stop management decided to run the contest again during the winter, with a two-week break for the Christmas season. As Mike had not expected the former team to show up, he was surprised when he walked into the bar on the evening of the first round of the new contest, to see Hannah and some of her friends seated in their old booth.

"Care to join us?" asked Hannah. "I think we have a really good chance of winning this time."

QUESTIONS

1. In what ways was the team that Hannah and Mike put together similar to a formal organization, and in what ways was it not?

2. Why were the team members not motivated to continue coming to the bar after the end of the contest? Would it have been different if they had won the contest?

3. Given the difference in skill between Mike's group and the rest of the team members, would different styles of leadership and communication have resulted in improved social harmony? If so, what styles?

4. Could Jack Stanley have intervened in any way to prevent the poor sales results that ultimately occurred?

5. Do you think an effective team will form again for the new contest?

The Ready-to-Eat Department

Universal Foods Inc. is a large distributor and retailer of general food products in Canada. It has provided quality products and services to its customers for the past 35 years and employs over 50,000 people in more than 700 branches across Canada. The company structure is tall, with many layers of management: from department managers, assistant store managers, store managers, area managers, regional managers, Assistant Executive Officer, and Chief Executive Officer. Common policies covering most administrative matters for all branches are set at head office and implemented throughout the country, with minor regional differences. Individual store managers have authority to adjust the product selection to suit local tastes (from an approved list), hire permanent and part-time staff up to the level of department manager, and allocate non-managerial staff throughout the store according to workloads.

Branch X is one of Universal's stores in Toronto. Like others, it is divided into a number of different departments. Within the branch, every department has its own challenges, but the Ready-to-Eat Department, in particular, seems to face numerous problems, giving it a high profile with the branch's store manager as well as with the regional manager.

The Ready-to-Eat Department is the "Prepared Foods" section of the store, and many Universal branches have this department. The department is further divided into different stations, such as prepared meals, pizza, pastry, baked goods, sandwiches, salads, and coffee. This department at Branch X employs about 40 people, and priority for assignments to the more attractive postings and work shifts is largely based on seniority. Susan, the new department manager, tries to exert a strong control over her employees. The staff, including Susan, are all under pressure to deal with a range of consumer attitudes, requirements, and complaints. These are more frequent than in other departments of Branch X because the food is prepared in the store for direct consumption. Unlike most of the other products sold in the branch, the quality of the items is directly under the control of the department, and customer feedback can sometimes be intense and immediate.

This work is based on original work by Sheryl To.

Some of the challenges in the Ready-to-Eat Department originated with the department manager, Susan, who herself has been there for less than two months. Susan had been a long-term, loyal Universal employee at Branch Z, another Toronto branch. Six months ago, she had been selected to succeed the manager of her department in Branch Z. Her promotion had been long delayed. Although she was a good worker and reliable, she did not have a post-secondary education and her written communication skills were deemed to be less than acceptable for management. However, after more-junior employees were promoted over her, Susan voiced her displeasure to the store manager. Since he was unsure of Susan's suitability, the store manager consulted with the regional manager, and they jointly decided to promote her on the condition that she would attend a remedial English course. She did attend, but the improvement in her writing skill was only marginal. Her leadership of the group was also not optimal. It was exercised only by giving orders and expecting to hear "Yes, Susan" in return. She seemed unwelcoming to any feedback or suggestions from her subordinates and would become angry if challenged. Within three months of becoming department manager, an employee in Susan's department claimed that she was harassed and discriminated against by Susan, and two other employees said they had witnessed this behaviour towards their colleague. During a subsequent interview with a regional human resources specialist, it was felt that Susan's behaviour was not acceptable, but it was not intended to harass or to discriminate against her subordinate. Instead, it was a defensive overreaction of a manager who felt insecure and unprepared in her post. It was noted that Susan had not as yet received formal leadership training.

Universal is reluctant to give up on loyal employees. So, rather than demote or terminate Susan, she was transferred to Branch X as the department manager for the Ready-to-Eat Department, a position that had just come open. The condition for this placement was that she attend a course in leadership as soon as possible. Ultimately, she would have to show better supervisory skills. The next leadership course was due to start in two-and-a-half months, and Susan readily agreed to the posting and the condition.

The previous manager of the Ready-to-Eat Department favoured participation in key decisions and had been on good terms with most of the group. The staff found out about the situation at Susan's previous posting, and some had adopted a negative bias against her almost immediately after she was introduced to the group by the store manager. One of Susan's first acts as their new manager was to post a notice for a staff meeting on the bulletin board outside her office. The notice contained several grammatical errors, and some staff members who were gathered there wondered out loud how someone with such poor English skills could be appointed as their manager. Susan was sitting in her office with the door closed but heard much of what the group was saying.

The stress of the failed placement at her previous store, the bad start with her new staff, and her urgent need to do well at Branch X seemed to bring out behaviour that steadily worsened her relationship with her new subordinates. She became intensely dictatorial with the majority of the staff, whom she felt resented her, and favoured those few whom she perceived as "on her side". The latter group received preferential treatment concerning work shifts and duties, and their requests for time off were considered ahead of others. Her interactions with most of the staff were kept to the bare minimum, with Susan giving orders and the staff member listening. For the following six weeks, since the staff were generally very experienced and still wished to keep their jobs, this did not affect performance greatly. The main effect was less-cheerful employees to deal with customers and a lot of informal negative comments exchanged among staff members. However, the changed atmosphere in the department did increase complaints from customers, who had some less than friendly encounters with staff. The store manager was sensitive to these developments. She had not been enthusiastic when the regional manager had insisted on placing Susan with Branch X, but she understood that giving Susan a second chance was part of Universal's corporate culture, and the position was available.

At this time, another branch in the Toronto area had a fairly severe problem with cockroaches. While the store was attempting a quiet cleanup, several customers noticed the cockroaches, and the news media publicized the story. The spotlight of negative public attention produced stern warnings from head office to all stores nationwide to be vigilant against any form of infestation. New inspection and cleaning guidelines were to be introduced immediately according to the guidelines issued from the top.

When the news story broke, Branch X's store manager was away for several days attending a meeting of all the region's store managers in another city. She was aware of a potential mouse problem at Branch X, which had been at a low level. However, considering the attention the media were now giving to Universal, a customer report of mouse droppings anywhere near the food would certainly create another serious public relations problem that would reflect on the entire chain and, of course, her reputation. She wanted to ensure that new inspection and cleanup procedures were immediately implemented, and she called the senior assistant store manager to get it started as soon as possible. The assistant store manager called a meeting of all the department managers. He pointed out that the guidelines would need to be customized for each area in the store. He realized that the Ready-to-Eat Department with its open displays of prepared foods was especially vulnerable, so Susan was instructed to immediately draw up procedures based on the head office guidelines and to have them implemented within 24 hours. She did so, after submitting them first to the assistant store manager for review as he had requested. However, two hours after that meeting, he went for an emergency dental procedure and booked off the next day as well. Susan was not aware that he was gone for so long. When she received no feedback by noon the next day, she assumed his acceptance of her procedures, posted them on the bulletin board, and distributed them to each of the staff members via their mailboxes in the staff room. Due to the ongoing tense situation with her staff and her prior experiences, she did not want to risk a group meeting to discuss them.

The staff members who had been antagonistic to Susan scanned the notice for more grammatical errors. They found three, which were not very serious, as well as some awkward sentences. They focused on them and the lack of consultation to proclaim to other staff members that they could not implement these procedures. The following day, when the procedures were to be fully implemented, Susan talked to individual staff members about putting the procedures into effect. Having received a mumbling reply rather than assurance of implementation from the first two staff members, she insisted on a proper reply from the third. This started a loud argument, with the staff member claiming that the procedures were hard to understand and impractical.

The argument was overheard by the manager of an adjoining department. The problems of the Ready-to-Eat Department had become well known throughout the store, and normally he would have ignored the conflict since it was not his direct concern. But given the risk to the entire store's business that would be created by a failure to implement inspection and cleanup procedures in the Ready-to-Eat Department, he decided it was essential that he inform the store manager of the situation when she returned the next day. The store manager was dismayed by what she heard. It required immediate action, but what action should she take?

QUESTIONS

1. Was it appropriate to promote Susan, given that she lacked the formal educational qualifications? Is the rationale that the promotion represents prevailing corporate culture a valid one?

2. After Susan's severe conflict with her subordinate in the first store, was it appropriate that she be given another chance as department manager in Branch X? If not, what else should have been done?

3. Once Susan had been appointed department manager in Branch X, what advice would you have given her concerning how to manage her new group of subordinates?

4. What should the store manager of Branch X do now, and why?

Reduced Hours

Fraser Shilling, the manager of the head office training department of a large insurance company based in Calgary, is reviewing a proposal submitted by Nairobi Hanson, who occupies a mid-management position.

Nairobi is a female in her late 30s who has decided to return to university part-time to complete a B.A. degree with a major in Fine Art that she had begun some 20 years earlier. There is no overlap between her career and her chosen area of study. Her job entails analyzing the training requirements of employees at various levels across the organization and designing training material appropriate to their needs. Each of her peers in the department manages their own project(s), and deadlines are set according to the scale of each individual project. There is only an occasional need for cooperation among department staff members.

The organization's policy regarding continuing education is proactive, provided the studies are job-related, and would develop skills that enhance on-the-job performance. Courses falling into this category are paid for in full by the company.

In this particular case there is no perceived benefit to the organization by this employee pursuing studies in fine arts. The work arrangement she proposes includes covering the cost of the course(s) herself and working a three-day week at 60% of her regular salary. She will continue to work on the projects currently assigned to her; deadlines, however, will have to be extended to accommodate the reduced work week. The work arrangement is to remain in effect for an indefinite period.

Mr. Shilling is quite well-disposed towards Ms. Hanson's proposal. She is one of the most productive members of the department, and he fears that she might leave entirely if refused.

In addition, he is quite supportive of a more flexible approach to employer-employee relationships. His regret is that the courses she intends to take will not be professionally oriented. Fraser Shilling believes that a career can and should be developed through a life-long commitment to supplementary education.

Nairobi's peers are not unanimously supportive of her proposal. There is the suspicion that although her attendance will be reduced and her salary will be pro-

---

This case was written by Marian McLennon.

rated, her performance and output might be undiminished. This would make everyone who is remaining full-time look very unproductive. Two of the people who felt this way have already spoken to Fraser Shilling, and said that they thought a person should have the right to a full leave for a period of time, but that the job could not be properly done part-time. They also indicated to Nairobi that it would be "difficult" to cooperate with her once she began her reduced hours.

QUESTIONS

1. Is Nairobi Hanson's proposal a reasonable one? Would it be a better proposal if the educational program was professionally related?

2. Assuming that he was willing to approve the proposal, should Fraser Shilling attempt to deal with the concerns of the other staff members? In what way?

3. Should Nairobi try to restrict her output to about 60% of its former level once she goes on reduced hours?

4. Should Fraser Shilling accept the proposal:
   (a) as it is?
   (b) with qualifications? State any that you believe are warranted.

The Reorganization

Lilly Jones has been with the Department of Regional Industrial Expansion for four years. During this time she received several pay increases in recognition of her superior performance as an Economic Analyst and as Manager of the Economic Analysis unit. Recently she was promoted Director of her branch in the Economic and Regional Policy Division of the department, which employs some 250 people, most of whom are professionals: economists, sociologists, lawyers, and accountants.

As Director, Ms. Jones has three unit managers reporting directly to her: Charles Thompson, Strategic Policy Analysis; Karen Smith, Economic Analysis; and Stan Cooper, Regional Policy Analysis. The Strategic Policy Analysis unit has the most employees, with over 120 analysts whose function is to process private sector applications for regional development grants and subsidies. Economic Analysis is the smallest unit, with about 30 employees who study economic trends to ensure that the department is aware of the developments in national economic conditions. The Regional Policy Analysis unit evaluates projects to ensure monies have been properly spent and assesses the effectiveness of the development policies of the department as determined by priorities established by the Economic Analysis unit.

Ms. Jones worked closely with Ms. Smith in the past, and was instrumental in her appointment as manager to succeed Ms. Jones as head of the Economic Analysis unit. Ms. Smith's promotion, however, has caused resentment among some of the professional staff of the Economic Analysis unit. Some of them feel that Ms. Smith was promoted because she is a woman and worked closely with Ms. Jones.

Mr. Thompson, on the other hand, resents Ms. Jones' recent appointment because he feels he deserved the director's position in the branch by virtue of his seniority and breadth of experience. Mr. Thompson has worked in the department for the last ten years, has contributed to the success of many projects, and has served on various interdepartmental committees during this time.

Mr. Cooper is one of the longest serving members, not only in the branch, but also in the department, and is close to retirement. For this reason he did not expect to be appointed to the director's position and, in fact, had lost interest and enthusi-

---

This case was written by Jim C. Simeon.

asm for his job some time ago. This was evident to most of the staff in the Regional Policy Analysis unit, who thought he would coast for the next few years before he retired. Accordingly, many of the more ambitious types in the unit were "jockeying for position" in the hopes of succeeding Mr. Cooper in the manager's office.

The other day Ms. Jones received a directive from her assistant deputy minister that an impending budget cut would require the department to cut $50 million annually and a minimum of 35 PY (Person Years). The bad news was that her own branch would have to take the lion's share of the personnel cuts because of a pending internal reorganization of various branches of the department. As the director of the branch, Ms. Jones had to recommend the reallocation or dismissal of 35 PY, of which at least two would be in the management category, and the cut of up to $15 million from her branch's current year budget.

The assistant deputy minister (ADM) of the division called Ms. Jones to his office this morning to discuss the reorganization of the department, the effect of the required cuts to the branch, and its possible impact on the division. During their meeting the ADM made it clear that Stan Cooper was one of his old friends, and was personally close to the Deputy Minister as well. The ADM then made it clear that Mr. Cooper should perhaps be allowed to stay on for the next several years in order to qualify for his full pension. The ADM also said a number of positive things about how "Charlie" Thompson had been such a hard and dedicated worker for the department over the years. This left Ms. Jones with the distinct impression that perhaps Mr. Thompson should also be spared from any impending cuts in her branch. The ADM concluded their meeting by saying that he would like to see her preliminary recommendations on how the impending cuts to her branch should be handled by 10:00 a.m. tomorrow.

QUESTIONS

1. What are the moral, ethical, and organizational issues in this case?

2. Is the ADM acting properly when implying that Mr. Cooper and Mr. Thompson should be spared from the cuts?

3. What do you recommend that Lilly Jones put in her preliminary recommendations?

4. What will be the consequences of your recommendations?

Returned Goods

My name is Lynn. I am a factory worker here in Mississauga, Ontario who is now about eight years away from retirement. I've spent my whole life working in the west end of Metropolitan Toronto, which is common in my family. In fact, I'm the third generation of factory workers. My grandfather was originally a farmer, but he sold his farm and went to work in a factory. My father made skates, my oldest brother made bicycles for CCM and my other brother worked in a printing factory. As a young girl, my mother worked in a munitions factory during World War II. My sister and I are the youngest of her children, and the only ones still working. She is a foam cutter in a furniture factory. My husband works in a factory as well.

Factory work has been pretty good to me, at least until lately. I didn't finish high school, so my career options weren't that many. Being a rocket scientist wasn't in my future. But industrial work is better than most service work or "Mac" jobs, as the kids call them. My husband and I have enough trouble making ends meet on our two wage packets, and it would be very difficult to do it on the minimum wage paid by those employers. Most factory jobs start at about one and a half times minimum wage, and I currently make twice the minimum wage. The work itself can be tiring, because it is usually repetitive and, frequently, physically demanding, with heavy loads to be lifted. However, usually I have worked in places that are fairly clean and warm, and protected from the elements. I have always enjoyed the company of my fellow workers. Factory life usually provides opportunities to talk to your neighbour a bit while doing your work, and the fellowship at breaks is good. We all seem to share the same interests and problems. The men talk about sports and the women about family.

One of the nice things about factory work is that you can't take it home with you. When you walk out the door at quitting time, you leave your work behind you. That means lots of time for other interests. My husband is active in community affairs, and was recently recognized for his volunteer work by our city. I am quite active in Girl Guides, which takes me out a couple of nights a week and gets me to

---

This case is based on original work by Donna Olde Weghuis.

a few weekend campouts each year. My sister and I have a small handicraft business. We have always been quite good with crafts in our family, and we make goods to sell at craft shows in our area. Some of my relatives are stamp collectors, and my brother has made a small "retirement" business of selling stamps at stamp shows. My husband is also becoming active in that.

I haven't worked in the same factory continuously, as I have been out of the workforce to raise my kids. That is a bit different from my father and older brother who worked at the same places until they were shut down. However, I have worked for my current employer for the past 11 years, and I would say I have been a good employee. I am strong and I get along with people. I do my job and I am rarely off sick. My only health problem is a sore arm that may be a repetitive strain injury from my work. Usually it is tolerable, and I have always tried to not let it affect my performance.

I work in a factory that processes returned goods. I call it a factory because it works like a factory in many ways. Material is brought in; we process it, and then send it out. We have a busy shipping and receiving department. Compared to most factories, everything goes backwards. We receive things from retail stores, and then we ship to manufacturing plants. When customers return defective products, the store has to make sure that the item is returned to the manufacturer for credit. Actually, it is more complicated than that. Some goods can be repaired by the store if it has a repair depot, or by the retail chain if it has a repair depot. Other goods are so defective, perhaps through damage that happened in the store or in transit, that the manufacturer doesn't want it back. These items can be written off, with the cost charged to the responsible party. It isn't even simple when goods are actually destined to be returned to a manufacturer. They all have many factories, and the factories can change what products they produce. This means an item may need to be returned to a different destination than where it was made.

These factors make the management of returned goods a complex and significant activity for major retail chains. Most chains now centralize that activity. The work involved is sufficiently specialized that they have found it more efficient to have all returned goods sent to a central location for processing. Originally, my organization was a part of Media Mania, a large chain that sold electronic equipment for the home. Each retail outlet assembles their returned goods onto pallets to be shipped to our factory. The pallet contains everything returned to the store by customers. The store makes the decision as to whether the item is a repair, a return, or a write-off by giving it a close look and following the policy that applies to that product. Typically, this is the one and only time that anyone will actually look at the product. Thereafter, it is processed according to its skid and product number. We add what we call a licence plate, which directs the return to its ultimate destination.

My job involves taking a pallet of returned goods, recording each item so that the computerized inventory control system can track the item, the store, and the manufacturer, and make the appropriate adjustments in the inventory and sales records. Likewise, the chain adjusts its accounts with the manufacturer. I record serial number, store id, country of manufacture, batch number, skid number, and the decision that was made about what to do with the item. To do this I must physically unload the pallet, scan each item, attach its licence plate, place it on a conveyer belt and send it on its way to be repaired, returned to the manufacturer or written off. The items can be large or small, and are usually boxed, but sometimes bagged. All of us doing this work are women. Although we are pretty strong and used to moving heavy items, we do occasionally need help lifting an item onto the conveyor belt. The skids are moved around by men driving fork lift trucks and we get one of them to help us with the heavy items.

Not all of the information we need is found on the returned goods. Often we need to look up information, such as country of manufacture. Generally, we got to know this information, as it was shared among the workers. If I didn't know what to put down for an item, I would call out to one of the other women. Somebody would know where it goes. This was faster than looking it up.

Goods that we can repair are routed to our repair depot. Sometimes they send items back into the loop if they decide it can't be repaired or if they are too busy. If it is to be returned, it goes to our area sorting workers, who collect products according to manufacturers, and then to the shipping department, which packages them for the return and sends them on their way

Until two years ago our factory was fairly small, with only about twenty full time employees and about ten temporary workers. Only four of us scanned. We scanned about 7,000 items each day, so you can see why this activity needs to be organized. I liked working for Media Mania. We had our targets to meet, but they were fairly easy going so long as we got the work done. I'm the oldest of the four scanners, and I'm not as quick as I used to be. Media Mania was okay about the fact that we didn't all work at the same rate. We each had our strengths. For example, I'm really good at remembering the information not found on the products, so the others always asked me for help. We cooperated, had lots of fun and got the job done on time. In all my years with Media Mania, I always got excellent annual and semi-annual reviews.

Media Mania was a Canadian owned and operated business. Then, two years ago, they became part of a large American chain. They do things much differently. The first change is that they outsourced the returned goods business. We no longer work for Media Mania, but for Retco, a North American returned goods business that acquired our factory. We all kept our jobs, and we work in the same place, but Retco deals with several chains, and our business is growing as more chains are signed up. So far, Retco has kept these new operations in separate locations but we expect to be merged soon into a larger building with many more workers.

We now have new managers with an entirely different outlook and rules. They put a huge emphasis on output. All we ever hear is, "Scan faster", and, "Get the products off the skids and onto the conveyer." They have also become more particular about talking on the job. We aren't supposed to talk to each other. They have a new system of recording employee "misbehaviour". They write up "occurrences", which are reports of things they think we have done wrong. Taking a sick day is an "occurrence" unless you bring in a doctor's note. Talking is an "occurrence". Going to the bathroom too often is an "occurrence". After five "occurrences" you get a verbal warning. After seven, you receive a written warning, and after ten you are fired. One of the men got fired this year. He was a good worker, but he tended to complain loudly once in a while. He was just "blowing off steam", and would calm down quickly, but the new management didn't like that.

While all of the workers seem to get some "occurrences", several of us are getting more than others. Those of us who have been around longer, generally older, and are at the top of the pay scale seem to be targeted. I'm having a hard time with these changes. I don't enjoy my job as much, but I can't afford to quit at this time in my life. I'm really having trouble avoiding "occurrence" reports. For example, when I need help with a heavy item, I still ask, but the fork lift operators aren't as willing to help out anymore. They say it isn't their main job and it keeps them from moving the pallets around as fast as possible. When a manager notices me asking, it gets recorded. Not being able to receive help once in a while slows me down. My arm is bothering me more now from all the heavy lifting. Also, we don't cooperate on the line anymore. If someone doesn't know the country code of a product, they can't ask anyone or they'll get an "occurrence". The managers also don't like to see them taking time to look up the information, so they just guess.

I know that the best thing for me to do is to just keep my head down, do my job, ignore everyone else, never talk to anyone, never answer anyone's request for help, and work as hard as I can. However, it isn't any fun anymore, and I wonder whether I can do a good enough job in this way. It is frustrating, and I'm finding it very stressful. Sometimes, I stay awake at night worrying about what is going to happen. I'm not enjoying my hobbies as much anymore.

I'm fifty-seven years old and I know I'm not going to find another job easily, especially one that pays as well. I can't afford to quit, but my niece, who works in the human resources department of another company, says it looks like Retco is trying to get rid of me. If they can't drive me out, they will probably fire me. She says they appear to be laying the groundwork for it now.

I don't think this is fair. I've worked hard for this business, and I could still do useful work for this company. Perhaps I am getting a bit too slow to work on the line but there are other jobs I could do for them in the office or in shipping. My product knowledge must be of value somewhere, but this is making *me* feel like returned goods.

QUESTIONS

1. Describe Lynn's motivational situation before and after the takeover by Retco.

2. How has her perception of the job and sources of satisfaction changed?

3. Identify all the sources of Lynn's stress.

4. Retco would claim that their policies are designed to maximize performance. Do you agree or disagree, and why?

5. Describe the type of organization that existed before the takeover by Retco and the type it became afterwards.

6. Evaluate Retco's behaviour from the standpoint of ethics and corporate responsibility.

7. What should Lynn do now, and how should she go about it?

8. As a human resources consultant to Retco, what would you suggest concerning Lynn and others in the same job?

Ridgway Furniture Limited

Ridgway Furniture Limited started manufacturing on a small scale about 20 years ago but now employs over 700 people, producing a wide range of wood and metal home and office furniture. The firm enjoys a good reputation in the furniture industry, and its products, sold in the medium-to-high price range, are considered good quality products by the general public. The firm is also recognized for its own special furniture stylings. To produce its furniture, the firm uses the latest in modern technology. The firm's rapidest expansion took place in its first ten years of operation. However, although the firm has kept growing since then, the rate of growth is now much slower.

Donald Carson, who has been with the company since it started, is the head of the Furniture Design department. Dick Prindles, who also joined the firm at that time, is now the company president and Donald's boss. They are good friends, and have together witnessed the company's growth to its present size.

Carson is regarded as one of the pillars of this organization because of the many contributions he has made towards the growth of the enterprise. He is well recognized for his creative abilities, which have led to the firm's unique furniture designs, one of the hallmarks of the company.

Until five years ago, Carson had a small staff of eight employees engaged in the task of creating new furniture designs. Five of them were male and three female. They were all hand-picked, bright, young individuals. They were all highly creative, and most of them had received formal training in the art of furniture design at various community colleges. Carson rated them as "high performers".

Carson's department has expanded considerably, and the number of employees engaged in designing had jumped from 8 to 19, which included two clerical employees and a secretary to the head of the department. In addition to these 19 employees, Carson had hired John Gilbert as his assistant. His title was somewhat vague, but it is believed that Carson created this position so that the new person could assist him in running the department. Carson's workload had become unusually heavy, and John Gilbert's appointment came in response to this problem. It was

By Anwar Rashid. © L & S Management Publications.

expected that Gilbert would relieve Carson of much of the supervisory work, and also take care of many administrative details, thus releasing Carson to perform developmental work, relate to customers, and plan for the future. John Gilbert was hired from outside the firm, and was regarded as particularly suitable for the position because of his supervisory experience as well as his knowledge of furniture design. He shared a large office with the other artists and designers.

The relationships in the department were very informal, and people felt free to approach Carson any time. Carson's office door was always open. The employees liked him as a boss, and many admired him. Carson was always willing to listen to their ideas as well as their problems. Quite often they discussed their personal problems with him, and they never failed to get "good advice". They even had his home telephone number so that they could reach him after office hours in case of an emergency.

Three years ago Carson decided to hire another supervisor who would look after the specialized work being done by a group of six designers involved in the development of "modular furniture". A young and dynamic person by the name of Martin Starke was chosen for the newly created position. Starke was respected in the industry for his designing ability, and had come to the company with excellent credentials. It was believed that he would bring new vitality to the group, and would be responsible for the training of his workers. It was also expected that his work group would gradually increase in size, since there appeared to be a strong demand for the kind of furniture they were designing. In the new organizational structure, Starke was responsible to Gilbert for his work, but he would have free access to Carson, the head of the department. It was assumed that the other employees would report to Gilbert and receive their instructions from him.

During the next two years, new practices and patterns of relationships developed in this organization. While it was understood that some of the employees would report to Gilbert and some would report to Starke, it did not work that way in practice. The designers had acquired the habit of keeping in touch with Carson for almost everything they did, and they looked to him for all sorts of decisions. They even approached Carson with work-related problems that could have been handled by Gilbert or Starke. The six designers working under Starke went to Carson for every detail. Perhaps for reasons of expediency, Carson went along with this. He never turned the designers away or referred them to the supervisors concerned. Perhaps because he had been hired by Carson, or because he was easier to talk to, Starke also frequently approached Carson directly with his problems, rather than going to Gilbert.

As time passed, Gilbert began to show strong signs of resentment towards Carson's policy of discussing work with the designers, but he never lodged a formal protest or confronted Carson with his "beefs". Since Starke was still fairly "new" to the company, he preferred to lie low and adopt a do-nothing approach. In fact, he had never seriously tried to assert his position as a supervisor, except recently when he had a showdown with his group, who were now openly defying his authority. As a result of this incident, Carson arranged a meeting with the six designers, Starke, Gilbert, and himself. During the meeting Starke was accused by the designers of "not being around" when help was needed! They also complained that Starke had made very little effort to train them in design techniques. Two of them complained about not getting straight answers from him to any of the questions they had raised in the past. Starke responded by saying that he was involved with a lot of other work, which caused him to overlook some of the routine activities. He apologized to the group and promised to develop a "think-tank" type of training program for his designers. Starke took a defensive approach during this meeting. Gilbert never said a word. Carson pointed out to the designers that, in accordance with the organizational structure, they were responsible to Starke and they should go to him with their problems. He also suggested that another meeting should be arranged to be attended by the remaining employees, Gilbert, and Carson to clarify departmental policies.

In the meantime, another development had taken place. The president had informed Carson that the company would soon undertake a major expansion program, creating an additional position for a vice-president. Prindles had made it clear that he would like Carson to take over the new position. But Carson realized that if he were to move into the vice-president's office, a gap would be created in the Design department because, in his estimation, Gilbert was not ready to assume the responsibility of department head. Carson felt that Gilbert had lately become quite uninvolved and uninterested in the affairs of the department. It was Carson himself who was dealing with all the administrative work, as well as carrying out the necessary supervision of the employees. The only things that Gilbert attended to were those of a semi-clerical nature and, on occasions, answering simple questions raised by some of the customers. It seemed to Carson that, because of Gilbert's apathetic attitude, the employees preferred to come directly to Carson. Also, they seemed to be satisfied with the answers he gave them. However, Carson was now spending too much time supervising the tasks being performed by various people in the Design department. In fact, some of them should have been dealt with by Gilbert, and some by Starke. Together, these two should have run most of the departmental activities, leaving Carson free to attend to other developmental types of work. Carson realized that there was something wrong with the organization of this department, and some action had to be taken to rectify the situation. He decided to have a quiet chat with Gilbert, as well as with Starke, to remind them of their responsibilities and of the fact that the morale of the entire department was being affected. He told them over coffee to assert the necessary authority over their subordinates and insist that they come to them for instructions and decisions, and not to Carson. Both the supervisors gave certain reasons for their present dilemma or predicament, and promised to "put things into harness" for the future.

Over the next few months, Carson failed to perceive any change in the prevailing practice followed by the Design employees; nor did he notice any change in the attitudes of Gilbert and Starke. Employees continued to come directly to Carson and, when he tried to discourage them, they explained that "they had come to him after failing to get a satisfactory answer from the supervisor." Motivation and morale had gone down considerably in the past few weeks. It was virtually impossible for Carson to deal with his own departmental work, which had been increasing all the time, and to relate to market developments and at the same time be involved in organizational changes. He had to make his choice now and set priorities that would be acceptable to himself as well as to the others. He had to encourage Gilbert to use discretion and take control. He must also ensure that Starke, a brilliant man in many ways, would come up to his expectations, as well as to the expectations of his subordinates. Both these men must perform as supervisors or team leaders by taking the initiative, demonstrating ambition, and making decisions. Carson knew well that there was no lack of technical knowledge on the part of these two. They had the "ability", but did they have the "willpower"? If things remained unchanged, it would not be possible for Carson to move up to the new position likely to be open soon.

QUESTIONS

1. Draw the organizational structure of the company. Indicate the problems of authority, roles, and relationships. Point out the main problems and the reasons for their occurrence.

2. How do you evaluate the performance and role of Carson as the head of the department?

3. What problems do you see in the leadership of Gilbert and Starke?

4. How would these problems affect the motivation of the Design employees?

5. What recommendations would you make in order to rectify the situation?

Robert Bart

Robert Bart has been employed with the Ministry of Consumer and Corporate Affairs for the past six months on a probationary contract; that is, Mr. Bart's contract for employment with the federal government will expire in the next few months unless he is given an offer of permanent employment. His immediate supervisor is Ellen Clark, Manager of the Commercial Practices and Investigations unit where Mr. Bart is a junior investigations officer.

When Ms. Clark initially hired Mr. Bart, she did so because her unit was short staffed with a number of deadlines over the next few months, and also because Mr. Bart was a young, energetic, and enthusiastic university graduate with an exceptionally strong academic background — he had achieved the highest standing in his Bachelor of Commerce graduating class. However, the projects are now completed, and there is no longer any immediate pressure on her unit.

Mr. Bart, to his surprise, found his job exhilarating and challenging. He had never wanted to pursue a public service career, but the ministry's offer of employment was the best he had received, and he thought it might be a useful stepping stone to get an offer from one of the top corporations in the country. His first months at the ministry not only taught him a great deal about how governments operate, but also about business-government relations. He felt that he even had a better appreciation and understanding of the world of business.

Mr. Bart was aware that he would need at least a "fully satisfactory", but preferably "outstanding", review rating from his manager to remain on as a permanent employee. This did not trouble him, since he felt he was doing well and seemed to be fitting in with the other members of the unit. He found his work engrossing and took great pride in the quality of his investigative studies.

Ellen Clark called Mr. Bart into his office to go over his Performance Review and Appraisal Report. She gave him a copy of his performance review. Ms. Clark started by indicating that she had been satisfied with Mr. Bart's overall contribution to the unit. She stated that she thought his strengths were in research and writing and that his weaknesses, unfortunately, were in the area of interpersonal relations.

This case was written by Jim C. Simeon.

This was particularly evident in Mr. Bart's dealings with the companies that the ministry dealt with on an ongoing basis. Ms. Clark documented several complaints she had received from different companies about Mr. Bart's arrogant attitude and his lack of sensitivity to their circumstances and concerns. On this basis alone, Ms. Clark said, she would have to give him low scores on "Exercise of Judgment", "Tact and Diplomacy", and "Relationship with Others". As a consequence, Ellen Clark concluded, she was unable at this time to give him a rating of higher than "Satisfactory".

Mr. Bart was stunned. However, he recovered quickly, and said that Ms. Clark's assessment was totally unfair, and stated, he would not sign the report.

QUESTIONS

1. From the evidence in the case, do you think Ellen Clark's assessment was accurate? Why?

2. What should Robert Bart do now?

3. What should Ellen Clark do now?

4. What should someone in Robert Bart's situation do during the term of his employment to maximize the possibility of a permanent job offer?

Sandra Beaumont

Sandra Beaumont was on the fifth day of her new job as the Benefits manager for the Toronto Ball Bearing Company (TBBC) when she received a letter from TBBC's insurance company. The letter outlined that the rates for TBBC's Prescription Drug Plan would have to be raised by 18% to maintain the same level of coverage — the fifth substantial raise since the plan was introduced ten years ago.

When Sandra had been hired by the company's president, she had been told that the Benefits department had not been very well run — in fact, the manager's position had been vacant for the last six months. Normally, the company would try to hire from within; however, when the president received Sandra's application, he was quite impressed with her background and experience.

The president mentioned that, on the whole, he thought the company-funded Benefits Plan was a good one — although he wasn't quite sure whether all the employees really understood what was going on, or whether some understood only too well how to use the plan. The president had made it quite clear that he cared for the individual well-being of each of the company's 235 employees, and wanted to have the best plan that his limited resources could buy. He wondered whether he was getting the best for his money.

TBBC's employees came from various ethnic backgrounds, and many of them had been with the company for over 20 years. Even though many of them could barely speak the same language, they all got along well and were quite willing to help each other out. The managers were mostly people who had made it up through the ranks, and who also felt part of the TBBC family.

Sandra had noticed that few of the managers had dropped by to welcome her to her new job. She wondered why. Perhaps the previous manager had not gotten along well with them, and they were just testing her out. Or perhaps they were expecting another man to fill the position. (Most of the managers were men, while quite a few of the employees were women.) Regardless, she certainly sensed some hostility when she approached a few of the managers to talk about the benefit plan. Equally, the few employees she had approached were not very open. Some had

---

This case was written by Peter Kells.

mentioned that if they had any problems, they could always speak to their supervisor.

After looking through the few records that were available, Sandra noticed that the Prescription Plan seemed very popular with the employees. It certainly was easy to use, since the employees had only to buy the drugs, and the pharmacy would then submit the bill directly to the insurance company. Since no receipts had to be submitted, Sandra couldn't even determine the kind of drugs being bought, and would also find it hard to see exactly how much each employee was spending on prescriptions.

As Sandra sat down to have a cup of coffee, the phone rang. It was the floor supervisor, who wanted to know how to get reimbursement for one of the employee's dental bills. Could she send him down some information? . . . As Sandra sipped her coffee, she thought about what she had observed over the last few days. In two hours, her first week on the job would be over. She wondered what she should do starting Monday morning, and how she should go about doing it.

QUESTIONS

1. What difficulties is Sandra Beaumont likely to face in her new position?

2. What should she do to build good relationships with the other managers?

3. How should she go about reforming the benefit plan?

Sarah Hannigan

Sarah Hannigan is the manager of a small human resources (HR) unit of five employees serving a financial services company of about 200 employees. Her current, temporary position is "acting HR manager". She had only been at the company two months as a human resources generalist when her supervisor became ill, and she was offered the acting position by the president. The opportunity came as a surprise. As a new employee of the firm, she had conflicting thoughts about whether to accept the position. She realized the longer-term employees were expecting that one of them would have the position.

Sarah's entrance into the unit had gotten off to a shaky start. The president of the company is married to her second cousin. This caused a certain amount of gossip and resentment. In addition, the fact that she possessed a professional human resources qualification, which neither her supervisor nor her colleagues had, made for a tense situation in the unit. Any work-related suggestion that she made seemed to be perceived as flaunting her credentials. During the initial period, sensing the negative atmosphere she was inadvertently creating, she tried to put her colleagues and boss at ease by being as pleasant and friendly as possible. However, she was treated formally and somewhat distantly by the other members of the unit.

When her boss went on leave for treatment and recuperation, Sarah was put in charge. She had to learn all the company procedures and issues quickly. The two employees she had hoped to rely on for assistance, the training manager and an HR assistant, seemed reluctant to answer questions, share information, or volunteer direct assistance. In particular, the training manager was very withdrawn. She strongly felt that she had been overlooked for the acting position. When Sarah forced her to communicate by asking her direct questions, Sarah received the impression that the training manager knew nothing beyond her immediate functions. The other employee, the HR assistant, behaved differently, but was equally unhelpful. He either became quiet and unresponsive or loud and aggressive, if Sarah persisted. His favourite phrase seemed to be, "This isn't the way we do things here."

This case is based on original work by Caryl Registe.

He seemed particularly resentful when asked to perform assignments that were not part of his normal routine.

It is a busy time for the HR unit because it is the start of a new fiscal year and salary adjustments, bonuses, etc., are being implemented. Along with the adjustments, each employee receives a letter commending or reprimanding her or him for the work done. Sarah felt that the letter reflected the way HR was practised in the "old" days. The letter did not invite the employee to discuss the results and ways to effect improvement with his or her supervisor, when the letter identified deficiencies in performance. Early one Monday morning, Sarah gave her HR assistant some changes to make to the standard letter for each group of employees and rushed off to a meeting. She had pointed out the need for changes to him late on the previous Friday afternoon. On her return from the meeting, she found letters to 40 employees awaiting her signature. They did not contain her changes.

After lunch, she asked the HR assistant to come into her office and confronted him. He informed her that he had called the previous manager (now on leave) at home, who asked him not to make the changes. Sarah closed her office door and severely reprimanded him for his disrespect and failure to carry out her instructions. She then required that the letters — all 40 of them — be redone. Through her closed door she could hear him expressing his displeasure very audibly. Sarah felt the walls closing in on her. She had received a directive from the chief executive that morning to plan a general staff meeting. She cannot do so without the help of her HR staff.

QUESTIONS

1. Who is mainly responsible for the situation that is occurring in the HR unit at the end of the case and why?

2. Characterize the leadership style of Sarah Hannigan.

3. Should Sarah Hannigan have dealt with the staff of her unit differently and, if so, how?

4. What should Sarah Hannigan do now?

Terra Company

Ty Davenport had just been appointed CEO of Terra Company, the local business unit of a large multinational telecommunications corporation situated in a small, tropical country (population 265,000) located in the Pacific Ocean. The firm's head-quarters were in the U.K. A degree in engineering, an MBA, numerous training courses in business, and a series of carefully selected international appointments had propelled him from technician to chief executive officer (CEO) in 15 years. Ty's previous appointment had been for two years in the London head office where he gained administrative experience as an executive assistant to the vice-president of international operations.

Terra consisted of the following departments:

- Finance
- Sales and marketing
- Customer service
- Engineering
- Human resources and administration
- Corporate communications

There were 300 employees, all host country nationals except for the popular manager of HR who was from a neighbouring country.

Ty's London experience had provided him with a strong focus for changing Terra to reflect the multinational corporation's mission and operational practices. Having worked at Terra for a number of years and having aggressively and openly spoken out against perceived unfairness and the laid-back attitudes among some of the workforce, he was happy to finally be in charge and excited about the changes he could make to improve performance. Over the years, Terra had moved from a focus on engineering to a focus on sales and marketing, and more recently on customer service. Due to the volatility of the telecommunications market as a whole and deregulation in local markets, Terra needed something other than technology

---

This case is based on original work by Caryl Registe.

to differentiate it from its competitors. Ty fully endorsed the corporate value that excellent customer service was the key to success in the market. He was full of enthusiasm and eager to bring change to Terra.

Ty believed that improved staff morale was a prerequisite for better relations with the public. However, right from the beginning, he was under pressure from the parent company to achieve strict profit targets, both by reducing costs and maximizing sales, as Terra was not performing as well as most other branches. A recent cost savings directive from head office was to reduce the staff complement, since it was too heavy in comparison with operations in other countries. He realized that staff cuts would certainly reduce morale, at least in the short run.

Given that day-to-day supervision was principally exercised through the administrative function of the HR department, Ty also saw the need to restructure and perhaps change reporting relationships in order to exert more direct control to implement his plans.

Ty was the first national to be selected to head Terra. He had been appointed by head office ahead of his peers, who had remained working for Terra while he had been on international assignments. He had actually reported to a number of his peers at various times during his extensive career with the company. These factors seemed to lessen the respect given to him and diminished his overall authority. There were instances where managers booked overseas travel, conferences, etc., without his knowledge. There were also occasions where company equipment needed for meetings, etc. were "stored" at managers' and employees' homes. And employees at all levels could be seen using company vehicles to transport their families to and from school or work, and to popular entertainment spots on weekends. An order given by Ty to curb this behaviour had resulted in a further loss of his popularity with a number of staff members.

Ty had also been experiencing a strained, uncertain and sometimes rocky relationship with his manager of HR-administration, and he was wary of her. After a couple of run-ins, Ty made it clear to her that he did not trust her. He found out that she had lobbied various members of the management group to boycott decisions he had made that she did not favour. Furthermore, his corporate communications manager was sympathetic to her cause. When Ty asked both of them to attend a meeting to discuss how employee attitudes in their departments could become more "customer friendly" when dealing both with internal staff and external clients, it resulted in open hostility between Ty and the two managers. In the days following, Ty noticed that the staff members of their two departments were avoiding him.

A second incident occurred when the HR-admin manager leaked a plan for reducing travel costs that Ty had begun to work on with her. Employees were up in arms since their expense allowances would be reduced. Many employees had benefited financially from travelling by receiving the full allowance and then spending much less. Third, Ty was particularly annoyed when he found out that an HR-admin employee was allowed to jump the queue for educational funding, when there were five employees from other departments waiting longer for study grants from the same fund.

The final straw for Ty came when the HR-admin manager signed a contract with the present security service provider without his knowledge, thus granting $200,000 to a company of her choosing. He had expressly asked her to forward all tenders to the tenders committee according to the standard company process. (Later, she claimed that her action stemmed from her fears that he would grant the contract to his brother, whose tender for the security contract was being considered.) A severe letter of reprimand was placed in her personnel file.

These incidents convinced Ty to implement a restructuring plan. Less than a month after the last incident, citing cost and efficiency issues, he restructured Terra as follows:

- Sales and marketing became two separate departments reporting to the CEO.
- The admin function was removed from HR and shifted to the manager of customer service (a supporter of Ty).
- HR and corporate communications would report directly to the CEO.

The positions of manager of HR-admin and manager of corporate communications were then declared redundant, and both employees were dismissed. A few of their subordinates were also laid off. The managers were replaced by lower level supervisors, who were given the lesser title of head of department. Much of the authority that the previous managers had was removed.

These changes served to further lessen Ty's popularity, but with an 18% rate of unemployment in the small country, there was no open rebellion. Few employees wanted to risk losing their jobs. Ty felt that after some time had passed Terra would settle down. Now able to exert more direct control over operations, he felt that he would ultimately be able to increase morale and reach his goal to improve attitudes and customer service.

Two months after the restructuring, Ty granted a six-month contract to a former employee (a distant relative) who was returning to the country with newly acquired HR qualifications. In a small country with a limited pool of professionals and limited high-level employment opportunities, hiring relatives was not unusual. The new position she occupied reported to the head of HR, who in turn reported to the CEO. She was on special contractual assignment, but everyone believed that she was being groomed to take over the position of head of HR, as the incumbent would soon go on maternity leave. After a short time, the incumbent did leave and she was appointed acting head of HR. Terra was immediately served with a $700,000 lawsuit for wrongful dismissal of the former manager of HR, who claimed that she had been manoeuvred out of the way simply to make room for Ty's relative.

Ty was shocked by the lawsuit and realized that even a successful defence of the suit could be expensive, create bad publicity for Terra, and stain his reputation. If Terra lost the lawsuit it would be a disaster. Then he received word that the vice-president of international operations of the parent company would be arriving in three weeks to check on how Terra was doing under Ty's leadership. Feeling very depressed over these developments, Ty wondered how all this had happened to him and what, if anything, he could do now about it.

QUESTIONS

1. Why did Ty's appointment as CEO and subsequent actions cause animosity and resistance?

2. How did Ty's appointment as CEO affect motivational levels and attitudes among his immediate subordinates and the employees as a whole?

3. Assess Ty's plan for organizational change. Identify and explain its weak points and its strong points.

4. What would you have done differently throughout the case if you were Ty, and why?

5. What should Ty do now?

Victory Fashions

INTRODUCTION

Phil Mager, President of Victory Fashions, has been mulling over the same issue ever since the new shareholder's agreement was signed in January 1991. He wanted more control of the strategy of his company. He was increasingly dissatisfied with the financial progress of his company, and was even more dissatisfied with his role in it. He didn't know whether to dissolve the company and strike out on his own, or to continue the company in the hope of a better future.

GENERAL BACKGROUND

Victory Fashions is a manufacturer of high fashion ladies' tailored clothing. In Canada, the ladies' garment industry consists of over 2,000 establishments employing about 115,000 workers. Affectionately known as the "rag trade", this industrial segment represents an important economic factor in Canada. In 2000, these 2,000 establishments shipped nearly $4 billion worth of goods.

Victory Fashions was started in 1928 in Montreal by Sheldon Gerber, an enterprising immigrant who saw an opportunity to break into the apparel business, which was then dominated by few major manufacturers. His strategy was to sell large quantities to major retailers. He was able to do so because of his strategy of using the most modern and efficient machinery instead of cutters, tailors, and other expensive labour. This strategy was continued into the 1960s by the new owner, Sam Greenberg, a former shipper who had worked his way up into the executive suite. Greenberg dreamed of opening an even more technologically advanced plant and closing the original plant. His dreams were realized, and the old plant was scheduled to be shut down as soon as the new plant became fully operational in 1972.

However, in 1970, the clothing industry took a downturn. Changes in government regulations caused a massive influx of low-priced imports. The new, modern plant, which could compete with the imports, was still having start-up problems, and

---

This case was written by Monica Belcourt.

the old plant began suffering losses for the first time in its history. The situation continued until 1975, when a creditor called a loan.

Greenberg and his executive team scrambled for funds. During a very tense month, they managed to persuade the creditors that everyone would be paid within one year, with the conditions being that the old plant would be allowed to close, and that credit would be extended to the new one. The creditors agreed, but required that Greenberg, nearly 65 then, get the commitment of his merchandising manager to run the business. Reluctantly, Greenberg sold one-third of the business to Phil Mager, the merchandising manager who had a "hot" reputation in the clothing industry. Mager paid for the share by mortgaging his house and releasing part of his salary. In return, he was made a vice-president.

The new plant of Victory Fashions was established in 1973. At its peak in 1991, it employed 400 workers, produced 1,000 garments daily, and had sales of $15 million. The plant was unionized, and there were strict divisions of labour between the cutters, the needle workers, the taggers, and the shippers. Within the office, approximately 20 white collar workers (non-unionized) did whatever they were told to do or saw was necessary to do. Even the cleaning lady would do clerical jobs when necessary. The four partners tended to cross functional lines quite frequently. For example, the Vice-President, Accounting would sell directly to discounters, and the President would negotiate with suppliers and work directly with designers.

The structure of Victory Fashions resists easy classification. The production department is typical of a mechanistic organization. The work to be accomplished tends to be predetermined, routine, mechanical, and repetitive. However, the merchandising department (styling and sales) tends to be market-oriented and organic. There is little division of labour, no goals, little work that is predetermined or analyzed, and communication tends to be informal. The internal structure of Victory Fashions appears to be composed of disparate departments.

The nature of the environment in the fashion business is extremely important in understanding Victory Fashions. The fashion industry could be characterized as being in a turbulent environment in which governments change import quotas unpredictably, competitors produce nearly identical lines and steal logos and ideas, suppliers are unreliable in terms of delivery dates, etc. The environment is also dynamic in the sense that the product line is uncertain and unpredictable due to client demands for novelty, changing department store buyers, and the high bankruptcy rate among retailers. The environment is not complex in the sense that it requires sophisticated knowledge about the products or customers. In the fashion business, the manufacturer can easily comprehend the markets and technology, although the styles or colours are unpredictable.

Within a year, the creditors were paid off. However, this left the company seriously undercapitalized. This precarious financial position was further threatened by a new blow to the company. A recession hit in the late 1970s, and consumers stopped spending on luxury items such as ladies' tailored clothing. Interest rates reached 22%. The company was scrambling for sales and money. The creditors were beginning to re-evaluate the new plant.

The provincial government was approached for a loan under the Business Development Incentives Program. Government officials quickly noticed how little capital ($300,000) the company had invested on sales of $15 million. In order to approve the loan, the government demanded additional personal investment. The two owners, Greenberg and Mager, could extend themselves only so far. They were forced to ask members of the executive team to invest, and thus become part owners of the company. The members of the executive team took second mortgages on their homes, and together the executives raised $250,000.

In return, Greenberg, now in his early 80s, sold all of his shares, to be paid for by profits over the next 15 years. The total sum to be paid was $300,000. Greenberg gave up his voting rights, and was no longer active in the day-to-day operations of the business. He continued to come to work every day to read and talk to friends.

The new ownership agreement gave two-fifths of the company to Mager (because of his earlier investment), and three other executives received one-fifth each. Mager was made President.

Sales continued to be difficult to obtain, and the floating interest rates the company had previously negotiated were burdensome. During the previous five years the company had reinvested the very small profits that were generated. Two divisions that were started by Mager were profitable and were, in fact, supporting the divisions on which Victory Fashions had originally made its reputation.

PHIL MAGER, PRESIDENT

Mager, 38 years old, was married with two children. He had spent ten years as a very successful merchandising manager on the retailing side. He was well known in the fashion business for his considerable talent to spot fashion trends. He had started a number of divisions since his arrival at Victory Fashions in 1973. Some proved profitable; others were phased out.

Mager had started a children's wear line targeted at the grandmother market. The potential profits were high, but there was little time to establish contacts with the children's wear retailers, and so the line slowly died. Another unsuccessful operation was the establishment of a factory outlet open to the public. This store was to act as a dumping ground for unsold merchandise and surplus fabric. However, the factory outlet had to be located at some distance from other retailers in order to avoid price conflicts. This resulted in little traffic to the outlet, which was subsequently closed.

The two most successful operations were the designer line and the import program. Even during a recession, consumers continued to spend money on designer clothing, and Phil had obtained the production and distribution licence for an important designer. Mager had approached the designer for the rights to Canada, and the contract proved to be exceptionally profitable. The import business, too, had been successful because the low price of these imports enabled the company to appeal to a low-end retailing clientele. Overall, these two profitable areas channelled enough money into the company to keep the company afloat in spite of losses in the other areas.

The profitability of these two divisions had convinced Mager that he had a good feel for the market. He felt restricted by the lack of capital needed to finance his other marketing projects. More important, he felt restricted by the new shareholder's agreement, which required a majority vote for the approval of any new venture. (As will be seen later, this clause had been inserted by one partner, and signed by Mager under extreme pressure and with reluctance.) Mager had felt betrayed by this clause which reduced his power in the company. He had lost control, and for him, control was critical. He hated feeling powerless — he had never wanted to work for anybody because he didn't trust others.

There was also a business reason. Mager disagreed with this clause. He reasoned that, in the fashion business, merchandising innovations were the key to survival, and no innovations could come from a team that included an accountant and a production manager. How could Mager justify his gut feelings on a balance sheet to Carl Deacon, the accountant who was more like a bookkeeper? Deacon's idea of financial planning was to resist paying bills in order to accumulate pennies worth of interest, while in the long run antagonizing the suppliers, who Mager had to then placate. Manny Kesper, VP Production, was even worse. Kesper, an old friend Mager had brought into the company, wanted to keep that production line moving. His idea of profitability was that "the more you make, the more you make". It was impossible to explain to him that maximizing profits was more critical than maximizing sales. Both Deacon and Kesper resisted anything new and potentially risky. The fourth partner, David Cleary, VP Merchandising, understood fashion, but Cleary had some peculiar social democratic political views on how to run a company. Cleary believed that all partners should be equal, with equal pay, equal prerequisites, and equal votes. During the last financial downturn, Cleary had persuaded Deacon and Kesper to support him.

Together, they forced Mager, who was desperate to salvage his original investment and his company, to consider a parity shareholder's agreement.

Despite 12 hours of threats and protests, Phil reluctantly signed. His discomfort with the agreement persisted, particularly when he saw that his whole merchandising strategy had to be changed as a result. Previously, when he had an idea, he acted on it. He made the contact, told the designers to prepare the samples, got production moving, and, in effect, set up the entire apparatus to produce a new line or open a new division.

Now, however, when he had an idea, he would approach each partner separately, sell them on the idea from their unique viewpoints in order to obtain their vote, and then attempt to hold them to it in an open meeting. His success rate was very low, and he felt increasingly frustrated as he saw opportunities slip by. Phil felt that innovative merchandising ideas were the key to survival, and no innovation could come out of a group of equals. He wanted his old powers back — it was essential for the survival of the group. "It's this damn one-person, one-vote proposition that David forced on us. Not only do I own 40% of the company, but I'm President. I'm the one with the ideas that will keep this company alive . . . The others belong in a soap company, with their traditional ideas of accounting and production. And I don't see why I should be paid the same when I have a larger investment and the top job. If I can't have control, I'll ... I don't know," Mager fumed.

Mager decided to enlist the support of the external auditors and the company's lawyers in an attempt to rewrite the shareholder's agreement. The lawyers refused to unilaterally rewrite an agreement that might favour one partner. They insisted that they represented the company interest, and the company consisted of the four partners. The lawyers would be present at a meeting of the four executives, and would attempt to chair it. Following is a transcript of the meeting between the lawyers, Cohen and Cohen, and the Victory Fashions management group that met to discuss the effectiveness of the present shareholder's agreement.

HIGHLIGHTS OF THE TRANSCRIPT OF THE MEETING (Executive Group of Victory Fashions Limited, Held on June 15, 1991)

Present: Messrs Cohen, Cohen, Mager, Kesper, Cleary, and Deacon

Cohen: Phil approached me several days ago, indicating his continued dissatisfaction with the shareholder's agreement. He feels that it would be to the company's benefit, and therefore to each of the partners' benefit, that the agreement be revised.

Mager: Yes, as you all know, I never liked the equal division of votes from the beginning. I only agreed to it because I was forced to make a decision within one day — you sprung it on me the day before we had to get that loan. I was very tempted to lose everything and go out on my own. I know you thought it was just that I didn't like losing power, but it was more than that. In a fashion business like ours, we have to react quickly. We're not the federal government. We can't make decisions by committees. It's too slow. I'm proposing that we create a structure whereby the president can use his 40% voting power ...

Cleary: Look — we didn't force you into anything. The times have changed, and you can't just follow any idea to see if it works. We need planning now, we have to work as a team, look at financial projections, determine if the idea is profitable ...

Kesper: David's right. We have to look at the impact on production. Just because we're a fashion business doesn't mean that we can't have plans. Besides, we need a stable line — just to keep production moving. We can't switch lines all the time. The costs are too great, and my people don't like it.

Mager: Your people are damned lucky to have jobs. If we don't meet the market demands, we go out of business. It's that simple. You two are always talking about formalizing this business, about setting objectives, doing analyses. I'll tell you what my objective is — to survive one more season. How can you plan in an environment like this? The government changes the import regulations monthly, the interest rates can double in two years. In the past, we went from a boom to a recession in three years. Look, unless we can react quickly and not be blinded by plans made under different assumptions, we're going to die like dinosaurs.

Cleary: I think that the new partnership agreement meets all our needs. It was drawn up to reflect the fact that all of us invested the same amount of money this time around. Phil had an earlier investment, but his risk is less if the company goes under ... All of us lose our houses, except for Phil. He lives in a mansion; he can afford the loss. So because we have greater risk, we should have at least equal votes. I know that in the past, Phil, you ran the company the way you wanted to, and you made a couple of good decisions that are basically keeping the company afloat. But what about your factory outlet idea . . . and your children's wear program? They both bombed. You see, if we can just tap the best of your ideas, and screen out the others through our executive committee, then we'll be a better company. I'm not arguing for rigid planning. It's just our need to be more professional in our management.

Mager: But how will you know which are the good ideas and which are the bad ones until they are tested in the market? So far, you've turned down every venture I've proposed, or belaboured it so long that the economics have changed or someone else got it. Committees just don't work in this business.

Kesper: But neither do people who just follow their whims ... You're great on ideas, but you don't understand production and projections and ...

Cohen: Why don't we take a break? People seem to be getting a little excited. Let's reconvene in half an hour and explore this some more.

During the break Phil Mager left his partners and went back to his office. The old conflict was there, and it looked like there would be no new solutions. In his view, Victory Fashions had to be market-oriented, and not a rigid organization run by MBO: "Management by Obsolescence." He mused, "Where there's a problem or a need, the company can't be handcuffed by job descriptions and memos. The market is not predictable. If we were manufacturing widgets — I'd let them win. We could have routines and schedules and goals — but we're in fashion, and strategic plans and formal management will kill us!"

QUESTIONS

1. Describe the structure of Victory Fashions as of the end of the case. Is it well-suited to the external environment of the firm?

2. What are the pros and cons of a management group of four all having equal power?

3. Describe the motivational state of Phil Mager. What are his salient needs, and how can he best satisfy them?

4. Can the disparate values of the partners be reconciled? Explain your answer.

5. Take the role of one of the mediating lawyers and state, in detail and step-by-step, what you would do when the meeting resumed.

WD Inc.

WD Inc. is a Canadian company with a parent company in the United States, UWD Inc. WD Inc. is a leading marketer, manufacturer, and distributor of gypsum wallboard products and interior finishing materials. The company was established in 1905 and is a key participant in Canada's dynamic building materials industry. It supplies innovative wall and ceiling products to different sectors of construction. WD Inc. has several plants across North America. The Canadian subsidiary imports its supplies, mainly from the United States. The Canadian branch, located in London, Ontario, is large and is primarily divided into financial, marketing, and human resources departments. Recently, the corporation was audited by the Canada Border Services Agency (CBSA). The audit resulted in the detection of incorrect valuations of imported commodities. The firm was required to comply with import regulations by making adjustments to the value of all goods it imported from the United States and other countries since 2007.

Ali was a junior accountant working for WD Inc. on a fixed work term as a voluntary intern to gain experience. He was assigned by the financial department to work on a rush assignment, due in 60 days. Ali reported to Tony, an accounting manager and Ali's direct superior. Tony was helpful at the start of the internship when Ali was working on small, simple projects. Soon, however, Ali was left on his own and was given larger, more complex projects to complete. He found it difficult to contact Tony for assistance, and Ali frequently had to work overtime to complete his tasks. One morning, when Ali was working on the transfer-pricing rush project, Tony came to speak to Ali. It was a rare appearance.

Tony: Good morning Ali, how are you? How was your weekend?
Ali: I'm fine. The weekend was great. I watched movies, and had a family get together.
Tony: Always fun. I was wondering, how is the transfer-pricing project going? Once this is done, we can start working on an urgent project regarding Canada Customs files. We're having some problems with

---

This case is based on original work by Muzammil Kukaswadia.

the government that require us to recover data concerning our imported goods. I will want you to start with the easier files. Later, we will have to tackle the bigger files, and that will mean lots of work. I want all the Canada Customs files to be done by a deadline we have been given by the CBSA.

Ali: Okay, I'm almost done with these transfer-pricing files.

Tony: That's good to hear. Let's see what you have so far. [Tony pauses to look over Ali's work.] Well, there is some more analysis for you to do, but overall, it looks good. Okay, then, I'll check with you later today. Until then, you keep working on them because I have to give them to my boss.

Ali: All right, Tony. I'll get it done.

The day passed, but Tony did not show up. The next morning, Ali went to see Tony and found him in his office.

Ali: Hello, Tony. I was hoping to see you yesterday.

Tony: Oh yeah. Sorry, I had a meeting to rush through and then I went home.

Ali: I finally finished the transfer-pricing files.

Tony: Great! I will look it over and hand it to my boss for further analysis. Now we can start working on the Canada Customs files. We have to match up the reference numbers on our documents with the Customs files. If they match, we should compare the amount we declared with the actual amount. All this has to be done in Excel. You can use our Oracle databases and the broker's site to track these references. All right? I'll leave you with the files, and I'll get back to working on our corporate taxes.

Ali: Okay, Tony, I'll start working on it. I was wondering what happens when the reference numbers don't match?

Tony: Well, in that case, you have to manually go through the records to match the data and exchange rates. After that, you'll most likely get the right price. This is a great project for you as an intern, Ali. It will really contribute to your professional development. I'm looking forward to seeing how you handle it.

Ali: I will give it my best. But, honestly, I may need your help with this. I'm still feeling my way around at WD and may have trouble matching the data.

Tony: No problem. Anytime you need some advice, just send me an email or leave a message.

After several weeks of work Ali noticed that although most of the reference numbers matched, one-quarter of them remained unmatched. He tried many methods to track those, but huge amounts of data seemed to be missing. He also believed that matching the dates with exchange rates would result in a flawed analysis. He had to assume the amount by coordinating the import dates with exchange rates, but there were strong daily fluctuations and differences between buy and sell rates.

Which would apply in this situation? Ali decided to discuss all this with Tony. He went to his office on several occasions, but Tony was either out, on the phone, or in a meeting. Ali could not get hold of him until Tony appeared a week later, after Ali had sent an email and left a phone message asking Tony to come over to his desk.

Ali: Hello, Tony. How are you? Busy?

Tony: I'm fine, just working on these taxes. How's your work going on the files?

Ali: Tony, I noticed that at least a quarter of the data does not match, and some are not even on our system. I have tried all the methods, but I cannot track them. I also believe that matching dates and exchange rates is a faulty analysis because we could be picking an exchange rate that might not apply.

Tony: Well, I guess we will have to contact the CBSA and get their files. They have all the declaration transactions, so you will have to go through the matching process again with their files, or maybe you can figure out a way by using formulas.

Ali: So we will have to redo the whole project!

Tony: No, not really. Maybe you just need to merge the data you have with what you get from Customs. Or, perhaps you could make a template. Anyway, concentrate on the goal. We really need to match these numbers quickly.

Ali: Okay, Tony. I'll try my best to finish this as quickly as I can. But, you know, I will need some help.

Tony: Absolutely. But our staff accountants are either tied up with me on our corporate taxes or have other projects on the go, I can't assign anyone else to work with you. However, if you send me an email, I'll make sure that I'll reply. right away.

Ali was very frustrated with the discussion with Tony. He actually thought of leaving WD Inc., even though he was only part of the way through his work term. It seemed he was being asked to redo the most of the project with no help, and time was running short. However, a successful internship was important for his future career prospects.

Although there were usable formulas in Excel, all the manual analysis would have to be done again. Using Customs documents, he had to match invoices with the B3s (declaration documents of goods crossing the border). It was not easy because he had to track the invoices and use different methods to link the two. There were too much data, including all the invoices and B3s from 2007 to the present. Ali was dealing with about 30,000 invoices per year, of which about 95% were declared incorrectly in some way. There were misplaced numbers and errone-ous, as well as missing, declarations. As Tony had requested, Ali tried to ask his questions by email, and typically received a reply from Tony within 24 hours. How-ever, Ali's detailed questions and discouraging progress reports were not met with very helpful replies. Mostly he received back were generalities and continual urges to get the work done on time.

A typical email from Tony in response to a detailed question or disclosure of difficulty was: "Yes, I can see your challenge. There isn't a lot I can do because of the taxes and other urgent projects that are on my desk, but I am confident that you will find a way to make it work before the deadline. You can be sure that we are taking note of the situation you're dealing with, and we will certainly be adopting measures to prevent it from recurring in the future."

Ali began to feel that this project was too large for him to handle on his own, and he was sure that none of the permanent staff were willing to be involved. Assigning a team of external accountants to work on it might be a way to get the job done, but it would cost many thousands of dollars, considering the complexity and volume of the work. He learned from other staff that the company frequently appointed student volunteers to complete senior accountants' tasks, and he wondered if this was intentional, because of the leverage the firm had over interns. The time remaining for the completion of the project was used up with little progress, although Ali continued to spend many long hours at work. As usual, he received little, if any, supervision, guidance, or help from Tony.

Ali had observed that most staff at WD Inc. seemed to be working very informally, and with minimal attention to following set procedures. Most employees had been there for a long time and worked according to their long-established habits. Newly hired employees would frequently be teamed up with longer-term staff to learn the "traditional" way of doing things. Subordinates and supervisors would chat and laugh endlessly throughout the office. Ali almost never witnessed managers actively supervising. He worked late almost every day, and rarely were there any others in the office with him after 5 p.m. He felt that the company did not have optimal procedures, and those the company did have were not enforced. WD Inc., he felt, was neither up-to-date with its technology and hardware nor serious in its attempt to establish good internal record-keeping and accounting practices. Instead, the firm relied on the experience of the employees. This practice was now causing serious problems as the business expanded, and the workflow became more uncoordinated with the staff less able to handle the increasing scale of operations.

The general disorganization that Ali perceived severely affected his own project. It made it difficult for him to track some of the entries, while some others perhaps could never be found. To reconstruct data from the external Customs documents was extremely tedious and time-consuming. Although he tried his best, as the deadline approached Ali became more certain that it would not be npossible for him to complete the job on time, or even during his work term, which ended two weeks after the deadline. He spent his remaining time at WD Inc. in a futile attempt to accomplish the impossible.

At the end of his internship, Ali's departure from the firm took place quietly. Tony briefly thanked him for his efforts, but it was clear that Tony was not happy with the incomplete project. Tony's previously friendly attitude was replaced by a more formal and distant one. Although Ali knew that no single person could have finished that project on time, and even though the project probably could never have been finished, due to the poor quality and limited availability of the data, Ali still found himself apologizing to Tony for his failure to complete the work. After leaving Tony's office for the last time, Ali regretted that he did not say what was really on his mind.

As a result of not being able to challenge the irregularities found in the audit by the CBSA, WD Inc. was penalized significantly by the government. With his internship now behind him, Ali does not know whether he could ever use Tony as a reference for future job applications.

QUESTIONS

1. Identify and assess issues of fairness and justice in this case.

2. Compare and contrast the intent and goals of the communications between Ali and Tony.

3. How should Ali have better handled his relationship with Tony throughout his internship?

4. Apparently, the managers and staff at WD Inc. are generally satisfied with their jobs. To what would you attribute this?

5. If WD Inc. wants to implement proper recording procedures to avoid similar problems in the future with the CBSA, describe the problems that might be encountered with the staff — supervisors and subordinates — and identify the root causes.

6. Design a change procedure that would enable an effective implementation of proper recording procedures.

Weston Tire Corporation

Weston Tire Corporation is a multinational corporation with major operations located in Canada, the United States, and western Europe. The company employs more than 30,000 workers in all its operations. The Canadian subsidiary, majority owned by the parent, has a workforce of over 5,000 employees, including managerial, supervisory, and factory personnel. There are several unions covering various categories of employees in the company, but the largest number of workers is covered by the United Rubber, Cork, Linoleum, and Plastic Workers of America.

The company has been operating in Canada for more than 30 years, and enjoys a high reputation for its products. The Canadian operations of the company are quite profitable. Although the products of this company are not cheap, they do have a reputation for good quality, and, because of this, they enjoy a fair share of the market.

With regard to its personnel policies and practices, the company has built a good public image. People in the community regard Weston as an excellent company to work for. Pay is above average, working conditions are quite good, and employee services are excellent. The company has a record of good industrial relations, and there has not been a strike, lockout, or serious work stoppage in the past eight years.

Weston has a reputation for promoting people from within. Almost all of its 180 foremen have been internally promoted, and many of the production superintendents have also risen from the ranks. The personnel director prides himself on the upward mobility of the firm's employees. The president of the company made a particular point of mentioning this aspect at the last board meeting. Three out of five corporate directors have been with the company for more than 15 years, and have risen to their present levels from fairly humble beginnings within the company. The R&D director is a recent recruit from outside, but the president was forced into this situation because a suitable man was not available from within the company. Besides, they needed a man with wider experience and familiarity with developments in related industries.

By Anwar Rashid. © L & S Management Publications.

The company's welfare programs are beyond reproach. Weston has excellent health programs that are looked after by three medical doctors and a chief medical officer, who are all trained in industrial medicine. The older employees are looked after by the company, even after their retirement. The nurses from the company's medical department pay visits to ailing employees during their time of employment as well as during retirement if necessary. The firm has an excellent retirement program for its employees.

Compared with many other organizations of the same size, Weston Tire has a large personnel department headed by Mr. Jenkins, the personnel director. Mr. Jenkins enjoys a powerful position and tremendous status within the company hierarchy. He is assisted by more than 40 staff members responsible for recruitment, training, safety, welfare, security, and union affairs. In addition, he has a separate section concerned with management development programs. Mr. Jenkins is eminently qualified for the post. Over the years he has diligently and conscientiously worked toward the development of a viable and credible personnel function within the organization. He has been instrumental in getting a comprehensive set of personnel policies established and consolidated. These are now strictly followed by line management and other departments within the company. The company takes a dim view of executives who fail to follow personnel policies laid down by the board of directors. The personnel director is one of the more powerful board members, and is considered by divisional heads as a formidable opponent and, consequently, an individual not to be tangled with.

Weston's wage levels, incentive schemes, profit-sharing plans, and welfare programs, etc., are more than impressive and far better than programs offered by other industries in the area. The company has a large number of long-service employees, and they have excellent social clubs in which they and their families participate. The present president of the company was formerly the company's director of personnel.

Jim Maloney is one of the firm's project engineers and has been with the company since he graduated from university about eight years ago. From time to time he has attended various courses organized by the company and last year was sent to the United States to attend a residential training program for potential managers. Not long ago, Jim began working closely with Dickson Chemicals, a company that received a substantial amount of subcontracting work from Weston Tire Corporation. In fact, that company depended upon Weston Tire for the largest part of its income. The chief executive of Dickson Chemicals was very impressed by Jim Maloney's work, and got to know him quite well during the term of a project at Dickson's. Jim was just the man they were looking for. There was an opening as Chief Project Engineer at Dickson Chemicals, and the position was offered to Jim at a very attractive salary and with the prospect of challenging work. Actually, the salary earned by Jim at Weston Tire was no less attractive, but somehow he had started to feel that he had reached a dead end, and the projects had started to become somewhat mundane. Jim was tempted by the offer, as he was looking for a change of pace. The opportunity seemed to have presented itself at just the right time. Jim accepted the job offer in principle, but the contract had to be formalized. However, it was decided that, since Dickson Chemicals received a substantial amount of work from Weston Tire, it would be wise for Dickson Chemicals to let the personnel director of Weston know about it in advance, so that a replacement could be found for him well before he took up his new assignment. In fact, it was Jim himself who went up to see Mr. Jenkins in order to inform him about his proposed move. Jim was quite surprised at Mr. Jenkins' reaction, as he seemed very upset about it. Jim had already discussed it with his own director (production), who was reluctant but agreeable.

On the same day that he spoke to Jenkins, Jim received a note from the company president stating that he wished to see him the next morning. Jim presented himself at the president's office at 9:45 a.m., and found the president to be very upset — almost in a rage. The president informed him that the company took a very dim view of those employees, particularly at professional levels, who quit the company for better prospects with a subcontracting company. The president would do everything in his power to put a stop to this move. If necessary, he would wreck Dickson Chemicals if they "poached" any of Weston's managerial personnel. As far as Jim could make out, the president had already phoned Dickson's chief executive, who received the message loud and clear, and he immediately washed his hands of Jim.

QUESTIONS

1. Analyze the general work environment and policies of Weston Tire, highlighting the positive and negative features.

2. Comment on Jim's action as an employee. Bearing in mind the work environment of Weston Tire, how would you have behaved with respect to the Dickson offer if you were Jim?

3. Did the president act properly when faced with the prospect of Jim's departure? What type of leadership is he exhibiting by his actions?

4. What should Jim do now?

Zimmer Engineering Limited

Howard Pearson is a management consultant located in Dartmouth, Nova Scotia, and holds a faculty position with the University of Eastern Canada. During a recent social event at the Dartmouth Boat Club, he was asked to undertake a consulting project by a fellow club member, Will Browning, senior vice-president, Zimmer Engineering Limited.

The firm's business chiefly involved the design and sales of fluid flow equipment for industrial applications. All the required engineering was done "in-house". The supply of components, such as high-capacity pumps and the fabrication, of custom installations was subcontracted to outside suppliers and metal fabricators. In 1991, with a new competitor on the scene, business had slowed noticeably. Will Browning was concerned that the firm's structure and job descriptions needed change if the company was to regain its market share.

On a regular basis, Zimmer Engineering employed 11 people (see Figure 1). The staff complement could swell to 17 when the workload was heavy. Will Browning saw the firm's problem as one in which certain key people had responsibilities inappropriate for their abilities and preferences. In particular, he pointed to the Zimmer brothers, Allan and Bernard, who served as president and vice-president, Engineering, respectively. Allan Zimmer attempted to guide all aspects of the business, even though his educational background was in finance. And Bernard, although a competent engineer, had recently acquired a time-consuming "hobby" farm that prevented him from concentrating fully on his job responsibilities. According to Will Browning, he was not effectively supervising the design and production functions. Moreover, Bernard stated that he was not interested in devoting any additional time to the firm at the present time. This meant that Allan was becoming even more involved in the technical aspects of the business, and expensive design and production errors were being made that generated poor customer relations. As an engineer with extensive business experience, Will Browning was usually called upon to sort out these problems after the fact. However, due to the existing structure and reporting relationships, he had no authority to prevent them from occurring and to eliminate the damage they caused. When he had suggested that Allan consult him prior to making decisions on technical matters, he was received coolly by the

FIGURE 1 ORGANIZATIONAL CHART OF ZIMMER ENGINEERING LIMITED

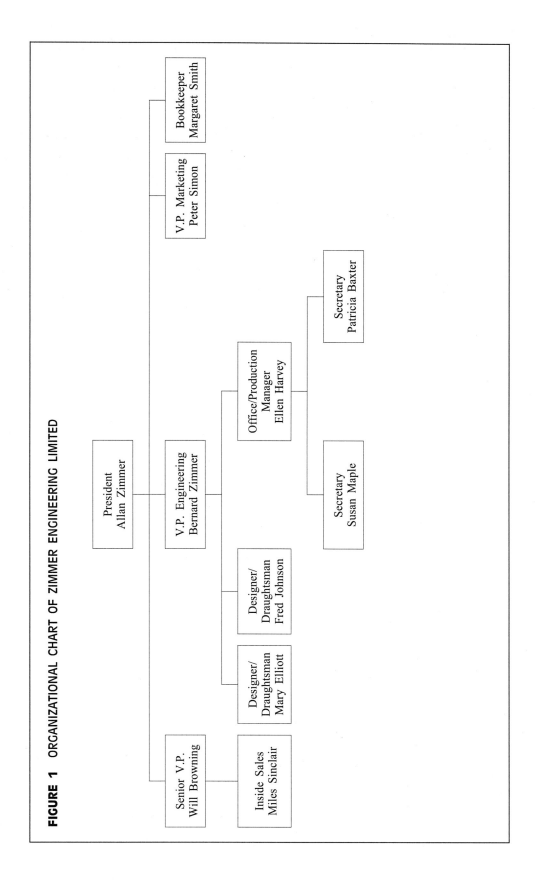

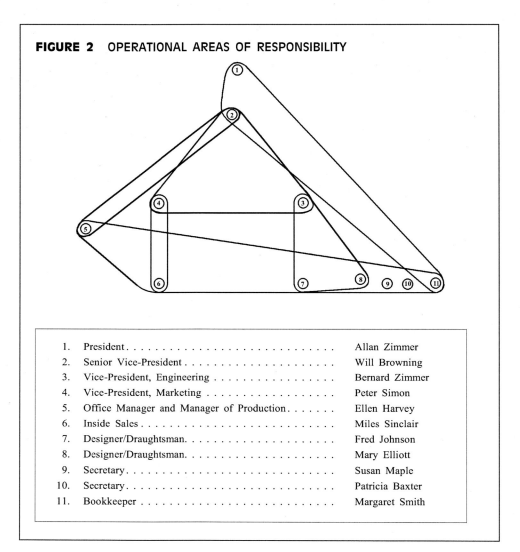

FIGURE 2 OPERATIONAL AREAS OF RESPONSIBILITY

1.	President.	Allan Zimmer
2.	Senior Vice-President.	Will Browning
3.	Vice-President, Engineering	Bernard Zimmer
4.	Vice-President, Marketing	Peter Simon
5.	Office Manager and Manager of Production.	Ellen Harvey
6.	Inside Sales	Miles Sinclair
7.	Designer/Draughtsman.	Fred Johnson
8.	Designer/Draughtsman.	Mary Elliott
9.	Secretary.	Susan Maple
10.	Secretary.	Patricia Baxter
11.	Bookkeeper	Margaret Smith

president. It seemed to be a matter of pride for Allan Zimmer to try to handle any sort of issue that arose.

With the quiet support of the rest of the employees, including Peter Simon and the one outside director of the company, Will Browning wanted to alter the role descriptions, authority, and responsibilities so that he would have effective control over the marketing, production, and engineering functions. The difficulty was that the Zimmers owned over 70% of the company's shares, and they certainly would not relinquish the status of their family willingly.

Howard Pearson was impressed by the work of Rensis Likert, a well-known organizational behaviourist. He decided to suggest a Likert linking pin model to reallocate responsibilities, as shown in Figure 2. In this model, functional responsibilities for each job are restricted to those other positions that are also included in the same link or links that enclose that job. For example, under the new plan Allan Zimmer would be involved only with Will Browning and the bookkeeper. The revised structure would leave Allan in the position of president, but it would remove his influence over areas in which he had no expertise. Will Browning would become the buffer between the president and the technical side of the firm. Howard felt that Bernard Zimmer would probably accept the relationship of directly reporting to Will Browning as long as Allan was still to be president. Bernard might even feel some relief, as his responsibilities were diminished. Will would be able to step in directly to supervise design and production when Bernard was busy with his farm, and to manage personally some of the more critical projects.

Howard also prepared a very brief job description for each management position (see Table 1 on the following page). His intention was to involve the whole management group in filling in the details once the main thrust of the change was accepted. Will Browning totally approved of the plan, as it seemed to meet all his goals for changing Zimmer Engineering. However, he wondered how he would get Allan Zimmer to accept it.

QUESTIONS

1. Is Bernard Zimmer's attitude towards the firm irresponsible?

2. Evaluate Howard Pearson's plan. Do you think that it will be effective? What drawbacks does it have?

3. What alterations or additional measures are necessary?

4. How would you:
   (a) introduce the plan to Allan Zimmer?
   (b) implement the structural changes and new role descriptions? Answer in detail.

TABLE 1 ROLE DESCRIPTIONS

PRESIDENT

1.0 Areas of Responsibility and Reporting Relationship
  1.1 Administration and reporting for the Company Budget.
  1.2 Co-responsibility (along with Senior Vice-President) for financial planning.
  1.3 Administration and reporting for strategic planning studies.
  1.4 Bookkeeping, finance, and auditing.
  1.5 Coordinating these areas with the Senior Vice-President.

2.0 Areas for Which Objectives Should Be Set
  2.1 Company tax planning.
  2.2 Company borrowing.
  2.3 Administration costs.

3.0 Areas of Authority
  3.1 Financial statements and audit.
  3.2 Supervision of bookkeeper.
  3.3 Cheque signing authority (with Will Browning and Bernard Zimmer).

SENIOR VICE-PRESIDENT

1.0 Areas of Responsibility and Reporting Relationship
  1.1 Participation in objectives, strategies, and policies which are set and implemented for the functional areas of:
    (a) Marketing
    (b) Engineering
    (c) Office Management
    (d) Strategic Planning
    (e) Production Management
  1.2 Formulation of Company Budget.
  1.3 Evaluation of performance within above functional areas.
  1.4 Definition of role descriptions as well as reporting and coordinating functions.
  1.5 Co-responsibility (along with Vice-President, Engineering) for marketing of engineered systems.
  1.6 Chair of the Executive Committee which will convene regularly to provide consulting assistance in matters of strategic and general management.
  1.7 Report to Board of Directors.

2.0 Areas for Which Objectives Should Be Set
  2.1 Return on investment.
  2.2 Net profit.
  2.3 Contribution margin.
  2.4 Development of new initiatives.
  2.5 Market areas:
    • types of customers
    • types of products
    • geographical areas

3.0 Areas of Authority
  3.1 Review of all personnel terminations.
  3.2 Final arbitration of salaries.

Table 1 continued

3.3 Cheque signing authority (with Bernard Zimmer and Allan Zimmer) and review of all expenditures.

3.4 Final authority in determining acceptance of sales and engineering contracts.

3.5 Final arbitration of objectives, strategies, and policies that apply to individual functional areas of the company.

VICE-PRESIDENT, ENGINEERING

1.0 Areas of Responsibility and Reporting Relationship
  1.1 Marketing of hardware and technology.
  1.2 Co-responsibility (along with Senior Vice-President) for marketing of engineered systems.
  1.3 Job functions of draughting personnel.
  1.4 Research and development in areas of environmental control and engineered systems.
  1.5 Report to Senior Vice-President.

2.0 Areas for Which Objectives Should Be Set
  2.1 Sales of products and technology.
  2.2 Sales of engineered systems.
  2.3 Contribution margin of engineering area.
  2.4 Fixed costs of engineering area.
  2.5 Productivity of draughting personnel.

3.0 Areas of Authority
  3.1 Cheque co-signing authority (with Allan Zimmer and Will Browning).
  3.2 Supervision of draughting personnel.
  3.3 Salary review of draughting personnel.
  3.4 Engineering area budget.

VICE-PRESIDENT, MARKETING

1.0 Areas of Responsibility and Reporting Relationship
  1.1 Marketing of standard products.
  1.2 Development of new products and improvement of existing products.
  1.3 Research and development in area of industrial air handling and conditioning products.
  1.4 Report to Senior Vice-President.

2.0 Areas for Which Objectives Should Be Set
  2.1 Sales of standard products.
  2.2 Contribution margin of market area.
  2.3 Fixed costs of sales area.
  2.4 Productivity of inside sales personnel.

3.0 Areas of Authority
  3.1 Supervision of inside sales personnel.
  3.2 Salary review of inside sales personnel.
  3.3 Marketing area budget.

Table 1 continued

PRODUCTION MANAGER

1.0 Areas of Responsibility and Reporting Relationship
    1.1 Administration of outside manufacturing services relating to standard product lines.
    1.2 Purchasing of components from outside suppliers.
    1.3 Scheduling of purchased items and manufacturing priorities (for both standard products and engineered systems).
    1.4 Report to Senior Vice-President.

2.0 Areas for Which Objectives Should Be Set
    2.1 Product quality/warranty expenses.
    2.2 Manufacturing costs.
    2.3 Contribution margin of manufactured products.

3.0 Areas of Authority
    3.1 Decisions as to outside manufacturers of standard products.
    3.2 Quality control.

OFFICE MANAGER

1.0 Areas of Responsibility and Reporting Relationship
    1.1 Office administration.
    1.2 Personnel administration.
        • time keeping
        • vacation scheduling
        • absenteeism.
    1.3 Report to Senior Vice-President.

2.0 Areas for Which Objectives Should Be Set
    2.1 Office efficiency.
    2.2 Personnel morale.
    2.3 Office expenses.

3.0 Areas of Authority
    3.1 Hiring and firing of clerical staff.
    3.2 Purchasing and maintenance of office equipment and supplies.

Exercises

∎ ∎ ∎ ∎ ∎ ∎

Earn Your Mark

Equity Theory

PURPOSE

To apply equity theory to a familiar situation.

PREPARATION

None required.

INTRODUCTION

You are a member of a study group that has recently submitted a major paper in your Organizational Behaviour class. Different group members took on different responsibilities in the preparation of the paper. The list below describes the different contributions that people made. For the purposes of this exercise, you will be assigned one of the following roles:

Conceptualizer: Contributed to the theoretical discussion of the issues and critiqued the drafts of the paper.

Primary Data Gatherer: Collected the raw data needed to meet the requirements of the assignment.

Data Analyst: Conducted a sophisticated statistical analysis of the primary data.

Secondary Source Analyst: Did the review of the literature and prepared the bibliography and references.

Organizer: Called the meetings for the group, scheduled the work, arranged for word processing, photocopying, and delivery of the paper. Provided the pizza.

Politician: Took charge of "professor politics", ensuring that the professor was constantly aware of the progress of the group.

Writer: Actually wrote the paper.

Ghost: Assigned to the group, attended the first meeting, announced the intention of doing an individual paper and then vanished. Received the group mark.

This is a group assignment and a group mark will be given. The exercise provides an application of equity theory, and you will have the opportunity to assess the equity of your grade in light of your contribution and that of the others.

EARNING YOUR MARK — SCORE SHEET

Group Mark: _____					
ROLES	**A**	**B** $\left(\dfrac{\text{Group Mark}}{\text{Column A}}\right)$	**C**	**D** $\left(\dfrac{\text{Column C}}{\text{Column A}}\right)$	
Conceptualizer					
Primary Data Gatherer					
Data Analyst					
Secondary Source Analyst					
Organizer					
Politician					
Writer					
Ghost					

Step 1:   In Column A, give your assessment of the contribution of each member of the group, including yourself. Express this as a percentage. Do not consult with any other members of the group. For example, if you thought the conceptualizer did the most work, you might decide he or she deserved a high mark, such as 87%. Rate each member's contribution.

Step 2:   In Column B calculate your equity ratios by dividing the mark your group earned for the assignment by your assessment of the contributions of the different members. This group mark is the mark given to you by your instructor, and can be recorded at the top of the score sheet. For example, if your contribution was 50% and your group mark was 75%, then your equity ratio is 1 ½. Your final mark was inflated by 1 ½ times as a result of the group effort.

Step 3: Assess your feelings of equity from the group mark method of evaluating your contribution. Any ratio greater than one shows that the grade was inflated by the group mark. Any ratio less than one shows a loss associated with the group mark.

Step 4: Hold a group discussion to assign individual marks to each member based on their contribution. The individual marks must be ordinary percentages, and the group average must remain as the original group mark. Record these new marks in Column C.

Step 5: Calculate new equity ratios in Column D by dividing Column C by Column A. Express all marks as a percent.

Step 6: Discuss the following issues with your group:

- How successful was your effort to achieve equity by adjusting the outcome?

- Evaluate the role of perceptual differences in achieving equity. What misperceptions occurred?

- Transfer this case to a work setting where you are involved in a team project. Imagine that you have been assigned to develop a new product for your high technology firm. Include the product manager as a team member.
  - Identify possible effort and outcome variables that would be associated with this project. Look for more than one outcome variable.
  - Develop strategies to minimize feelings of inequity amongst team members.
  - Distinguish long-term strategies that could be applied to future projects.

- A key difference between a unionized workplace and a non-unionized workplace is in method of determining pay. Non-union workplaces usually reflect the employer's interest in rewarding employees individually on the basis of merit as judged by the employer. Unionized workplaces typically have a small number of "pay bands", and employees advance on the basis of seniority. Use equity theory to explain the union position on pay.

Improving Communication

Perception and Attribution

PURPOSE

To improve interpersonal communication skills through an understanding of how behaviour is perceived by other people and how individuals make attributions based on those perceptions.

PREPARATION

Your instructor may request that you complete the questionnaire prior to class.

INTRODUCTION

Read the four conclusions provided for each statement. Think of them as four points on a ruler: points numbered two, four, six, and eight. Use them to determine a score from zero to ten that you think best describes your own situation.

1. If I heard from a third party that my best friend has described my personality,

I would be quite worried about what the description would be.	2
It would be fairly likely that it would be news to me.	4
I would not mind hearing it, since I rather doubt I would be surprised.	6
I am quite sure I would know exactly what they were talking about.	8

    Score 0 to 10 ☐

2. One of the things that I think is most important about a best friend is that

I would not feel that I would have to share my thoughts or feelings.	2
The relationship would have lots of room for personal privacy.	4
We would share some things but not others.	6
We would be completely open with each other.	8

    Score 0 to 10 ☐

3. If I had a performance review by my supervisor in which I was told things about how I did my work,

I would not want to hear any of it because I expect my supervisor would describe things about my work that I did not know about. 2

I think there would be some things that I would be familiar with, but a lot of it could be news. 4

I rather suspect I would know most of what was going to be said. 6

I look forward to my performance reviews because I want to know how my supervisor sees me. 8

Score 0 to 10 ☐

4. I think that when I am at work it is important that

The distinction I make between work life and private life is absolute. 2

I do not always have to tell other people what I am doing in my private life. 4

I can share some of my personal feelings with others if I want to. 6

I do not keep any secrets from my co-workers. 8

Score 0 to 10 ☐

5. If I was married and my spouse and I went on one of those TV shows where husbands and wives have to guess what their spouse is thinking or feeling,

I would dread going on such a show because I would be worried that my spouse would come up with all sorts of things about me that I was not aware of. 2

My spouse probably knows quite a number of things about me that I don't know. 4

I would not expect many surprises. 6

I think that kind of experience would be very helpful, as my spouse is intimately familiar with me. 8

Score 0 to 10 ☐

6. If I was married, the kind of relationship I would like would be one where

I could still maintain a strong sense of privacy about my personal beliefs and feelings. 2

The two of us could share a few things of mutual interest. 4

I could tell my spouse about a lot of the things that I was feeling. 6

I would be completely open and exposed to my spouse. 8

Score 0 to 10 ☐

Scores

Feedback: Add scores for questions 1, 3, and 5 = _____

Self Disclosure: Add scores for questions 2, 4, and 6 = _____

JOHARI WINDOW (Reference: Joseph Luft, *Group Processes: An Introduction to Group Dynamics*. Palo Alto, California: Mayfield, 1984.)

Plot your scores in the window below. The upper-left corner represents a zero score. Scores rise to 30 moving to the right and downward. Draw your window and label the panes in the window.

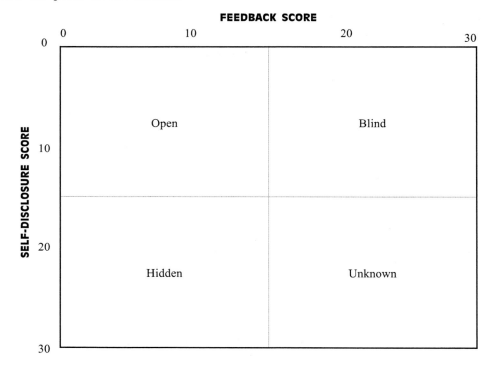

Task

After plotting your JoHari window, analyze for potential change. The area over which you have most control is that of self-disclosure. There are problems associated with both too much and too little self-disclosure.

Rate yourself using the following list of reasons for self-disclosure, and then identify areas for potential self improvement.

Reasons for Self Disclosure

1. **Catharsis:** Used to relieve a personal burden, e.g., regretting past behaviour that was harmful.

2. **Self Clarification:** Talking things out people can sort out beliefs, opinions, thoughts, attitudes, feelings.

3. **Self Validation:** Getting others to confirm the wisdom of your thoughts or actions. Checking it out.

4. **Reciprocity:** A self disclosure by one person encourages self disclosure by others. Can be used to get others to reveal themselves.

5. **Impression Formation:** Using self disclosure to create a particular impression of yourself. Bragging.

6. **Relationship Maintenance and Enhancement:** Ongoing openness helps to maintain existing relationships.

7. **Social Control:** Telling tales about others for personal gain includes "squealing" or "tattling".

8. **Manipulation:** When the self disclosure includes a hidden agenda, which remains hidden.

Analysis
Share your findings with a partner.

Classical Conditioning in Advertisements

Learning and Reinforcement

PURPOSE

To analyze the use of classical conditioning principles in advertising.

PREPARATION

Bring at least one copy of a magazine to class. Several different magazines would be better. Scissors are useful.

INTRODUCTION

This is a small-group project. The task of your group is to find a variety of ads that illustrate classical learning theory and two of its characteristics.

Classical learning theory can be used to analyze a wide variety of modern ads. In a typical ad the viewer is exposed to an image of the product as well as to some seemingly unrelated image that provides a diverting message. The advertisers have learned that such ads help the viewer to recall the product for a longer period of time and in a more favourable light. Classical learning theory explains this benefit through the process of conditioning.

The first step involves selecting a stimulus for which the viewer has already acquired a suitable response. In the use of sex in advertising, the image of a provocative pose or exposure (the stimulus) will evoke feelings of excitement or pleasure in some viewers (the response). Since this stimulus-response pattern was not learned in the ad, the elements are called the UnConditioned Stimulus (UCS) and the UnConditioned Response (UCR). The purpose of the ad is to cause an association between a new stimulus (the product) and the existing response. Since this stimulus-response pattern is learned by the viewer, it is called the Conditioned Stimulus (CS) and the Conditioned Response (CR). The conditioning is done through repetition of the ad, although perceptual factors such as size, location, colour, movement, novelty can affect the learning.

PART I

Look through your magazines and find five ads that employ classical conditioning. Select ads that use different UCS–UCR bonds. Identify, to the members of your group, the elements of the ad: the UCS, the UCR, and, of course, the conditioned stimulus. Discuss whether the UCS–UCR bond has been selected because of a real association with the product (as in the strength of the Rock of Gibraltar for the Prudential Insurance Company) or whether it has been selected on the basis of the power of the bond (as in any ad using sex when the product is not sex).

Stimulus Generalization and Stimulus Discrimination

Another aspect of classical conditioning that can be analyzed in advertisements is the related processes of generalization and discrimination of the stimulus. When people respond to a stimulus, they may in fact be capable of giving a similar response to a whole class of stimuli that are similar to the one for which the response was originally learned. This learning phenomenon has been eagerly adopted by advertisers and is most clearly apparent in the marketing of clones. The advertiser hopes that the favourable S–R bond for the original can be generalized to include the new stimulus of the clone. Sometimes the product is not a clone, but nonetheless hopes to ride famous coattails. The ads vary in terms of the honesty of the pitch towards generalization, because some are virtual knock-offs of the original.

Stimulus discrimination is the reverse process. In this situation, the viewer has a pre-existing S–R bond that applies to a whole class of stimuli. The advertiser wishes his product to stand out from the rest and must, therefore, get the viewer to discriminate and respond only to his stimulus. The popular Smirnoff Vodka ads are a good example of stimulus discrimination ("There's vodka and then there's Smirnoff!"). This is a common problem for products that don't develop strong brand loyalty, because the consumer tends to think they are all alike.

PART I   CLASSICAL CONDITIONING WORK SHEET

NAME: _____

Ad #1   Description: _____

UCS: _____

UCR: _____

CS: _____

Relationship of UCS–UCR bond to the product: _____

_____

_____

Ad #2   Description: _____

UCS: _____

UCR: _____

CS: _____

Relationship of UCS–UCR bond to the product: _____

_____

_____

Ad #3   Description: _____

UCS: _____

UCR: _____

CS: _____

Relationship of UCS–UCR bond to the product: _____

_____

_____

Ad #4   Description: _____

UCS: _____

UCR: _____

CS: _____

Relationship of UCS–UCR bond to the product: _____

_____

_____

Ad #5   Description: _____

UCS: _____

UCR: _____

CS: _____

Relationship of UCS–UCR bond to the product: _____

_____

_____

PART II

Find two ads that illustrate stimulus generalization or stimulus discrimination, and explain the elements to the members of your group.

PART II STIMULUS DISCRIMINATION AND
STIMULUS GENERALIZATION

Ad #1 Description: _____

General stimulus: _____

Discrete stimulus: _____

Description of generalization or discrimination: _____

_____

_____

Ad #2 Description: _____

General stimulus: _____

Discrete stimulus: _____

Description of generalization or discrimination: _____

_____

_____

Worker Monitoring
Learning and Reinforcement

PURPOSE

To examine the growing trend of worker monitoring systems and the implication of learning theory on these practices.

PREPARATION

None required.

INTRODUCTION

A growing trend in personnel supervision practice has been the use of computerized methods of monitoring the work of employees. Often these systems are a spin-off from computerization for some other purpose, such as inventory control or scheduling. A typical example that is familiar to shoppers at a modern supermarket is the cashier at the checkout counter. In addition to the price, the checkout process records the item and the quantity purchased for inventory control. These records are maintained for each cashier, and, with the addition of a timer, the store is able to tell how long it takes the cashier to register the sale. Even a fairly simple system can conduct several analyses of this database: How many sales can the cashier record per hour? How many are not committed to memory and have to be looked up? How many errors are corrected? Word processing in the office provides additional methods of automated supervision. Computers can count keystrokes, words, and documents, and produce a performance report based on these variables. Generally the analyses are of speed and accuracy.

Modern telephones also provide opportunities for monitoring of worker behaviour. Calls can be monitored for personal use as well as to ensure the employee is projecting the correct image on business calls.

Relatively cheap video cameras have encouraged more companies to use them for security purposes. Often the security issue is internal, and it is an easy step to move from checking for pilfering to checking for performance.

Companies using these systems cite the following benefits:

1. **Cost:** These monitoring systems usually have a low operating cost, although the initial set-up may be expensive.

2. **Quantity Control:** The systems usually provide good measures of speed and accuracy.

3. **Face Validity:** The employer usually has a strong feeling of providing effective supervision.

PROBLEMS

1. **Worker Resentment:** Monitoring often leads to union grievances and reduced worker morale. Better workers may leave.

2. **Job Stress:** A typical worker complaint is that of increased job stress resulting from the monitoring.

3. **Gender Bias:** Monitoring systems are more common in female-dominated jobs.

4. **Unintended Consequences:** Employers may ignore the qualitative side of employee performance; workers may be motivated to beat the system rather than to do their actual work.

EXERCISE

Objective
To apply the concept of behaviour modification to employee monitoring.

Method
Working in a group of up to six students, complete the following tasks.

Step 1: Briefly review the following concepts of employee behaviour modification.

- Establish clear goals for employees.
- Have the employees provide accurate information on their performance.
- Give positive reinforcement for all improvements in behaviour as well as for accurate and honest record keeping.
- Use shaping and the scheduling of reinforcement to modify behaviour toward the goals.
- Use extinction to eliminate undesired behaviour.
- Use praise, recognition, and intrinsic rewards from the job itself as positive reinforcement; in particular, identify feedback mechanisms that serve as automatic reinforcers.
- Avoid punishment.

Step 2: Make a list of five different examples of worker monitoring. Draw upon your own experiences as a worker and as a customer.

Step 3: Evaluate each example in terms of the effectiveness of the behaviour modification.

• Outline the strengths and weaknesses of each system.
• What behaviours are being monitored?
• What behaviours are being reinforced?

Step 4: Propose ways to improve each worker-monitoring method.

Step 5: Evaluate each in terms of its ability to motivate towards better performance. Has it dealt with qualitative as well as quantitative methods of measurement? An ideal system of worker monitoring is one that provides the worker with the most information about their performance and, thus, the greatest opportunity for self-control.

Step 6: As a group, discuss the question, "Do these worker-monitoring systems interfere with the dignity of the worker?"

The Model Boss

Learning and Reinforcement

PURPOSE

To evaluate the impact of role models on individual behaviour and in the formation of corporate culture.

PREPARATION

Your instructor may request that you complete the steps listed below prior to class.

INTRODUCTION

One of the most powerful forms of learning is through the process psychologists call modelling. According to this theory, we learn behaviours as a result of copying them from people we think are important or admirable. This is most apparent with fads and fashions, where some particular celebrity will set a style for dress or mannerism or even language. With celebrities, the mass media plays an important role in communicating the new style. We also copy the behaviour of our peers, particularly those we consider to be leaders. Indeed, one useful definition of leadership is the ability to establish a fashion in a group. With peers, the contact is more immediate and intimate and, as a result, can be very powerful.

In each case the learning process is the same. First, we have a favourable attitude toward the person, and then we begin to associate their specific behaviours as part of their overall image. Our positive view about them as a person is carried over into what they do, or say, or wear, or whatever. We accept these other aspects of the person uncritically and, often, unconsciously as part of the whole "package". Part of admiring someone involves wanting them to admire you, and so we imitate their behaviour in the expectation that this admiration will be reciprocated. Since "imitation is the sincerest form of flattery", this return of admiration usually occurs, and the cycle is reinforced.

We are not normally aware of the influence of modelling on our behaviour. We may think about it at the level of fashion (i.e., what people wear at the office), but otherwise the process is largely unconscious. The purpose of this exercise is to dig into this unconscious material.

Step 1:   Identify a person who you think is a model for you. To look for corporate influences, you should choose one of your supervisors or managers; it need not be your immediate supervisor. Your respect for that person might be moderated by your daily work relations. It should be someone you have some interaction with, so that when you see them and hear them speak, you can observe mannerisms and other aspects of behaviour. If you do not have a current "boss", then find some other person, perhaps from a sports team you are on, or a volunteer group, or a friendship group or, perhaps, even a family.

Step 2:   Over the next two weeks, observe the behaviour of this person and those around him or her. Identify those behaviours that seem to be imitated by you and by others. You may find it easier to see the modelling in other people's behaviour than in your own, at least at first. List the behaviours under the following categories:

1. **Clothing:** This is the easiest, so start here. Businesses often have a quite pronounced but unofficial dress code. The boss will set the code by personal behaviour.

_____

_____

_____

_____

_____

_____

2. **Language:** Business, like any other subculture, has developed its own language, words, and expressions that relate to daily worklife. This language is in part practical because it is a shorthand reference to things normally used in the business. Some of it is faddish in that it is a popular expression, but you could get along very well without it because there is a plain English word that would do just as well. Sometimes it is just an inappropriate overuse of a particular word or expression. Taken together, special language serves to identify who is in the know and who is not.

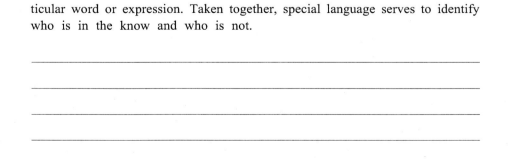

3. **Routine Behaviours:** The official work day might be nine to five, but there will be some additional norm about how early you should be and exactly when you can leave. If you punch a time clock, this might not vary a lot, but in a white collar office this is often quite important. Also check out routines about coffee breaks, lunch hour, etc. Employees who do not model their behaviour correctly may learn of their error.

_____

_____

_____

_____

_____

_____

4. **Mannerisms:** This category includes the little pieces of personal behaviour that we all have but are not very conscious of. They include the behaviours we have that others might think are funny or eccentric. Sometimes these become quite stylish in the sense that everyone does them. They can include our non-verbal communication patterns that we use to supplement our verbal communication. This one is trickier, so you will have to look harder.

_____

_____

_____

_____

_____

_____

Step 3: Report your findings to your discussion group. How similar are the different observations people have marked? How strong was the modelling?

Cognitive Learning in Trade Journals

Learning and Reinforcement

PURPOSE

To apply the principles of cognitive learning to advertising.

PREPARATION

Your instructor may request that you analyze five ads prior to class. In any event, you will be asked to get access to a copy of a trade journal. Your library may be willing to provide an old issue for this purpose.

INTRODUCTION

Commercial advertisements are designed to shape our attitude about particular products and services. One of the methods used by advertising agencies involves what psychologists call cognitive learning. This is learning that involves our ordinary thought processes and is the kind of learning that you most frequently use. When you read a textbook or listen to a lecture and your brain processes the information it receives, this is cognitive learning. Along with this cognitive processing of information, our brain also undertakes an evaluative processing of the information being received. Is this information worthwhile or not? This may occur at various levels of awareness.

In cognitive oriented ads the message at the front is quite clear: here are the features of our computer, these are the advantages of our credit card as compared to others, and so forth. Typically the ad contains a lot of information. The image of the product might be quite obscure or even absent.

At another level the ad provides a different message: Are you computer literate? Ours is a technological society, are you part of it? How up to date are you?

This second level of ads can be very powerful when ads are looked at within a particular category. For example, the Toronto Star runs a regular section of computer ads. The main products are personal computers and business software. This market is still dominated by a large number of small suppliers, each of whom can only afford a small ad in a large circulation paper like the Star, so the paper groups the ads together. The effect of this is twofold: to display the competition amongst the companies and encourage technical advertising of their features, and to convey an overall positive image of the relevance of computer applications to modern business. The ads themselves rarely focus on the image theme that you need computers to be in business today.

For this exercise, use trade journals as a source of data. Pick one trade journal. For the purpose of this exercise, a trade journal could include something outside of business, e.g., a magazine for a particular sport, such as running or sailing, or some specific hobby. The idea is to get a focused journal. Collect at least five cognitive ads and analyze them at the two levels: first for the overt content, and then for the underlying attitude or value set being conveyed. Compare the ads looking for common sets of values and attitudes.

Your instructor will direct you to either hand in this exercise or to provide a verbal report.

JOURNAL: Name the journal and briefly outline its target market.

NAME: _____

TARGET MARKET: _____

AD #1: Content of Ad _____

_____

_____

_____

AD #2: Content of Ad _____

_____

_____

_____

AD #3: Content of Ad _____

_____

_____

_____

AD #4: Content of Ad _____

_____

_____

_____

AD #5: Content of Ad _____

_____

_____

_____

Underlying Attitudes and Values of the Ads:

_____

_____

_____

_____

_____

What's the Use — Innovation

Creativity

PURPOSE

To experience the "creative" demands of business.

PREPARATION

Your instructor may request that you complete the questionnaire prior to class.

INTRODUCTION

Your supervisor has given you a very strange job. After a corporate merger and restructuring, there are some leftovers, and she has sent you a list of this "stuff" for your input. She expects that you will make good use of these "things".

PART I

Look over the list and come up with as many possible uses as you can think of. Be creative in your ideas, and don't censor your own work. Your supervisor will think any idea is worth looking at right now.

The "Stuff"

1. Fifty gross, black rotary dial telephones.

_____

_____

_____

_____

_____

_____

2. Seventy-five office sets including large, double-pedestal oak desks (Empire style) as well as chairs, credenzas, etc.

_____

_____

_____

_____

_____

_____

3. Approximately 3,000 copies of annual reports from past years. All are printed on glossy paper in full colour. All refer to companies that no longer exist.

_____

_____

_____

_____

_____

_____

4. Complete fixtures for two company cafeterias: one seating 100 using cafeteria service, and the other seating 20 with full dining room service.

_____

_____

_____

_____

_____

_____

5. Approximately 10,000 hub caps for assorted cars of various ages.

_____

_____

_____

_____

_____

_____

6. One corporate art collection of 400 pieces, but of little appraised value.

   _____

   _____

   _____

   _____

   _____

   _____

7. A remote fishing camp used by executives. Completely equipped and ready for the next season. The staff were not advised of the restructuring.

   _____

   _____

   _____

   _____

   _____

   _____

8. The public goodwill of a now disbanded furniture company.

   _____

   _____

   _____

   _____

   _____

   _____

9. One hundred and thirty-five employees.

   _____

   _____

   _____

   _____

   _____

   _____

PART II

Compare your ideas with the others in your group. There are no right or wrong ideas, but you are looking for ideas that go beyond the conventional use. Try to grade them in terms of conventionality: i.e., strictly conventional, same use but very different target, very different use, off the wall.

Use your group to add to the lists. Follow the brainstorming technique of avoiding judgments about ideas; just list them all.

Look for combinations of ideas from the different items. Synthesis is a higher form of creativity. List the combined ideas below.

_____

_____

_____

_____

_____

_____

_____

_____

PART III

Evaluate the process in terms of the creativity achieved. What were the major barriers to creativity? What were the major stimulants of the creative process?

Self-Esteem Inventory

Personality and Attitudes

PURPOSE

To analyze the concept of self-esteem and to examine various elements of that overall concept.

PREPARATION

Your instructor may request that you complete the questionnaire prior to class.

INTRODUCTION

Self-esteem is the term popularly used to describe positive feelings of self worth and a belief in personal ability to perform effectively and to cope in a variety of situations. It is not a measure of actual ability, but rather a measure of personal attitude. Such attitudes can have a powerful effect on personal performance since behaviour is the result of a combination of ability and motivation. Of the two, motivation may well be the more important. A key ingredient of motivation is a personal belief in one's own potential. Self-esteem inventories measure that belief system.

The following questionnaire is easy to use and is self-scoring. Each of the following 45 words and phrases relate to aspects of self-esteem. Decide how well each of them fits you. Be as honest as you can with yourself. Rate them as they apply to you. A common problem with instruments like these is that people put down the answer that they think the examiner wants to hear or that they think is the most socially desirable. Try to avoid this bias when picking your answer.

After you have filled out the questionnaire, use the scoring key to tabulate the results. Meet with your group to analyze the instrument, compare your results, and discuss the questions found at the end of this activity.

The original version of this self-esteem inventory was developed by Keitha Davey, Gail Higginson and Barbara Learn.

Rate as follows:

A	NEVER describes me	
B	RARELY describes me	
C	SOMETIMES describes me	
D	MOST OF THE TIME describes me	

1	helpful	_____	24	achiever	_____
2	easily discouraged	_____	25	cooperative	_____
3	makes decisions easily	_____	26	dependent	_____
4	likes to succeed	_____	27	problem solver	_____
5	tries hard	_____	28	capable	_____
6	pleasant	_____	29	sets own goals	_____
7	easily embarrassed	_____	30	agreeable	_____
8	leader	_____	31	pessimistic	_____
9	shy	_____	32	assertive	_____
10	practical	_____	33	high aspirations	_____
11	cheerful	_____	34	peacemaker	_____
12	timid	_____	35	follower	_____
13	persistent	_____	36	skilled	_____
14	self-confident	_____	37	popular	_____
15	ambitious	_____	38	feels inferior	_____
16	likeable	_____	39	analytical	_____
17	self-doubting	_____	40	creative	_____
18	shows initiative	_____	41	blaming	_____
19	intelligent	_____	42	flexible	_____
20	accepts new ideas	_____	43	realistic	_____
21	confused	_____	44	independent	_____
22	planner	_____	45	enduring	_____
23	competent	_____			

SELF-ESTEEM SCORE SHEET

This self-esteem inventory has five sub-scales. Transfer your answers from the above sheet and circle the score for each choice. The item number is provided to help in transferring the score. Do NOT change any of your answers. Notice that the responses in the second factor score in a different direction to the others. Add up the score for each sub-scale, and then combine the two for a total self-esteem score. Compare your score to the norms provided.

AMIABILITY				
# ITEM	**A**	**B**	**C**	**D**
1 helpful	1	2	3	4
6 pleasant	1	2	3	4
11 cheerful	1	2	3	4
16 likeable	1	2	3	4
20 accept new ideas	1	2	3	4
25 cooperative	1	2	3	4
30 agreeable	1	2	3	4
34 peacemaker	1	2	3	4
37 popular	1	2	3	4
40 creative	1	2	3	4
42 flexible	1	2	3	4
45 enduring	1	2	3	4
TOTAL SCORE = =	+	+	+	

CONFIDENCE				
# ITEM	**A**	**B**	**C**	**D**
2 easily discouraged	4	3	2	1
7 easily embarrassed	4	3	2	1
9 shy	4	3	2	1
12 timid	4	3	2	1
17 self-doubting	4	3	2	1
21 confused	4	3	2	1
26 dependent	4	3	2	1
31 pessimistic	4	3	2	1
35 follower	4	3	2	1
38 feels inferior	4	3	2	1
41 blaming	4	3	2	1
TOTAL SCORE = =	+	+	+	

ACHIEVEMENT					
#	ITEM	A	B	C	D
4	likes to succeed	1	2	3	4
15	ambitious	1	2	3	4
24	achiever	1	2	3	4
29	sets own goals	1	2	3	4
33	high aspirations	1	2	3	4
	TOTAL SCORE =		+	+	+
	=				

CONTROL					
#	ITEM	A	B	C	D
3	makes decisions easily	1	2	3	4
8	leader	1	2	3	4
13	persistent	1	2	3	4
18	shows initiative	1	2	3	4
22	planner	1	2	3	4
27	problem solver	1	2	3	4
32	assertive	1	2	3	4
36	skilled	1	2	3	4
39	analytical	1	2	3	4
43	realistic	1	2	3	4
	TOTAL SCORE =		+	+	+
	=				

COMPETENCE					
#	ITEM	A	B	C	D
5	tries hard	1	2	3	4
10	practical	1	2	3	4
14	self-confident	1	2	3	4
19	intelligent	1	2	3	4
23	competent	1	2	3	4
28	capable	1	2	3	4
44	independent	1	2	3	4
	TOTAL SCORE =		+	+	+
	=				

PROFILE CHART

Percentile

	10	20	30	40	50	60	70	80	90	100
Amiability	36 37	38	39	40	41 42	43	44	45	47	48
Confident	20	24	25	26 27 28	29	30	31	32	35	
Achievement	15	16		17	18	19	20		21	
Control	25	30	31	32	33 34	35	36	37	39	
Competence	21	22 23	24		25	26		27	28	
Self-esteem	130	135	140	145	150	155	160	165		

SUB-SCALE FACTOR	SCORES
Amiability	
Confidence	
Achievement	
Control	
Competence	
SELF-ESTEEM	

Interpretation

1. **Amiability:** Amiability refers to a positive attitude about getting along with others. Personal values stress the importance of interpersonal processes rather than on a task orientation.

2. **Confidence:** Confidence relates to a positive belief in one's own ability, and is the result of a feeling of emotional security.

3. **Achievement:** The need to achieve has long been recognized as a hallmark of business success. It is usually defined in terms of a person who gets positive reinforcement from achieving recognized goals. A corollary of this value is that the person is not motivated by unachievable or unrealistic goals.

4. **Control:** This factor is most closely aligned to the values associated with a manager. The control referred to involves the control of others.

5. **Competence:** The value factor is a subjective rating of personal competence. Positive self-esteem requires a strong belief in one's own ability.

DISCUSSION QUESTIONS

1. Analyze the items in each sub-scale to broaden your understanding of the factor. Was there a relationship in your score between the items?

2. Describe the kind of "organizational persons" who would score highest in the different factors: i.e., who would you find in top management, personnel, marketing, research and development, etc.? Is there a fit between your score and your career plan?

3. Attitude and motivational factors are subject to personal development; indeed, a large part of management training would fall in this category. Prepare a personal development plan and present it to your group.

4. Discuss any minority group bias you suspect may exist in the concept of self-esteem. To what extent is self-esteem an ethnocentric concept of Western, industrialized, male culture?

Risk Taking

Personality and Attitudes

PURPOSE

To measure individual differences in risk taking.

PREPARATION

Your instructor may request that you complete the questionnaire prior to class.

INTRODUCTION

See Part II.

PART I

Complete and score the following questionnaire. Score each item as True or False as it pertains to you and your past behaviour.

_____ 1. I am a smoker.

_____ 2. At least once in the past I have quit my current job before finding a replacement for it.

_____ 3. Over the past two years I have received two or more traffic tickets.

_____ 4. My recreational activities over the past three years have included at least one that could be considered risky, such as downhill skiing, water skiing, motor vehicle racing, mountain activities, sky diving, hunting, white-water sports, etc.

_____ 5. At least once in the past I have disagreed with my supervisor about a business issue in a private meeting.

_____ 6. At least once in the past I have disagreed with my supervisor about a business issue in a group setting that included my supervisor's peers and supervisor (i.e., the next level of management).

_____ 7. I have been a passenger in a motor vehicle when the driver was clearly impaired by drugs or alcohol.

_____ 8. I have driven a motor vehicle when I was clearly impaired by drugs or alcohol.

_____ 9. I have critically evaluated the work of my peers knowing that my comments would get back to them.

_____ 10. I never buy trip or flight cancellation insurance.

_____ 11. In a business venture I have risked the equivalent of at least one year's income.

_____ 12. I regularly eat high cholesterol "junk food".

_____ 13. I have applied for a transfer or promotion to another department knowing that my supervisor will resent what I am doing.

_____ 14. I have applied for a transfer or promotion to another department without discussing it with my current supervisor.

_____ 15. When driving on a crowded street, I never leave room in front of my car for another car to get in.

_____ 16. I would not mind a sales job that had good earning potential but involved a very large proportion of "cold calls" (i.e., no previous contact with the potential customer).

_____ 17. I wager at least $20 per week in various forms of gambling, including lotteries and office pools.

_____ 18. When planning a vacation, I much prefer to visit some place new, some place that neither I nor my friends have previously been to.

_____ 19. Most of my personal investments are either in the stock market or directly invested in my own business.

_____ 20. In the past year I have been asked by at least one friend or acquaintance to join them by investing in a business venture.

[ ] TOTAL NUMBER OF "TRUE" ANSWERS

GROUP SCORE: Record the number of people with each score		
0 =	7 =	14 =
1 =	8 =	15 =
2 =	9 =	16 =
3 =	10 =	17 =
4 =	11 =	18 =
5 =	12 =	19 =
6 =	13 =	20 =

PART II

A modern psychological theory has evaluated the usefulness of risk taking behaviour in people. The theory assesses Risk Utility, and evaluates the way in which individuals will give a positive evaluation to risk taking by crediting certain benefits, such as unloading stress, showing aggression, impressing others, showing independence, taking self-control, opposing authority, coping with anxiety, gaining acceptance into a peer group, etc.

The theory further states that people vary in the level of their need to take a risk, and will even deliberately undertake risky behaviour if they perceive things as being too safe. This process is called risk homeostasis.

In your study group, examine the question of risk taking as a personality style. Compare people's scores, looking for categories. Can you distinguish the risk takers from the risk avoiders? Let these individuals discuss how they see this label fitting themselves.

This risk-taking scale includes items from a wide variety of activities. This is based on the concept of cognitive dissonance, which states that individual belief systems should be internally consistent. Therefore, people are unlikely to be risk takers in one part of their life and risk avoiders in another. How does this fit with your experience?

Take a few minutes in your group to evaluate the theory and the questionnaire.

What Matters in a Job?

Drives and Needs

PURPOSE

To measure individual differences in needs.

PREPARATION

Your instructor may request that you complete the questionnaire prior to class.

INTRODUCTION

Think about your future career. Think about the ideal job you would like to have. What matters the most to you? What matters the least to you? Listed below are the same three groups of characteristics about jobs. Rank each group separately, from 5 for the most important to 1 for the least important. Do this on your own.

CAREER		
#	**RANK THIS GROUP FROM 5 (MOST) TO 1 (LEAST)**	
1	_____	My co-workers will be very friendly
2	_____	The company will protect me from harassment by customers, fellow employees, and supervisors.
3	_____	The working conditions will protect me from bad weather.
4	_____	The work will be creative and challenging.
5	_____	My supervisor will recognize the value of my work and praise me for it.
#	**RANK THIS GROUP FROM 5 (MOST) TO 1 (LEAST)**	
6	_____	I will be able to participate in decision making.
7	_____	The company will sponsor social activities both on and off the job.
8	_____	The pay and fringe benefits will be good.
9	_____	There will be good opportunities for promotion to a higher status job.
10	_____	The company will work hard to maintain safe working conditions.

CAREER (CONTINUED)	
#	**RANK THIS GROUP FROM 5 (MOST) TO 1 (LEAST)**
11 _____	I will get along well with my supervisor.
12 _____	There will be a merit pay system based on performance.
13 _____	The company will provide a cafeteria for its employees.
14 _____	The work itself will have a flexible schedule and I will have a lot of autonomy.
15 _____	There will be excellent job security.

Think about your current job (or if you don't have one right now think about the last job you had). What are the best things about that job? What are the worst things about the job? Listed below are three groups of characteristics about jobs. Rank each group separately from 5 for the best thing to 1 for the worst thing. Do this on your own.

CURRENT JOB	
#	**RANK THIS GROUP FROM 5 (BEST) TO 1 (WORST)**
1 _____	My co-workers will be very friendly.
2 _____	The company will protect me from harassment by customers, fellow employees, and supervisors.
3 _____	The working conditions will protect me from bad weather.
4 _____	The work will be creative and challenging.
5 _____	My supervisor will recognize the value of my work and praise me for it.
#	**RANK THIS GROUP FROM 5 (BEST) TO 1 (WORST)**
6 _____	I will be able to participate in decision making.
7 _____	The company will sponsor social activities both on and off the job.
8 _____	The pay and fringe benefits will be good.
9 _____	There will be good opportunities for promotion to a higher status job.
10	The company will work hard to maintain safe working conditions.
#	**RANK THIS GROUP FROM 5 (BEST) TO 1 (WORST)**
11 _____	I will get along well with my supervisor.
12 _____	There will be a merit pay system based on performance.
13 _____	The company will provide a cafeteria for its employees.
14 _____	The work itself will have a flexible schedule, and I will have a lot of autonomy.
15 _____	There will be excellent job security.

Scoring

The items in this list represent the five levels of need found in Abraham Maslow's Hierarchy of Needs. Each of the groups of five has an item that refers to one of Maslow's needs as applied to the workplace. Use the number in the left-hand column to sort out the items. Add the scores together for each level of the hierarchy.

The instrument also differentiates between your needs as they exist as an ideal and the way in which your current employer is meeting your needs. These are also scored separately.

YOUR CAREER:
WHAT IS YOUR HIERARCHY OF NEEDS?

Self-actualization: Add together the ranks for items 4, 6, and 14

(4) _____ + (6) _____ + (14) _____ = _____

Self-esteem: Add together the ranks for items 5, 9, and 12

(5) _____ + (9) _____ + (12) _____ = _____

Social: Add together the ranks for items 1, 7, and 11

(1) _____ + (7) _____ + (11) _____ = _____

Security: Add together the ranks for items 2, 10, and 15

(2) _____ + (10) _____ + (15) _____ = _____

Physiological: Add together the ranks for items 3, 8, and 13

(3) _____ + (8) _____ + (13) _____ = _____

CURRENT JOB:
HOW ARE YOUR NEEDS BEING MET?

Self-actualization: Add together the ranks for items 4, 6, and 14

(4) _____ + (6) _____ + (14) _____ = _____

Self-esteem: Add together the ranks for items 5, 9, and 12

(5) _____ + (9) _____ + (12) _____ = _____

Social: Add together the ranks for items 1, 7, and 11

(1) _____ + (7) _____ + (11) _____ = _____

Security: Add together the ranks for items 2, 10, and 15

(2) _____ + (10) _____ + (15) _____ = _____

Physiological: Add together the ranks for items 3, 8, and 13

(3) _____ + (8) _____ + (13) _____ = _____

TABLE OF RESULTS		
HIERARCHY OF NEED	**YOUR CAREER**	**CURRENT JOB**
Self-actualization		
Self-esteem		
Social		
Security		
Physiological		

TASK

Analyze your results and compare them with those of the other members of your discussion group.

1. What is your strongest need? Is it being met in your current job?

2. Where differences exist between your needs and your current job, discuss ways of redesigning the job to better meet your needs.

3. In your group, analyze the 15 job characteristics and categorize them in terms of their relationship to the job. Are they an integral part of the job, or are they external to the job? For example, being able to participate in decision making is intrinsic to the job, whereas the existence of a company cafeteria is external to the job.

Occupational Values

Motivation

PURPOSE

To analyze Frederick Herzberg's two factor theory of worker motivation.

PREPARATION

Your instructor may request that you complete the questionnaire prior to class.

INTRODUCTION

Step 1: Read the list below. It describes 16 characteristics you are probably looking for in the job you are in or the one you will seek after graduation. They will not all be of equal importance to you. For the purposes of this exercise, you are to rank them in your order of importance.

It is difficult to rank order a long list. Try this method: place a 1 beside the most important characteristic, then place a 16 beside the least important characteristic. Follow this with the second most important, then the 15th, and so forth.

Step 2: Frederick Herzberg distinguished between those characteristics of a job that could lead to job dissatisfaction (hygiene factors) and those that could lead to satisfaction (motivational factors). The hygiene factors are usually related to job context and are external to the job itself, whereas the motivational factors are related to job content, and are internal to the job. Return to your previous list and, in the column headed H\M, indicate whether you think the job characteristics are hygiene or motivational factors.

Step 3: Tabulate the frequency of your factors according to the listed ranges of ranks.

RANK	G	JOB CHARACTERISTIC	H\M
		The pay is good	
		The boss provides lots of direction	
		The job provides a chance to use your mind	
		The work environment is very attractive	
		You are free to decide how to do your own work	
		The company is an "equal opportunity employer"	
		The job has well-defined responsibilities	
		"Voluntary overtime" is NOT expected	
		Your professional development is supported	
		You find the work itself to be very interesting	
		The job provides very secure job tenure	
		You can achieve your career path	
		Individual achievement is formally recognized	
		Workers participate in decisions regarding work	
		Your co-workers are very nice	
		The job title reflects its importance	

YOUR RANKINGS		
RANK RANGE	**HYGIENE FACTORS**	**MOTIVATIONAL FACTORS**
Ranks 1 to 4		
Ranks 5 to 8		
Ranks 9 to 12		
Ranks 13 to 16		

Step 4: In your discussion group of six to eight students, compare your findings:

1. How much agreement did you have on the rankings? A good way to do this is to attempt to come to a group consensus on the value of the different job characteristics. Record the group ranking in the column headed G.

2. Discuss the Herzberg categories and review your decisions about them. Herzberg's most controversial hygiene factor is pay. If it means pay as in the money you use to live on, then it is clearly external to the job, but if it means pay as a symbolic recognition of your achievement by your employer, then it is internal to the job. Record your group rankings below:

GROUP RANKINGS		
RANK RANGE	**HYGIENE FACTORS**	**MOTIVATIONAL FACTORS**
Ranks 1 to 4		
Ranks 5 to 8		
Ranks 9 to 12		
Ranks 13 to 16		

3. Discuss whether there is a relationship between job factor and ranking. What conclusions can your group reach regarding age- or gender-related preferences about job characteristics?

Job Enrichment

Motivation

PURPOSE

To evaluate the job enrichment possibilities of a variety of modern workplace systems.

PREPARATION

Your instructor may request that you complete part of the work prior to class.

INTRODUCTION

A great deal of attention has been given in recent years to reorganizing work. These efforts fall under the general name of job enrichment, but their effect goes beyond the job itself. While the overall purpose has been to improve worker productivity, there are other goals of maximizing the long-term use of the workforce, of treating all members of the workforce equitably, and of improving the corporate image. Modern companies typically adopt goals that stress the need to help their employees reach their highest potential. They are often employed by Quality of Work Life programs.

The list below is a fairly comprehensive set of these modern alternatives. For each of them, discuss the goals that the alternative will best achieve, and how they will be achieved. Use this framework:

1. **Classical Job Enrichment:** Use Herzberg's two factor theory to evaluate the alternatives as to their emphasis on hygiene and motivation factors.

2. **Long-term Workforce Development:** The most successful companies really do believe that their workforce is their most valuable asset, and will take steps to develop and maintain this resource over a longer period than the current financial statement.

3. **Corporate Values:** Do these alternatives represent certain statements about the value system of the corporation? These can include moral and ethical values that do not have any immediate bottom-line consequences.

4. **Corporate Image:** For some organizations, this might be related to the previous item; however, you may identify some alternatives that have a high value as corporate image builders.

5. Discuss any personal experience you may have had with some of these alternatives. A major issue with any planned change is the implementation process. What implementation strategies would you recommend?

THE NEW SYSTEMS

1. **Compressed Work Week:** Fewer days per week, each day is longer. Many hospital nurses work 12-hour shifts; also common is four days at ten hours. Firefighters work a two-shift day, with 8:00 a.m. and 6:00 p.m. shift changes.

_____

_____

_____

_____

_____

_____

2. **Councils:** Communication groups composed of a cross section of employees of the organization. Often used as a means of downward communication, but the real benefit is upward communication. Replaces some management functions.

_____

_____

_____

_____

_____

_____

3. **Cross-training:** Training people in skills beyond their immediate job area, sometimes at quite a distance, with office workers trained for shop work, etc.

_____

_____

_____

_____

_____

_____

4. **Fast-track:** Employees selected on the basis of either their ability and/or their membership in some targeted group (such as a minority) are given extra assistance in gaining promotion. The extras can include special training, a managerial mentor, and preferential selection. It is often combined with cross-training. The designation itself is usually valued.

_____

_____

_____

_____

_____

_____

5. **Flex Time:** Any system that gives employees some control over their starting or ending time during the day. Flex time does not usually refer to compressed or split schedules.

_____

_____

_____

_____

_____

_____

6. **Gain Sharing:** Any of a wide variety of systems that return part of the savings from improved productivity to the employees.

_____

_____

_____

_____

_____

_____

7. **Job Rotation:** Employees are moved through a group of similar jobs on a regular schedule. It usually replaces seniority as the basis of job assignment, and helps alleviate boredom and some aspects of fatigue.

_____

_____

_____

_____

_____

_____

8. **Job Sharing:** One job is shared by two people.

9. **Labour-Management Committees:** Formal union-management group that attends to matters outside the contract. It recognizes that many union grievances have nothing to do with the contract, but the union and its contract is the only vehicle available for workers to deal with management on an equal footing.

10. **Leaderless Work Groups:** The normal duties of a first line supervisor are turned over to the work group. The group sets its own schedules within general goals and objectives.

11. **Matrix Organization:** A reporting system where employees are responsible to two parts of the organization at the same time. It calls on greater self-management skills by the employee.

12. **Pay-for-Skills:** A pay system by which employees are paid for their skills and ability, whether currently used or not, rather than their actual job assignment. It encourages personal growth and development.

_____
_____
_____
_____
_____
_____

13. **Permanent Part-time Jobs:** Full-time benefits with part-time work.

_____
_____
_____
_____
_____

14. **Quality Circles:** Similar to the leaderless work group. Employee groups are given responsibility for their own quality control.

_____
_____
_____
_____
_____
_____

Feedback in Communication

Interpersonal Communication

PURPOSE

To demonstrate the need for feedback in developing effective communication.

PREPARATION

None required.

INTRODUCTION

In this exercise, you will experience one of the fundamental principles of communication: namely, that feedback increases accuracy. In this example, we will use the communication of spoken language. This is an appropriate application for the business world, where most communicating is done face to face. The concept being applied is that if you have the opportunity to check out what you are hearing, the speaker will be able to modify the message to increase its accuracy.

Three different members of your class will be called to describe an object to you. They will use different methods to describe these three objects to you. The objects are similar, but are not identical. After you have drawn them, you will score your accuracy.

Method One: One-way communication with no spoken or visual feedback.

Method Two: One-way communication with no spoken feedback, but with visual feedback permitted.

Method Three: Two-way spoken and visual communication.

Method One
Use this page to draw the first object described to you.

Number of correct shapes. Score one point for each correct shape in the correct order.	
Number of correct intersections. Score one or two points for each intersection.	
TOTAL	══════

Method Two
Use this page to draw the second object described to you.

Number of correct shapes. Score one point for each correct shape in the correct order.	
Number of correct intersections. Score one or two points for each intersection.	
TOTAL	

Method Three
Use this page to draw the third object described to you.

Number of correct shapes. Score one point for each correct shape in the correct order.	
Number of correct intersections. Score one or two points for each intersection.	
TOTAL	_____

ANALYSIS

Your teacher will collect the results from the classroom for the three methods and put them in a table on the board. Transfer the classroom results into the blank graph shown below. The scale for the Y-axis will depend on your class scores. Find the biggest score in the table, round it off, and make it the top of that axis.

**FREQUENCY DISTRIBUTION OF SCORES
FOR THE THREE METHODS**

| 2 | 4 | 6 | 8 | 10 | 12 | 14 | 16 |

Accuracy (Number of Points)

TASK

1. How accurate are the three methods of communication? What happens to accuracy when feedback is added to the communication? Pay particular attention to differences between Methods One and Two.

2. What effect does class size have on the three methods? What do you think would be an optimum size for each method?

3. What implications can you draw from this exercise for the workplace? What would it mean if you were trying to communicate a new operating procedure for a machine? What if you were trying to communicate the company's new anti-harassment policy to all employees?

Linear Communication

Interpersonal Communication

PURPOSE

To evaluate the impact of passing information through a chain of command on the accuracy of communication.

PREPARATION

None required.

INTRODUCTION

This exercise is a scientific version of the game you played as a child, when a story was passed down the line in whispers, and the final version was compared to the original. Usually the discussion afterward centred around where the story went wrong. That childhood game is of considerable value to modern business communication because most communicating at work is done through spoken communication. It is important to have realistic knowledge about the accuracy and sources of error in oral communication.

You will listen to a group of your fellow classmates pass on a story, and you will record the parts of the story they get correct. Use the score sheet below for that purpose. The first time you hear the story, it will be read to a student and should be completely correct. Each successive telling will be based on the recall of the previous student. It is not unlike receiving a series of instructions from your supervisor about how to perform a particular job.

SCORE SHEET

#	STORY ITEM	1	2	3	4	5
1	Alice Bigelow worked for the Beaver Basket Company					
2	newest member of their sales department and the first woman					
3	an old and established Canadian company					
4	manufacturing wooden baskets					
5	used by the fruit and vegetable industry					
6	used in the home as laundry baskets					
7	switched to more modern packaging methods					
8	serve the growing manufacturing industry of southern Ontario					
9	from Minesing which had an abundant forest					
10	to Ajax which was close to major highways					
11	visited manufacturers and helped them package their product					
12	make the packages and ship them to the manufacturer					
13	importers who required domestic packages for their products					
14	current packages made of paper and plastic					
15	still privately owned by the original family					
16	corporate culture was filled with the traditional rural values of the founders					
17	they no longer manufactured any wooden laundry baskets					
18	problem was with her expense form for her first sales trip					
19	for a week her actual expenses came to $730					
20	one of the older salesmen asked to see it					

#	STORY ITEM	1	2	3	4	5
21	far too low and ought to be padded the same way as the men					
22	he showed her how to do this by faking receipts and adding charges					
23	past average for her trip was around $800–$850.00					
24	put in that much or the accountants would wonder about the previous expense forms					
25	if she wanted to be one of the boys she had better play ball on their team					
26	her great grandparents were from Minesing and had founded the Beaver Basket Company					
27	first member of her family in a generation to actually work for the business					
28	had not told anybody that she was a part of the family that owned it					
29	whether to blow the whistle on the salesmen or choke on it					
30	she decided to save it for a rainy day					

Consolidate your results in the following table:

YOUR RECORD					
ITEMS	1	2	3	4	5
1 – 5					
6 – 10					
11 – 15					
16 – 20					
21 – 25					
26 – 30					
TOTAL					

Your instructor will assemble class data, which you should copy into the table below. You will use it to analyze the results of the exercise.

THE CLASS RECORD					
ITEMS	1	2	3	4	5
1 – 5					
6 – 10					
11 – 15					
16 – 20					
21 – 25					
26 – 30					
TOTAL					

ANALYSIS

1. Describe the accuracy of the story as it was passed from person to person.

2. What points caused the greatest difficulty?

3. Compare the accuracy in the six groupings. Was there improved accuracy at the end of the story over the middle? If so, why might that be?

4. Did the novelty of the "fact" have any effect on accurate recall? Why might that occur?

5. Describe the major barriers to accurate recall of the story.

Bidding Exercise

Group Decision Making

PURPOSE

To investigate different modes of resource allocation and the effect of communication on these modes.

PREPARATION

Divide into groups of seven or nine students each. One person in each group acts as "banker", and the others divide into subgroups of two persons each.

INTRODUCTION

Decision making in competitive circumstances occurs when there is a limited amount of resources to be distributed among individuals, groups, or entire organizations according to the strategies and tactics employed by all the decision makers. Among firms, such competition is a necessary and desirable facet of a private enterprise-based economy. Regulatory measures are employed by governments to help maintain these competitive activities, as well as to protect the public interest against monopolistic practices.

Within organizations, the various divisions and work groups must also often compete for finite resources in order to carry out desired and necessary programs. Sometimes hostility and lack of co-operation among managers predominate during negotiations for the allocation of these resources. In other situations, conflict is avoided and a mutually acceptable allocation of the resources is achieved. In this simulation, the class is divided into units of seven to nine students. These units are further divided into three or four groups of two students each, who act together, and the remaining student takes the role of "banker". The simulation is carried out by each group of two students competing for resources with the other two or three groups within their unit. There is no interaction between units, all of which operate separately.

INSTRUCTIONS

1. Each group of two students is issued $200 in simulated funds by the banker.

2. The simulation consists of a series of rounds, all of which begin by each group paying in $20 and the bank paying in $30 to a central "pot" (managed by the banker). No group still participating can avoid this payment.

3. Then, each group in turn bids for the total in the pot in an auction run by the banker. All bids must be in multiples of $5. There is no maximum. A bid is accomplished by handing the amount to the banker, who retains it permanently.

4. When a bid is received that no other group wishes or is able to surpass, the round ends. The group who submitted the highest bid wins only the amount originally put in the pot. That amount does not include any of the bid funds, which are all forfeited to the bank (including the winning bid) when the bids are made.

5. The simulation ends when:
   (a) A pre-selected number of rounds has been played.
   (b) All groups except one have gone bankrupt. This occurs when a group possesses less than $20.

6. The winning group is the one possessing the largest amount of funds when the simulation ends.

7. Members of each group of two may discuss their bids with each other quietly. Your instructor will inform you whether any communication **between** groups within the units is allowed. Under no condition are payments permitted between groups.

8. The banker also has the role of referee. His or her word is final concerning enforcement of the rules of the simulation.

9. The banker must record the number of rounds played, the total amount taken in by the bank in forfeited bids, the amount paid out by the bank to the pot, and the amount held by the winning group at the end of the simulation.

Span of Control

Leadership

PURPOSE

To determine differences in the number of people that a supervisor can effectively control.

PREPARATION

Your instructor may request that you complete the questionnaire prior to class.

INTRODUCTION

An important issue in administration in organizations is the question of how many people a manager can effectively supervise. This question is usually described by the term "span of control" when referring to an individual supervisor, and, when referring to an organization, the distinction will be made between tall (and narrow) structures as opposed to wide (and short) structures. In this activity, you will rate your own span of control if you are a supervisor, or that of your supervisor if you are not one yourself. The premise on which this scale is based is that a supervisor's core activity is to manage the personal aspects of working with employees: that is to say, understanding them as individuals, determining how best to motivate their performance, etc. Any time that a supervisor spends on other aspects of management detracts from this core task, and therefore reduces the time available for the personal aspects of management and, as a corollary, reduces the number of people who can be effectively supervised.

The criteria used for determining span of control, therefore, are those that have an impact on the managerial workload, and include the following:

1. **Similarity of the Jobs Being Supervised:** The more alike the work of the people being supervised, the less time that will be required by the supervisor in learning and keeping up-to-date on the activities being performed. If all those being supervised do the same thing, then more can be supervised than if the employees all do totally different jobs.

2. **Physical Proximity:** Does the supervisor need to spend a lot of time travelling between those people being supervised? If so, this will reduce the amount of time available for direct contact with the employees.

3. **Complexity of the Work Being Supervised:** Simple, repetitive work requires less training than complex tasks and less supervisory time spent on the training function.

4. **Direction and Control of the Work:** Can the work run itself or does it require close supervision? Will the manager be frequently called upon to solve task problems as opposed to focusing on personal aspects of the supervision?

5. **Coordination Outside the Department:** Does the supervisor spend a lot of time coordinating the work with other parts of the organization or with other external organizations? If so, the span will be reduced owing to the competition for the supervisor's time.

6. **Planning of Work:** Does the supervisor have responsibility for planning and scheduling or for developing and interpreting company policies? How well-formulated are these policies?

Rating Scale

Supervisor's job being rated: Give the job title and describe the nature of the work. Are you the supervisor?

_____

_____

_____

_____

_____

_____

    For each of the six factors, pick the one choice that most closely fits the job being evaluated. Write the accompanying score in the column.

SIMILARITY OF JOBS

_____ 1 Fundamentally distinct jobs. Not just different tasks, but also different work routines. No transfer from one job to another.

_____ 2 Inherently different. Some slight possibility of transfer between jobs.

_____ 3 Similar jobs. Fairly common hiring pool. Transfers, routine.

_____ 4 Essentially alike. Job rotation, common.

_____ 5 Identical jobs.

PHYSICAL PROXIMITY

_____ 1 Dispersed, more than one city or region. Overnight or full-day trips required to visit locations.

_____ 2 Separate locations, one urban region.

_____ 3 Separate buildings, one location.

_____ 4 All located in one building, but separate rooms.

_____ 5 All together.

COMPLEXITY OF WORK

_____ 2 Extremely complex and varied, requiring constant supervision of the tasks being performed. Supervisor is the task expert.

_____ 4 Complex but less varied.

_____ 6 Less complex.

_____ 8 Routine.

_____ 10 Simple and repetitive.

DIRECTION AND CONTROL

_____ 3 The workers require constant, close supervision with frequent re-training.

_____ 6 Frequent and continuing supervision.

_____ 9 Moderate, periodic supervision.

_____ 12 Limited supervision.

_____ 15 Minimum training and supervision.

COORDINATION

_____ 2 Extensive relationships with other organizations that are non-repetitive in nature. Constantly making new arrangements.

_____ 4 Considerable, close relationships.

_____ 6 Moderate number of relationships that can be easily controlled.

_____ 8 External relationships are limited to defined courses of action.

_____ 10 Almost an autonomous department.

PLANNING

_____ 2 Extensive planning function. New policies and missions are developed as a regular part of the work. No "book" to follow.

_____ 4 Policies are developed as guided by mission statements.

_____ 6 Feedback is expected on policy development. Supervisor is "consulted" on policy changes.

_____ 8 Planning, only in strictly local applications.

_____ 10 Minimum planning. Follow the "book".

_____ TOTAL SUPERVISORY SCORE

Use this guide to determine the span of control. Circle the score and then read the number below it. This is the ideal number to be supervised.

SUPERVISORY SCORE												
10	15	18	21	24	27	30	33	36	39	42	45	50
1	2	3	4	6	8	10	12	14	16	18	20	22

SUGGESTED SPAN OF CONTROL

☐ Actual number of employees supervised.

The suggested span of control should be interpreted as a range rather than as a specific number. Other factors not included above would have an influence on the number of employees a supervisor could manage.

DISCUSSION QUESTIONS

1. How does the suggested span of control compare to the actual number of employees supervised?

2. If there is a strong difference between the two, discuss how that difference is reflected in supervisor effectiveness.

3. Evaluate the supervisor's job and determine ways of improving any difference between the actual and the suggested span of control. Would this be best accomplished through changing the number of people supervised, or could it be done by changing the supervisor's job? Discuss.

4. As the manager at the next level, how would you increase this supervisor's span of control?

5. Discuss the reasons why you would normally expect different spans of control at different levels of management in an organization.

6. Use the span of control evaluators to measure and evaluate the span of control of a supervisor found in one of the cases in this book.

Sources of Power

Power and Influence

PURPOSE

To understand some of the ways others can influence your behaviour.

PREPARATION

Your instructor may request that you complete the questionnaire prior to class.

INTRODUCTION

Beginning with the work of Max Weber, social scientists have analyzed power in terms of its various sources. The following is a fairly typical current list of these sources:

1. **Charisma:** This source of power is within the personality of the leader. We will do as they wish because we respect or admire them, and want them to respect us.

2. **Expertise:** An expert can correctly manipulate and interpret data. This special skill can be of benefit to others and, as such, puts the expert in a position of power over those who are dependent on that expertise.

3. **Force:** Compliant behaviour can be gained through fear of punishment, whether actually used or not. Punishment is anything the subject of the power would like to avoid.

4. **Information:** Any person who has accurate information that is of use to others has power over those people. It is the desirability of the information that provides the power.

5. **Networks:** People with good connections have power. The strength of the power is directly related to the influence of the people in the network. Compliance is based on a desire to have a favourable evaluation in the network.

6. **Position:** Formal positions carry formal powers that are accepted as right and proper by all those who are subservient to that position. This power is legiti-

mate in that it is well understood and agreed upon by all parties to the relationship.

7. **Reward:** Just as force is based on the fear of punishment, rewards can be used as a basis of gaining compliance. The leader must have the ability to deliver a reward. A reward is anything desired by the subject of the power.

PART I

Think about the bases you believe the ideal manager should have for his or her power. Should it largely be from one source, or should it be spread over several? Which ones should be the most important?

Rate each of the seven power sources on a scale of 0–20.

- Give it a zero if you think this source of power is of no value whatsoever in business management.
- Give it a 20 if you think that this is the absolute apex, and one need not look any farther for a source of management power.
- Give scores that are in between for less-extreme sentiments.
- Give each source a different score.
- Consult the definitions if you need help with the meaning of the words.

IDEAL MANAGER	
	SCORE 0 – 20
1. Charisma	
2. Expertise	
3. Force	
4. Information	
5. Networks	
6. Position	
7. Reward	

PART II

Now rate yourself. How do you respond to different kinds of power?

- Give it a zero if you absolutely reject the use of a particular type of power on yourself.

- Give it a 20 if you think you would follow this person anywhere.
- Give it an intermediate value for less-extreme positions.
- Give each source of power a different score.

YOURSELF		SCORE 0 – 20
1.	Charisma	
2.	Expertise	
3.	Force	
4.	Information	
5.	Networks	
6.	Position	
7.	Reward	

PART III

Plot these two profiles on the graph below.

		0	5	10	15	20
1.	Charisma					
2.	Expertise					
3.	Force					
4.	Information					
5.	Networks					
6.	Position					
7.	Reward					

Analysis

1. Where are the major disagreements?
2. Why are they there?
3. Where are the major agreements?

PART IV (OPTIONAL)

Rate your supervisor using the same scales. Look for trouble spots in your relationship. Identify possible opportunities for improvement. Would you really like to have your supervisor know how to exercise more power and influence over you? What could be done to improve trust in your relationship?

SUPERVISOR	
	SCORE 0 – 20
1. Charisma	
2. Expertise	
3. Force	
4. Information	
5. Networks	
6. Position	
7. Reward	

Let's Make a Deal!

Conflict

PURPOSE

To identify issues involved in developing cooperative strategies of conflict resolution.

PREPARATION

None required.

INTRODUCTION

You are an employee of Canramco, a modest-sized automobile parts manufacturer located in the industrial heart of southern Ontario. Like much of the auto industry, your company is unionized and is represented by local 10822 of CAW. As the expiry of each contract approaches, the company and the union select negotiating teams to work out a new deal. In this simulation, you will be assigned to either the management or the union negotiating team.

Each team has its own power base. The union can either decide to settle, or go on strike. The decision to strike will be influenced by the union strike fund and the support it receives from other locals. This information is their secret and is not available to the management team. In effect, they can decide to strike or settle at will. The management position is similar. They can either settle or lock out their workers. The decision to lock them out would in part depend on their orders and inventory. This information is their secret, and not available to the union team.

Most of the contracts are for one year, but three of them are for more than one year. The negotiating process has been greatly simplified for the purpose of this simulation. The teams can choose to settle or not. After an opportunity to discuss strategy in caucus (the members of each team privately), the teams meet to air their views and to agree on a strategy for this contract. At a pre-determined time, the conciliator will call for the teams to show their intent for the current contract. The team leaders will then show a card indicating whether they will settle of not. The round will then be scored, and the next round of negotiations will begin. A large part of the challenge is to build trust, so that agreed-upon deals will in fact be carried out.

The overall goal is the long-term growth and health of the company and its workforce.

CANRAMCO ECONOMICS

The basic structure is that both parties will agree to settle when the deal conforms to the industry norm. As a small company, they do not want to be very different from their competition. For the sake of simplicity, this norm is given to be 6%. If the union gets more than the norm, then the company will cut back on the size of the workforce growth to cover the increase in wages. Similarly, if management steals a contract, it will have more money to hire more workers but end up with a disgruntled workforce, which will lower product quality at a cost in quality bonuses to the company.

THE PAYOFF SCHEDULE		
UNION	**MANAGEMENT**	**PAYOFF**
Settle	Settle	6% increase in wages, sales
Settle	Lock Out	2% wage, 8% workforce
Strike	Settle	8% wage, 2% workforce
Strike	Lock Out	6% decrease in wages, sales

CONTRACT LENGTH	THE CHOICES		THE CHANGED STATUS		
	UNION	**MANAGEMENT**	**WAGES**	**SALES**	**WORKFORCE**
	Circle the Decisions		$16/hr.	Starting positions $10 million/yr.	100
1 year	Se St	Se LO			
1 year	Se St	Se LO			
2 years	Se St	Se LO			
1 year	Se St	Se LO			
3 years	Se St	Se LO			
1 year	Se St	Se LO			
3 years	Se St	Se LO			
1 year	Se St	Se LO			
1 year	Se St	Se LO			
1 year	Se St	Se LO			

DEBRIEFING

After you have negotiated the ten contracts, meet as a whole group to evaluate the outcome.

1. How has Canramco thrived as a company?

   _____

   _____

   _____

   _____

   _____

   _____

2. What were the major barriers to sticking with the win-win solution?

   _____

   _____

   _____

   _____

   _____

   _____

3. Were there key personality interactions that particularly helped or hindered the process? Discuss these.

   _____

   _____

   _____

   _____

   _____

   _____

4. Give your evaluation of this simulation.

   _____

   _____

   _____

   _____

   _____

   _____

Mediating Conflict

Conflict

Mediation is a process that helps people resolve conflict. It differs from arbitration in that an arbitrator renders a judgment as to the resolution of the dispute. An arbitrator is a judge of the facts, and makes a decision. A mediator helps the parties to the dispute find their own solution.

The word "mediation" usually brings to mind the activities we hear about in the news where the parties to a labour dispute meet with a mediator to resolve their conflict and reach an agreement. This is formal mediation, and involves processes designed to guarantee a binding agreement and to protect the liability of the mediator.

Mediation can also exist as an everyday activity for managers. One of the most time consuming activities of managers involves managing conflict. It might involve conflict between two subordinates, or between the manager and a subordinate or between the manager and someone else in the organization. And of course it might involve parties outside the organization. Managers have historically relied on their "right to manage" as the basis for making a decision in conflict. It seems to go with the job. Subordinates and others see managers as judges to whom they can take their conflicts for a resolution. The managers act in the role of arbitrators.

The manager as a judge or arbitrator is almost always in a lose-lose situation. Often the manager has little stakes in the actual conflict itself. Their main interest is in getting it over with so that people can get back to work. Conflict itself is quite de-motivating in the workplace. The longer it goes on, the firmer the positions, the larger the factions and the greater the disruption. And, of course, the manager's decision may be resented by one or another party to the conflict.

An alternative role for the manager is to act as a mediator to the conflict. Mediators help the parties to the conflict find their own solutions to the conflict. Such solutions, when they can be found, are usually more acceptable to the combatants than one imposed from on high. As a bonus, once employees know that a

---

This exercise was originally developed by Fred Ruemper, Kate Beattie and Wendy Ruemper for the purpose of staff training at Georgian College.

manager won't always make a judgment call, fewer people will bring forward complaints.

Mediation is based on the negotiating theory that assumes that the positions people take in a conflict or dispute are an imperfect or incomplete representation of their true interests or needs. A classic example of this exists with labour unions that represent employees who want to be treated with greater respect. This is hard to achieve at the bargaining table or to put in a contract, so they bargain for more money as a way of showing they have power and ought to be respected. Problems of respect are poorly solved by throwing money at them.

Step One: The first step in the informal mediation process is to have the parties express their true interests and needs. Through a question and answer process the mediator/manager can help the parties identify and confront the issues about which they disagree. Often a dispute will be a mixture of facts and values. Value conflicts can be hard to change, but issue conflicts can be resolved. The mediator/manager can help the parties separate the issues and get them on the table. Real needs and interests can be separated from irrelevant power plays. A clear understanding of the needs and interests of the parties can reframe the conflict away from irresolvable positions.

Step Two: The second step is to develop a list of options or alternatives to meeting these needs and interests. At this stage the original positions are ignored in favour of dealing with the needs and interests just revealed. The mediator/manager helps the parties find creative solutions to these needs and interests. These may bear little resemblance to the original positions taken. Often the mediator/manager makes a substantial contribution at this stage, calling on their greater experience, contacts etc.

Step Three: The third step is to build a bridge between the options and a solution. Once the options are clear, the parties need help in moving toward accepting one of them. At this stage the parties to the dispute take ownership of their ideas for resolving it, since they must ultimately accept them as a solution. The mediator/manager can be persuasive in helping the parties move towards a solution.

TASK

In groups of three, work through one of the following cases. They have been structured to have an independent mediator to avoid any confusing overlap with a manager role. It can be tempting to step back into a power role and impose a solution in a conflict. Mediation assumes that the parties to the conflict have the resources to solve their own problem, with a bit of help from a neutral third party.

Step One: Each person will take on a role and read it over. At this step, do not look at the other roles. The mediators will then take charge of the process, bring the parties together and endeavour to identify the real interests and needs, as outlined in Step One above.

Step Two: Rotate roles and continue with Step Two above.

Step Three: Rotate roles a final time, and complete the role play with Step Three above.

A. The Profane Professor

Complainant: You are Janet, a 25-year-old student who has decided to return to school after "stopping out" for a few years while experiencing teenage marriage and parenthood. Neither experience was easy, and you are now a single parent and sole support of two youngsters in Kindergarten and Grade Two. Your youthful pregnancy and marriage caused you to drop out of high school prior to graduation, even though you had always been a good student.

A year ago you started to pull your life together. The first step was to rid yourself of an immature and dependent spouse. The next step was to take upgrading to prepare yourself for post secondary education. Your plan has been on track, and things are going well. You are now enrolled in first year in the Music Technology Program. Prior to returning to school you had supported your children and husband with some part-time work as a disc jockey. You found that you liked it, and were quite successful. You hope to work at a more technical level, and are confident of your future success.

Right now you are really upset with your Popular Music Professor, Jefferson Smith. You can't believe that the college would tolerate such behaviour from one of its faculty members. He uses profanity in class, and never misses an opportunity to talk about sex. His sexual references seem to centre on his own fantasies and life experiences. He seems to want to impress the younger people in the room with his liberated approach to life and his breadth of experiences. You don't see how any of this has any relevance to the course content. You checked the course outline and read the book. There is no sexual or profane comment or reference in either of them. You want him to stick to the course and stop his in-class sexual and profane diversions. You aren't a prude, but you haven't made this major investment in your education to be diverted by this teacher. As far as you know, you are the only student to complain, but you know you aren't the only one to be unhappy with him.

Respondent You are Professor Jefferson Smith, and you are a professor in the Music Technology Program. You have been a popular member of the faculty for the past 20 years, and have basically been doing things the same way ever since you first arrived. Your speciality was in popular music at university, and you have always seen yourself as a pretty with-it guy.

Your student evaluations have always seemed excellent. Your self-esteem is strong, and you feel good about your ability to relate to the young people of today.

You were very surprised when the Human Rights Officer asked you to make an appointment to receive a complaint. The complaint is from one of the women students in your Popular Music Course, and she is upset with what she says is your inappropriate use of profanity in class, and she further says that you never miss an opportunity to talk about sex. The complaint has you mystified. You never had a complaint before, and this one seems really harsh. The student has taken everything out of context. You don't think you dwell on sexual matters, but it is a theme in popular music and a topic of interest to young people.

Mediator   Your name is Martha, and you are a long-standing member of the student counselling services at the college. A student by the name of Janet has filed a complaint with the Human Rights Officer about a Professor by the name of Jefferson Smith. The complaint is that he uses profanity in class and makes sexual references about most of the subject matter in his course.

You have been selected as mediator because of your participation in a recent mediator training workshop and your background in the student counselling department. You don't know the complainant, but the respondent is well known to you. For years, there has been talk about him around campus, and you have heard student complaints in your counselling role; however, there are no previous formal written complaints on record.

B. The Group Mark

Complainant   Your name is Raj, and you were assigned by your teacher to a team to complete a major assignment for your course in Management Practices. The project counts for 30% of the final grade in the course, and it is important to you that you get an A in the project and the course. Your group received only a C+, and you are quite unhappy about it. Your goal is to make the Dean's List, and the poor mark you received in this project will make it hard for you to keep up your class average.

For the most part you blame the other members of the team because of their lack of interest in getting an A in the project, but you are also upset that the teacher deliberately structured the groups so that the good students were spread around and didn't have a chance to work together. The teacher said she was replicating the real world of work.

Doris and Herb are the two other members of the team, and it is your view that they didn't make enough of a commitment to the project to warrant an equal share of the mark. Both of them have stated that a C+ is just fine and completely within their personal expectations. Neither are strong students, and have stated that it was an extremely educational experience working with you on this assignment.

Your request is that you be granted an A for your major contribution to the assignment. You don't care what happens to the others. They can keep their C+, or take a lower mark so that a C+ average for the group is maintained.

You made this request to your professor, but she rejected it out of hand. You can't understand her inflexibility on this issue.

Respondent   You are Prof. R.B. Ramcharan, and you were approached by Raj, who was the member of a group doing an assignment in your Management Practices Course. Raj didn't like his mark on the assignment, which is the group mark, and appealed to you for a different mark than that given to the other members of the group. His case was based on his belief that he had contributed more than the other group members, and ought to be given a greater reward. You rejected Raj's request for a separate evaluation of the group project. Your goal was to teach teamwork and, in your view, Raj didn't demonstrate much learning. You are most displeased that he has made a "federal case" out of it by appealing the grade to the Academic Director. If Raj thought you were inflexible earlier, he will have lots to learn as you take him through advanced studies on this one.

You have already had several conversations with your colleagues in the faculty lounge, and they all agree that this is a key issue of academic freedom and integrity.

Mediator You are Dr. Sandy, the Academic Director, and it is ordinarily your duty to arbitrate marks appeals that come up from the faculty. Recently, the Vice-President, Academic took you to a workshop on conflict mediation and announced to you at the end of the workshop that she didn't want any more appeals settled by arbitration, but rather that they should be settled by mediation. You were told that the difference between arbitration and mediation is that an arbitrator is like a judge who makes a decision, whereas a mediator helps the parties to resolve the dispute themselves. As she saw it, mediated settlements wouldn't be appealed, and it would mean happier students and less acrimony in the department. You suspect that the real attraction is that mediated settlements will mean a lot less work for her, since she is the next step in the appeal process.

Your first opportunity to try this out will be with Prof. Ramcharan and one of his students who is unhappy about his mark on a group project.

C. Who Needs Professional Development?

Complainant You are Juan, and you are a relatively new faculty member of the business program of your college. For the past year you have had your heart set on attending the upcoming annual conference of the Professional Market Research Society (PMRS) in Ottawa. You have prepared and submitted an important paper, and it has been accepted for presentation at a workshop. This is the first time anyone from the program has had a paper accepted for presentation at this meeting, and you believe it will bring much prestige to you and to the program. The cost of the conference is about $1,000 including: conference fees, air fare, single accommodation at the hotel and a few incidentals. This represents the balance of the money in the business program conference pot. As far as you are concerned, this is a just and fair reward for all of the effort you have put into upgrading the level of academic excellence in the program which, frankly, is desperately in need of all the upgrading it can get. It seems to be top heavy with tired old business types.

Unfortunately you may not get the money. Meng-Che, the Academic Director, has recommended that the money go to Henry, one of those "tired old business types", a crony of his from the old days. In your view the only useful contribution Henry could make would be to apply for early retirement. He still teaches from the same notes and overheads he developed twenty years ago.

You have appealed to Meng-Che to reconsider his decision, or at least offer a satisfactory explanation for his lack of support for your initiative. While he said he was pleased that your paper was accepted for presentation he nonetheless wants

Henry to go and he won't explain his support for Henry. Your personal finances are such that you cannot afford this on your own, as you are the father of a young family and have been struggling with the burdens of a sick child.

You and Meng-Che have agreed upon contacting Anthony from the Benefits Department to see if he can mediate the dispute and avoid an unappealing choice.

Respondent   You are Meng-Che, the Academic Director for the Business Programs. For some months now you have been trying to revive a rather moribund department. The problem, as you see it, is that you have an aging and somewhat tired group of faculty who lack enthusiasm for the job. Some of these old cronies of yours seem to spend their days watching their investment portfolios shift with the market tide and counting down the years until they can retire on a decent pension. Unfortunately, most of them are too far from retirement for that to be a viable option. Recently, you have been working on Henry, and have convinced him to get involved with the Professional Marketing Research Society, just as he was some years ago, and see if it will fire up his juices. Your inducement was to supply him with funding to attend the annual conference in Ottawa.

Juan then applied for money to attend the same conference. Apparently, he will be presenting a paper on his recent innovations. You would really like to encourage Juan's initiative. He is a resourceful and enterprising young faculty member who is a key element in your plan to renew the program. Unfortunately, you only have $1000 left in the budget, and you have been working on Henry for quite a while, and feel committed to your renewal plan with him.

Mediator   You are Anthony from the Benefits Department, and you have been asked to mediate a dispute between Juan of the Business Program and Meng-Che, his Academic Director. The issue has to do with the allocation of professional development resources for an upcoming conference in Ottawa. You know that Meng-Che wants to allocate the money to Henry, a very senior faculty member.

You know Juan because he is the father of a young family who has been having some financial struggles lately with a sick child. You know Henry because he is one of the old timers who is part of the "burned-out burden" that senior management has been talking about lately.

D. The After Pub Class

Complainant   You are Professor Viola Lopiccolo, and you have had a struggle with students attending class after lunch in the student pub. The lunch seemed to feature too many glasses of beer. The only problem is with the Wednesday afternoon class. The other two classes are in the morning. You have already had two sessions with the students about this problem. At first, the issue was that the students were skipping the Wednesday class. When you dealt with this in class, the result was that several of them came to class intoxicated. When you then dealt with the drinking, it seemed to clear up the problem, except for Tom.

Tom has insisted on his "right" to drink and to attend class afterward. He denies that he is impaired, and is quite aggressive about this. His aggressive behaviour has you worried for your own safety. Last week, when you asked him to leave the class, he refused and started waving his arms in your direction.

You have filed a complaint about Tom's behaviour, and have asked that he be permanently removed from your class.

Respondent You are Tom, a senior student at the college. Professor Viola Lopiccolo has filed a complaint against you, and has asked that you be permanently removed from her class. She claims that on several recent Wednesday afternoons you have come to class while intoxicated.

This is an extension of an earlier issue of attendance at the Wednesday afternoon class. You and several of the students in the class had developed the routine of going to the campus pub at lunch prior to Professor Lopiccolo's class. When she found out what was going on she "raised the roof", and so you started showing up with beer on your breath. She didn't like that either.

None of your other Professors care what you do at lunch. All they care about is that you do the work. They don't seem to mind if you don't show up all the time.

You believe that as a mature student you can do what you want with your life. Professor Lopiccolo isn't a morality cop, and it's none of her business whether you drink. Besides, you can handle your own booze.

You would be in serious trouble if you were barred from her class. It is the only section of this course and you need it to graduate.

Mediator You are Kevin Kralik, a student and member of the Student's Advisory Council. You have been called on to mediate a dispute between a student and a faculty member. Professor Viola Lopiccolo has filed a complaint against Tom, a senior student and has asked that he be permanently removed from her class. She claims that on several recent Wednesday afternoons he came to class while intoxicated and exhibited threatening behaviour.

One reason you have been selected as mediator is because you are the President of Bacchus, the student organization for responsible drinking. You know that there is a problem with on-campus pubs, and that some students don't always exercise the best judgment. You also know that not all faculty see the pub as a problem. You were a student of Professor Lopiccolo, and know that she sets high standards for her students.

Mechanistic or Organic

Organizational Design

PURPOSE

To measure individual preferences in organizational design.

PREPARATION

Your instructor may request that you complete the questionnaire prior to class.

INTRODUCTION

How well does each of the following statements describe your views about an ideal place to work?

Score 5 if it is a perfect description. Score 0 if it is totally wrong. Score 4, 3, 2, or 1 if it fits somewhere in between.

_____ 1. I get most of my motivation to work from the job itself rather than from the rewards the company gives me for doing it.

_____ 2. I respect my supervisors for what they know rather than for the fact that the company has put them in charge.

_____ 3. I work best when things are exciting and filled with energy. I can feel the adrenalin rushing through me, and I like it.

_____ 4. I like it best if we can play things by ear. Going by the book means you do not have any imagination.

_____ 5. People who seek security at work are boring. I don't go to work to plan my retirement.

_____ 6. I believe that planning should focus on the short term. Long-term planning is unrealistic. I want to see the results of my plan.

_____ 7. Don't give me a detailed job description. Just point me in the general direction, and I will figure out what needs to be done.

_____ 8. I don't expect to be introduced to new people. If I like their looks, I'll introduce myself.

_____ 9. Goals should be set by everyone in the organization. I prefer to achieve my own goals rather than those of someone else.

_____ 10. One of the things I most prefer about a job is that it be full of surprises.

_____ 11. I like a job that is full of challenges.

_____ 12. Organization charts are only needed by people who are already lost.

_____ 13. Technology is constantly changing.

_____ 14. Supervision and control should be face-to-face.

_____ 15. If organizations focus on problem solving, the bottom line will take care of itself.

_____ 16. I would never take a job that involved repetitive activities.

_____ 17. Organizations are constantly in a state of change. I don't worry about how the players line up.

_____ 18. Every decision I make is a new one. I don't look for precedents.

_____ 19. When people talk about efficiency, I think they really don't want to do a good job.

_____ 20. The people who know the most about the work should be put in charge.

Scoring

Total scores of less than 50 suggest a preference for mechanistic or formal organizations; scores above 50 suggest a preference for organic or informal organizations.

TASK

1. Within your group compare scores and discuss the kinds of work that you think go with your preferred organizational style.

2. Describe, in general, the kinds of jobs most characteristic of an organic and mechanistic design.

3. Rate the following organizations in terms of whether you would expect them to be mechanistic or organic.
   - a fast food chain
   - a business college
   - a car factory
   - a car design centre
   - a beauty parlour
   - a pollution control plant
   - the maintenance department in a factory
   - a bus company
   - a taxi company
   - a computer programming department

- a data coding department
- a summer camp
- the management team for a large company
- an army combat unit
- a police detective department
- the editorial staff of a newspaper
- the creative department of an advertising agency
- this class

Enriched Job Design

Organizational Design

PURPOSE

In this exercise you will design an enriched managerial job.

PREPARATION

None required.

INTRODUCTION

An enriched job is one that incorporates a fair degree of autonomy and participative power sharing between the job holder and her or his supervisor. The key problem to be faced is the question of which aspects of the duties and the responsibilities of the position need to be specified by the hierarchy, and what aspects should be delegated to the job holder. The assumption for this exercise is that this is a newly designed position. The hiring exercise that follows uses the job design you create.

In an enriched job, the job holder has significant delegated and/or shared power over at least one and, possibly, all three of the following components:

1. Objective-setting, where targets for key-result areas will be formulated by the job holder alone (delegated power) or with a direct supervisor (shared power).

2. Resource budgets, which specify what resources may be employed in meeting the targets.

3. Work plans or procedures, which specify what work methods will be employed.

With the high degree of autonomy attached to enriched managerial positions, the organization must ensure that sufficient control is still maintained, so that the diminishment of authoritarian control over individual employees does not result in an uncoordinated and ineffective structure. If that occurs, the motivational advantages of job enrichment are lost to organizational inefficiency. Following are four categories over which upper management may exercise relatively complete control even when managing an enriched position.

1. **The performance responsibilities of the job**, as defined by key-result areas in which the job holder will be expected to set and achieve objectives. For example, instead of telling a production supervisor what the quota should be, the job description may state "the production supervisor will (perhaps in consultation with the general manager) establish the production targets that are to be met." This establishes the key-result area of production volume as critical without removing the authority for target-setting from the job holder. The key-result areas may also be listed in order of their importance for organizational effectiveness.

2. **The custodial responsibilities of the job.** That is, which organizational resources the job holder must maintain, protect, and replenish.

3. **Overall budgetary allocations** to the position that still allow the individual to make the division of sub-allocations within the overall budget.

4. **Any universally applicable organizational policies,** such as compensation packages, vertical and lateral communication responsibilities to other organizational units, etc.

THE PROBLEM

You are the Mid-Canada District Sales Manager of Hi-Tech Corporation with four branch offices under your supervision in Manitoba, Saskatchewan and, soon northwestern Ontario. With head office in Calgary (where you are located), Hi-Tech supplies computerized instrumentation to a variety of industrial plants across Canada. The company has decided to open a new branch office in Thunder Bay, Ontario, to serve industrial customers from Kenora to Sault Ste Marie. You must now design, as an enriched job, the branch manager's position. This is the most junior management position in the field sales group. The following information forms part of the job description:

- The only activity of the branch office will be the solicitation of sales to industrial customers and directly associated activities. All promotional activities, order processing, and service arrangements are performed by head office.
- There will be sufficient funds allocated to maintain the branch manager, a maximum of five salespersons, and one secretary.

Each group of students is to draft the rest of the job description, containing:

1. A set of from six to eight key-result areas, listed in order of priority, for which the branch manager must set and attain objectives. Give your reasons for each one selected.

_____

_____

_____

_____

_____

_____

_____

_____

_____

_____

2. A list of, from five to seven, custodial responsibilities for which the branch manager must also develop policies and work procedures.

_____

_____

_____

_____

_____

_____

_____

_____

_____

_____

Remember to avoid over defining work procedures. This is to be an enriched job, in which the branch manager must develop his or her own methods of fulfilling the job requirements. When you have performed the two steps above, refer to the three components of individual control listed at the beginning of this exercise. Will the branch manager have an enriched position? Will Hi-Tech Corporation and the district manager still have sufficient control over the Thunder Bay branch?

Personnel Selection

Organizational Design

PURPOSE

To learn principles of personnel selection in the challenging context of an enriched job.

PREPARATION

The job design exercise preceding this one must have already been completed.

INTRODUCTION

Modern management theories support the notion that human behaviour is context or situationally specific. It is not practical to describe behavioural traits or patterns for any individual unless the situation in which the individual is placed is also specified. The same person might behave quite differently in an altered environment. In personnel selection, it is necessary to first identify the behavioural patterns that would facilitate high performance on the job. These should be quite specific. For example, when attempting to hire an accountant, instead of simply saying, "should act intelligently", it would be better to state, "should be capable of rapid and accurate quantitative analysis even when under stress." This defines the desirable behavioural pattern in much more detail. The former statement could apply to almost any job, while the latter is targeted at the requirements derived from the task environment of an accountant.

Once the appropriate behavioural patterns have been decided, a strategy for selecting a person who is likely to display those patterns when on the job must be devised. In the Hi-Tech Corporation example, you have already defined the task environment. Assume that the educational and experiential backgrounds have already been defined for the branch manager position, and you are to carry on from there.

1. From the prioritized list of key-result areas, define a set of from six to eight behavioural patterns that would likely lead to successful performance. Concentrate on those pertaining to the leadership of the branch. Be as specific as pos-

sible, and be realistic. Remember that this is a junior management position that will not be filled by a senior executive.

2. From Job Application (A), Job Interview (I), Previous Experience (E), Testing (T), and Dynamic Assessment (D), indicate which mode(s) would be useful to evaluate whether each job applicant would be likely to exhibit the selected behaviour patterns if she or he was hired. Note separately the reasons for selecting each mode, any disadvantages or biases that mode might have, and how they might be overcome.

DESIRABLE BEHAVIOUR PATTERN	MODE OF PERSONNEL SELECTION

Measurement Scale

Quality of Work Life

PURPOSE

To measure those aspects of job satisfaction that are enclosed by the concept of Quality of Work Life and to measure five core dimensions of jobs of this scale.

PREPARATION

Your instructor may request that you complete the questionnaire prior to class.

INTRODUCTION

Use the following instrument to evaluate a job you have recently held. How well does each of the following statements describe the job? Score 5 if it is a perfect description. Score 0 if it is totally wrong. Score 4, 3, 2 or 1 if it fits somewhere in between.

_____ 1. My job provides me with different tasks to perform throughout each hour.

_____ 2. Everyone who works where I do is aware of how all of the jobs fit together to achieve our company goals.

_____ 3. The other workers depend on the job I do to accomplish their work.

_____ 4. I am my own boss.

_____ 5. I know right away if there is a problem, with the way I am doing my job.

_____ 6. My job requires a large variety of different skills.

_____ 7. Our work is mostly custom work with each project being unique.

_____ 8. My employer has a mission statement, and I am familiar with how my job supports it.

_____ 9. I get to control my own work.

_____ 10. I know at the end of each week whether I have been successful on my job or not.

_____ 11. My employer arranges job rotation so that we are given different tasks on different days.

_____ 12. One good thing about my job is that at the end of the day I know what I have accomplished.

_____ 13. In my job I hear back about how people react to what I do.

_____ 14. I feel responsible for getting my whole job done.

_____ 15. My supervisor provides me with accurate production reports on a frequent basis.

_____ 16. We are cross trained to handle different jobs in our business.

_____ 17. At the end of my career I will be able to look back and identify what I achieved through my work.

_____ 18. On my job I know exactly why I perform each task.

_____ 19. My supervisor only checks up on me when something goes really wrong.

_____ 20. I get regular information on how well my work is going.

_____ 21. When I get to work each day, I do not really know for sure what task will be assigned to me.

_____ 22. Our work is organized so that each of us does a complete job.

_____ 23. When people ask me what I do for a living, I am able to tell them exactly what I have done.

_____ 24. My supervisor likes it if I figure out a better way of doing my job.

_____ 25. My work is monitored, so that I have daily reports on my progress.

The questions above are each related to one of the core dimensions of a job as described by Hackman and Oldman (J. Richard Hackman and Greg R. Oldman. "Development of the Job Diagnostic Survey", _Journal of Applied Psychology_ Vol. 60, 1975). Use the table below to add up your score for each of the core dimensions. The numbers in the cells identify the questions that are related to each dimension.

CORE DIMENSIONS OF JOBS: HACKMAN AND OLDMAN						
1. Task variety	1 =	6 =	11 =	16 =	21 =	
2. Task identity	2 =	7 =	12 =	17 =	22 =	
3. Task significance	3 =	8 =	13 =	18 =	23 =	
4. Autonomy	4 =	9 =	14 =	19 =	24 =	
5. Feedback	5 =	10 =	15 =	20 =	25 =	

QWL PROFILE

The Quality of your Work Life is best viewed as a snapshot at a particular point in time. The result is that it is usually presented as a profile graph of the scores. Plot your QWL profile on the graph outline below.

QUALITY OF WORK LIFE PROFILE									
CORE DIMENSIONS		**5**		**10**		**15**		**20**	
Task Variety									
Task Identity									
Task Significance									
Autonomy									
Feedback									

Interpretation

The five core dimensions that Hackman and Oldman have identified provide a useful basis on which to analyze jobs. They represent core dimensions of a job, and should not be taken to be a complete basis for job analysis. All should be present to provide a job that is psychologically satisfying and will motivate employees to greater performance.

1. **Task Variety:** Task variety involves performing different tasks that require different talents. Workers typically see jobs that require more of their talent as more challenging and, consequently, more motivating. Variety relieves monotony, and can also help avoid the muscle strain caused by repetitive movements.

2. **Task Identity:** One of the keys to effective worker motivation is the satisfaction that comes from being able to identify that they have done a whole job, or that they can point out what it is they have built or achieved. This is best exemplified in the problem of extreme job division, where the work has been divided into so many parts that each has lost all meaning to the worker. To extend the old analogy, while working on a twig, they have trouble seeing the tree, let alone the forest.

3. **Task Significance:** Not only must the task be identifiable, it must be seen as important or worthwhile. This is a particular problem with routine work, especially if there is a widespread worker belief that whatever they do will be checked and repaired by someone else later on.

4. **Autonomy:** How much responsibility is the employee given for their own work routines? Are employees given specific detailed instructions about their

work, or are they given broader goals and invited to share in their achievement? While autonomy is usually associated with the managerial level of work, there have been major breakthroughs in achieving autonomy in jobs on the factory floor.

5. **Feedback:** Workers need information about their performance, and they need it before their exit interview. Misunderstandings about performance expectations are easily avoided. Frequency of feedback varies with the job, but the lessons of psychology are that feedback should be provided at almost the same instant as performance, and that its impact diminishes with time. Feedback must be positive as well as negative. "No news" is not "good news", it is simply no news.

TASK

1. After drawing your QWL profile, do an analysis of your job and determine its strengths and weaknesses.

2. Identify areas needing improvement and develop ways to improve your job. Use the five core dimensions as the basis of this job redesign.

3. If you are working in a study group, share this with the members of your group to get their feedback.

Measure and Evaluate

Organizational Culture and Values

PURPOSE

To measure and evaluate employee values as an aspect of corporate culture.

PREPARATION

Complete Steps 1, 2, and 3 prior to class.

INTRODUCTION

This is a group activity. The purpose is to develop a picture of one aspect of corporate culture: namely, the value system of the ideal employee as seen from the company point of view. We will measure this using a ranking of a list of typical human values. A value is any trait that people believe is important, and is used as the basis of behaviour. If people think it is important to be helpful, then they will act on this value by providing assistance to others. Norms are based on values.

Step 1: Rank the values on the sheet on the next page in the order you think they are important for employees in a corporation. Use one of the score sheets. You may find it easier to fill this out with a particular company in mind; if so, read the case called Mason Electric, and analyze the corporate values found there. View them from the perspective of the company or its management. Try to avoid thinking about a specific manager. Use a generalized ideal.

Long lists are hard to rank, so use this method: Place the number "1" next to the value you think is most important and the number "16" next to the one you think is least important. Then number the second, and the fifteenth, and so forth.

Step 2: Get three people to give you their rankings. The previous sheet can be folded in four, or cut into four rectangles so that people will not be influenced by how other people responded. Explain to these people how they should rank the items.

	Ambition		Ambition
	Broad-mindedness		Broad-mindedness
	Competence		Competence
	Cheerfulness		Cheerfulness
	Cleanliness		Cleanliness
	Courage		Courage
	Helpfulness		Helpfulness
	Honesty		Honesty
	Imagination		Imagination
	Independence		Independence
	Intelligence		Intelligence
	Obedience		Obedience
	Politeness		Politeness
	Responsibility		Responsibility
	Self-control		Self-control
	Tolerance		Tolerance
	Ambition		Ambition
	Broad-mindedness		Broad-mindedness
	Competence		Competence
	Cheerfulness		Cheerfulness
	Cleanliness		Cleanliness
	Courage		Courage
	Helpfulness		Helpfulness
	Honesty		Honesty
	Imagination		Imagination
	Independence		Independence
	Intelligence		Intelligence
	Obedience		Obedience
	Politeness		Politeness
	Responsibility		Responsibility
	Self-control		Self-control
	Tolerance		Tolerance

Step 3: Compile your results and calculate a rank order based on the four sets of data that you have. Do this by first adding up the ranks that the four sheets give for each value. Use this total for each value, and assign new ranks from one to 16.

Step 4: Meet with your group and repeat this procedure with your group data. You should end up with one list of the values with ranks from one to sixteen.

Step 5: Discussion questions for your group:

1. What agreement was there among the members of your group about the importance of these corporate values? How much agreement was there about the most important? The least important?

2. What does your list reveal about corporate culture? What value judgments would you make about it? Make predictions about behaviour based on these values.

3. Compare your list of corporate values to the list below of values held in general society. Discuss similarities and differences. There are norms for both males and females. Discuss the extent to which values are related to gender or, perhaps, other minority group status.

RANK ORDER OF VALUES FOR GENERAL SOCIETY		
MALE	**FEMALE**	**VALUE**
2	4	Ambition
4	5	Broad-mindedness
8	11	Competence
12	9	Cheerfulness
9	8	Cleanliness
5	6	Courage
7	7	Helpfulness
1	1	Honesty
16	16	Imagination
11	13	Independence
14	15	Intelligence
15	14	Obedience
13	12	Politeness
3	3	Responsibility
10	10	Self-control
6	2	Tolerance

Census and Climate

Organizational Culture and Values

PURPOSE

To become familiar with the concept of a "corporate census", which measures minority group composition in the organization, and with the related concept of corporate climate, which measures the "atmosphere" as it exists for the different members of the corporate community.

PREPARATION

Your instructor may request that you complete the questionnaire prior to class.

INTRODUCTION

Record the number of your choice in the column on the left-hand side of the page. After completing the questionnaire, turn to the scoring key to calculate your census and climate index scores.

CENSUS QUESTIONS

_____ 1. What is your sex?
(a) Female
(b) Male

_____ 2. Are you a member of one of the Aboriginal peoples of North America (North American Indian, Inuit, Métis)?
(a) Yes, I am a North American Indian
(b) Yes, I am Inuit
(c) Yes, I am Métis
(d) No, I am not an Aboriginal person

_____ 3. Are you a member of a visible minority? Members of visible minority groups are persons of colour or race who are identifiable minorities in Canada. Please note that this question does not refer to the country in which you were born, your citizenship, or your religion.
(a) Yes, I am Black (including African Black, American Black, Canadian Black, West Indian Black)

(b) Yes, I am East Asian (including Chinese, Japanese, Korean, Polynesian)

(c) Yes, I am South Asian (including Indian, Pakistani, Bangladeshi, Sri Lankin)

(d) Yes, and I am of another visible minority

(e) Yes, and I am of mixed race

(f) No, I am not a member of a visible minority

_____ 4. Do you have a disability? Please include your disability, even if it does not preclude your employment. Do not include temporary disabilities, such as those caused by injury that will heal. The World Health Organization defines disability as "a major limitation that substantially limits an individual from performing one or more of the major life activities in a manner considered normal."

(a) Yes, I am blind or visually impaired (do not include problems correctable with lenses)

(b) Yes, I am deaf or hard of hearing

(c) Yes, I have a medical disability (including arthritis, diabetes, epilepsy, hemophilia, heart condition, multiple sclerosis, muscular dystrophy, psychiatric illness)

(d) Yes, I have a mobility disability, such as the need to use a wheelchair

(e) No, I do not have a disability

_____ 5. What is your native language, that is, the language you first learned to speak and still understand?

(a) English

(b) French

(c) Chinese

(d) Italian

(e) Portuguese

(f) Other

_____ 6. Do you believe that the variety (dialect) of English or French that you speak limits your employment opportunities?

(a) Yes   (b) No

_____ 7. Do you have any children?

(a) Yes   (b) No

_____ 8. Age at present time:

(a) 17–20

(b) 21–24

(c) 25–30

(d) 31–40

(e) 41 or more

_____ 9. Citizenship:

(a) Citizen of Canada

(b) Not a citizen of Canada

SCHOOL CLIMATE QUESTIONS

Answer these questions with reference to the class you are now attending.

_____ 10. This course is:

(a) A core course for my program

(b) A general education or elective course

_____ 11. Does your instructor know you by name?
    (a) Yes
    (b) No
    (c) Don't know

_____ 12. How often do you voluntarily answer questions or contribute to class discussions in this class?
    (a) Never
    (b) One to three times during the course
    (c) An average of once a week
    (d) An average of two to three times a week
    (e) An average of one or more times a day

_____ 13. How often does the instructor call on you or ask you to respond to a question or comment?
    (a) The instructor does not call on anyone
    (b) One to three times during the course
    (c) An average of once a week
    (d) An average of two to three times a week
    (e) Never

_____ 14. How does the instructor most frequently call on you?
    (a) By name
    (b) By pointing with hand
    (c) By eye to eye contact/looking at me
    (d) The instructor never calls on me

_____ 15. Are there times when you raise your hand to ask a question or make a comment, but do not get called on by the instructor?
    (a) Once or twice
    (b) Three or more times
    (c) I am called on when I raise my hand
    (d) I never raise my hand

_____ 16. Why do you think the instructor does not call on you when you raise your hand? (Select the **one** answer that best reflects your opinion.)
    (a) Too many students want to respond
    (b) Others beat me to it
    (c) The instructor does not see or hear me
    (d) The instructor ignores me
    (e) This situation never occurs

_____ 17. Are there times when you want to participate in class by asking a question or making a comment, but choose not to do so?
    (a) Once or twice
    (b) Three or more times
    (c) Nearly every class
    (d) No, because I participate when I want to
    (e) I do not want to participate

_____ 18. If you have wanted to participate in class by asking a question or making a comment but did not do so, what was your reason for not doing so? (Select the **one** response that most closely corresponds with your feelings.)
    (a) Felt insecure, inadequate, or uncertain
    (b) Another student asked question or commented first
    (c) Too many students in class
    (d) Disagreed with the instructor, but chose not to speak out
    (e) This situation never happens

_____ 19. In your opinion, which students most frequently participate in class? (Select the **one** answer that best represents your opinion.)
(a) Those who are most knowledgeable or most interested in the subject
(b) Those who are seeking clarification or want more information
(c) Those who are trying to show off or get attention
(d) I have not noticed

_____ 20. In your opinion, which students ask the most questions and make the most comments in class?
(a) Male students
(b) Female students
(c) Male and female students equally
(d) Have not noticed

_____ 21. How does the instructor react to the questions you make in class?
(a) Encourages me to question or comment again
(b) Discourages me from commenting or asking a question again
(c) Neither encourages nor discourages me
(d) I never participate

_____ 22. In your opinion, how does the instructor react to opinions and comments given by other students in the class?
(a) Respects the opinions of students in this class
(b) Does not respect the opinions of students in this class
(c) Embarrasses or "puts down" students for their opinions
(d) I did not notice

_____ 23. Does your instructor use humour or make humorous references that you feel are offensive, embarrassing, or belittling to any individuals or groups?
(a) Never
(b) One time
(c) Occasionally
(d) Frequently

_____ 24. How often do students participate in this class by asking questions or making comments?
(a) Never
(b) Rarely
(c) Occasionally
(d) Frequently

_____ 25. Sex of the instructor
(a) Male
(b) Female

_____ 26. Class Size _____

WORK CLIMATE QUESTIONS

Answer these questions with reference to your current place of employment. If you are not currently employed, make reference to your most recent job. Use either full-time or part-time work.

If you have more than one supervisor, pick the one with whom you have the most frequent contact; that is, the one who is most regularly involved in overseeing your work.

_____ 27. How well does your supervisor know you?
(a) Not at all
(b) Knows my name
(c) Knows my work
(d) Understands my personality

_____ 28. How often do you voluntarily answer questions or make suggestions about work routines?
(a) Never
(b) Every month or so
(c) An average of once a week
(d) An average of two to three times a week
(e) An average of one or more times a day

_____ 29. How often does the supervisor call on you or ask you to respond to a question or comment?
(a) Supervisor does not call on anyone
(b) Every month or so
(c) An average of once a week
(d) An average of two to three times a week
(e) Never

_____ 30. How does the supervisor most frequently call on you?
(a) By name
(b) By pointing with hand
(c) By eye to eye contact/looking at me
(d) Supervisor never calls on me

_____ 31. Why do you think the supervisor does not call on you for help? (Select the **one** answer that best reflects your opinion.)
(a) Too many workers want to help
(b) Others beat me to it
(c) Supervisor does not see or hear me
(d) Supervisor ignores me
(e) This situation never occurs

_____ 32. Are there times when you want to offer suggestions, but choose not to do so?
(a) Once or twice
(b) Three or more times
(c) Nearly every day
(d) No, because I participate when I want to
(e) I do not want to participate

_____ 33. If you have wanted to participate by offering a suggestion or making a comment but did not do so, what was your reason for not doing so? (Select the **one** response that most closely corresponds with your feelings.)
(a) Felt insecure, inadequate, or uncertain
(b) Another worker spoke first
(c) Too many workers
(d) Disagreed with supervisor, but chose not to speak out
(e) This situation never happens

_____ 34. In your opinion, which workers most frequently participate? (Select the **one** answer that best represents your opinion.)
(a) Those who are most knowledgeable or most interested in the work
(b) Those who are seeking clarification or want more information
(c) Those who are trying to show off or get attention
(d) I have not noticed

_____ 35. In your opinion, which workers offer the most suggestions and make the most comments?
(a) Male workers
(b) Female workers
(c) Male and female workers equally
(d) Have not noticed

_____ 36. How does the supervisor react to what you have to say?
(a) Encourages me to question or comment again
(b) Discourages me from commenting or asking a question again
(c) Neither encourages nor discourages me
(d) I never participate

_____ 37. In your opinion, how does the supervisor react to opinions and comments given by other workers?
(a) Respects the opinions of workers
(b) Does not respect the opinions of workers
(c) Embarrasses or "puts down" workers for their opinions
(d) I did not notice

_____ 38. Does your supervisor use humour or make humorous references that you feel are offensive, embarrassing, or belittling to any individuals or groups?
(a) Never
(b) One time
(c) Occasionally
(d) Frequently

_____ 39. Sex of supervisor
(a) Male
(b) Female

_____ 40. Is this a part-time or full-time job?
(a) Up to 24 hours per week
(b) More than 24 hours per week

CENSUS QUESTIONS		
Q#	RESPONSE	SCORE
1	a =2 b =1	
2	a =8 b =9 c =5 d =1	
3	a =5 b =4 c =6 d =7 e =8 f =1	
4	a =9 b =8 c =3 d =7 e =1	
5	a =1 b =3 c =6 d =5 e =7 f =8	
6	a =2 b =1	
7	a =2 b =1	
8	a =1 b =1 c =1 d =2 e =3	
9	a =1 b =3	
TOTAL CENSUS SCORE =		

\multicolumn{3}{c}{**SCHOOL CLIMATE QUESTIONS**}
Q#	**RESPONSE**	**SCORE**
10	a =1 b =2	XXXXX
11	a =1 b =3 c =2	
12	a =5 b =4 c =3 d =2 e =1	
13	a =0 b =4 c =3 d =2 e =1	
14	a =1 b =2 c =3 d =4	
15	a =2 b =3 c =1 d =4	
16	a =1 b =2	XXXXX
17	a =1 b =3 c =2	
18	a =5 b =4 c =3 d =2 e =1	
19	a =0 b =4 c =3 d =2 e =1	
20	a =1 b =2 c =3 d =4	
21	a =2 b =3 c =1 d =4	
22	a =1 b =2 c =3 d =0	
23	a =1 b =2 c =3 d =4	
24	a =4 b =3 c =2 d =1	
25	a =4 b =1	
26	XXXXX	
\multicolumn{2}{r}{TOTAL SCHOOL SCORE =}	

\multicolumn{3}{c}{**WORK CLIMATE QUESTIONS**}
Q#	**RESPONSE**	**SCORE**
27	a =4 b =3 c =2 d =1	
28	a =1 b =2 c =3 d =4 e =5	
29	a =0 b =4 c =3 d =2 e =1	
30	a =1 b =2 c =3 d =4	
31	a =1 b =2 c =3 d =4 e =0	
32	a =2 b =3 c =4 d =1 e =0	
33	a =3 b =2 c =1 d =4 e =0	
34	a =1 b =2 c =3 d =0	

| \multicolumn{3}{c}{**WORK CLIMATE QUESTIONS (Continued)**} |
Q#	RESPONSE	SCORE
35	a =3 b =2 c =1 d =0	
36	a =1 b =3 c =2 d =0	
37	a =1 b =2 c =3 d =0	
38	a =1 b =2 c =3 d =4	
39	a =3 b =1	
40	a =2 b =1	XXXXX
\multicolumn{2}{r}{TOTAL WORK SCORE =}	

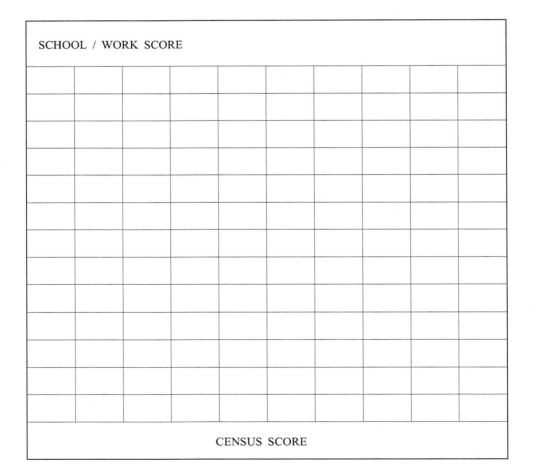

SCHOOL / WORK SCORE

CENSUS SCORE

Plot the status and climate scores for your group on the graph paper. Use separate sheets for school and work scores. If you have only a small number of group members, you may wish to combine your data with that of other groups.

DISCUSSION QUESTIONS

1. Describe the relationship, if any, between status and climate.

2. What variables other than status might contribute to a chilly or a warm climate?

3. What corporate costs would be associated with a chilly climate?

4. What strategies might be undertaken to warm up too chilly a climate?